THE ENCYCLOPEDIA OF
CHINESE COOKING

THE ENCYCLOPEDIA OF CHINESE COOKING

KENNETH LO

Galahad Books · New York City

Chinese calligraphy by Hsiao-Ying Chinnery

This edition published in the United States of America in 1985 by Galahad Books, 149 Madison Ave., New York, N.Y. 10016 by arrangement with William Collins Sons & Company, Ltd.

Library of Congress Catalog Card Number: 78-58765

ISBN: 0-88365-532-2

Printed and bound in the United States of America

To Anne, Robert, Michael, Vivienne, and Jennifer
for providing strong tea and loud background music.

CONTENTS

FISH

To retain their fresh, sweet juiciness, fish are best cooked only briefly, after a period of seasoning and marinating. The principal ways of cooking fish are to steam, clear-simmer, bake, deep-fry, pan-fry, slow stir-fry, and braise. They are often brought to the table whole to be dismembered by the host before the guests.

SEAFOOD AND SHELLFISH

Abalone, bêche-de-mer, crabs, shrimp, prawns, lobsters, clams, and squid. Although many seafoods are cooked fresh in China, as many are used dried, as a flavoring. As variety is the keynote of Chinese food, and since seafoods and shellfish have such a distinctive taste and texture, they almost invariably appear in the midst of a multi-course Chinese dinner.

EGGS

"When a pinch of chopped scallion and some dry sherry are sprinkled over eggs during the last and final stages of cooking, they generate between them a wonderful aroma." Savory Steamed Egg Custard and Yellow Flowing Eggs (Liu Huang T'sai) are particularly popular dishes.

SWEETS AND SNACKS

In China, sweet dishes are either served during a multi-course party dinner or for nibbling between meals. There is a wide range of delicious savory snacks which are eaten at the numerous Chinese tea-houses, or at any time of the day or night.

THE ENCYCLOPEDIA OF CHINESE COOKING

INTRODUCTION

The introduction of Chinese food to the Western world and its sudden rise to universal popularity during the post-war era must be something of a puzzle to all believers of Kipling's dictum that 'East is East and West is West and never the twain shall meet'.

There are several reasons for the phenomenal advance of Chinese food, a culture which now extends over so many frontiers—over the Pennines, the Pyrenees, the Dolomites, the Alps, Andes, and the Rocky Mountains. Various political and social factors have undoubtedly contributed to its galloping spread—factors such as the population explosion in Hong Kong after 1950 and the advent of the affluent society in the West, both of which have triggered off the culinary curiosity of a now much more mobile population. But, at the base of it all, I feel there is a more persistent and fundamental factor which is powering the drive of Chinese food; and this factor is the basic savoriness and sensual appeal of Chinese food which is acceptable to such a wide range of human palates!

Everybody who has lived through the last couple of decades in the West has noted the tremendous expansion in the desire for increased sensuality; for the freer and fuller use of our senses of sound, sight, taste, and touch. Color, texture, movement, food, drink, and rock music—all these have become much more a part and parcel of the average person's life than they have ever been. It is this increased sensuality and the desire for greater freedom from age-bound habits in the West, combined with the inherent sensual concept of Chinese food, always quick to satisfy the taste buds, that is at the root of the sudden and phenomenal spread of Chinese food throughout the length and breadth of the Western world.

What, then, are the elements which contribute to the wide sensual appeal of Chinese food, which make it so acceptable to people from all points of the compass—a food which requires some measure of love to create, and ardor to consume?

First of all, because Chinese meals are communal meals, and communal dishes served on the table are of necessity bigger and fuller than the average dishes, they are therefore bound to create a greater visual impact, and are more sumptuous in appearance. The exoticism of size and variety is further enhanced by the Chinese use of heat as an integral part of flavor—the use of heat to induce, ignite, and set ablaze all the latent desires in our appetites. Hence, in a well-served Chinese meal, the time-lapse between the food leaving the hot pan and stove and its arrival on the table is measured not in minutes but in seconds.

Secondly, because a Chinese dinner is a multi-dish or multi-course meal, it provides for the procession of a wide variety of dishes. This parade of variety is calculated to whet one's appetite by a kaleidoscope of changing temptations: if one dish does not tempt, many others might, or will!

The third contributory factor to the appeal of Chinese food is the frequent and deliberate exploitation of changing textural effects. Both the harmony of textures and the contrast of textures are exploited. The deliberate deployment of smoothness as well as crackling-crispiness over a wide area of food means that when the opposites meet they bring greater enjoyment. The marrying of the crunchiness of fresh vegetables to the flavor and qualities of dried or rich ingredients helps to further enrich the concept of the 'tapestry' of food.

Fourthly, the bulk intake of rice (which no connoisseur of Chinese food would do without during some stage of the meal) provides for that firm, tucking-in sensation, which is so essential to the production of the ultimate physical satisfaction in eating. This is further reinforced by the provision of several soups, situated at various strategic junctures of the meal, to chase down the rice and other foods with a delicious 'hot-wash' sensation which results in Chinese food being more 'torrential' in its savouriness than other types of cuisine which are able to command only one soup per meal.

Finally, because of the Chinese discovery and wide use of soy beans and their by-products (soy sauce, soy paste, soy cheese, soy bean curd, etc.), which, when used in conjunction with other ingredients are able to seduce our palate and taste buds as few other things seem able to do (a fact which is still mysterious to science), the Chinese are able to maintain a high degree of spiciness in their food without resorting to and relying on a wide range of rare exotic spices and sauces.

It is the combined and cumulative effect of all these characteristics of Chinese food—all the attributes and qualities of the femme fatale—which causes the affluent world of the West to succumb to its sensual charm and piquancy of appeal. Chinese food stimulates those desires which are so much in accord with the trends of our time—the demand for greater warmth, greater freedom, closer contact, and sharing of sensual experience and delights, and for something which is different and not handed down or re-hashed from the common ingredients of the age-worn past.

Because of the difference in the Chinese feeling for food and their enjoyment of it, there is a perceptible difference in the Chinese approach to this subject compared with that in the West. When a Westerner goes to a restaurant, he asks for the best table in the room, where he can see and be seen. He is not there just to eat but to be entertained socially. When a Chinese goes to a restaurant in China, he asks for and is given a room, or at least a partitioned-off compartment, with white-washed walls, as sparsely furnished as a waiting room in a country railway station. There he sees nothing of interest, and is seen by nobody, except by those in his own party. No sooner has he arrived than he takes off his jacket, and if the day is warm he would roll up his sleeves; then he and his friends are ready for business: the 'business' of eating. His intentions are both honorable and whole-hearted: to eat with a capital E.

This honorable and wholehearted attitude is possible only because of the great lengthy expectation of sensual satisfaction which is inherent in all good Chinese meals. What else can command such total and unquestioned devotion?

This book is largely about how the appeal of Chinese food and its accompanying charms are manufactured; and about the ingredients and techniques which go into their making. Another aim of this book is to reduce the mystique which still surrounds Chinese cooking, and to show that in the Western world, which is so richly endowed with all the wherewithals of foods and ingredients, there should be no difficulty in producing Chinese food of the first order in almost any kitchen, given the interest and a little love.

Any reader who feels inclined to move further into the not unexciting world of Chinese food and conduct his or her own experiments to some of its many sensual and aesthetic delights will find considerable areas to traverse in this book, but a reading of the introductory chapters should help in illuminating the somewhat lengthy journey, even if his intention is not to go on a general tour, but just to dwell on one or two selected dishes on a short culinary safari. As the author of the book I can only wish him or her very good luck, and some inspiring cooking!

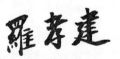

K.H.C.Lo

The Nature and Contribution of Chinese Cooking

One of the most exciting things about writing about Chinese food and cooking lies in the knowledge that one is writing about a subject which is undoubtedly one of China's unique contributions to the sum total of the world's civilization. If it is not her most important contribution, it is certainly one of the most living, extensive, and satisfying. And as such, its influence on the world at large must be considerable and quite immeasurable.

Few things in life are as positive as food, or are taken as intimately and completely by the individual. One can listen to music, but the sound may enter in one ear and go out through the other; one may listen to a lecture or conversation, and day-dream about many other things; one may attend to matters of business, and one's heart or interest may be altogether elsewhere. One can be bored and entirely indifferent.

In the matter of food and eating one can hardly remain completely indifferent to what one is doing for long. How can one remain entirely indifferent to something which is going to enter one's body and become part of oneself? How can one remain indifferent to something which will determine one's physical strength and ultimately one's spiritual and moral fiber and well-being?

Besides, in one's attitude towards food one can be driven by such a basic urge as gnawing hunger, and motivated by such a fundamental desire as physical appeal. For in food and eating, we are coming very near to that plane of life which is at the very root of human existence on earth, at which nobody is a bystander.

It is in this larger context and against this general basic human background that I should like to consider the subject of Chinese food and cooking. The significance of its conception and techniques has become a part and parcel of the Chinese way of life through the ages, and, it seems, will very soon become a measurable part of the heritage and practice of a good proportion of the human race.

For Chinese food and cooking have become, at first perhaps imperceptibly, and now during the past decade or two quite dramatically, easily the most universally accepted cuisine throughout the world. Soon it might be that all those who can afford to eat will be at one time or another during the week devouring Chinese food! Before that time comes, it is well that we take a closer look at Chinese food and cooking, and decipher the sources of their strength and meaning, instead of merely branding them as exotic.

In the many lectures I have given on this subject, I have used the title 'The Sources and Strength of Chinese Gastronomic Imperialism'! Whether the strength is derived from the materials used, from the technique of cooking, or from the conception of the completed dish, it is for us to investigate and determine. With the world growing smaller every day, we will all be living out of one another's pockets soon; therefore whatever any country or people has of significance to contribute will soon become the common possession of all of us and a part of everyone's common inheritance. What then is our common inheritance or legacy from the Chinese in the line of food and cooking, which we are about to embrace and claim as our own? In what way will this help in contributing to the enrichment of our daily lives? To answer this question, one has to take a look at the situation at closer quarters and examine it against a wider background.

First of all, the basic purpose of cooking is primarily to render food edible, and secondly to render it more enjoyable to eat. To achieve these purposes, two methods are generally employed: heating and flavoring. These two methods or processes are commonly used by people all over the world. The difference between one type of cooking and another, where differences exist, can really only lie in the degree of refinement and sophistication which is conceived or employed within each category of methods.

If refinement means the minuteness of adjustments, the delicacy of touch required in flavoring and heating, and the recognition and mastery of all the wide variety of interrelated factors which combine to produce the desired effect, then Chinese cooking must rank as one of the most refined and sophisticated in the world. For in ultimate refinement and sophistication, to outsiders at least, there is something which resembles the proverbial 'Chinese Puzzle' in Chinese cooking.

Perhaps it is only natural that it should be so, for refinement and sophistication have been the natural style and expression of the Chinese artistic instinct in more than one aspect of her culture and civilization. Here one can easily compare Chinese cooking with Chinese painting and calligraphy, where the aim is to achieve a very high degree of delicacy and refinement within a traditional and sometimes stylized framework, but at the same time never lose sight of the need for character, quality, and meaning which should be the foundation of every artistic expression.

Indeed, for Chinese cooking to have attained any style or character of its own, it is likely that it followed this broad stream of Chinese inclination and artistic tradition. It could hardly have been otherwise.

Take the heating of food, which is basically capable of only a limited number of variations, such as heating by air (roasting, baking), heating by fire or radiation (grilling, barbecuing), heating through the medium of water (steaming, boiling, stewing), heating by oil (frying), or heating by contact (any heating on or against a dry surface or object—such as a stone or a griddle). By combining the different methods, by varying the pace of heating (what we Chinese call 'fire-power'), by the speed or lengthiness of treatment, the stability or mobility (as in stir-frying) of food while being heated, we Chinese have developed some forty different accepted heating methods, each with its well-defined and established terms of reference and conception. These terms are used, more or less, as terms are used in ballet movements, to indicate some precise stylized execution, the purpose and details of which are well-known, accepted, and established. In the sphere of flavoring, the Chinese have perhaps developed and advanced even farther than in heating. This is probably due to the normal Chinese practice of cross-cooking different types of foods, which results in the large-scale cross-blending of flavors, arising from the blending of different basic constituents of the dish.

Although not all Chinese dishes are 'mixed' dishes—some consist of only one ingredient cooked in the simplest way, such as by long, slow boiling—many more are mixed, usually consisting of one predominant ingredient which gives bulk and character to the dish, with one or two supplementary ingredients, supported by a few flavoring materials in small quantities, and further enriched by a range of seasoning materials and sauces. These seasoning materials and sauces are often applied at the last stage of cooking, when the heat is frequently turned up to a crescendo, thus creating a situation of 'explosive orchestration'.

The flavoring in Chinese cooking is, therefore, achieved through a multi-layer process; that is, through the use of supplementary ingredients for cross-cooking (to provide variety and difference in material and texture), the use of flavoring ingredients, seasonings, and sauces to further enhance taste and flavor, and finally through the serving of table condiments to provide the individual diners with the opportunity to do

4

their own personal 'touch-ups' before consumption. Not that these categories or layers of flavoring can always be divided into clear-cut, water-tight stages—they are sometimes blurred and inter-merged—but in carrying out flavoring processes in the execution of Chinese cooking, the concept of the various stages of heating and flavoring should be quite clear in the chef's mind.

The fun and interest arise, therefore, when all the various different types and degrees of flavorings are being applied at different stages and by way of different methods of heating. In other words, it is when multi-angle flavoring is married to multi-phase heating, with all the possible variations involved, that possibilities multiply and add up to a degree of profundity (and occasionally absurdity). That is when Chinese cooking gets to take on the character of a Chinese puzzle.

In fact, perhaps in order to reduce confusion, it is the normal practice in Chinese kitchens to divide the job of cooking into two clear stages: preparation, and actual cooking over the stove or cooker. Here the Chinese concept of cooking is not unlike the Western practice in painting: first you have actually to lay out all the different colors and mixes of colors on your palette, and prepare the canvas and easel, before you begin the picture.

In Chinese restaurants, the task of preparation and the task of cooking are usually carried out by two different persons. The preparations and portioning of the principal and supplementary ingredients are usually carried out by the assistant cook, while the chef attends to the 'firing' (control of the heating) and all the work and 'orchestration' over the stove, including flavoring and the application of all the sauces and seasonings. While the first person is the expert in slicing, cutting and assembling, and portioning of ingredients, the second person, the chef, is the executor and manipulator who attends to the final formulation of the taste, color, shaping, and presentation of the dish. He is in fact the final arbiter, the conductor on his rostrum, which is his stove! It is his interpretation which makes the dish.

At home, it is, of course, the housewife who does most of the jobs. However, with all the things she requires at hand, and many of the items needed for a meal largely prepared or semi-prepared in advance, plus the use of various items left over from previous meals, the task of preparing a meal is not so onerous as one might imagine! One is constantly surprised at the speed at which a five-dish or five-course meal will come out of a kitchen—often in no more than 30 minutes—and dishes of a standard and appeal (though simpler) which only the very best establishments can be expected to produce. Indeed, Chinese cooking provides the housewife with a large area where she can exercise her creative ability and talent, and thereby fulfil herself through self-expression in a subject which is directly related to man's very existence and well-being.

Creativeness in Chinese Cooking

The description and analysis of Chinese cooking contained in the preceding pages may make it look as if it is a kind of chemical process, made more complicated by the numerous options open to the practitioner during the various stages of its preparation and execution. Nothing would be farther from the truth.

For it is not only that there exists neither formula nor equation in Chinese cooking which would provide it with some resemblance to chemistry, but during all the millennia that Chinese cooking has existed with a pronounced character of its own, there has hardly even been a book of recipes which has been handed down to us through all the centuries of Chinese history. A body of knowledge or practice which has not been committed to writing, nor systematized into book form so that it can be easily communicable, hardly merits the term science, least of all chemistry.

Yet scores of Chinese scholars, poets, and bureaucrats of the past, who had plenty of leisure to indulge, have written copiously about food and drink. In the Yuan or Mongol Dynasty there was a book called *The Principles of Food and Drink,* which was written by the Emperor of the day himself. It concerned mainly what he considered to be hygiene. There has, unfortunately, never been a single cookbook from which recipes could be taken. The bulk of writings of this type consisted of a load of philosophizing, flights of poetic imagination, and exercises in the use of words rather than in the use of foods, ingredients, and flavorings. They were literary exercises rather than instructions on food and the whys and wherefores of food. Consequently, in China we have inherited a great tradition of the spirit of food, of the philosophy of food, of the joy of eating superb meals; but very little of the technique of food.

Perhaps for this reason—without precise instructions—we are left with an attitude towards food and its preparation which embraces a great deal of creative licence. Food and cooking in China are, therefore, much more a liberal art than a precise science. This is perhaps what makes them so intriguing and absorbing, so much a challenge to people of artistic or creative bent.

What we know of the technique of food has been handed down to us through the generations, mainly by word of mouth, from master to pupil, from parents to children—perhaps like the technique of playing the violin or of painting. Indeed, the writings about food in the past in China are very akin to the modern art critics' writings about painting. You can spend the whole of a Sunday afternoon poring over art in galleries—its themes, spirit, style, and conceptions, but feel none the wiser as to how it was actually painted. Yet the challenge is there, and when aroused that artistic challenge sometimes becomes a physical urge.

It is perhaps true that the Chinese writers of the past have treated the creation of dishes very much in the spirit of works of art: the flavors are the colors, the sharpness in timing the clearly delineated lines, the firing and heating, the warmth and emotion which inform and unite the picture. So long as one feels that one has a good grasp of the theme, conception, and spirit, one feels drawn and tempted to answer the challenge, in spite of inadequate training or incomplete know-how. Many did in every generation. For it is a type of liberal challenge which, with the gnawing of the stomach and a constant and appreciative audience ever ready to indulge, can hardly be consistently ignored. Once the challenge is taken up, without detailed or conveniently available instruction (as in the case of all art), one has at once to fall back on one's own creative urge and instinctive ability. The more these urges and instincts are exercised and given free rein, the more competent and capable one feels. To compose and create become no longer exalted efforts but just a way of living, a way of living which has grown in China into a formidable tradition. All Chinese people of culture can talk about food as you talk about art or cricket in the West.

Because a good proportion of culinary exercises cannot be resolved into equations and formulas, Chinese cooking can only be regarded as very much a liberal art. Recipe books and precise recipes may now exist—mainly copies of Western models—but much of their contents is best used merely as a guide and reference. With so many different types of materials and ingredients often involved in a dish, a great deal has to be left to individual enterprise, initiative, and imagination. Since there are options and alternatives, there are few absolutes in Chinese cooking. This is probably the reason why Chinese cooking of a good standard can often be achieved by a competent practitioner with a minimum of ingredients, and sometimes with no Chinese ingredients at all. What he needs above all else is good sense and imagination. On the other hand, the opposite is also true, that is, with all the materials and ingredients in the world, an incompetent person who has no clear grasp of the theme and conception of a dish or what its ultimate feel and flavor are intended to be can easily make a hash. As with all art, composition is impossible without complete clarity of conception.

It is, perhaps, fortunate that the creative continuity of Chinese cooking has been maintained through the ages because it is a living art, and the enterprise and creativeness which have to go into it have had to be regenerated daily in order merely to keep pace with living. It is probably also fortunate that there has been no bible of Chinese cooking written by some cookery-Confucius during the time of the Great Sage, which was the most productive and effervescent period in the whole of China's history, otherwise much of the growth of the Chinese culinary art would have come to a halt by the time of the beginning of the Christian era. The strong, blanketing influence of Confucian traditionalism was largely responsible for the discontinuance or non-continuity of China's technological progress, in spite of many significant technical discoveries which were made in the long progress of China's checkered history. (The Chinese classical language remained the same from Confucian times to 1919!)

As it was, Chinese cooking just went marching merrily along, picking up a point here and an inspiration there, and asserting itself over whatever it came into contact with, as well as incorporating from other forms of cooking that had anything to contribute. Until today, it is probably true to say that all the cooking of Eastern Asia, whether it be Japanese, Mongolian, Korean, Vietnamese, Burmese, Malayan, or Indonesian, is peripheral to the cooking of China. The traffic has of course flowed both ways, but with China being by far the largest entity, the outflow from that country has been greater than the inflow.

This does not mean, however, that Chinese cooking, being so liberal in attitude, is traditional. It is only because it is such a massive tradition that it is able to accept extraneous elements without compromise. Freedom and unconcern are often the reflection of security. Like the English language, conscious of its Shakespearian weight and its unique style and massive literature, it has a large appetite for foreign expressions. It incorporates them without any trace of self-consciousness. So Chinese cooking, having been fed by so many tributaries, has now grown into such a large river that it is difficult to extricate and determine the origin of all its diverse dishes (Peking Duck, for instance, was originally Mongolian, but is now much more a favorite in Peking than in Ulan Bator).

The impact of Western cooking in China, and Chinese cooking in the West, is undoubtedly a major event in the culinary history of the world. The repercussions will be far-reaching. Which will absorb more from the other's traditions? If the blending of pure Marxism and Confucian ethical righteousness has produced the Cultural Revolution in China, what would the mixing of sweet and sour sauce and bechamel sauce produce? If a Long Island duckling, dried with an electric hair-dryer and roasted in a Massachusetts oven, produces as crispy and perfect a Peking Duck (and perhaps more readily) as in Peking, what would the impact of modern technology do to Chinese cooking? For what both Western and Chinese cooking have to face up to is not just each other but also the technological advances of the last quarter of the twentieth century.

These are, therefore, all exciting questions, which add spice to the problems of Chinese cooking of today.

To keep its creativeness alive, Chinese cooking should at this juncture take full note of the culinary arts of all the major schools of cooking in the West, as well as take into account all the exciting new avenues and possibilities afforded by modern technology, rather than always hark back to the Classics, which, although they set a pinnacle of standards, are inclined to be backward-looking and are bound by their limitations. Ancestral worship is all very well for the Confucians, but it is of little contribution to the production of a juicy pie in the future sky towards which we are all flying (I hope!). Yet it was Confucius himself who said that the purpose of reviewing the past is to comprehend the new and see the future. So we must all study and master Classical Cooking yet keep our eyes focused on the future.

If Chinese cooking is to engender a forward-looking spirit, it has only to encourage and keep alive the creativeness which is within its own nature and tradition. It is only thus that its contribution to the culinary world at large can be most useful and have the greatest effect.

For Westerners, of course, the first step is to get to know Chinese cooking—especially its theme, spirit, and liberal and classical practice—and to make acquaintance with as many well-established methods and dishes as possible, as much their eating as their preparation, for much of the spirit and theme of a dish lie revealed in its eating—an indulgence which can, after all, be an extremely pleasant vice.

Accepted Methods of Heating Food in Chinese Cooking

If one were to take into account all the differing provincial variations, there are probably twice as many verbs as the ones I have listed below indicating the different methods of heating food in Chinese cooking. The fact that even this short list contains more than three dozen distinct terms, each with its own accepted operative meaning, must be an indication of the refinement and importance which the Chinese attach to the art of heating—which is best described as 'fire control' 火候 He Hou—a term which we actually use to apply to the control of heating 火候 in our cooking.

In some Western cooking, the quality of the raw materials is the primary thing. In Chinese cooking three things are equally important: raw materials, 'fire-control' in heating, and flavoring.

Heating or fire control has come to assume such importance in Chinese cooking partly because we often practice multi-phase heating, which involves much more change of 'pace', and partly because in the case of quick stir-frying the temperature is so high that timing has consequently to be as often in seconds as in minutes. This latter process can almost be more appropriately described as 'scorch-frying lubricated with oil'. Western readers who are attuned to reading Chinese recipe books in the original (in Chinese) would probably at first be surprised to note the frequent instruction: 'heat the pan red'. After such an instruction nobody would be surprised to find that cooking time is often just a matter of seconds!

But Chinese cooking is like photography, where the exposure can be instantaneous or prolonged. In the case of the latter, the process can be almost interminable. In the case of quick stir-frying, the final blending of taste and flavor is usually done at such a high temperature that the heat itself becomes an essential part of the flavor. Dishes blended hot have usually to be eaten within a minute of leaving the pan to be at their best.

In some ways this aspect of Chinese cooking is not unlike the old-fashioned way of heating and beating iron: a piece of iron may take some time to heat, but it is only when it is red-hot that it can be beaten into shape. Hence the beating is often furious, since the iron will remain red-hot and malleable only for a short while. So, in Chinese cooking, this final process of blending flavors at high temperature has also often to be a very short one. This is partly because the food cannot often stay at that temperature for any length of time without burning or being overcooked; yet at the same time, without reaching that high temperature, the blending will be incomplete. Like a musician, the Chinese chef works up to a crescendo, although he may have begun slowly with an overture or a chorale. Over the cooker the chef is essentially a conductor, and for this reason Chinese cooking is probably the most enjoyable in the world. So much is in interpretation, and the interpreter has so much at his fingertips. Because both heating and flavoring are multi-phase, he can raise the heat here, and lower the heat there; he can add a dash of flavor here and a touch there; he can add a mighty injection of taste, ingredient, or seasoning at the beginning, middle, or towards the end. But all the time he must have in mind a clear concept of the design he wishes to achieve. This is what makes Chinese cooking so fascinating—it is 'artistic chemistry'—and the control of heating is an integral part of that alchemy.

Indeed, looking at Chinese cooking chemically, heating is so much a part of flavoring that they cannot be conceived separately. If you know heating, you will know flavoring, and that is two-thirds of mastering the business of cooking.

1.  Chu

'Chu' is the usual Chinese verb to indicate the general process of cooking; more specifically, it indicates cooking in water by boiling. As a culinary method, it has to be a well-controlled and well-timed process. The boiling must not be too long or most of the flavor and juices of the ingredient cooked will go into the water (soup), nor must it be too short, resulting in undercooking. In the accepted Chinese practice, the boiling is controlled by bringing the water initially to a full-boil, and then either by introducing small amounts of cold water at intervals or by lowering the heat to such a point that the boiling will continue only at a simmer.

Meat and poultry are often cooked whole in this manner. Once cooked, the meat is sliced or chopped into pieces of suitable size and eaten after being dipped into various dips at the table. These dips are made by mixing various sauces and ingredients, such as chopped ginger, chives, scallions, garlic, soy sauce, chili, sherry, mustard, plum sauce, and purées (tomato, apple, etc.). Alternatively the pieces of meat may be dipped into mixes, which usually consist of mixtures of dry condiments, such as salt, pepper, chili powder, and five spice powder (equal quantities of anise, cinnamon, cloves, fennel, and star anise).

Boiling is a very popular and well-favored method of food preparation, due primarily to the purity of flavor resulting from the plain cooking of the ingredients, which tend to retain more of their original tastes and flavors. The use of highly-seasoned dips allows the individual diners to flavor the food according to personal taste.

2. 燙 T'ang or 湯 爆 T'ang P'ao

This process can perhaps be described as 'steeping' or 'quick-boiling'. It is really a variation of the previous process of plain boiling. The method used here is to bring the soup, stock, or water to a high pitch of boiling; then the ingredients to be cooked are dipped into the hot liquid. The food is usually sliced or cut into suitably thin pieces and dipped into the hot liquid for the momentary process of quick-boiling. Alternatively, the hot liquid can be poured onto the food arranged in a serving bowl. The heat of the liquid seals and cooks the food quickly. Again, food cooked in this way is eaten by dipping into dips and mixes. The method is sometimes also called 'He'.

3. 涮 Shuan

When the previous method of cooking is carried out in a charcoal-burning, or methylated spirit-heated hot pot or fondue pot placed on the dining table itself (a sight particularly warming on a winter's evening), it is called 'Shuan'. The ingredients cooked are usually thinly-sliced meats, such as beef, lamb, kidney, liver, and chicken. The best known of them all is Peking Mongolian Sliced Lamb Hot Pot. This dish has a Chinese Moslem background, originating from the Central Asian grasslands and prairies.

4. 浸 Ch'in

'Ch'in' is the process of cooking in water by gradual reduction in temperature—that is, controlled heating achieved through natural reduction in temperature by removing the heated container from the source of heat.

The usual procedure followed in this process is first of all to bring the heating liquid (usually water) to the boil, immerse the food to be cooked, and after a very short period of boiling, remove the pan from the heat, allowing the rest of the cooking to be done by the remaining heat in the liquid.

In this case the length of the boiling can of course be varied to suit the ingredient being cooked, but it must be short (not more than one minute).

In China, this process is often used in conjunction with other processes of heating to complete the cooking of a given dish. When used alone, it generally applies only to young and tender food. A good example is Crystal Chicken, in which a pullet is immersed in boiling water for one minute and then allowed to cool in the liquid. When cold, the water is discarded, and the chicken is chopped into pieces of suitable size for eating along with various dips on the table. Alternatively, the chicken could be marinated with wine, liqueur, salt, chopped chives, ginger, and garlic, and served without further cooking as Drunken Chicken (an excellent item for hors d'oeuvres).

The advantage of this process is that by immersing the food in a liquid which is boiling, the shock of the immersion locks in all the flavorsome juices (provided, of course, the food is fresh and tender); and since the material is already tender, it requires no further cooking than that which the heat already present in the cooking liquid will do during the next 10–20 minutes, as the temperature recedes gradually from boiling point. Good fresh food is invariably found to be richer in flavor and fresher-tasting than if it had been boiled in the ordinary way (say for more than 20–30 minutes).

'Ch'in' is applicable not only to heating in water, but also in stock and oil. Hence the terms 'cooking in stock-receding-heat' and 'cooking in oil-receding-heat'.

5. 川 Ch'uan

'Ch'uan' is another process of water-heating or stock-heating which is allied to 'Ch'in'. Here the technique is to use re-boiling as the measure of the length or extent of the heating. Stock or water is brought to a rolling boil, and the food to be cooked is then introduced.

At the next re-boil, or the following re-boil (after a short period when the container is removed from the heat), or else at the third re-boil, the food will be cooked and ready. Again, only young and tender fresh food can be cooked in this manner. For thicker or larger cuts of meat, two or three, or even four re-boils might be necessary before the food is well-cooked.

Again, this form of cooking is frequently used in conjunction with other forms of heating. In China both meat and vegetables are often cooked in this manner first before being subjected to other forms of heating, such as quick-frying, deep-frying, or deep-frying-and-steaming. In Western cooking this process, when used in conjunction with other forms of heating, is sometimes loosely called parboiling. 'Ch'uan' is, however, a much more refined process, in that it has its precise timing and, unlike parboiling, can be used as an independent form of cooking.

6. 煲 Pao

'Pao' is the process of deep-boiling, the equivalent of deep-frying. The quantity of water used should be at least three to four times greater than the amount of food cooked. As a rule, the heat applied is low, and the process is one of 'time-cooking'—a long-term affair. In this connection, it might be mentioned that although the Chinese are renowned for high-heat cooking, as in 'Chow' (quick-stir-frying), Cha (deep-frying), and Pao (high-heat stir-frying), they also possess extensive methods of low-heat cooking.

7. 燜 Men

'Men' is very similar to the Western process of stewing. The procedure is to fry the main ingredient first in a little oil, together with various seasonings and supplementary ingredients and materials. A reasonable quantity of water or stock is then added, and the contents brought to the boil. The heat is then reduced, and a long period of slow-simmering follows.

The apparent difference between 'Men' and Western stewing lies in the fact that the Chinese concept involves somewhat lower heat and a longer period of cooking. Hence anything which is 'Men' tends to be cooked to almost jelly-like tenderness, and because of the use of soy sauce, an ingredient which does not seem to change character whatever amount of cooking it is subjected to, the chances of success here are much greater.

11

Again in contrast to Western stewing, in Chinese cooking of this type generally just meat alone is used without vegetables, at any rate to start with. Meat such as beef (especially shin), lamb, pork (pigs' feet, knuckles, etc.) is cooked in this way. In any case, because of the length of time involved in cooking, any vegetables cooked with the meat would mostly have disappeared by the end of 3–5 hours of slow-cooking, during which time their flavor-imparting qualities would have become negligible. Hence in 'Men', unlike stewing, when vegetables and other supplementary ingredients are used, if they are introduced at all, they are added only towards the last 20–45 minutes of cooking time.

The most frequent forms of 'Men' are Brown Stew and Red Stew (using brown sugar, red bean cheese or red wine-sediment paste in addition to soy sauce).

8. 燒 Shao

'Shao' is one of the most commonly employed terms in Chinese cooking. The process is very similar to the preceding 'Men' in that it involves frying first in a little oil, then continuing by cooking and simmering in stock or water.

The difference lies in that in the second phase in the process of 'Shao', there is a period of conscious reduction of liquid (as in French cooking), when small amounts of fresh ingredients and seasonings are often added, leaving ultimately only a small amount of thickened gravy to go with the meat. In 'Men' there is usually more gravy.

9. 义 燒 Cantonese Cha Shao (Spit-roast)

In the Cantonese 'Cha Shao' method, there is not only a process of reduction of liquid at the last phase, but in addition, the meat is placed over a fire or in the oven for a period of barbecuing or roasting. Often the 'Cha Shao' process involves cutting the meat (usually pork) into strips, then thoroughly marinating them before 'hang-roasting' them in the oven. The strips of meat are brushed with a specially prepared marinade at regular intervals until cooked.

In the cooking of 'Cantonese Roast Pigling', the head and tail of the animal are subjected to a period of 'Shao' (that is, cooking in the pan with the flavouring ingredients) before the whole animal is barbecue-roasted.

10. 滷 Lu

'Lu' is a process of cooking food (usually meat, liver, kidney, other variety meats, poultry. eggs, and sometimes fish), in a strong, aromatic, soy-herbal stock. The stock is initially prepared by simmering meat in broth with quantities of rock sugar, soy sauce, sherry, dried tangerine peel, ginger, garlic, and five spice powder (a mixture of cinnamon, fennel, cloves, anise, and star anise). The first stock produced is called the 'original stock' and as more meats and food are simmered in it the stock assumes the name of 'master stock'.

The master stock is used again and again, and every three to four times it is used more fresh herbs have to be added and boiled in it. The herbal strength of the stock, as well as the strength of the other ingredients, can be varied according to taste or requirement.

The master stock is further enriched each time fresh materials are cooked in it; it is not only enriched but renewed. So long as the stock is used with some frequency, and its herbs strengthened and renewed, it can be used more or less forever. Some master stocks can be ranked as living antiques!

11.  Ch'eng

'Ch'eng' is a form of steaming. There are two accepted forms of steaming in China: steaming in an open bowl or plate and steaming in a closed receptacle.

'Ch'eng' is 'open steaming'—here the bowl, plate, or basin is usually placed on a wire or bamboo rack, set inside a large pot, with the water kept at a rolling boil some inches below. Or the process can be carried out in multi-layer baskets with enclosed sides which fit on top of one another in a top-hat fashion, and which are placed on top of the rice-boiler. Thus the dishes can be cooked while the rice is being steamed or boiled.

In 'Ch'eng' the food to be cooked is usually pre-marinated or treated with all the necessary seasonings, garnishes and decorations before being placed in a steamer. Sometimes the food is given only a short blast of vigorous steaming. 'Ch'eng' is most often used when the food to be cooked does not require prolonged cooking—indeed, a short, sharp blast of steam is one of the few ways that certain foods may be cooked in order to retain their original freshness, flavor, and juiciness. Fish, being usually tender in flesh, is most often and best cooked in this manner. Because of the prevalence of 'Ch'eng', we Chinese have been recognized as expert fish and seafood cooks.

12. 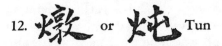 Tun

In contrast to 'Ch'eng', 'Tun' is closed steaming, that is, steaming in a closed receptacle; and in China the mouth of the receptacle is often sealed with paper which is stuck down or glued on. In the West this can be done by covering with a piece of aluminum foil, but with so many different types of casseroles with lids available, it is rarely necessary to have to resort to this.

It is always the practice in 'Tun', before the cooking proper starts, to place the food in boiling water for 1–2 minutes. This is followed by a quick rinse in cold water before placing the food in a casserole or closed pot for steaming.

The boiling and rinsing help to cleanse the food of impurities as well as to lock in the juices. All the seasoning, marinating, adding of supplementary materials, garnishing, and decorating should be completed before the actual steaming starts.

Often in 'Tun' only a very few ingredients and supplementary materials are added to the main ingredient, which is usually meat. This is in order to achieve an end-product of impeccable purity.

Because of the great desire and tradition of achieving purity, this method is very much favored in invalid cooking; besides, the prolonged steaming, which is habitual in this process, also ensures that the food will be extremely tender. Pure and tender food is considered ideal for the sick and aged.

Again in contrast to 'Che'ng', 'Tun' is, as a rule, a lengthy process—30–40 minutes upwards to 3–6 hours. Another cooking process called 'Kao', which is very long simmering over a low heat, produces very nearly the same results. In this process, as in 'Tun', the food is subjected to a short, sharp boil, followed by rinsing in cold water, before the actual cooking starts.

13.  P'eng

'P'eng' is a process which involves frying the foodstuff on either side until brown, then introducing a limited amount of stock or water and supplementary ingredients. The cooking is then continued over a low heat until all the liquid has been reduced to dryness. This is, in a way, fairly akin to 'Cantonese Ch'a Shao', except that in the latter process the complete drying of the food is achieved through barbecue-roasting.

14.  Hui

'Hui' can perhaps be described as 'hot assembly in thickened soup' (the soup is usually thickened with cornstarch or water chestnut flour).

The ingredients used in this cooking process are usually in long, strip form, or cut into shreds. Transparent bean-thread noodles are frequently used. Normally a number of different types of food, both cooked, semi-cooked, and fresh are cooked together with a wide range of vegetables. The meats and tougher ingredients are usually fried first in a small amount of oil which impregnates the food, and thereby, together with some seasonings, provides the first phase of flavoring. This is followed by the addition of soup (the quantity of soup should not exceed the total amount of ingredients used). A period of cooking together with a further range of food and some seasonings (perhaps wine) follows, thus providing a second phase of flavoring.

The mixed contents of the pan are then brought up to a boil and, after a short burst of high boiling and some scrambling together, cornstarch and a small amount of monosodium glutamate are added, transforming the soup into a gravy. If the transparent noodles have absorbed nearly all the soup, the result would be what might be termed 'solid gravy'. This is probably the best form of Chinese mixed vegetable dish, flavored with meat and swimming in gravy, which does not spill easily.

The last build-up in flavor is carried out by placing a drop or two of sesame oil on top of the mixed composite food—it invariably provides a warming and earthy aroma. The famous 'Lo-Han Chai' (Chinese Monastic Vegetable Ensemble) is a dish essentially in this tradition, except that in this case all the ingredients used are vegetarian.

15. Pan

'Pan' can be described as 'hot toss-and-scramble', except when cold is expressly indicated, resulting in the production of a composite dish which can almost be described as a 'hot salad'. It is a process of cooking which is very similar to 'Hui'. They differ in that 'Pan' is a dry process—no soup is added; the different strip-foods (or foods reduced to strips) are tossed and scrambled together in flavor-impregnated oil, which is used almost as a savory lubricant.

Again in 'Pan', all the constituent foods must be sliced into long matchstick strips, while in 'Hui' only some of the constituent foods need be in strip form. They differ again in that while in 'Hui' transparent bean-thread noodles are frequently used, in 'Pan' ordinary wheat-flour noodles are usually used.

In conception, and as a process, it differs from the Italian idea of how pasta foods should be produced in that a much greater range of constituent ingredients is incorporated. These ingredients generally fall into two distinct categories: cooked ingredients and uncooked or fresh ingredients. Because of the juxtaposition and incorporation of both cooked and uncooked foods, each with their prior treatment, flavoring, or cooking, the resultant 'hot salad' has a very distinctive quality of its own. As in the process of 'Hui', a little sesame oil is generally used as a final flavoring.

16. 炸 Cha

'Cha' is the equivalent of deep-frying. As a form of cooking, it is sometimes much the same thing as Western deep-frying, where food is first of all dipped in a batter, and then given a period of deep-frying until it is ready for serving.

But as often as not in China, 'Cha' is only one of two or three stages of heating in the cooking of a given dish. In Crispy and Aromatic Duck the duck is first marinated and steamed before it is finally deep-fried to give it that final crispiness; or in the case of Crackling Wonton dumpling, the thin-skinned ravioli with meat filling is steamed or simmered first before being finally deep-fried, again to achieve that final crispiness.

On the other hand, deep-frying is sometimes used as an initial process where food (usually meat) is given an initial deep-fry, until it is nearly cooked, and then it is given a phase of seasoning by marinading. It is only after a period of well-adjusted flavoring that it is given a short sharp, final frying (usually this time only in a limited amount of oil), before being served piping-hot. Diced Meat in Soy Jam or Chicken Cubes in Hot and Sour Sauce or Sweet and Sour Sauce belong to this category.

In general, in the Chinese process of deep frying, the food often requires two or three immersions in hot oil to complete the cooking, and the oil in these cases is divided into three degrees of heat-temperature: 'hot oil', 'very hot oil' and 'fierce oil'. In many cases it is necessary to break up the deep-frying process into several phases, as the food could easily burn if the frying were to be maintained as one continuous process. Besides, the intermission (when the food is given a chance to cook in its own heat) can often provide an opportunity for the food to be treated with additional flavoring.

Deep-frying in China is conventionally divided into three categories: 'plain-fried', when the food material is cooked or deep-fried on its own; 'soft-fried', when sauces and seasonings are added to the food, especially during the latter part of the frying, when the excess oil has been drained away; and 'dry-fried', when the food is rolled in flour or cornstarch or dipped in batter before being fried.

17. 永 Yung

'Yung' is cooking in one continuous deep-frying process or deep-frying in one phase. The oil used in this one-phase deep-frying is usually 'just hot'. Because the heat of the oil is not too fierce, and the sizzling noise after the food is introduced is just barely audible, the food can be cooked for 10–15 minutes without burning. In 'Yung' the food must be suitable for cooking in one continuous process.

18. 炒 Chow (or Ch'ao)

'Chow' is distinguished from 'Cha' in that it is stir-frying and only a small amount of oil is used in the cooking (almost as a lubricant). The ingredients being fried are kept in more or less continuous movement throughout the process of cooking. A metal spoon (ordinary or perforated), or a pair of chopsticks, is used to keep the food in motion.

The materials to be cooked are usually cut into strips or small pieces, so that more of their surfaces come into contact with the pan, and are exposed to the heating-oil and seasonings. 'Chow' is usually a quick process (often translated as 'quick-frying'), and is probably one of the fastest cooking methods for a tasty dish. The process seldom takes more than 2–3 minutes—often only a few seconds.

19. 爆 Pao

'Pao' is a term employed to indicate rapid cooking over a high heat, either in oil or in stock. 'Yiu Pao' means oil-rapid-cooked and 'Tang Pao' means stock-rapid-cooked.

When oil is used, the method differs from the ordinary 'Chow' or quick-frying in that the cooking is for a shorter period of time, and over a higher heat. Besides, 'Pao' is always the finale in any multi-stage cooking process, while 'Chow' or 'Cha' quick-frying and deep-frying can take place at an earlier stage. In 'Pao', the foodstuff being cooked is usually already seasoned and flavored, or has been cooked at a previous stage. 'Pao' is never lengthy, and it is a phase in the oil frying process which can be described as 'frying up to a crescendo'. In China, the term 'Pao' is the same word used to describe an explosion. The process can, therefore, also be described as 'explosive-frying' or 'explosive-boiling'.

When water or stock are used in the cooking, 'Pao' is usually a process of dipping thinly sliced meat or vegetables into the liquid, which is kept in a state of rolling boil.

Food which has been 'Pao', that is 'explosively-fried' or dipped in high-boiling stock or water should, as a rule, be eaten red-hot from the pan—for the heat in the food is taken as an integral part of the flavor.

A well-known example of the process of 'Pao' is Quick-Fried Diced Chicken in Soy Jam. In this case the chicken meat is first of all diced into cubes, and semi-deep-fried until almost cooked. It is then 'explosively-fried' in a hot marinade of soy jam with sugar, wine, and vinegar for about 15 seconds to one minute to complete the cooking.

20. 煎 Chien

'Chien' is a process of cooking in oil, in which only a small amount of oil is used, and the cooking is static for a period of time (usually longer than 'Chow' and much longer than 'Pao'). The food to be cooked can be in larger chunks or pieces than in the case of 'Chow' or 'Pao', hence more time is required for them to cook through. A typical case of 'Chien' in Western cooking is fried bread. 'Chien' can be used as one phase in a multi-phase cooking process. The gravy or sauce used in the dish can be prepared separately and poured over the food afterwards.

21. 淋 Ling

This is a process which might be called 'splash-frying'. In other words, the food is not actually immersed in the oil during the frying; instead it is suspended above the oil, and a ladle is used to pour and splash the food with hot oil which is then allowed to run down into the pan containing the oil. A well-known dish cooked in this manner is 'Yiu Ling Chi' or Splash-Fried Chicken. Here the chicken can be suspended over the oil in a wire-basket and ladles of oil are poured steadily over the chicken until the bird is brown and well-cooked. Because in this manner of cooking, the heat, i.e. the oil, is applied by hand, it is a well-controlled process. Chicken cooked in this manner is considered much more special than 'Deep-Fried Chicken', and is suitable for serving at a banquet. The seasoning of the chicken, whether through marinating, rubbing with a mixture of salt, pepper, and ginger, or by treatment in some other manner, before or during the cooking, is something which can be varied according to the taste or inclination of the chef. In any case, poultry so prepared is the result of craft-work, which evolves and matures visibly into a finished dish under the eyes of the chef. Thus it is more of a prized product, created with more justifiable pride than run-of-the-mill deep-fried dishes.

22. 溜 Liu

'Liu' is a form of wet-frying in which a thickened sauce (invariably involving cornstarch, sugar, and vinegar) is made or introduced during the middle or later stage of frying.

In 'Liu', the frying is comparatively static compared to 'Chow' or 'Pao': the food is not subjected to a rapid movement of stirring and scrambling. Hence in 'Liu' a flat, wide pan is favored, so that more of the foodstuff being cooked can be in direct contact with the metal of the hot pan, without continual movement. Movements are confined to the steadier, gentler type of turning over of ingredients, without too much rapidity or violence.

The sauce mixture used in 'Liu' is usually prepared beforehand in a separate bowl, and added into the frying pan soon after both sides of the food have been fried, or during the final phase of the cooking. 'Liu' is one of the favorite methods of cooking sliced fish, in which case some wine or spirit is often introduced into the sauce mixture, and the fish slices themselves are initially fried in oil with a little garlic, ginger, and onion to heighten the flavor.

In Canton the term 'Hua' is often used to describe the process. Both these terms, 'Liu' and 'Hua', are used to describe skating on ice, or that slip-sliding, lubricated movement in the pan, when the sauce-mixture is added for the final phase of the cooking.

23. 貼 T'ieh

'T'ieh' resembles 'Chien' in that it is a static, non-scramble form of frying, in which not too much oil is used. It is different from 'Chien' in that normally only one side of the food is fried—the food is not turned over as in the frying of bread. In fact, it is quite often the practice to sprinkle the top side of the food with water or stock while the frying is going on, to keep it soft on top. Thus in the case of 'Kuo T'ieh' (Peking Pot-Stuck Ravioli), the aim is to produce something which is crispy underneath, soft on top, and juicy inside. (In the cooking of Kuo T'ieh a lid is placed over the large, flat pan for a while to help the cooking.)

'T'ieh' is, however, also a term which is sometimes applied to the frying of large slices of food on both sides (as in the case of frying a veal scallop), and after cooking is completed and the food is removed from the pan, it is sliced into smaller pieces before being served.

24. 熿 Pien

'Pien' is a type of frying which is used mostly in vegetable cooking; about 10–15% of oil is used in relation to the weight of the vegetables being cooked.

It is the practice to first of all fry a small quantity of onion, garlic, and ginger or pickles, so that the oil will be impregnated with their strong taste and aromatic flavor. The main vegetable is then fried in the oil, to take on to a lesser degree the same appealing taste and flavor, further enhanced by the heat of the frying.

After 2–3 minutes of continued frying, and when the vegetable is thoroughly oil-impregnated, a small amount of water or stock is introduced. This has the effect of preventing burning, and also provides quick-steaming. Furthermore, flavoring is added when a good stock is used. The result is tender, glistening vegetables which have in fact been cooked primarily in their own juices; and if some seasonings (such as soy sauce, monosodium glutamate, sesame oil, chicken fat, wine, or sugar) are added, it should make an extremely palatable dish. 'Pien' is the usual way in which most vegetables are cooked in China.

25.  Ao

'Ao' is really a compressed form of 'Pien'. It starts with the food or vegetable being fried in a small amount of oil, with the addition of some ingredients and seasonings. When partly cooked and well-covered and impregnated with oil, a little water or stock is introduced. Thereafter the cooking is finished or rounded off with both a 'high-boil' and 'high-fry' over a high heat, resulting in the food being part-fried and part steamed. Here the steam is, however, of special quality, being impregnated with the flavor and aroma of the strong-tasting vegetables.

'Ao' is, therefore, a compressed process of rapid frying, followed by rapid cooking or steaming. It is a process often used in cooking crabs and lobsters, where the seafood is subjected to the blast of flavor-impregnated steam with results which can only be called advantageous.

26.  Wen

In timing and method, 'Wen' is the cooking process which is nearest to the Western concept of braising. The food material is here first of all fried in oil with the addition of a few seasonings and other ingredients. After the initial quick stir-frying, a small amount of water or stock is introduced. The cooking pan is then moved to a low heat or the heat can be reduced, to cook for 10–15 minutes with some gentle stirring. Just before serving, a small amount of cornstarch and a dash of monosodium glutamate (both mixed in water and wine) are introduced for a final fry-up to thicken the gravy and accentuate the flavor.

27. Chüeh

'Chüeh' is a variation of 'Wen' in that some supplementary ingredients (usually garlic, ginger, and onion or chili) are fried in oil first before the introduction of the main material. Once the latter is cooked or browned, the seasonings and stock are added. The contents of the pan are then simmered over a low heat for 10–20 minutes. Thereupon the solid food is removed and placed on a well-heated serving plate, to await the sauce. The sauce is produced by the addition of a little cornstarch mixed in water, a dash of monosodium glutamate, and some wine to the remaining liquid in the pan, which is then heated for 1 minute. When the sauce is ready it is then poured over the main ingredients in the dish or plate. The only difference between this method and the previous one is that in 'Chüch', the gravy or sauce is produced at the last moment, separately from the main ingredients of the dish.

28.  Chü

'Chü' is another variation on the braising theme. It involves an initial frying of the main and supplementary ingredients over a high heat, followed by the addition of further ingredients and the introduction of water, soup, or wine. The process is then continued along one of two lines, both involving a reduction of the liquid: prolonged simmering over a very low heat, and controlled braising over a somewhat higher heat, so that the liquid can be reduced visually to the desired thickness and quantity.

Another meaning of the term 'Chü' denotes pot-roasting or casserole cooking, where only a minimal amount of liquid is used.

29.  Ts'ang

'Ts'ang' is a term generally applied to the method of frying and braising in which the ingredients are generally stir-fried in the usual manner and placed on a serving dish. A sauce is then made from a previously prepared mixture which is quickly heated in the pan. The sauce is poured over the food in the serving dish and left to cool. The dish is served cold.

'Ts'ang' is a term which is also used to describe the process of treatment, seasoning, and marinating involved in 'cold mixing' or 'cold tossing' (as in salad making). Here the customary seasonings and ingredients are used: sesame oil, vinegar, soy sauce, good stock, chopped scallions, ginger, and garlic. 'Cold mixing' in China generally applies not to the preparing of a vegetable dish, but to a pasta dish (noodles), involving both cooked and uncooked ingredients and supplementary materials, which are all seasoned and marinated, together or separately, prior to being served cold.

30.  T'a

'T'a' (as in 'Kuo T'a') means deep-frying food in batter, then draining it of oil and cooking and braising it with various supplementary ingredients. 'T'a' is also used to describe the same process with an additional phase of initial steaming, before the deep-frying and braising.

31. 烤 K'ao

'K'ao' is a term which indicates exactly the same process as in Western roasting. However, in China, without the modern oven, fire control is much more difficult. A great deal of art and skill has to go into fire-building and timing. Usually a large pile-up of wood is first of all burned in a stove, like a bonfire. The resulting smoldering wood and charcoal are then scraped and piled up on the sides, and the food to be cooked is hung up in the middle of the stove for roasting—as in the cooking of Peking Duck.

In denoting the process of roasting, 'K'ao' differs from the term 'Shao', in that the latter word when used in this sense denotes the type of roasting where the heat is applied entirely from below, such as barbecue roasting where the food is generally turned on a spit over the fire; or it can also indicate pot-roasting. In 'K'ao' the cooking is effected largely through air-heating (convection), or direct-level radiation.

32.  Hung

'Hung' indicates open barbecue-roasting. It involves the frequent turning of raw food on a spit over an open fire. The term 'Shao' sometimes indicates the same thing, but 'Hung' is the more specific term. It means heating mainly by radiation.

33.  Wei

'Wei' is the process of cooking by 'burial', that is the burying of food in hot solids, such as charcoal, smoldering coal, heated stones, sand, salt, or lime (heat evolved by the addition of water). Foods cooked in this manner are generally of the type with a thick crust or skin, or foods which can easily be wrapped in a cover—such as in lotus leaves, a mudpack, or a sheet of suet. (Sweet potato baked in its jacket by burying in hot coal and earth is a typical case.)

Without the modern oven, we Chinese resort to cooking by burial much more frequently than in the West. 'Chiao Hua Chicken' from Amoy is a case of heating by burial in lime, over which water is then poured.

34.  Hsün

'Hsün' is to smoke. In Chinese smoking, the food material used has usually been cooked beforehand. It is often previously seasoned in salt, wine, onion, and ginger.

The food is suspended over the smoke/fire on a wire rack. A few pieces of red, smoldering coal or charcoal are first placed under the rack inside a pan or tin fitted with a cover or in a proper Kilu. The coal or charcoal is then covered with a handful of sawdust, sugar, or dried tea leaves. This immediately creates a heavy smoke. The lid is then closed and the food left to smoke for 15–20 minutes, depending upon the degree of smokiness required. In Cantonese cooking, smoking with tea leaves is called 'Hsüng', and with sawdust 'Yen'.

35. 扣 K'ou

'K'ou' is a double process—usually frying first and steaming afterwards, and the food is then turned out from the steaming bowl on to a plate (like a pudding).

The main ingredient to be cooked is usually fried first, then sliced into smaller pieces. It is then neatly packed with several supplementary and flavoring materials in a heat-proof bowl. The ingredients are arranged in layers, and placed in a steamer for a period of prolonged steaming. When the foods are cooked, they are then turned out on a serving plate. The term 'K'ou' in Chinese actually means 'turn out': the result is usually a 'meat-pudding'.

36. 朴 Pa

'Pa' is just the reverse process of 'K'ou', in that here the food is steamed first, then fried. In the final frying the food is often given a last flavoring by the addition of supplementary materials, ingredients, and seasonings. This last 'treatment' has the effect of sharpening and livening up the flavor of the food.

37. 醉 Tsui

'Tsui' is the process of marinating fresh or cooked food in wine or liqueur before serving, thus giving it a 'drunken' effect, as in Drunken Chicken. Food treated in this way in China is usually only lightly cooked (often by the process of 'Chien') and then subjected to a period of marinating in wine, liqueur, scallions, ginger, and garlic. Meat, fish, and seafood can all be prepared in this manner. But when meat is used it is usually poultry meat; and in a majority of cases the marinating needs only to be for a short length of time (although several days is more usual).

38. 醬 Chiang and 糟 Chiaow

'Chiang' and 'Chiaow' are processes of food preparation which are closely related in method to 'Tsui'; the difference lies mainly in the difference between the marinating ingredients used. In 'Tsui', as already pointed out, the marinade is composed principally of wine or liqueur. In 'Chiang' the main ingredients are soy sauce and soy jam. In 'Chiaow' the principal ingredient used in the marinade is a paste made from wine-sediment (the dregs or lees from the bottom of a wine jar), which is called 'wine-sediment paste'. These pastes exist in different colors such as red, purple, brown, and cream. When these ingredients are used to marinate, a small amount of ground ginger and salt are often added. The foods are usually first of all lightly cooked, then placed in an earthen jar where the marinating is carried out, often lasting several days or weeks.

39. 醃 Yien

'Yien' is the general term for salting and marinating, but more specifically, 'Yien' is the process of salting—usually with coarse salt.

The food to be salted is rubbed with coarse salt and a little saltpeter and placed in an earthen jar. It is turned over once every three days. After nine days a heavy weight (usually a stone) is placed on it to squeeze out any remaining liquid. Meat thus treated is capable of keeping for a good length of time and even inferior meat can become flavorsome after a period. Heating in one form or another usually precedes or follows the salting.

40. 風 Feng

'Feng' is the above process when it is carried out by drying in the wind, instead of by compressed marinating in a jar. Although these preserved meats and fish are edible, have a very distinctive taste, and are very appealing to many, they are often used in conjunction with fresh food, to impart to the latter their distinctive taste contribution. In the case of salted fish, it is usually fried up to a crispy state for eating with rice. It is a great help in downing rice as it acts as a kind of 'non-dairy cheese'. Not infrequently it is cooked with meat to give an anchovy flavor. Therefore, in these cases, the salting, drying, and heating are all part of a triple or multi-phase process in the preparation of a food material. Although the materials can be used independently, they are more frequently used in conjunction with one another.

There are many more cooking terms in China than the foregoing forty. Every province and region has its own expressions and peculiarities. Some of the cooking terms are related to the material and ingredients used. But forty is a round number, and the various local terms and expressions, although they may run into dozens more, are really only variations of these principal, basic terms.

The Chopsticks and Chinese Cooking and Cutting

I am not certain of the origin of chopsticks, nor how far back in history they were first introduced in China. Mythology has it that when we first came down from the trees and started to make fire to heat food to make it more edible, we found it too hot to handle with fingers. Hence twigs and branches were used to pick up pieces of food.

In the early period of Chinese history (3000 BC—100 BC) the cooking utensils were usually made in the form of tripods (solid metal pots with three squat legs, which can still be seen in museums). These were simply stood on top of bonfires to do the cooking. It seems that some of the greedier ladies and gentlemen who witnessed the delectable spectacle could not wait for the pot to cool before dipping in (the large solid pots take an hour or two to cool). They manipulated the food with sticks in order to make an early start and pick out the choicer pieces for themselves. Such circumstances are likely to have been the origin of the technique of chopsticks.

However, their general adoption by polite society has probably something to do with the Confucian abhorrence of the appearance of weapons of slaughter (knives and forks) on the dining table. Confucius remarked on a famous occasion that a man's attitude towards animals, if he is an honorable and upright man (that is, in the Confucian sense, if he is a man at all), should be that if he sees an animal alive, he would hate to see it dead; and that if he heard the noise and screams of the killing, he would refrain from eating the flesh of the killed. Hence he said 'The upright and honorable man keeps well away from the kitchen and abattoirs'. It has been deduced from this that the Sage would never have countenanced the display of knives and forks—the weapons of slaughter—on the table, far less their actual sharpening at the table, activities which are indulged in with masterly ritual and masculine pride nowadays, at the best tables in some other parts of the globe!

Today, the use of chopsticks, apart from eating with bare hands and fingers, is one of the two accepted ways by which civilized human beings eat in the world. They have, in fact, a much more far-reaching effect and influence on how we Chinese cook and prepare our food than may be at first supposed.

Once chopsticks have been adopted for eating, foods have to be reduced to a size or state suitable for eating with them. In other words, foods have to be cooked to a degree of tenderness, so that they can be taken apart with a pair of chopsticks, or cut to the convenient size of a sugar lump or at the very most the size of a match-box, so that they can be picked up and chewed with some semblance of delicacy or elegance. Otherwise food must be rendered into elongated strips (such as noodles) so that it can be absorbed in the manner in which the larger reptiles gulp down the smaller ones, a kind of exercise which produces a physical satisfaction only known to the healthiest of connoisseurs!

To be eaten efficiently with a pair of chopsticks, foods in grain form have to be lifted up in a bowl and scooped into the mouth, a practice at which the Chinese are adept. The average Westerner needs practice to eliminate any self-consciousness, since the raising of dishes or bowls to one's mouth is unusual at a Western table, to say the least.

Since the longer methods of cooking which reduce food to jelly-like tenderness require a great length of time and a large consumption of fuel, the bulk of Chinese dishes are prepared from foods which have been reduced to small, uniform sizes. Hence Western people have gained the impression that Chinese cooking consists largely of 'chop, chop, chop', which is of course only too true in a majority of cases. The cutting or reduction of food to manageable and masticable sizes, which can easily be handled with a pair of chopsticks, has the following far-reaching effects on Chinese cooking.

1. Cross-cooking of different types of foods and materials is made much easier and this in turn creates the possibility of a vast number of recipes arising from different combinations of foods. It is possible, therefore, that Chinese cooking possesses a greater range and number of dishes than any other known form of cooking.

2. It has made quick stir-frying popular; when food is cut into smaller pieces, the pieces present a far larger cooking and seasoning surface both to the heating medium (oil, stock, water, or metal) as well as to the flavoring ingredients. This reduces the time required for cooking, and in the long run fuel consumption is reduced, factors which are of considerable importance whether in restaurant cooking, where dishes have to be prepared quickly and individually, or in home-cooking where time and budget are short, or in mass-catering, where the consumption of fuel has to be reckoned with.

3. Because food can be used in smaller pieces, all the left-over bits and pieces can be much more easily used up without at all impairing the quality or presentation of the dish. This makes for a much more complete use of food, and, therefore, for much greater economy, a factor which is of paramount importance in any level of human livelihood.

With these built-in advantages and economy, backed by the natural industry of the Chinese, there should be little wonder that Chinese food is now galloping around the world and making inroads everywhere.

Since most things Chinese appear to go back to Confucius, it might even be that through his advocating the substitution of chopsticks for the lethal implements on the dinner table, and because of his insistence that diners should behave and conduct themselves with all propriety, he was one of the most important originators of China's gastronomic strength.

The Technique of Chopsticks

One of the most frequently-made mistakes in the use of chopsticks is to fall into the 'baby' method, which is to cross the two sticks like a pair of scissors, and to use the fingers as best you can to close the opened ends when trying to pick up food. This appears to be the method most commonly employed by babies (up to 2½ years old) when first introduced to chopsticks, and is sometimes used not without success.

The correct way to use, as well as to learn to use a pair of chopsticks, is first of all to hold the upper of the pair with the tips of the index finger, thumb, and the longer finger—with the latter slipping and protruding a little under the chopstick (about ½ inch). Once you can hold the first chopstick firmly in place, try to move it up and down freely. Having done this, insert the other chopstick under the first one, between the thumb and the hand, crooking the fourth finger to press in the opposite direction to the thumb, which will help in holding this chopstick in place firmly. This latter chopstick is meant to be fixed and non-moving. Only the first chopstick moves. When picking up an object, the upper chopstick is moved to press the object against the lower chopstick, which should be held firmly (see figure below).

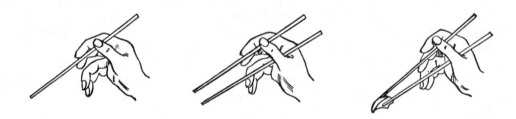

Once you have learnt to hold and manipulate the two chopsticks, the next most important thing is to *relax*. By relaxing you will forget that you are actually using a pair of chopsticks, and by practising with lumps of sugar and a matchbox you should master the technique in five minutes. Within a single meal you will have achieved one of mankind's basic techniques and forgotten altogether that you had once never used chopsticks.

Cutting

Too much can be easily made of cutting, as too much can be made of carving. Over-elaboration only creates a mystique, which dissuades interested people from undertaking what are, in fact, only simple and logical procedures in tackling specific jobs. Chinese cooking is too big to need to cloud itself over with any mystique to command reverence.

However, something has to be said about cutting, as it is more of an integral part of Chinese cooking than of Western cooking. A good part of the necessary cutting of Western food is done on the dining table, for example, carving. In Chinese cooking, practically all the cutting is done in the kitchen, and much more of it has to be done than in Western food preparation. This is due, as already mentioned, to the fact that we Chinese use chopsticks, and that the most widely used form of Chinese cooking is quick stir-frying, which necessitates reducing different types of foods to uniform sizes before cooking commences. In the main, the following are the principal shapes and sizes to which the foods and materials have to be reduced through cutting: chunks, slices, strips, shreds, dice (cubes), grains, mince.

Chunks are further divided into mah-jong-pieces, triangular (or water nut) pieces, and miniature chops (spare-ribs cut into 1 inch lengths).

Slices are divided into autumn leaf slices, willow-leaf slices (or slivers), nail-piece slices, long-oblong slices (about 3 inches thick), and very thin slices (for rapid dip-boiling in stock).

Strips are usually about the size of matchsticks, sometimes twice as long; and shreds are thinner and more thread-like in size.

Diced cubes usually vary in size from the size of an average sugar lump to half that size.

The larger type of mince is about the size of grains, and the smaller is what we call 'velvet mince'. In neither case would we Chinese resort to use of the meat grinder or blender, as we feel that through the latter's squeezing action, most of the valuable meat-juices are squeezed out and lost. We prefer to do it with two choppers at a drum-beat!

In order to perform Chinese cutting and chopping efficiently, it has to be done on a chopping board (or rather block) which is at least 6 inches thick and 12–15 inches in diameter—usually a hardwood block from a tree-trunk. Since the Chinese kitchen cleaver is a razor sharp implement, it has to be used on a very firm and steady base.

Although the Chinese kitchen cleaver is able to perform all the functions which a knife or cleaver is expected to do, the professionals in China use three weights of cleaver: the thin cleaver, heavy cleaver, and bone cleaver. The thin cleaver is used for slicing, dicing, shredding, and cutting into strips. This cleaver is used more frequently than any other. The thick or heavy cleaver is used for graining or mincing. Here the sides and top of the cleaver (opposite to the side of the blade) are constantly used for beating, hammering, flattening, and mashing, and the weight of the cleaver provides that additional gravitational power to each chop. The bone cleaver is, of course, used for cutting through the bone, as well as pushing through the joints. Bone chopping or cutting has to be done far more frequently in Chinese cooking than in Western cooking—with chopped chicken, or duck, or Chinese spare-ribs (which are cut into $\frac{3}{4}$–$1\frac{1}{2}$ inch lengths) the bones have to be chopped through at least a score of times even in the preparation of a single dish. Although it is a Western saying 'The nearer the bone, the sweeter the meat', it is the Chinese who eat the meat with its bone. The bone cleaver is also the implement used for deboning, at which Chinese chefs are masters. All these cleavers—thin, heavy, and bone—are rectangularly shaped.

The Chinese, of course, also use the cleaver for scoring. Although scoring is frequently practised in cooking thick chunks of meat or fish, it is sometimes even more important in quick stir-fry cooking, especially in the frying of kidneys and tripes, in which the action of the hot oil on the food has to be very thorough and even throughout, so that the texture and crunchiness resulting from the cooking will be uniform. In such instances the depth of the scoring has to be very even, and the cuts at almost exactly the same distance apart, so that when cooked the food will be evenly crunchy throughout.

Finally, while so much has been said about always cutting meat across or against the grain, we Chinese confine this mainly to the cutting of beef. With pork, which constitutes over 60% of all Chinese meat dishes, the cutting should usually be with the grain, for the reason that the muscles and fibers of pork are much weaker and more tender than those of beef, and if the cutting is performed against the grain, after more than 30–35 minutes cooking, the chunks or cubes of meat will begin to fall apart. You would thus end up with a dish in which the meat had broken up into all kinds and sizes of loose pieces. The same applies to chicken, which in any case does not provide enough thick meat to cut into any length or thickness against the grain.

In the case of diced pork or chicken, since the meats are cut into cubes, whether the cutting should be with or against the grain is neither here nor there; and in such cases cooking seldom exceeds ten minutes and is usually under five minutes, so there is no likelihood of the meat falling apart.

As a rule, the shape and size of cutting follows upon the original size and shape of the principal ingredients, or the sizes or shapes into which they have been cut. Diced pork or chicken will be cooked with diced vegetables; shredded beef will have shredded vegetables or bean sprouts to go with it. Noodles always have meat and vegetables sliced into strips to go with them. It is only occasionally that supplementary materials in different shapes from the principal ingredients are cooked together; a fact which only proves the rule.

Variation is found or allowed to exist in cutting only when a shorter-cooking food is sliced into somewhat thicker pieces to cook with a food which requires longer cooking time, and which is cut into thinner or smaller pieces. It is all a matter of logical timing and harmony.

Texture in Chinese Food, and the Names of Chinese Dishes

As a rule, the title of Chinese dishes consists of the name of the principal ingredient and the main method of cooking involved. Occasionally the name of the chief supplementary ingredient is tagged on, together with the style of cutting or slicing adopted. The following examples show this rule: Pure Steamed Bass, Red-Cooked Pigs' Feet, Shredded Pork Stir-Fried with Bean-Sprouts, Duck Ribbons Quick-Fried in Shredded Ginger.

The names or titles are, therefore, pretty much down to earth. It is only occasionally that they take on more fanciful flights, and assume such titles as: The Four Great Crispies (Peking), Casserole of Lions' Heads (Peking), Long-Simmered Southern Snakes (Eels: Canton), Beef with Triple Winter (Canton), Pork of Four Happiness (Metropolitan China), Great Fry of the Phoenix and Dragon (Metropolitan China).

Not infrequently, dishes are named after their originator. The best-known is Tung-Po Pork, which was named after the great poet Soo Tung-Po, who was said to have invented it.

Much more often dishes incorporate the name of their geographical origin. Thus: Canton Fried Noodles, Yangchow Fried Rice, Peking Duck, and Yellow River Sweet and Sour Carp.

Certainly, in more than half the cases, the actual method of cooking employed is incorporated in the title. For this reason alone, if not for any other, it is extremely useful to be acquainted with, or at least have an impression of, the principal features of the forty accepted methods of heating (cooking) commonly in use in China. For once you have achieved an impression of or acquaintance with these forty methods of cooking which are in effect far less complicated than they may at first appear, you will be able to achieve a grasp of the general principles behind the preparation or creation of each of the dishes, simply by reading the title. In this manner, you will find yourself much more at home, and gain an insight into the whole geography of Chinese cookery by a short cut.

Texture

It is a popular thing to talk about texture in food and cooking these days. But it is in Chinese food and cooking that texture suddenly takes on a fresh meaning and reality.

26

This is for two reasons. First of all, because a Chinese meal consists of many dishes, whether served at once (as at home), or one after another (as at a party or banquet), the contrast between the texture of dishes is more of a concrete reality which has to be taken into account in the planning of the menu. It is only at a Chinese meal that you can have two or three soups, two or three casseroles, stews, and steamed dishes, a couple of semi-soup dishes, three or four or even half a dozen quick-fried dishes (of which one or two will be dry-fried in contrast to wet-fried, that is, frying with the addition of sauce), and several cold dishes as appetizers. Perhaps there will also be a sweet dish or two—one of which will probably be a sweet soup.

People have sometimes wondered why we Chinese have sweet soups. If you have had the experience of half a dozen or more highly savory dishes, one following the other, you will understand what a welcome and refreshing thing it is to have something so very different in taste and texture from what has been served previously, especially if it is chilled. Savory soups are generally used for breaking up the run of drier, quick-fried or deep-fried dishes, in addition to their function of washing down morsels of food, as table water is used in Western meals. The same applies to China's many semi-soup dishes—which are generally clear-simmered or long-steamed dishes, with meat or poultry cooked to jelly-like tenderness, sitting in clear consommé, perhaps supported by a small choice of vegetables added during the last stage of cooking. Here all the items which make up the dishes stand out in great purity and clarity. Such dishes act as an excellent contrast to the quick-stir-fried dishes, which usually make up the bulk of the dishes in a Chinese meal.

Among the quick-stir-fried dishes themselves, there is contrast and variation in the tastes and textures of the principal and supplementary ingredients used, and also in the way in which the foods are cut or shaped—whether diced into cubes, cut into match-stick strips, shredded into threads, left in chunks, or shaped into balls—like deep-fried shrimp balls or meatballs. After a wet-fried dish, which in Chinese we call 'Liu', we would have a dry-fried dish, which we call 'Gan Shao'. The taste and texture of these two types of dishes are entirely different; one is smooth and soft and should melt in the mouth, and the other is usually hot, spicy, and crispy and needs to be bitten or chewed before it can be swallowed. These dishes are excellent accompaniments to wine, or to the blandness of plain-cooked (boiled) rice.

Another excellent type of dish to follow a 'Liu' dish is the aromatic and crackling type—for example, Aromatic and Crackling Duck or Four Great Crispies—where the crackling qualities are used to provide contrast with the soft smoothness of the 'Liu'.

Often diced dishes such as Kung-Po Chicken, which is a dish of hot diced chicken breast meat, pink-red in color, are arranged to follow a dish of Shredded Beef Stir-Fried with Shredded Green Pepper. Here, not only are there different flavors to provide a contrasting sensation in the mouth, but there is also a difference in shape and color to provide variety in presentation.

Then there is another type of Chinese dish, which is all runny and soft, like 'Yellow Flowing Eggs' ('Liu Huan T'sai' of Peking), or 'Savory Sesame Bean Curd' (Ma Po Dou-Fu' of Szechuan), which we Chinese love to eat with our rice. These hot creamy or soft-textured mixtures run like savory lava into the rice.

Transparent noodles (or bean-thread noodles) have a unique texture of their own, and one of their great qualities is the ability to absorb at least four times their own weight or quantity of rich gravy when cooked with meat. This type of gravy-laden noodle dish, which never gets soft or mushy however long it is cooked, has a very distinctive quality and texture of its own, which I have often described as being China's 'solid gravy'. Transparent noodles are used extensively to cook or fry with vegetables which have been cut into strips: this type of dish is one of the pillars of, and gives added dimension to, Chinese vegetarian cooking.

Crunchiness is another very important quality in the Chinese conception of texture. I have often suspected that the reason for bamboo shoots being used so extensively in Chinese dishes is entirely related to their crunchy texture—since bamboo shoots, although subtle to taste, have, in fact, very little flavor of their own. However, they possess an undeniable and inimitable crunchiness, whether in soup, fried, or in stews: a quality which is hard for them to lose in any combination, hence their popularity in all kinds of cross-cooked dishes.

Another popular way in which we Chinese introduce the quality of crunchiness into a dish is to use various raw vegetables, including cucumber, scallions, carrots, turnips, and celery which are either cut into matchstick strips, or diced into small cubes and cooked for an instant, usually by quick-frying with the other materials which constitute the bulk of the dish. An example of this is the very popular northern dish, Quick-Fried Sliced Lamb with Scallions, which was as popular with the coolies as with the Emperors. Here the scallions are given only a very short time in the oil and gravy with the sliced lamb.

The concept of texture of food applies not only in the difference between the textures of different dishes, but also to differences and contrasts in the feel of the different constituents within a single dish. Here, because of the extensive Chinese practice of cross-cooking different types of foods and materials, texture has a reality and meaning, which give it greater interest and significance than are generally apparent in other styles of cooking.

Take, for instance, a water chestnut, which possesses an exceedingly crunchy texture. Because of this quality it is mixed or blended into all types of ground or minced meats to produce crunchy meat balls or shrimp balls. It is also used as one of the constituents of various types of meat fillings, which are used in steamed buns, dumplings, and transparent-jacketed raviolis. This is one of the reasons why meatballs, shrimp balls, and fillings in Chinese cooking possess a quality which is often missing from Western counterparts—the element of crunchiness.

A parallel instance is the case of Chinese noodles, which are the equivalent of Italian spaghetti, macaroni, etc. While spaghetti and macaroni are usually served with one or two types of meat sauce, such as milanese or bolognese, Chinese noodles can be cooked or fried with every type of meat as well as with such things as oysters, lobster, crabs, and shrimp. Noodle dishes can often be composed of ingredients with different or even contrasting textures. Bamboo shoots sliced into matchstick strips, sliced strips of raw vegetables, such as chives, scallions, celery, chicory, or cucumber, which have been previously dressed or marinated, and soaked, dried vegetables such as dried mushrooms and tiger-lily buds can be used with noodles. All these ingredients have a distinctive flavor of their own, and are combined only in small quantities. They are often tossed together with one or two varieties of cooked or smoked meats, such as strips of plain boiled chicken, smoked duck, or ham. As all these foods and materials possess distinctive textures of their own, especially as they have been subjected to different types of prior cooking and preparation, their joint or combined effect is one which can only be described as 'textural tapestry'. Here the different 'threads' which make up the texture can be incorporated according to taste or inclination.

In such instances it is very seldom that a sauce of one single flavor is poured over the whole dish: it might destroy the whole 'finely knitted' textural artistry. More often, after some frying or tossing in vegetable oil, only one teaspoon or less of sesame oil is added to give that earthy, unifying effect, while allowing the individual textures and tastes of all the ingredients which constitute the dish to achieve their fullest expression.

This short excursion into texture in Chinese food might, I hope, do a little to lift up a small corner and reveal the vast area of Chinese cooking which unfortunately is seldom done justice to in Chinese restaurants abroad, but upon which so many Westerners must base their impression or judgment of Chinese food. Fortunately, the standard of Chinese food and cooking abroad seems to be improving everywhere, although more slowly and painfully in some places than others.

Chinese Flavorings and Food Materials

The flavorings in Chinese food, and their numerous variations, appear to be derived from five main sources, and are applied at different stages of the cooking and eating. It is the orchestration of this multi-stage flavoring with multi-stage heating, which in many instances acts to solder together the flavors, that gives the preparation of Chinese food its mystery and sophistication.

The five main sources of flavoring in Chinese cooking are:

(i) the principal food on which a dish is based, which always provides the main source of flavor in any style of cooking. Often it is the very purpose of the cooking to bring out the distinctive flavor of the main ingredient in a dish.

(ii) the supplementary materials, with which the principal ingredients are cooked or cross-cooked. In Chinese cooking, the use of supplementary materials is practiced to a point where, in many instances, it is difficult to say which is the principal ingredient and which are supplementary materials. In such cases, there is usually a great deal of cross-blending of flavors, and here the supplementary ingredients are present not only to enrich and vary the taste of the dish, but also to provide additional substance. They often also contribute to the variations of texture and color in the dish.

(iii) the flavoring ingredients, which are small amounts of materials, either fresh, prepared, or preserved, are introduced in limited quantities purely to enhance or vary the taste of the food. We Chinese are not inclined to use a great many herbs (although there are innumerable medicinal herbs which sometimes wander into the dishes), but we command a good range of preserved and dried foods, which are used extensively for this purpose.

(iv) seasonings and sauces—the seasonings used in Chinese cooking are quite conventional, and we do not go in a great deal for made-up sauces, as the French do. Chinese sauces might be called natural sauces, as they are the natural by-products of the process of cooking. They are usually concocted during the very last stage of cooking, when the ingredients of a dish are frequently heated up to a crescendo, with the addition of a little savory but neutral stock and small quantities of seasonings and basic sauces.

(v) Chinese table condiments, or 'dips' and 'mixes', are probably more numerous than those customarily used in the West. They are often made-up condiments which are traditional in origin and are an essential part of the dishes which they accompany. They are usually concocted just before they are served, and are invariably served in small dishes or saucers—never in bottles—and arranged strategically on the dining table.

From the foregoing, it must not be assumed that all Chinese dishes must go through all the stages of flavoring before they are complete. Indeed, many dishes are hardly flavored at all until they arrive on the dining table. Some are cooked with a few fresh supplementary materials, but without much flavoring; these depend again on the table condiments for their flavoring. Some dishes omit the supplementary materials and flavoring ingredients altogether and use only seasonings and sauces for their flavoring. They require no condiments on the table as the seasonings and sauces are added at the beginning. These, together with the principal materials, cook up to a sufficiency of richness which requires no further touching up. Other dishes are cooked 'native', with the seasonings and sauces added only at the end. Still others use very little in the way of seasonings and sauces but start by cooking the flavoring materials in the heating medium (oil or lard), and it is only when the cooking medium is thoroughly impregnated that the cooking of the principal ingredient begins. There are some dishes which, to be complete, must have flavoring ingredients at every stage of the cooking. The application of flavorers is often very closely tied to the method of heating adopted. The possible combinations here are sufficiently numerous to justify a special study and survey to achieve a degree of clarification.

Principal Materials

One of the reasons why Chinese cooking is so easily acceptable in the Western world is because the principal materials used are almost identical to those used in Western cooking, except for dairy produce which is seldom used in China.

We use the same fish, flesh, and fowl, as well as the whole range of vegetables which are used in Western cooking, and perhaps a few more. If there is any difference in the principal materials used it is only a question of emphasis. We use pork more than any other type of meat, probably because pigs are difficult to use otherwise—for example, as beasts of burden. We eat and value fresh-water fish more than salt-water fish (except in coastal areas), because China is in the main a continental country, and Chinese farmers are habitual fish-farmers: the country-side is littered with millions of ponds and lakes in which fish are kept, fed, and grown. In addition, there are thousands of rivers, streams, canals, and tributaries from which fresh fish and other water-food can be obtained.

Although duck is one of the favorite fowls, chicken easily leads as the most popular of all poultry used. Next to pork, it is probably the most extensively used meat in China, even before the era of mass-produced chickens. Indeed, even in China today, domesticated chickens are still probably unknown. As free-range chickens are used exclusively, Chinese chicken dishes are much more tasty than those we are now used to in the West. It is essential in many Chinese chicken dishes that the fowl itself provides nearly all the flavor, as it is intended to be only very lightly cooked, with very little seasoning. In other dishes, where the chicken is highly seasoned and flavored, for example, curried chicken, the true flavor of the fowl is less essential.

Taken in the main, it is possible to produce good dishes without the use of supplementary and flavoring materials or seasonings only when the quality of the principal material used is excellent, as in Western cooking. In such cases, cooking becomes merely a process or art of rendering food edible and palatable through controlled heating. Chinese Moslem cooking is inclined to favor this method as in the case of the famous Peking Duck, and many long-simmered dishes, which are in effect cooked through a process of long, slow boiling or simmering. The sophistication here comes from the refinement of the heating, and the manner in which the dish is eaten and treated on the table. In the case of Peking Duck the skin is made crispy by overnight hanging and airing, and it is then eaten together with some duck meat, strips of raw crunchy vegetables—such as scallions and cucumber—all heavily brushed with plum sauce or blended soy paste and wrapped in a pancake. Thus the rolled pancake combines the qualities of crispiness, crunchiness, pungency, and meaty-richness all at once. Peking Duck, and the various long-simmered dishes are typical cases of Chinese dishes where the principal materials are subjected only to simple cooking. Such methods are usually adopted where the principal materials are of good quality and are cooked in large pieces.

In Chinese cooking, more often than not, the materials used are chopped, cut, or sliced into smaller pieces so that they are more easily eaten with chopsticks. The use of flavoring materials, seasonings, and sauces during various stages of cooking is therefore more extensively practised. In dishes of this type, the method of heating adopted is usually 'quick-frying'—the time required here for the food to cook and for the seasonings to penetrate is practically instantaneous. This not only helps to save time and fuel, but by cutting or slicing the principal materials into matchstick-size strips, even fairly tough food can be made to appear reasonably tender. Thus a tough steak is uneatable, but when produced as Quick-Fried Beef Ribbons with Onion, it is most acceptable. Typical dishes in which the principal materials are reduced to small pieces and cooked with only a minimum of supplementary materials are Diced Pork (or Chicken) Quick-Fried in Soy Jam, Hot and Sour Diced Chicken, or the well-known Sweet and Sour Pork. Although first quality materials are always preferred in Chinese cooking, the Chinese can manage with second class materials when necessary.

Steaming is a method of cooking which is usually used in conjunction with marinating. When steaming, the principal ingredients are normally fully prepared, that is marinated and garnished before being placed in the steamer to be cooked.

On the other hand, there is another method of Chinese cooking in which the food is steamed first, then marinated, and garnished afterwards or just before being brought to the table. A whole series of excellent dishes produced in this manner are known as 'drunken' dishes, since many of the marinades used are composed of wine and liqueur—Drunken Chicken, Drunken Shrimps, and Drunken Crabs are only a few.

In considering the principal materials used in Chinese cooking, I have written here mainly about methods used in cooking and cutting the foods. This is because, as already stated, the principal ingredients in Chinese cooking are practically the same as in Western cooking.

In meat dishes we use bacon, beef, chicken, duck, ham, lamb, pigeon, pork, turkey, and venison.

In fish dishes we use abalone (or awabi), bass, bêche de mer, bream, carp, clams, cod, crab, eel, flounder, haddock, halibut, herring, jellyfish, lobster, mackerel, mullet, oyster, perch, pike, prawns, rock salmon, sardines, shad, sharks' fins, shrimp, sole, squid, sturgeon, trout, tuna, turbot, and whitefish.

In vegetable dishes we use asparagus, bamboo shoots, beans (and their various products), bean sprouts, bitter melon, broccoli, cabbage, celery cabbage, mustard cabbage, carrots, cauliflower, celery, chives, corn, cucumber, eggplant, leeks, lettuce, lily buds, lotus roots, melon, mushrooms, onions, parsley, potatoes, pea pods, peas, pepper, radishes, snow peas, spinach, squash, string beans, tomatoes, turnips, water chestnuts, and watercress.

In addition, we also use numerous variants and allied foods of the above principal materials. As far as food is concerned, the economically advanced countries are more amply supplied than China, therefore the Westerner taking up Chinese cookery should concentrate more on the treatment and cooking of the materials than on the materials themselves since they have the principal ingredients in plenty. Let not the mystique of Chinese cooking give the impression that we Chinese eat differently from you. We eat almost precisely the same things. If there is any mystery it is in the cooking, cross-cooking, flavoring, and heating.

Supplementary Materials

Because of the extensive Chinese practice of cross-cooking different foods (especially those of different genre and texture), supplementary materials play a much bigger role in Chinese cooking than in Western food preparation. Indeed, as already said, there are situations where the materials used are so evenly balanced that it is difficult to decide which is the principal material and which are supplementary ones.

As a rule, the principal material is the one which lends the dominant bulk, flavor, or character to the dish; all the other materials which are cooked in conjunction with it, to provide a difference or balance in flavor, color, and texture, are the supplementary materials. Sharks' fins generally represent only a small proportion of the bulk of a dish, but since they give it its character, they are the principal ingredient.

Theoretically, it might almost seem that anything, if chopped into small pieces, can be cooked or combined with almost anything else, which is, of course, not quite true. However, it is the possibility of combining a wide range of ingredients—especially as one type of food can be cooked or cross-cooked with many supplementary materials—which makes for the vast number of Chinese dishes.

What then can be combined with what? This is determined not only by the flavors of the foods concerned, but also by shape, size, texture, and toughness which determine the time required for cooking different ingredients.

Take the example of pork, which is the most versatile of meats. When it is meant for long-cooking, such as in red-cooked stews, casseroles, long-steamed or long-simmered dishes, it can be combined with carrots, turnips, Chinese cabbage, tiger lily buds, bamboo shoots, chestnuts, walnuts, abalone, transparent noodles, etc., which all require a long period of cooking.

On the other hand, when the pork is sliced thinly or shredded, it can be combined and cooked, sometimes in an instant, with all the quick-cooking vegetables, such as mushrooms, scallions, celery, green peas, sliced mustard greens, sliced peppers, sliced bamboo shoots, cucumber, cauliflower, and spinach. The method adopted in such cases is usually stir-frying in oil over a high heat, with the oil acting as a very hot lubricant; a lubricant imparting both flavor and heat.

When pork is finely chopped it is often, if not invariably, mixed with water chestnuts to provide that characteristic crunchy texture, and with chopped onion to give it an appealing aroma when fried. Other foods such as salted fish or crab may be used. When pork is cut into larger slices it may be combined with liver and kidney to vary and heighten the flavor.

The same principle applies to chicken, which is another very versatile meat. When chicken is cooked for a long period, the tougher, longer-cooking vegetables, such as walnuts and bamboo shoots, can be cooked with it. However, turnips and carrots, which are considered too strong and too rough, are never cooked with chicken. But when it is meant to be stir-fried and quick-cooked, in slices or shreds, a whole variety of vegetables which do not require long-cooking—also ready-soaked or ready-cooked materials, such as ham, dried mushrooms, or tree fungus—can be combined with chicken.

Noodles come in varying sizes and lengths. When meats or vegetables are cooked with them, they are usually cut into the same matchstick strip shapes. The purpose of all these supplementary materials is therefore not only to contribute to the flavor of the dish, but also to its color and texture, and in this way, to its interest and appeal to all appetites.

When one investigates the importance of supplementary materials, one comes to the conclusion that their presence in a dish serves two principal purposes: in the case of flavorsome principal materials such as meat or fish, supplementary materials add variety and interest to the general flavor; in the case of bland or neutral principal materials such as rice or noodles, supplementary ingredients provide some appealing taste and flavor. Of the two functions, the latter is probably the more important. For in any economically underdeveloped country, where meat and fish are not in plentiful supply, the need for making bulk-food tasty is of paramount importance. The Chinese ability and expertise in doing this is one of the high points in Chinese culinary art, and is what makes Chinese cooking so economical—and incidentally—so profitable!

To achieve this general purpose with greater effect, Chinese cooking advances one stage farther from supplementary materials to the use of flavoring ingredients, both fresh and dried.

Flavoring Ingredients

The one thing which is common to both Chinese fish and vegetable cooking is that supplementary materials are seldom employed to any great extent in their cooking, and when they are used, it is as garnishing. Fish and vegetables are usually cooked with a selection of flavoring ingredients, either to enhance their interest and flavor, or to reduce or eliminate their inherent but less appealing tastes (such as fishiness in fish), or for both purposes. These flavoring ingredients are, of course, also used for the same purposes in the cooking of meat, rice, and pasta.

The flavoring ingredients used in Chinese cooking are of two main types: fresh, strong-tasting vegetables and dried, preserved, and salted items. The fresh, strong-tasting vegetables employed in Chinese cooking are not very different from those used in Western cooking, for example onions, chives, garlic, ginger, and coriander. It is in the area of dried, preserved, and salted materials that we Chinese seem to possess greater variety. It is well-known that the flavor of food becomes much more concentrated and intensified when it is dried. This intensity of flavor is not lost even if the dried foods are soaked in water. Thus soaked Chinese dried mushrooms have a much stronger taste than fresh mushrooms. In Chinese cooking the dried ingredients are frequently fried in oil together with fresh ones to impregnate the oil with their varied flavors, which are in turn imparted to the principal and supplementary ingredients in the process of cooking.

The most popular dried flavoring materials of animal origin include dried shrimps, dried scallop (stem muscle), dried oyster, dried mussels, dried squid, dried abalone, clam, salted duck, duck feet, duck liver, salted egg, salted fish, smoked or cured ham, small Chinese sausages, and Fukien meat wool.

Those of vegetable origin are far more numerous. The most popular of these are: dried mushrooms, dried tree fungus (wood ears and cloud ears—used more for texture than taste), dried tangerine peel, golden needles (tiger lily buds), a whole variety of preserved cabbages (such as Szechuan cabbage, Shanghai cabbage, or Winter cabbage), preserved turnips, parsnips, dried chili peppers, pickled mustard green, lotus seeds, lotus roots, melon seeds, dried lychees, longans (or dragon eyes), dried kumquats, dried dates, cinnamon bark, black beans (salted and fermented), anise, star anise, and all the varieties of herbs, which are often used in a combination called five spice powder, which is a ground powder made from anise, star anise, fennel, cloves, and cinnamon. It is used very frequently in meat cooking, especially with beef.

When fresh flavoring materials are used in conjunction with dried, preserved, or salted ingredients of both animal and vegetable origin, and when these are further combined with the principal ingredient and the various supplementary materials, great avenues of flavor-blending are opened to us. Indeed, the possibilities are exciting, intriguing, and almost fathomless! This is what prompted a French scientist to remark to me that Chinese cooking is not cooking, but alchemy!

Seasonings and Sauces

Chinese seasonings and sauces can be subdivided according to their order of application into marinades, seasonings, sauces, dressings, and table condiments in the form of dips and mixes.

In a Chinese restaurant kitchen, the tasks of food preparation and cooking are clearly defined and divided. Although the greater part of the work involved in food preparation is attended to by the assistant chef, it is the chef who presides over the stove and exercises the heat control, and who makes the decisions regarding the all-important seasonings and sauces. Although he usually conducts his cooking with a flourish, he generally applies the seasonings and sauces with moderation, so as not to obliterate the blending of flavors already achieved, except in cases where there has been no previous cross-cooking of ingredients, or cross-blending of flavors. In these latter cases, where the principal ingredients are straight-cooked, he may administer a good dose of seasoning or sauces towards the end to give the dish a last necessary boost.

Except for the frequent use of sugar as an ingredient in the preparation of savory dishes, all the other basic seasonings used in Chinese cooking are much the same as those employed in Western cooking, namely, salt, pepper, vinegar, mustard, and chili, which is usually in the form of dried chili or chili oil, rather than in powdered form.

The main difference between Chinese cooking and Western cooking in the area of food seasoning arises in the use of soy beans and their various by-products. First of all, there is soy sauce, which is already well-known in the West and which comes crudely in light, dark, and heavy forms. It is, of course, capable of much finer gradations. Then there are fermented, salted black beans, soy bean jam or paste (usually made from mashed brown beans, mixed with salt, sugar, garlic, and soy sauce), and soy cheese. When these four soy bean products are combined in varying quantities with varying amounts of wine, sugar, and monosodium glutamate, the combination makes almost anything highly tasty. I have often called this mixture the Chinese gastronomic gunpowder.

According to an eminent French immunologist, there is something extremely 'active' in soy beans, which he said we have yet to put our finger on, and which holds an element or substance that may have an influence on man's capacity for appreciation of food. He believes that the Chinese may have stumbled on a secret which may yet have to be defined, analyzed, and exploited to the full.

Whatever there is in soy beans, we Chinese have certainly employed it and exploited it fully. The use of soy beans and their by-products has certainly accounted for the biggest difference between Chinese and Western cooking.

Apart from soy beans, the Chinese also make extensive use of oyster sauce, fish gravy, and red wine-sediment paste (also in other colors) to vary and enhance taste and flavor.

34

We also use sesame oil and paste to provide an earthy smoothness and an appealing aroma, and this practice appears to have something in common with Middle Eastern cooking, which has been largely ignored by the French. In addition, there are the fruit-based and vegetable sauces such as plum sauce and hoisin sauce.

Except for fish gravy sauce, wine-sediment paste, and fermented, salted black beans, which can only be applied to food during the cooking process, all the other basic sauces and seasonings can be used as ingredients for marinades, as seasonings during cooking, or even as table condiments in the form of dips and mixes.

The following are some of the basic sauces and seasonings generally employed in Chinese cooking. They do not include the natural sauces which are produced during cooking, or the sauces which are made up for special dishes and preparations.

Sauces

Taking all in all, we Chinese do not appear to approach sauces in the grand manner of the French. Nor is there as much mystique about Chinese sauces, except for what is carried over from the Western reverence for the French sauces.

As a rule, sauces are produced in Chinese cooking almost as a matter of course, as we proceed with our cooking—usually through the addition of stock (mostly chicken, meat, or bone stock) to the food we are preparing, often towards the last stages of its heating. Seasonings, thickenings (cornstarch or water chestnut flour), and perhaps wine are also added at the same time.

Chinese chefs generally proceed with their cooking, producing the sauces as they go along, without giving them a second thought. To them, sauces are just a small cog in the large wheel of the exercise of cooking as a whole. They assume that anyone who knows the arts of cutting and the proportioning of supplementary materials, who has a sense of flavor-blending and the use of flavoring materials, and who has mastered the difficult art of heat control must therefore be able to make the sauces, which after all, are only a small part of the flavor orchestration.

Since sauces are not usually applied to wet, soupy dishes such as casseroles, steamed dishes, long-simmered dishes, and the numerous Chinese semi-soup dishes, their use is mainly confined to plain-cooked dishes, deep-fried dishes, quick stir-fried dishes, and bland rice and pasta dishes, which need additional flavoring to heighten their appeal.

Since the number of plain-cooked or deep-fried dishes is not quite so great as the quick stir-fried dishes, the larger proportion of sauces in Chinese cooking results from the process of quick stir-frying. Hence, although there are probably a vast number of sauces which are actually produced in the normal course of Chinese cooking (running probably into hundreds), they are so closely related to the main ingredients and supplementary materials of the dishes that they are seldom awarded an independent name, or, for that matter, given individual consideration. They are so much an integral part of the dishes themselves that they are seldom regarded as having a separate identity. Because of this lack of identity, the Chinese are much less preoccupied with sauces than the French. In actual fact, we probably produce as many sauces as the French, possibly many more. However, as the famous saying goes: 'We have it, but we don't talk about it!'

In one area, however, the French must possess a far bigger repertoire of sauces than the Chinese: these are the cold sauces, the mayonnaises, vinaigrettes, and dressings. This is probably only because, except for a very few dishes, the Chinese hardly eat cold food at all. They are obsessed with the fear of getting a chill in the stomach!

Although both the French and Chinese insist on good stock with which to make their sauces, there appears to be a basic difference in their attitude to and concept of the use of sauces. In Chinese cooking, when a sauce is consciously produced for a dish, it is usually produced from materials which are in contrast to the principal ingredient on which the dish is based. We Chinese, for instance, would not dream of using a fish sauce for a fish dish which, in the Chinese concept, would only double its fishiness. We would, in this instance, probably use an egg sauce, chicken sauce, or meat sauce, strengthened with onion, ginger, garlic, chili, sugar, wine, and preserves, and served with ample garnish. The Chinese idea here seems to be to heighten the contrast of flavors and to increase the blending of savoriness, as well as to reduce the fishiness of fish.

Following the same principle in the production of sauces for meat dishes, the constituents of the sauces are usually fermented bean pastes, bean cheese, minced preserves, wine-sediment pastes, vinegar, fruit juices, chopped vegetables, and almost invariably a small amount of sugar. In addition, we also use coarsely ground rice (fried golden brown), sesame seeds, sesame oil, and sesame pastes for producing an appealing aromatic effect.

A quick survey of the Chinese cookery landscape will reveal that the majority of Chinese dishes which result from the cross-cooking of a number of ingredients usually generate ample gravy or natural sauce in themselves, and are therefore not in need of any additional made-up sauces to go with them. In the production of these natural sauces, those with wine, vinegar, and ginger content are usually used to counteract and balance the qualities of fish, and those made from preserves or fermented beans, and having a sharp piquant saltiness, are used to give a distinctive savoriness to meats. In the main, Chinese sauces consist of these natural sauces which are distilled out of the foods during the process of cooking, through the addition of a limited quantity of stock, seasoning, and flavoring ingredients.

On the other hand, the use of made-up sauces is therefore confined to plain-cooked meat and chicken dishes, to plain deep-fried dishes, to egg or Fu-Yung dishes and to some fish dishes, where some contrast and a garnish are essential. Above all, made-up sauces are used to contrast with the neutrality of rice and noodle dishes, particularly with noodle dishes which in China are served in four principal forms: fried, in soup, tossed with chopped scallion, garlic, bean paste, and sesame oil or paste (or both), or finally in thickened gravy, or sauces. These identifiable, made-up sauces are in fact not many. The recipes for the majority of them are provided below in this chapter. What gives capacity and potential to Chinese sauces is their liberal tradition which is the possibility of cross-blending natural sauces, and cross-blending natural sauces with made-up sauces. It is these possibilities which give Chinese sauces something of the character of savory cocktails and allow for their almost limitless repertoire.

The following recipes for sauces, dressings, dips, and mixes are sufficient for four to eight people, depending on how many other condiments are served.

Sauces for Noodles or Rice

Although the sauces in this section may be served with either noodles or rice, the Chinese themselves prefer to eat rice plain.

Basic Pork Gravy Sauce for Noodles

Preparation Chop the pork coarse.

Cooking Heat the oil in a frying pan. Add the bacon, onion, and salt, and stir-fry for 4–5 minutes over medium heat. Add the soy sauce, stock, sugar, and monosodium glutamate. Bring the mixture to a gentle boil and cook for 4–5 minutes, then stir in the cornstarch, blended with ¼ cup water. Stir until the mixture thickens.

Serving Pour over noodles in individual bowls.

½ lb slab bacon

2½ tablespoons peanut oil *or* corn oil
2–3 tablespoons chopped onion *or* scallion
½ teaspoon salt
2½ tablespoons soy sauce
¾ cup stock
1 teaspoon sugar
¼ teaspoon monosodium glutamate
½ teaspoon cornstarch

Fancy Pork Gravy Sauce for Noodles

Preparation Soak the Chinese mushrooms, then slice them into matchstick strips. Chop the celery into 1 inch segments. Chop the onion or scallion, crush the garlic, and shred the ginger. Chop the bacon finely.

Cooking Stir-fry the bacon and onion in hot oil for 3 minutes over a high heat. Add the salt, garlic, ginger, celery, and mushrooms, and stir-fry for 3 minutes. Add the soy sauce, sugar, stock, sherry, and monosodium glutamate, bring to a gentle boil and cook over a medium heat for 3 minutes. Stir in the cornstarch, blended with ¼ cup water, and continue stirring until the mixture thickens.

Serving Pour the sauce over the noodles in individual bowls.

½ lb slab bacon

¼ cup Chinese dried mushrooms
½ cup chopped celery
¼ cup chopped onion *or* scallions
1 clove garlic
1 slice ginger root
3 tablespoons vegetable oil
½ teaspoon salt
2½ tablespoons soy sauce
1½ teaspoons sugar
¾ cup chicken stock
2 tablespoons sherry
¼ teaspoon monosodium glutamate
2 teaspoons cornstarch

Beef and Tomato Sauce for Noodles

Preparation Shred the beef, onion, and ginger root. Peel and quarter the tomatoes. Crush the garlic.

Cooking Stir-fry the onion, garlic, and ginger in hot oil for 30 seconds. Add the beef, salt, and tomatoes and stir-fry over medium heat for 3 minutes. Add the soy sauce, sugar, sherry, and stock, bring to a gentle boil, and cook for a further 3 minutes. Stir in the cornstarch, blended with ¼ cup water, and continue stirring until the mixture thickens.

Serving Pour the sauce over the noodles in individual bowls.

½ lb lean beef
6 medium-sized tomatoes

3 tablespoons chopped onion
2 slices ginger root
1 clove garlic
3 tablespoons vegetable oil
½ teaspoon salt
2 tablespoons soy sauce
1½ teaspoons sugar
1 tablespoon sherry
¾ cup stock
2 teaspoons cornstarch

Ham Sauce for Noodles

¼ lb ham

1 medium-sized onion
¼ cup chopped celery
1 slice ginger root
2½ tablespoons vegetable oil
½ teaspoon salt
1 tablespoon soy sauce
¾ cup chicken stock
¼ teaspoon monosodium glutamate
dash of pepper
1 egg
1 tablespoon cornstarch
2 tablespoons chopped parsley *or*
    fresh coriander

Preparation Chop the ham coarse. Chop the onion, and cut the celery into ½-inch segments. Finely chop the ginger.

Cooking Stir-fry the ham, onion, celery and ginger in hot oil for 2 minutes over a medium heat. Add the salt, soy sauce, stock, monosodium glutamate, and pepper; simmer for 3 minutes. Beat the egg lightly and blend it with the cornstarch and ¼ cup water; stir this mixture into the pan in a thin stream. When the sauce thickens, sprinkle with chopped parsley or coriander.

Serving Pour over the noodles in individual bowls.

Vegetarian Sauce for Noodles

¼ cup Chinese dried mushrooms
6 golden needles (tiger-lily buds)
1½ tablespoons wood ears
⅛ cup bamboo shoots
¼ cup lotus roots
3 scallions
2 slices ginger
1 clove garlic
¼ lb (1 cup) spinach
3 tablespoons vegetable oil
½ teaspoon salt
¾ cup vegetable stock
1½ tablespoons soy sauce
1 teaspoon sugar
¼ teaspoon monosodium glutamate
1 tablespoon cornstarch
1 tablespoon sesame oil

Preparation Soak the mushrooms, golden needles, and wood ears separately. Retain ¼ cup of the mushroom water. Cut the mushrooms into matchstick strips. Cut the golden needles into ½ inch segments. Rinse the wood ears. Cut the bamboo shoots into matchstick strips. Slice the lotus roots and chop the scallions into 1 inch segments. Mince the ginger and crush the garlic. Wash the spinach carefully.

Cooking Stir-fry all the vegetables in hot vegetable oil with the salt for 3 minutes. Add the stock, soy sauce, mushroom water, sugar, and monosodium glutamate, bring to the boil and simmer gently for 5 minutes. Blend the cornstarch with ¼ cup water and pour the mixture into the pan. Stir until the sauce thickens.

Serving Sprinkle a drop or two of sesame oil over each bowl of noodles, pour the sauce over; then arrange the vegetables neatly on top as a garnish.

Plain Chicken Sauce for Noodles

2½ cups chicken stock

2 tablespoons cornstarch
1 teaspoon salt
pepper to taste
¼ teaspoon monosodium glutamate
2 tablespoons vegetable oil *or* lard

Cooking Blend the stock with the cornstarch, salt, pepper, and monosodium glutamate. Heat the oil or lard in a saucepan and pour in the stock mixture. Heat, stirring, until the liquid thickens and is smooth; then serve.

Mushroom Sauce for Noodles or Rice

Preparation Soak the dried mushrooms for 20 minutes, then remove the stalks and cut the caps into strips. Cut the button mushrooms into thin slices.

Cooking Fry both types of mushroom in oil for 2½ minutes. Add salt, pepper, sugar, stock, and monosodium glutamate. Bring to the boil and simmer gently for 3 minutes. Blend the cornstarch with ¼ cup water; then blend in the soy sauce and sherry. Stir this mixture gently into the pan until the liquid thickens.

Serving Pour the mushroom sauce over rice or noodles in individual bowls.

¼ cup Chinese dried mushrooms
½ cup canned button mushrooms *or*
   ¾ cup fresh mushrooms

2½ tablespoons vegetable oil
½ teaspoon salt
dash of pepper
¾ teaspoon sugar
¾ cup chicken stock
¼ teaspoon monosodium glutamate
1½ teaspoons cornstarch
1½ tablespoons soy sauce
1 tablespoon dry sherry

Peking Soy-Meat Sauce for Noodles

Preparation Finely chop the pork and marinate it in the sherry for 15 minutes. Chop the scallions and crush the garlic.

Cooking Heat the oil in a pan, then add the scallions, garlic, and pork and stir-fry for 4 minutes over a high heat. Combine the bean paste with the soy sauce and hoisin sauce, and mix into a smooth paste. Stir-fry this paste with the scallions, garlic, and pork for 3 minutes over a gentle heat. Blend the cornstarch with 6 tablespoons water and pour into the pan. Stir-fry until the mixture is well-blended and smooth, then cook gently for another 1½–2 minutes until the sauce thickens.

Serving Do not pour this sauce over the noodles, but serve it in a bowl so that each person can dab 1–2 tablespoons of it on top of his own bowl of noodles.

Peking Soy-Meat Sauce Noodles are usually eaten accompanied by a variety of shredded raw vegetables, such as radishes, cucumber, scallions, blanched bean sprouts, and spinach. It is very much a native Peking dish.

½ lb lean pork
2 tablespoons soy sauce

1 tablespoon dry sherry
3 scallions
2 cloves garlic
3 tablespoons vegetable oil
2 tablespoons brown bean paste
1 tablespoon hoisin sauce
1 teaspoon cornstarch

Master Sauce

Makes 5 cups

1 lb piece of beef *or* fowl
¾ cup soy sauce
¾ cup red wine *or* dry sherry
1 medium onion, chopped
2 cloves garlic, minced
5 tablespoons rock sugar
1½ teaspoons salt
1 small piece dried tangerine peel
pinch of each of the following:
    anise, star anise, five spice pow-
    der

The term 'Lu' is used in China to indicate foods which have been cooked or braised in Master Sauce.

Preparation Simmer meat or poultry in 5 cups of water and the remaining ingredients for 1 hour. Any kind of meat or in-nards of animals, including heart, kidneys, liver, tripe, or intestines, which are to be cooked in the sauce, should be simmered in it for a further 30 minutes to 1½ hours. Remove, drain, and cool, then slice thin and alternate on an attractive serving platter. This makes a particularly good cold hors d'oeuvre. Hard-boiled eggs simmered in Master Sauce are known as Soy Eggs. When cold, they are sliced and served with the other Lu items

The Master Sauce is kept 'alive' by refilling it daily with water and fresh meat, and replenishing the herbal ingre-dients every two to three days.

Sauces for Fish

Plain Sauce for Fish

3 slices ginger root
3–4 tablespoons chopped scallions
1 tablespoon vegetable oil
2½ tablespoons soy sauce
2 teaspoons sugar
1 tablespoon vinegar
½ cup water *or* stock
1 tablespoon cornstarch

Preparation Shred the ginger into matchstick strips.

Cooking Stir-fry the ginger and scallions in hot oil for 1 min-ute over a medium heat. Add the soy sauce, sugar, vinegar, and water or stock, bring to the boil and simmer gently for 1 minute. Blend the cornstarch with 2 tablespoons water and stir into the pan. Continue to stir until the sauce thickens.

Serving Pour over shallow-fried or deep-fried fish.

Fancy Meat and Vegetable Sauce for Fish

¼ lb lean pork

¼ cup Chinese dried mushrooms
6 golden needles (tiger-lily buds)
¼ cup bamboo shoots
3 slices ginger root

Preparation Soak the mushrooms and golden needles separ-ately. Slice the mushrooms into matchstick strips and cut the golden needles into 1 inch segments. Shred the pork, bamboo shoots, and ginger. Cut the leeks into 1 inch pieces.

Cooking Stir-fry the pork, leeks, ginger, bamboo shoots, mush-

40

rooms, and salt in hot oil for 3 minutes. Add the golden needles, water, sugar, soy sauce, and sherry; then simmer for 5 minutes. Stir in the cornstarch, blended with 2 tablespoons water, and stir until the sauce thickens.

Serving Pour the sauce over steamed or deep-fried fish. Arrange the vegetables on top as a garnish.

¼ cup leeks
½ teaspoon salt
¼ cup vegetable oil
6 tablespoons water
1 teaspoon sugar
2 tablespoons soy sauce
1 tablespoon dry sherry
2½ teaspoons cornstarch

Five Willow Sauce for Fish

Preparation Shred the green pepper, cucumber, and carrot. Peel and slice the tomatoes. Crush the garlic, and cut the scallions into ½ inch segments.

Cooking Stir-fry the ginger, garlic, and scallions in hot oil for 1 minute over a medium heat. Add all the other vegetables, the pickles, and the salt; then stir-fry for 2 minutes over a high heat. Add the sugar, vinegar, soy sauce, sherry, and water and continue to stir. As the mixture comes to the boil, stir in the cornstarch, blended with 5 tablespoons water, and continue to stir until the sauce thickens.

Serving Pour the sauce over the fish and arrange the vegetables on top as a garnish.

1 small green pepper
2 inch section cucumber
1 small carrot
2 medium-sized tomatoes
2 cloves garlic
2 scallions
2 slices ginger root
2 tablespoons vegetable oil
1½ tablespoons mixed sweet pickles
½ teaspoon salt
1 tablespoon sugar
2½ tablespoons vinegar
1½ tablespoons soy sauce
1½ tablespoons dry sherry
6 tablespoons water
1 tablespoon cornstarch

Hot Five Willow Sauce for Fish

Preparation Repeat the recipe for Five Willow Sauce, adding 1 tablespoon red chili pepper or 1 teaspoon dried chili pepper to the ginger, garlic, and scallions during the initial stir-frying.

Egg Sauce for Lobster,
Crab, or Jumbo Shrimp

Preparation Soak and mash the black beans. Crush the garlic, mince the ginger, and chop the scallions into 1 inch segments. Mix together the black beans, garlic, and ginger. Blend together the soy sauce, sugar, sherry, and water; then add the scallions. Beat the eggs.

Cooking Heat the oil in a pan and stir-fry the black bean mixture for 30 seconds. Add the pork and stir-fry for 2 minutes. Pour in the soy sauce mixture, bring to the boil quickly and simmer for 2 minutes. Stir in the cornstarch, blended with 2 tablespoons water. Pour in the beaten eggs slowly in a thin stream along the prongs of a fork, and stir into the sauce.

Serving Pour it over lobster, crab, or shrimp; then serve.

2 eggs

1 tablespoon fermented, salted black beans
2 cloves garlic
2 slices ginger root
2 scallions
1 tablespoon soy sauce
1 teaspoon sugar
1 tablespoon dry sherry
6 tablespoons water *or* stock
2 tablespoons vegetable oil
¼ cup finely chopped lean pork
2 teaspoons cornstarch

Sauces for Chicken

Soy-Celery Sauce for Deep-Fried Chicken

3 stalks celery
2 tablespoons soy sauce

3 scallions
2 tablespoons vegetable oil
1 tablespoon dry sherry
6 tablespoons rich chicken stock
dash of pepper
1½ teaspoons cornstarch

Preparation Slice the celery and scallions into ¼ inch segments.

Cooking Heat the oil in a pan and stir-fry the celery and scallions for 3 minutes over a medium heat. Add the soy sauce, sherry, stock, and pepper. Bring to the boil and simmer for 3 minutes. Stir in the cornstarch, blended with 3 tablespoons water. Continue to stir gently until the sauce thickens.

Serving Pour the sauce over pieces of deep-fried chicken arranged on a serving dish.

Soy-Stock Sauce for Deep-Fried Chicken

½ cup rich chicken stock
2½ tablespoons soy sauce

2 scallions
2 slices ginger root
2½ tablespoons vegetable oil
1 tablespoon dry sherry
dash of pepper
¼ teaspoon monosodium glutamate
1 tablespoon cornstarch

Preparation Chop the scallions and the ginger root.

Cooking Stir-fry the scallions and ginger in the oil for 1 minute over a medium heat. Add the stock, soy sauce, sherry, pepper, and monosodium glutamate, bring to the boil and simmer for 2 minutes. Stir in the cornstarch, blended with 3 tablespoons water, and continue to stir until the sauce thickens.

Serving Pour the sauce over pieces of deep-fried chicken arranged on a serving dish.

Soy-Vinegar Sauce for Deep-Fried Chicken

2 tablespoons soy sauce
3 tablespoons vinegar

2 scallions
2 cloves garlic
2 slices ginger root
1 tablespoon vegetable oil
5 tablespoons water
1½ teaspoons sugar

Preparation Chop the scallions, then crush the garlic, and shred the ginger root.

Cooking Stir-fry the scallions, garlic, and ginger in the oil for 1 minute over a medium heat. Add the soy sauce, vinegar, water, and sugar. Simmer gently for 2 minutes.

Serving Pour over the pieces of chicken, and serve immediately.

Soy and Mixed Vegetable Sauce for Deep-Fried Chicken

Preparation Soak the mushrooms, then shred them. Shred the bamboo shoots and ginger root. Chop the scallions and leeks into ½ inch segments. Slice the water chestnuts thin.

Cooking Heat the oil in a small pan and stir-fry all the vegetables for 2 minutes. Add the stock, soy sauce, sugar, salt, and sherry; cook gently for 2 minutes. Stir in the cornstarch, blended with 3 tablespoons water, and continue to stir until the sauce thickens.

Serving Pour the sauce over pieces of chicken arranged in a serving dish.

2 tablespoons soy sauce

4 large Chinese dried mushrooms
¼ cup bamboo shoots
2 slices ginger root
2 scallions
2 leeks
2 water chestnuts
2 tablespoons vegetable oil
6 tablespoons chicken stock
1½ teaspoons sugar
1 teaspoon salt
1 tablespoon dry sherry
1½ teaspoons cornstarch

Sauces for Boiled or Steamed Chicken

Soy-Stock Sauce for Boiled, White-Cut, or Sliced Chicken

Preparation Blend the soy sauce, stock, salt, sherry, and monosodium glutamate together in a bowl.

Cooking Pour the sauce mixture into a small pan and bring to the boil. Blend the cornstarch with 3 tablespoons water and stir into the pan. Heat until the sauce thickens.

Serving Pour over pieces of chicken arranged on a dish.

1½ tablespoons soy sauce
6 tablespoons stock

½ teaspoon salt
2 teaspoons dry sherry
¼ teaspoon monosodium glutamate
1½ teaspoons cornstarch

Egg Sauce for Boiled White-Cut Chicken

Preparation Cut the scallions into 1 inch segments. Beat the eggs lightly with ¼ cup of the water. Blend the cornstarch with the remaining water.

Cooking Heat the oil in a small saucepan. Stir-fry the scallions for 30 seconds. Add the cornstarch mixture, salt, and sherry. Stir until the mixture is smooth and bubbling. Slowly stir in the beaten egg mixture, pouring it along the prongs of a fork. Continue to stir until the sauce is smooth and creamy.

Serving Pour over pieces of chicken arranged on a serving dish.

2 eggs

2 scallions
½ cup water
1½ teaspoons cornstarch
2 tablespoons vegetable oil
¾ teaspoon salt
1 tablespoon dry sherry

White Sauce for Boiled White-Cut Chicken

½ cup chicken stock
¾ cup milk
1 teaspoon salt
2 teaspoons lard *or* chicken fat
¼ teaspoon monosodium glutamate
2 teaspoons dry sherry
pepper to taste
2 teaspoons cornstarch

Cooking Heat the chicken stock in a pan; then add the milk, salt, lard or fat, monosodium glutamate, sherry, and pepper. Just as the mixture boils, stream in the cornstarch blended with 3 tablespoons water. Continue to stir over a gentle heat until the sauce thickens and becomes smooth and creamy.

Serving Pour over pieces of chicken arranged on a serving dish.

Sauce for Egg Dishes

Mushroom Sauce

3 large Chinese dried mushrooms
¼ cup shredded bamboo shoots
2½ tablespoons vegetable oil
3 tablespoons green peas
6 tablespoons good stock
1½ tablespoons soy sauce
½ tablespoon dry sherry
¼ teaspoon monosodium glutamate
1½ teaspoons cornstarch

Preparation Soak the mushrooms, then shred them into matchstick strips. Cut the bamboo shoots into matchstick strips.

Cooking Heat the oil in a small frying pan over a medium heat. Add the shredded vegetables and peas. Stir-fry for 1 minute. Add the stock, soy sauce, sherry, and monosodium glutamate. Bring to the boil and simmer gently for 2 minutes. Pour in the cornstarch, blended with 3 tablespoons water, and stir until the sauce thickens and is well-blended and smooth.

Serving Pour over the egg dish. This sauce goes particularly well with Chinese Omelets (see page 314).

Sweet and Sour Sauces

Basic Sweet and Sour Sauce

6 tablespoons water
2 tablespoons sugar
1½ tablespoons soy sauce
1½ tablespoons tomato puree
2 tablespoons vinegar
1 tablespoon cornstarch

This is the Sweet and Sour Sauce which has found so much favor in the West. In China, it is used in both the north and the south, with slight variations.

Cooking Heat the water in a small pan. Add the sugar, soy sauce, and tomato puree. Stir until the sugar has dissolved; then add the vinegar. Finally, stir in the cornstarch, blended with 3 tablespoons water. Continue to stir until the sauce thickens.

Strengthened Sweet and Sour Sauce

Preparation Crush the garlic and chop the ginger.

Cooking Heat the vegetable oil in a small saucepan or frying pan and fry the garlic, ginger, and scallions for 1½ minutes over a medium heat. Pour in the sugar, vinegar, tomato purée, soy sauce, sherry, orange juice, and water. Stir until the mixture is smooth and the sugar has dissolved, then increase the heat slightly, and stir in the cornstarch, blended with ¼ cup water. Stir until the sauce thickens.

2 cloves garlic
2 slices ginger root
1 tablespoon vegetable oil
1½ tablespoons chopped scallions
2½ tablespoons sugar
2½ tablespoons vinegar
2 tablespoons tomato puree
2 tablespoons soy sauce
2 tablespoons dry sherry
¼ cup orange juice
5 tablespoons water
4 teaspoons cornstarch

Cantonese Sweet and Sour Sauce

This is a southern version of the sauce.

Cooking Repeat the previous recipe, adding either 2 tablespoons tangerine juice or 2 tablespoons lychee juice to the sugar/vinegar mixture. Indeed, you could add both these extra ingredients if you wished.

Sweet and Sour Sauce for Fish

Cooking Repeat the recipe for Strengthened Sweet and Sour Sauce above, doubling the quantities of the ginger, scallions, and sherry, and adding some chopped pickles. Increase the heating time by 30 seconds.

Sweet and Sour Sauce for Pork Spare Ribs

Cooking Repeat the recipe for Strengthened Sweet and Sour Sauce, adding ¼ cup sliced green pepper, some onion, and 1 teaspoon soaked and drained black beans. Add an extra ½ tablespoon soy sauce and ½ tablespoon hoisin sauce to the sauce mixture; increase the heating time by 30 seconds.

Sweet and Sour Sauce for Chicken

Cooking Add 2 tablespoons sliced bamboo shoots, ½ teaspoon salt, and ½ teaspoon chopped mixed pickles to the recipe for Strengthened Sweet and Sour Sauce above.

Hot Sweet and Sour Sauce

Cooking Add 1 or 2 chopped chili peppers or 1 teaspoon dried chili pepper to the recipe for Strengthened Sweet and Sour Sauce. Alternatively, add 2 teaspoons of chili sauce to the sugar/vinegar mixture.

Sweet and Sour Sauce for a Chinese Omelet

1 tablespoon cornstarch
2 tablespoons water
1½ tablespoons sugar
1 tablespoon soy sauce
¼ teaspoon monosodium glutamate
1½ tablespoons vinegar
1 tablespoon dry sherry

Preparation Blend the cornstarch with 2 tablespoons water.

Cooking Mix all the ingredients in a small saucepan. Blend together over a medium heat. Stir until the liquid thickens.

Serving Pour the sauce over the omelet.

Sweet and Sour Sauce for Vegetables

1 tablespoon chopped pickles
1½ tablespoons chopped onion
½ teaspoon salt
1 tablespoon vegetable oil
1½ tablespoons sugar
¼ cup stock
2 teaspoons cornstarch
1½ tablespoons vinegar
1 tablespoon soy sauce
¼ teaspoon monosodium glutamate

Cooking Stir-fry the pickles, onion, and salt in the oil for 1½ minutes. Blend all the other ingredients together with 4 tablespoons water, then pour the mixture into the pan. Stir until all the sugar has melted and the liquid is smooth and begins to thicken.

Serving Pour the sauce over prepared blanched or cooked vegetables.

Marinades

In China marinating is extensively practiced for dishes which are steamed, deep-fried, or quick-fried. In steamed dishes, the flavoring of the principal ingredient to be cooked has to be complete or almost complete before the steaming starts. Because of the use of a large quantity of boiling oil for deep-fried dishes, little flavoring can be added to them during the cooking process, and consequently, much of it has to be imparted by marinating beforehand. In the case of quick-fried dishes, the flavors of some of the participating ingredients have to be kept as distinct as possible from the others, and therefore if the application of seasonings, sauces, and flavoring ingredients was effected during the final stir-fry, all the different tastes might intermingle to such an extent that they would become indistinguishable. This results in dishes of no character.

For the constituent ingredients to maintain their distinctive characters, they often have to be marinated separately and combined together in a final hot assembly only in the stir-frying.

Since the ingredients for Chinese marinades are fairly flexible, various types of purées and fruit juices can be added to the following recipes to give further variation. Fruit juices are used more extensively in the south than in the north.

Basic Marinade for Roast Pork, Barbecued Pork, Spare Ribs, or Fish

Preparation Chop the scallions into ½–1 inch segments. Blend all the ingredients together and use the mixture to marinate pork, ribs, or fish for 1–2 hours before cooking. Afterwards, use the remaining marinade to baste the meat during cooking.

As an alternative to soy paste, ½ tablespoon fermented, salted black beans can be used. They should be soaked for 30 minutes, then drained before use.

¼ cup chopped scallions
1½ tablespoons soy bean paste
¼ cup soy sauce
1½ tablespoons sugar
¼ cup dry sherry
¼ teaspoon monosodium glutamate
dash of pepper

Ginger-Garlic Marinade

Preparation Repeat the recipe for the Basic Marinade on page 47, adding 4–5 slices of ginger root, coarsely chopped, and 2 crushed cloves of garlic. This variation of the marinade is particularly suitable for fish.

Spiced Marinade

Preparation Repeat the recipe for the Basic Pork/Fish Marinade, adding ¼ teaspoon cinnamon, ¼ teaspoon ground cloves, ¼ teaspoon ground anise, 4–5 slices coarsely chopped ginger root, and 2 crushed cloves of garlic.

Chili Marinade

Preparation Repeat the recipe for the Basic Pork/Fish Marinade, adding 1 tablespoon chili sauce or 1 tablespoon chopped fresh chili pepper. Alternatively, fry ½ tablespoon dried chili pepper in 2½ tablespoons vegetable oil for 1 minute; then pour both the pepper and the oil into the marinade.

47

Marinade for Pork or Spare Ribs with Hoisin Sauce and Five Spice Powder

2 tablespoons hoisin sauce
2 tablespoons dry sherry
⅛–⅙ teaspoon five spice powder
2 tablespoons soy sauce
1 tablespoon sugar *or* honey
2 tablespoons water

Preparation Blend all the ingredients together. Marinate the pork or spare ribs in the mixture for 1–1½ hours.

There are two ways of varying this recipe. The first is to add 2 crushed cloves of garlic and 2 oz scallions, chopped into ½ inch segments, to the basic recipe. The second method of varying the marinade is to add 1 tablespoon chili sauce to the basic recipe; or to chop 2 dried chili peppers and fry them in 1½ tablespoons oil until slightly burnt; then add the mixture of oil and pepper to the marinade.

Brown Bean Marinade for Pork, Spare Ribs, or Fish

1½ tablespoons fermented brown beans

2 slices ginger
2 cloves garlic
1½ tablespoons soy sauce
¼ teaspoon salt
½ tablespoon sugar
6 tablespoons stock *or* water
1½ tablespoons dry sherry

Preparation Chop the ginger and crush the garlic. Mash the brown beans and add the ginger, garlic, soy sauce, salt, sugar, and stock. Heat the mixture, stirring, until near boiling point, and add the sherry. Marinate pork or spare ribs for 1–2 hours. Marinate fish for 30 minutes–1 hour. Use the remainder of the marinade for basting during cooking.

Honey Marinade for Pork and Spare Ribs

2 tablespoons honey

2 slices ginger root
2 cloves garlic
2 teaspoons salt
1 tablespoon sugar
2 tablespoons soy sauce
2 tablespoons dry sherry

Preparation Chop the ginger and crush the garlic. Rub the pork or spare ribs with the salt, ginger, and sugar, and leave to stand for 1 hour. Combine the soy sauce, sherry, honey, and garlic. Marinate the meat in this mixture for 30 minutes–1 hour, turning the meat over a couple of times.

Soy-Red Bean Cheese Marinade for Pork or Spare Ribs

2 tablespoons soy sauce
1 tablespoon red bean cheese

1 clove garlic
½ teaspoon salt
2 teaspoons sugar
1½ tablespoons dry sherry

Preparation Crush the garlic and combine it with the bean cheese. Mix in the soy sauce, salt, sugar, and sherry. Rub the mixture on the pork or spare ribs and leave to marinate for 1 hour.

Tangerine Peel Marinade for Roast Duck

Preparation Soak the tangerine peel in water for 30 minutes. Crush the garlic. Mince the tangerine peel and combine it with the garlic. Add the hot stock and the remaining ingredients, blending the mixture well. Turn the duck in the mixture and marinate it for 2 hours, turning every 30 minutes.

peel of 2 dried tangerines

2 cloves garlic
½ cup hot stock
3½ tablespoons soy sauce
½ teaspoon salt
pepper to taste

Dressings

Dressings have no great place in Chinese cooking because of the obsessive fear the Chinese have of getting a stomach chill from eating cold food. This fear would have been more soundly based if it had arisen because of a healthy respect for uncooked food in a country where previously there was no sterilized running water. Formerly, epidemics were prevalent during the summer, due to the unsterilized water. Things may have changed in China in recent years, but inclinations based on tradition take time to change and evolve.

Dressings were mainly used, therefore, on foods which had been lightly cooked, smoked, or at least blanched, steeped, or parboiled. In other words, they were served with cold, cooked dishes, such as the different 'drunken' dishes and hors d'œuvres. The Chinese 'tapestry hors d'œuvres' and similar dishes are a considerable contribution to the world of cold foods and their presentation. The Chinese use of wine, liqueur, sesame oil, sesame paste, and wine-sediment paste adds a great deal of interest to this sector of food preparation and to the culinary art. Since dressings in the Chinese tradition can be extremely good with American salads and other dishes, I have included here the following selection of recipes.

Basic Soy-Vinegar Dressing

Preparation Mix together the soy sauce, vinegar, ginger, stock, and sugar. Stir in the oil gradually, blending the mixture well. Pour over prepared vegetables.

2½ tablespoons soy sauce
2½ tablespoons vinegar

1½ teaspoons shredded ginger root
3 tablespoons strong chicken stock
2 teaspoons sugar
2½ tablespoons vegetable oil

Strengthened Soy-Vinegar Dressing

Preparation Add 1½ tablespoons chopped scallions, 1 tablespoon sherry, ¼ teaspoon monosodium glutamate, and 2 cloves of crushed garlic to the recipe for Basic Soy-Vinegar Dressing. Mix in these additional ingredients before stirring in the oil. This dressing should make any ordinary salad a great deal more interesting.

Hot Soy Dressing

2 red chili peppers
¼ cup soy sauce

1 slice ginger root
2 tablespoons vegetable oil
2 tablespoons vinegar
¼ cup chicken *or* meat stock

Preparation Chop the peppers and discard the seeds. Chop the ginger root.

Cooking Stir-fry the peppers in oil until they begin to turn black. Add the ginger, then stir in the soy sauce, vinegar, and stock, and blend well. Leave to cool.

Serving When cold, use the dressing on meat, cold cooked fish, or vegetables.

Soy-Sesame Dressing

3 tablespoons soy sauce
1 tablespoon sesame oil
1½ tablespoons sesame paste

1½ tablespoons vegetable oil
3 tablespoons chicken *or* meat stock

Preparation Mix all the ingredients together in a bowl, blending well. Use on cold meat or fish, or on cold, boiled noodles with blanched vegetables and shredded cold meats.

Soy-Onion Dressing

3 tablespoons chopped scallions
3 tablespoons soy sauce

2 cloves garlic
2 slices ginger root
¼ cup vegetable oil
3 tablespoons stock
½ teaspoon salt
2 teaspoons dry sherry
1½ teaspoons sugar
¼ teaspoon monosodium glutamate

Preparation Chop the scallions into ¼ inch segments. Crush the garlic and shred the ginger.

Cooking Stir-fry the scallions, ginger, and garlic in the oil for 2 minutes over a medium heat. Add the other ingredients and mix well; then leave to cool. Serve with cold cooked meat, fish, or vegetables.

Sesame-Vinegar Dressing

¼ cup sesame paste *or* peanut butter
2 teaspoons sesame oil
2½ tablespoons vinegar

1½ tablespoons soy sauce
1½ teaspoons sugar
¼ teaspoon salt
2 tablespoons water

Preparation Mix all the ingredients together in a bowl. Blend well. Use on cold cooked meat, fish, or vegetables.

Mustard Dressing

Preparation Combine all the ingredients in a bowl. Blend well. Leave to stand in a cool place or in a refrigerator for 2 hours to mature and develop. Use on cold cooked chicken, meat, or blanched vegetables.

1½ tablespoons powdered mustard

2 tablespoons soy sauce
2½ tablespoons water
pepper to taste
1½ tablespoons vinegar
2 teaspoons sugar
1½ tablespoons vegetable oil
1½ tablespoons dry sherry

Egg Dressing

This is a kind of Chinese mayonnaise.

Preparation Hard-boil the eggs. Crush the garlic, and shred the ginger. Mash the hard-boiled eggs; then mix them together with the garlic and ginger. Combine with all the other ingredients; blend well. Use on vegetables or blanched vegetables.

3 eggs

2 cloves garlic
2 slices ginger root
1 tablespoon soy sauce
¼ teaspoon monosodium glutamate
¼ cup chicken *or* meat stock
½ teaspoon salt
2 tablespoons dry sherry
pepper to taste
¼ cup vegetable oil

Table Condiments, Dips, and Mixes

Table condiments, dips, and mixes constitute the final phase in the multi-phase flavoring of Chinese food. As with Western food, dips and mixes are placed on the dining table for the diners themselves to add to the food. The main difference in presentation of Chinese and European condiments is that the Chinese ones are normally placed in small, open, saucer-like dishes into which the food is dipped; never in bottles for shaking over the food on the individual's plate. A second difference is that we Chinese blend the basic condiments into various mixes for the many types of dishes. Hence, although there are in fact only a limited number of basic sauces and condiments, there exists quite a variety of blended dips and mixes which are brought to the table to be eaten with different types of food. It is the cross-blending which increases and accounts for the large Chinese variety.

The Chinese attitude towards the use of dips and mixes, as towards cooking in general, is a liberal one; there is a high flexibility in practice. Although there are conventional condiments and mixes for different traditional dishes, there is no rule against using whatever one is inclined to use. Hence it is a frequent practice to arrange on the dinner table a number of basic dips and condiments, such as plain soy sauce, hoisin sauce, hot chili sauce, mustard, tomato sauce, and Salt and Pepper Mix, in addition to the few made-up mixes specially prepared for the dishes included on the menu, so that the diners will have a chance to follow their own inclinations. Besides, since many of the basic sauces are of contrasting colors, they provide an attractive color

51

display on the dining table, which should be particularly appealing to the color-conscious world of today.

When eating a range of Chinese dishes (e.g. Mongolian Barbecue of Meats) in a typical Peking restaurant, each diner is provided with two empty bowls, one for beaten egg, and the other to enable him to mix his own dip or sauce from the variety of basic sauces and condiments provided on the table. It gives the diners great satisfaction to mix their own dips after they have settled down at the dining table. They also have the anticipation of the barbecuing ahead, as a flaming earthenware brazier will be brought in and placed at the center of the table. To eat such a meal in Peking is one of the most interesting culinary·experiences in the world.

Partly to alleviate unnecessary labor in preparation—or likely confusion—and partly to conform to widely accepted Chinese practices, I have listed some basic dip-sauces and mixes under the headings 'Dips for Chicken' 'Dips for Pork,' and 'Dips for Shrimp' in the section which follows. The most suitable dips for the three types of food are given under the appropriate heading. Chicken, pork, and shrimp always require dips if they are to be perfect.

BASIC CONDIMENTS

The basic Chinese condiments are, in the main, the same as in the West: salt, pepper, vinegar, mustard, and tomato, with a few additions such as soy sauce, plum sauce, sesame paste, oyster sauce, shrimp sauce, chili oil, and hoisin sauce (a vegetable sauce, dark in color, available canned).

Soy sauce and hoisin sauce usually come ready-made, and nobody in China tries to make them. The other sauces, however, are sometimes home-made, and in America will frequently have to be made at home, since not all American towns and cities have Chinese markets. Both hoisin and soy sauce should be a boon for vegetarian and meat cooking alike when adopted for American use.

Soy Sauce

Soy sauce comes in many grades, especially in sauce-producing areas such as Foochow, where I was brought up, but in the main it is available in three grades, light, dark, and heavy. The heavy type is generally used for cooking materials such as beef and spare ribs, which require a strong, full-bodied sauce; however, it can also be used as a tasty dip for large chunks of white-cooked meat. Good quality, heavy soy-sauce has a flavor of its own which is not unlike a highly concentrated, rich beef consommé, and therefore it is very useful for any type of food which is not in itself highly savory or salty. The taste of soy sauce can perhaps be defined as the epitome of savory-saltiness.

For foods which are already fairly salty and savory, or for mixing with other condiments in cooking, the light and dark varieties are generally used, as they are not too thick to serve as table condiments.

The lighter types are more delicate, and therefore more suitable for mixing when preparing dips. They are invariably used in the preparation of soups, the various semi-soup dishes, and the numerous vegetable dishes; even if only to avoid colorization and the blanketing of taste. Shrimp sauce is also often used in dishes where there is a good proportion of soup.

Hoisin Sauce

Hoisin sauce normally comes in a much thicker form than soy sauce: it is almost a paste or jam, and is brownish-red in color, with a pungent sweet-spiciness. It is made from soy beans, garlic, chili, and spices, and looks almost like raspberry jam. It is used in cooking shellfish, spare ribs, pork, duck, chicken, and vegetables, and can be used as a table condiment for plain cooked food, such as pork and poultry, as well as roasted and deep-fried foods. It is sometimes called 'red vegetable sauce' or 'sweet vegetable paste'. I have found it very useful in frying vegetables, and as a dip in place of plum sauce. Hoisin sauce is very easily acceptable to the American palate and can be used almost like tomato ketchup, although since it is much stronger it should be used more sparingly.

Hot Chili Oil

This is a basic constituent ingredient for making up all the hot sauces in China, and can almost be classified as one of the basic sauces, although more often than not it is made in the kitchen. The red color in Kung-Po dishes and in a majority of all the hot dishes of Szechuan is attained by the use of hot chili oil.

8–10 red chili peppers or 2 tablespoons dried chili pepper
6 tablespoons peanut or corn oil

Preparation Remove the seeds from the chili peppers.

Cooking Heat the oil in a small saucepan. Add the peppers and cook gently over a low heat, stirring occasionally, until the oil turns dark red. Cool and strain. Use sparingly as it is extremely hot!

Plum Sauce

Preparation Peel, stone, and chop the plums. Blend all the ingredients in an electric blender for 30 seconds.

Cooking Pour the mixture into a saucepan and bring to the boil. Cover, and simmer very gently for 30 minutes, stirring occasionally. Store in a jar for 1 month to mature.

Serving Use for Peking Duck (to spread on the pancake) or with roast pork.

½ lb plums

2 tablespoons brown bean paste
2 tablespoons chutney
3 tablespoons apple sauce
2 tablespoons soy sauce
¼ cup sugar
¾ cup water
2 tablespoons vinegar
1 teaspoon salt

Salt-Cinnamon Mix

Cooking Heat the salt in a dry pan over a gentle heat until it starts to brown. Allow it to cool slightly, then stir in the cinnamon and add the five spice powder. This mix is best freshly prepared, otherwise it must be kept in a sealed jar. Use it in the same way as Salt and Pepper Mix.

2 tablespoons salt
1½ teaspoons ground cinnamon

dash of five-spice powder

Oyster Sauce

12 large oysters

½ cup chicken *or* meat stock
2 tablespoons dry sherry
3 tablespoons soy sauce
1 tablespoon hoisin sauce
1 teaspoon sugar
2 teaspoons vegetable oil

Oyster sauce is popular in CANTONESE (southern) cooking, especially with beef and quick-fried dishes. It is available ready-made at Chinese markets.

Preparation Shell the oysters; then strain and collect the liquid in a cup.

Cooking Heat the oysters, oyster water, stock, and sherry in a small saucepan. Simmer very gently for 10 minutes. Stir in the soy sauce, hoisin sauce, sugar, and oil and continue to cook, stirring gently, for 5 minutes. Cool; then strain, and keep in a cool place.

Hot Mustard Sauce

1½ tablespoons powdered mustard

½ teaspoon salt
1 teaspoon chili sauce
1 teaspoon vinegar
6–7 tablespoons water

Cooking Add the salt, chili sauce, and vinegar to the water. Bring to the boil and boil for 1 minute; then allow to cool. Stir the liquid very slowly into the mustard until the mixture becomes smooth and creamy.

Mustard is served as a dip with more or less the same types of food as it is used in America.

Salt and Pepper Mix

2 tablespoons salt
1 tablespoon freshly ground pepper

Salt and Pepper Mix is best prepared fresh, otherwise it must be kept in a sealed jar. It is a widely-used dip for many deep-fried dishes and for roasted food, such as shrimp balls, crackling chicken, or ordinary deep-fried chicken. (See illustration.)

Cooking Heat the salt and pepper in a small, dry frying pan over a gentle heat for 3–4 minutes, stirring constantly, until there is a strong smell of pepper.

Various Dips for Chicken

The following dip-sauces or basic sauces should be placed on the dining table for the diners to use at their own discretion. They can make their own choice of dips to blend together, or they can dip their pieces of chicken in any one or several of the mixes. Salt and Pepper Mix, Hot Mustard Sauce, soy sauce, tomato sauce, shrimp sauce, Soy-Oil Dip, Soy-Oil-Garlic Dip, Soy-Oil-Ginger Dip, and Soy-Sherry Dip should all be served. Such an array should satisfy even the connoisseurs.

Soy-Oil Dip for Chicken

This dip gives added smoothness to white-cooked chicken. The Chinese often use oil to give extra smoothness to the surface of foods which have been boiled or simmered. If the oil has had tasty foods fried in it, it adds to the flavor of the food. Soy-Oil Dip has these qualities.

Cooking Heat the oil until it is about to smoke. Let it cool, then stir in the soy sauce.

3 tablespoons soy sauce
2½ tablespoons vegetable oil

Soy-Oil-Garlic Dip

This mix can be used as a dip for clear-simmered, white-cooked chicken or for roast chicken. The same dip, using 3 tablespoons vinegar instead of oil, can be served with white-cooked pork. (As pork is fatter than chicken, it requires no oil.) The quantity in this recipe can be divided among three or four small sauce dishes and is sufficient for a table of ten.

Preparation Crush the garlic. Mix all the ingredients together, using an electric blender if possible.

4 cloves garlic
6 tablespoons soy sauce
3 tablespoons peanut *or* corn oil

½ teaspoon sugar

Soy-Oil-Ginger Dip

Preparation Shred and chop the ginger root. Mix all the ingredients together and blend well, using an electric blender if available.

Use the dip with clear-simmered, white-cooked chicken or with roast chicken. When serving it with white-cooked pork, substitute vinegar for the oil.

4 slices ginger root
6 tablespoons soy sauce
3 tablespoons vegetable oil

1 teaspoon vinegar

Soy-Ginger-Garlic Dip

Preparation Crush the garlic. Shred and chop the ginger root. Mix all the ingredients together, using a blender if available. Use with chicken or pork.

2 cloves garlic
2 slices ginger root
½ cup soy sauce
4 tablespoons peanut *or* corn oil
1 teaspoon sugar
2 teaspoons vinegar

Soy-Oil-Scallion Dip

3 scallions
6 tablespoons soy sauce
3 tablespoons vegetable oil

½ teaspoon vinegar

Preparation Chop the scallions very fine, then mix them with the other ingredients, using a blender if possible.

Serving Divide the dip among three sauce dishes. Serve with chicken or pork, but substitute vinegar for the oil if using with pork.

Soy-Mustard Dip

3 tablespoons soy sauce
1½ tablespoons mustard powder

2 tablespoons stock
½ teaspoon salt
1½ teaspoons sesame oil

Preparation Blend all the ingredients together, using a blender if available. Use as a dip for white-cooked or roast chicken and pork.

Hot Soy-Oil Dip

Preparation Add 1 teaspoon Hot Chili Oil (see page 53) to every 3 tablespoons soy sauce in any of the preceding Soy-Oil Dips. Use with chicken or pork.

Soy-Sherry Dip

¼ cup soy sauce
¼ cup dry sherry

2 teaspoons sugar
1½ teaspoons salt

Preparation Combine all the ingredients, blending well. Serve in two sauce dishes or saucers, as an accompaniment to Deep-Fried Chicken or Crackling Pork.

Hoisin or Plum Sauce for Pork

½ cup hoisin *or* 10 tablespoons plum sauce
2–3 teaspoons sesame oil

This dip appeals to those who like a sugary-sweet quality to contrast with the fatness of the pork. It serves the same function as red-currant jam or jelly in Western food, except that the Chinese sauce is slightly spicier.

Preparation Blend the sesame oil with the hoisin sauce or plum sauce, and serve as a dip with white-cooked, boiled, simmered, or roast pork.

Plum Dip for Duck

Preparation Combine all the ingredients, blending well. Serve in three sauce dishes.

6 tablespoons plum sauce

3 tablespoons soy sauce
1 tablespoon chili oil *or* 1 tablespoon Tabasco

Soy-Sesame Dip for Pork

Preparation Combine all the ingredients in an electric blender for 15 seconds. Divide the dip between two dishes.

¼ cup soy sauce
1 tablespoon sesame oil
3 tablespoons sesame paste *or* peanut butter

1 tablespoon vegetable oil
1½ tablespoons dry sherry
2 teaspoons minced ginger root

Various Dips for Pork

Arrange the following dips on the table: plain, heavy soy sauce, hoisin sauce, Hot Mustard Sauce, Chili Sauce, tomato sauce, Salt and Pepper Mix. You can also serve Vinegar-Garlic Dip (2 teaspoons crushed garlic with 3 tablespoons vinegar) and Vinegar-Ginger Dip (1 tablespoon chopped ginger in 3 tablespoons vinegar). The diners can use whichever dips they choose, or dip the food into several sauces at the same time, if so desired.

Basic Dip for Seafood

Preparation Shred or mince the ginger root. Combine all the ingredients, blending well. Divide the mixture among three sauce dishes.

6 slices ginger root
6 tablespoons vinegar
3 tablespoons soy sauce

Dip for Crab

Preparation Repeat the previous recipe, doubling the quantity of soy sauce.

As crabs are steamed, boiled, or fried with a light sauce, a saltier, heavier condiment is required to attune them to the average palate. Hence, a larger proportion of soy sauce compared with the previous recipe should be introduced.

Dip for Shrimp

Preparation Crush the garlic and shred the ginger root. Combine all the ingredients, blending well. Serve in four sauce dishes.

2 cloves garlic
2 slices ginger root
¼ cup soy sauce
2 tablespoons dry sherry
1 tablespoon hoisin sauce
1 tablespoon tomato puree
2 teaspoons hot chili oil

Dip for Deep-Fried Shrimp

Use the Salt and Pepper Mix recipe on page 54.

Dip for Deep-Fried Shrimp Balls

2 cloves garlic
2 tablespoons hoisin sauce
1½ tablespoons honey
2½ tablespoons dry sherry
3 tablespoons soy sauce
pepper to taste

Preparation Crush the clove of garlic and combine it with all the other ingredients, blending well. Serve in two sauce dishes. This recipe is sufficient for one large plateful of shrimp balls.

Various Dips for Shrimp

Arrange the following dips on the table: plain soy sauce, hoisin sauce, Hot Mustard Sauce, Chili Oil, Salt and Pepper Mix, Soy-Vinegar-Ginger Mix (which is the basic dip for seafood), and tomato sauce. With this wide selection of dips on the table, the diner can dip the shrimp in whichever dip or dips he prefers, thus giving him maximum satisfaction. Offering such a variety of plain dips is widely practiced in China.

Dip for Clams

3 slices ginger root
3 scallions
3 tablespoons soy sauce
1½ tablespoons dry sherry
1½ tablespoons vinegar
1½ tablespoons tomato sauce
1½ tablespoons vegetable oil
1½ teaspoons sesame oil

Preparation Shred and chop the ginger root and chop the scallions. Combine all the ingredients, blending well. Serve in three sauce dishes.

Dip for Deep-Fried Bean Curd

2½ tablespoons soy sauce
2½ tablespoons peanut butter
1 tablespoon sesame oil
2 tablespoons vegetable oil
¼ teaspoon hot chili oil *or*
    2 teaspoons Tabasco
3 tablespoons chicken stock

Preparation Combine all the ingredients, using a blender. Serve in three or four sauce dishes.

SOUP

Chinese soups, like Western soups, are mainly either thick or clear. We Chinese tend to have fewer thick soups than you do in the West, but on the other hand, the Chinese range of clear soups is immense.

Our variety is probably due to the Chinese concept of cross-cooking. A great many Chinese clear soups are only partly consommés in the Western sense, for they are clear soups with various meats and vegetables, in different sizes and shapes, floating or immersed in them. But the Chinese concept of soups provides that so long as the consommé is pure and crystal-clear, despite the many items in it, the soup can be classified as clear.

In other words, some Chinese soups are really big dishes in the Western sense. But these soups are never heavy, because although there is a variety of solids, these contrast with the light, clear purity of the broth in which they are immersed. The idea is of a clear, deep, mountain pool (albeit a hot savory one!), with many intriguing items of 'nature' in it, contributing to its form, color, and flavor.

The consommé of these Chinese clear soups consists mainly of chicken stock, meat stock, bone stock, a mixture of the two, or all three, in different proportions. The variety of flavors, colors, shapes, and appearances occurs only when other materials are added to the soups. Since these other materials can be fresh or cooked, dried, salted, or spicy meats, fish, or vegetables, the number of possible combinations rises into the sphere of permutations.

Take the basic chicken stock. If one were to add to it a few slices of abalone, smoked ham, or dried mushrooms or scallops, a few lengths of meaty pork ribs, or a tablespoonful or two of shelled shrimps or crab-meat, the resulting soup, after a short period of simmering, would have changed and achieved a distinctive flavor of its own, even without the addition of any further types of flavorers or ingredients.

If even more ingredients are added, perhaps in different stages of the preparation, the flavor of the stock undergoes a further subtle transformation. This is how the subtlety and differentiation in the flavor or taste of the stocks is gradually advanced and achieved in China—usually in stages, until each soup has a complete individuality and tradition of its own. It is this unique blending of *flavor* which the Chinese hanker for in their soups, when they look for traditional authenticity in their foods.

Texture also enters into the preparation and character of Chinese soups—not so much in the body of the soup itself, but in the texture of the various materials and ingredients which are added to it.

For example, there is a well-known and popular soup called the Triple Shred Soup, which consists of ham, white chicken meat, and bamboo shoots, all sliced into matchstick strips, and simmered for a while in good stock. If the strips are not cooked overlong in the stock they should retain their own color and texture, and at the same time contribute something to the flavor of the soup; the bamboo shoots should be ivory and crunchy, the ham, pink and salty, and the chicken, white and flavorsome. The combination of the three gives the soup its unique character, and although it is by no means a great soup, it can be very appealing and evocative to a Chinese when it is really well made. Like tea, the quality is all a question of the care taken in its preparation.

Two classes of materials which are very extensively used in Chinese soups are kidneys and chicken gizzards, and cooked pigs' and chicken blood. These foods are generally cooked for a very short time, sliced thinly and dipped briefly in boiling water before being simmered for a short time in stock. One of the qualities which all these materials contribute to the soup is the feeling of meaty-crunchiness (a quality which they retain so long as they are not over-cooked), quite apart from their individual contributions to the ultimate flavor.

When any meat is used in thinly sliced pieces in soup, it is usually first salted, then dredged in cornstarch. The latter treatment gives the slices a very smooth texture after a short period of simmering; this quality provides the added satisfaction of eating meat while one is drinking soup. Without such treatment all meats tend to become dry and fibrous after a period of cooking.

Another item frequently used in Chinese soup preparation is bean curd. The feel of the material is like that of a savory but spongy custard, which is able to absorb a great deal of flavor from surrounding ingredients and helps to give body to the soup. For instance, it is used very successfully to give added body to Hot and Sour Soup.

One aspect of Chinese soup which does not seem to be important in the West is shape. Shapes enter Chinese soup together with color in the various large and small chunks of foods and ingredients which are immersed in the soup. These may occur in the form of a whole chicken or duck, or in the smaller and browner pieces which have been previously roasted, and they contrast with the greenness of the whole tender heart of Chinese cabbage, greens, or broccoli (only lightly cooked), strands of transparent bean-thread noodles, the white roundness of fish balls, or the deep green of Chinese parsleys, a sprinkle of red chopped ham, or pieces of pink crab or shrimp, floating like red-hue petals in a steaming clear pond!

Indeed, a large tureen of Chinese soup is comparable to the art of a good landscape gardener!

This type of 'gardening' is often made easier by two of the most common methods in the last stage of soup-making. Firstly, all the different pieces or chunks of foods and ingredients (some cooked, some raw, some dried) are carefully arranged in a large tureen or dish, which is in turn placed in a steamer with a quantity of crystal-clear stock, and steamed for half an hour or so. The dish or tureen is brought steaming to the table, with all the various types of foods in the soup, quite undisturbed and all neatly in place as originally arranged.

The other, simpler way of making soup is to arrange foods and ingredients at the bottom of the dish or tureen, and pour in the boiling, concocted stock. One of the simplest of all Chinese soups, the Soup for Gods, is made by simply placing 1½ tablespoons of soy sauce, ½ teaspoon of salt, ¼ teaspoon of monosodium glutamate, 1½ teaspoons of sesame oil, 1 teaspoon of vegetable oil, and 1 tablespoon of chopped scallions at the bottom of the soup bowl, and pouring in 1 quart of boiling water! When you have several solid dishes to go with the meal, this can be quite a satisfactory dish of soup, a soup which can be made literally in 30 seconds flat, if you have a ready kettle of boiling water!

Since we Chinese do not use milk there are not many outstanding white cream soups in China; Chinese pea soups are not unlike the Western variety. On the other hand, the majority of meats can be combined with most vegetables to make soup, and the majority of vegetables can be combined with most meats; and since both kinds of resultant stock can be further combined with seafood, dried foods, salted foods, pickled foods, and spicy foods, to achieve distinct flavors, the avenues here are wide open for those who are creatively inclined. However, before one plunges into the production of a whole cacophony of flavors, it is best to take a look at the roads which are already well trodden—the soups which are well-established in China, and the flavors and appearance over the generations—whether classical, domestic, or regional.

To conclude, it should perhaps be said that the Chinese conception of soups is that they should not only be colorful—something which the soup manufacturers are nowadays so emphatic about—but they should also be picturesque. In other words, their impact should be derived not only from the flavor and color, but also from the shape and texture of the constituent materials and ingredients; these should be both original and attractively arranged.

Superior Stock

The traditional Superior Stock is usually produced in quantity in China, which is a long and stylized process. When dining in a restaurant in Peking, one can usually call for Superior Stock to be served as soup free of charge.

In its simplified and shortened form it can be made as follows: Remove the breast meat and 2 drumsticks from a 3 lb chicken, and boil the rest of the chicken for 15 minutes with 2 lb pork, 2 lb spare ribs, 2 lb pork bones, 1 lb pork belly bones, and 1 lb ham in 5 to 6 quarts of water, skimming off all scum and extraneous matters. Lift out the chicken and pork, then the pork belly and pork bones, and place them all in a bowl containing 2 quarts of cold water. After turning the chicken and bones around in the water, pour half of it into the stock, in which the chicken, etc. has been boiled. The sudden coolness of the water coagulates and precipitates more of the grease and impurities in the stock, and these can easily be skimmed off. Before returning the chicken, pork, and pork belly bones to the pan for a further period of boiling and simmering, pour a quarter of the now augmented stock into a separate bowl to cool. This cooling stock will be used later on in the same way as the cold water was used to precipitate and coagulate grease and impurities. After the chicken, etc. has been returned to the main boiler, bring the contents to boil and simmer gently for 1 hour. The materials are again lifted out, and the cooled broth water poured in, again precipitating and coagulating more grease, impurities, and extraneous matters which are once more removed.

The above process is repeated twice more over a period of 3 hours, after which the broth will have become much stronger as well as more purified.

The final phase of the preparation consists of some seasoning and double clarification. The seasoning is done by the addition of a small amount of ginger, onion, and soy sauce (according to your own taste). Chop the breast meat and the meat from the drumsticks of the chicken, keeping them separate. The chopped darker drumstick meat is used for the first clarification, and the minced white breast meat is then used as the second clarification. The clarification is achieved in each case by simmering the minced chicken in the stock for 10–12 minutes, then straining it. The important thing is not allowing the stock to come to a full boil at any time, thus creating what we call a stewed stock. The simmering has to be kept very gentle throughout to produce clear stock.

For making larger quantities of this Superior Stock a duck, where available, can be added to every 2 chickens used. But only chicken meat should be used for clarification. For the lighter and most refined stocks, the frog-and-chicken combination (in the ratio of 1:2) is considered the best.

A fascinating and established way of conducting the process of clarification in restaurants is to place only a quarter of the boiler over the open fire, and a filter at the opposite end just below the surface of the broth. Because of the heat, the stock at the fire-end of the boiler rises rapidly, carrying all the impurities with it. As the liquid reaches the top and pours over to the opposite end, the impurities are caught by the filter. As the process is circular and continuous, the stock becomes progressively and increasingly purified; and within the 10–12 minutes that the clarification is working, the stock will become crystal-clear.

Superior Stock is an essential in the preparation of soups and sauces if these are to be of the highest quality.

A note concerning quantity—10 lb of bones, chicken, pork, and ham should produce approximately 8 quarts of stock.

Clear Stock

Clear Stock is a term sometimes used for Superior Stock, but sometimes it indicates a stock which has a little less bone content than the normal Superior Stock. That is, instead of 2:1 ratio between bone and chicken, the ratio is reduced to 1:1.

Chicken Stock

Chicken Stock is a clear stock used for certain dishes such as Bird's Nest and Shark's Fin soups, and in making some sauces. It is produced by long, slow simmering of chicken, unadulterated by the addition of pork or bone, except perhaps a small amount of best ham. The stock is purified by the clarification method described above—that is, by the use of minced chicken meat for dredging during the last stage of cooking.

Secondary Stock

In the preparation of Secondary Stock, the only materials used are bones: chicken bones or carcase, pork bones, and pork belly bones in the ratio of 2:2:1, simmered slowly for $3\frac{1}{2}$–4 hours, starting with twice as much water as material. Necks of chicken or ducks may be added if available.

White Soup or Milky Stock

The White Soup or Milky Stock is made simply by boiling up all the remnants of the raw materials (bones) used in producing Superior Stock, with the addition of about 25% of fresh bones. The boiling should be vigorous, although not too vigorous, otherwise it might produce a burned taste, and it should be continued for 2 hours, until the liquid is reduced to just under half. The stock will then have become white. Strain carefully through a sieve and muslin and you have milky stock.

Today in Europe, Britain, and America, there is not the time to indulge in such lengthy and elaborate procedures as those described above. However the whole process of preparation of Superior Stock can be compressed by adding ready chicken stock cubes to pork bone, lean pork, chicken carcase and pork belly bones, which have been simmered very gently for 2½ hours, continually skimmed and finally strained and filtered, and have had seasonings, together with a small amount of onion and a bit of ginger, added to them. The resultant stock would only be marginally different from the traditional Chinese Superior Stock and can always be used as a substitute.

As for the preparation of White Soup or Milky Stock, with the use and availability of milk and dairy produce, the West is more advanced than the Chinese, and no problem should arise nowadays. The mixing of the Superior Stock or Chinese White Soup with milk or cream should make a good combination.

The number of Chinese soups which are based on the types of stock described above is inexhaustible. As a matter of fact, many Chinese soups can be produced even when you have not prepared any of these basic materials; for many quite respectable and palatable soups in China can, in fact, be produced in a reasonably short time from plain water. However, for good, tasty soups, stock is naturally preferable to water; and for first-class soups Superior Stock or Chicken Stock are preferable to Secondary Stock when the purpose is to produce a first class soup and not just a wash-down, which some Chinese soups are sometimes meant to be, especially after a succession of rich, savory, meaty dishes.

The following recipes are based on the assumption that either Superior Stock or Secondary Stock is available. However, if one is compelled to use tap water, a tablespoon of light soy sauce, a dash of pepper, and ¼ teaspoon of monosodium glutamate (or 1 chicken stock cube) should be added to every 2½ cups of water used instead of stock. Strangely enough, in some cases where quite a lot of ingredients are used in the cooking, it really makes little difference whether stock or water is used in the preparation of the soup. In soup making, we Chinese are basically optimists!

Casserole of Chinese Cabbage Soup

Preparation Clean the cabbage thoroughly and cut into 2 inch pieces. Soak the noodles and dried shrimp in warm water for 15 minutes, then discard the water. Slice the pork into thin 1 × 1½ inch pieces. Rub with half of the salt and all of the cornstarch. Shred the ginger.

Cooking Heat the lard in a large saucepan. Add the pork, shrimp, and ginger and stir-fry together over a medium heat for 2 minutes. Add the cabbage and soy sauce. Stir them together with the other ingredients for 2 minutes. Add the noodles, and pour in 5 cups of water or stock. Finally, when the contents come to the boil again, add the remaining salt and the wine and monosodium glutamate (or chicken stock cube). Place the casserole in a preheated oven to simmer for 30 minutes at 375°F (190°C). Serve in the casserole.

Since the principal attractions of this soup to the Chinese are its purity and the dominating flavor of the cabbage, it is equally acceptable whether made with water or stock.

Serves 4–6, with other dishes

1 medium-large (about 2 lb) Chinese celery cabbage *or* Savoy cabbage
¼ lb lean pork
5 cups water *or* stock

1 cup transparent noodles
1½ tablespoons dried shrimp
2 slices ginger root
2 teaspoons salt
2 teaspoons cornstarch
1 tablespoon lard
2 tablespoons light-colored soy sauce
2 tablespoons white wine *or* dry sherry
¼ teaspoon monosodium glutamate *or* 1 chicken stock cube

Spare Rib and Chinese Celery Cabbage Soup

Serves 4–6 with other dishes

6 meaty spare ribs (about 1–1½ lbs)
1 medium-sized Chinese celery cabbage *or* Savoy cabbage
6 cups superior *or* secondary stock *or* water

2½ teaspoons salt
pepper to taste
2 tablespoons dry sherry
¼ teaspoon monosodium glutamate *or* 1 chicken stock cube

Preparation Trim any excess fat from the spare ribs and chop them into 2 inch pieces. Boil in water for 5 minutes, then pour away the water. Clean and chop the cabbage into 2 inch slices.

Cooking Place the ribs in a large saucepan. Add 6 cups water or stock. Bring to the boil, reduce the heat, and simmer for 30 minutes. Add the cabbage, salt, pepper, sherry, and monosodium glutamate. Simmer over a low heat for the next 20–25 minutes; then serve in a large soup bowl or tureen.

After 50 minutes of cooking, the meat on the spare ribs will have become sufficiently detachable from the bone to be easily dipped into table dips, mixes, and condiments for eating.

Spare Rib and Bean Sprout Soup

Serves 4–6, with other dishes

Repeat the recipe for Spare Rib and Chinese Celery Cabbage Soup (see above), using 12 oz bean sprouts instead of cabbage, but simmer the ribs for 50 minutes before adding the sprouts and seasonings. Then only a further 5 minutes simmering is required before serving.

Spare Rib and Sliced Cucumber Soup

Serves 4–6, with other dishes

Repeat the recipe for Spare Rib and Chinese Celery Cabbage Soup (see above), using 1 lb cucumber instead of cabbage. Cut the cucumber into 2–3 inch pieces, then slice it vertically into thin matchstick strips (without peeling). Cucumber requires very little cooking, and should be added to the spare ribs in the soup only 5 minutes before serving.

Meatballs and Chinese Celery Cabbage Soup

Serves 4–6, with other dishes

½ lb slab bacon
1 medium-sized onion
2 tablespoons water chestnuts
1 medium-sized Chinese celery cabbage *or* Savoy cabbage

Preparation Finely chop the bacon, and chop the onion and water chestnuts finely. Mix them all in a basin with the egg white, cornstarch, and soy sauce. Blend into a paste and form into meat balls half the size of ping-pong balls. Clean the cabbage and cut into 2 inch pieces.

Cooking Boil the cabbage in water for 3 minutes. Pour away the water and place the cabbage in a casserole. Place the meat balls on top of the cabbage. Pour in the stock and sprinkle with seasonings. Cover the casserole and place it in an oven preheated to 375°F for 40 minutes.

Serving Remove from the oven, test the meat balls to make sure that they are cooked through, adjust the seasonings, and serve in the casserole.

5 cups stock

1 egg white
2 tablespoons cornstarch
1½ teaspoons soy sauce
2 teaspoons salt
2 tablespoons dry sherry
¼ teaspoon monosodium glutamate
   or 1 chicken stock cube
pepper to taste

Long-Cooked Spare Ribs and Carrot Soup

Preparation Trim the ribs and chop into 1½ inch pieces. Chop the carrots diagonally into similar pieces. Cut each tomato into four.

Cooking Place the ribs in 2 quarts water. Bring to the boil and simmer for 30 minutes. Skim away any impurities. Add the carrots and tomatoes, salt and pepper. Bring to the boil again, and reduce heat to simmer very gently for 1¼ hours. Add the wine and adjust seasonings; then serve.

This recipe originated in China during the height of the Cultural Revolution. Note that neither stock nor monosodium glutamate is used.

Serves 4–6, with other dishes

6 meaty spare ribs (about 1–1½ lbs)
1 lb carrots
2 quarts water

2 tomatoes
1 tablespoon salt
pepper to taste
3 tablespoons white wine

Sliced Pork Kidney Soup

Preparation Soak dried bamboo shoots in warm water for 1 hour, and discard water. Slice the kidneys and bamboo shoots very thin. Marinate the kidneys in a mixture of one third of all four seasonings.

Cooking Bring the stock to the boil in a saucepan. Add both types of bamboo shoots, and allow them to simmer gently in the stock for half an hour. Add all the remaining seasonings. When the contents come to the boil again, pour in the sliced kidneys and marinade for just 30 seconds, simmering rapidly but not boiling. Serve at once.

Note The shortness of the cooking time enhances the crispness of the kidneys.

Serves 4–6, with other dishes

3 tablespoons dried bamboo shoots
1 pair pork kidneys
1 cup bamboo shoots
5 cups superior stock

2 teaspoons salt
1½ tablespoons soy sauce
1½ tablespoons vinegar
2 tablespoons dry sherry

Pork Liver and Mixed Vegetable Soup

Serves 4–6, with other dishes

Preparation Slice the liver into 10–12 thin pieces. Boil in water for 3 minutes; then drain. Cut greens and celery into

6 oz pork liver
¼ lb mustard greens

65

¾ cup celery
6 cups good stock

1 medium-sized onion
1 tablespoon Szechuan hot pickled greens
3 large Chinese dried mushrooms
2 teaspoons salt
¼ teaspoon monosodium glutamate
  or 1 chicken stock cube
2 teaspoons sesame oil

Serves 4–6, with other dishes

6 oz lean pork *or* lamb
¾ lb turnip
5 cups superior stock

½ teaspoon salt
1 tablespoon cornstarch
3 tablespoons soy sauce
1 tablespoon vinegar
2 medium-sized onions
2 slices ginger root
2 tablespoons dry sherry
2 teaspoons sesame oil

Serves 4–6, with other dishes

¾ lb slab bacon
1½ cups mushrooms
5 cups good stock

1½ teaspoons salt
1 tablespoon cornstarch
2½ tablespoons soy sauce
pepper to taste
¼ teaspoon monosodium glutamate
  or ¾ chicken stock cube

Serves 4–6, with other dishes

¾ lb slab bacon
2 eggs
5 cups good stock

1½ teaspoons salt
1 tablespoon cornstarch
3 tablespoons soy sauce
pepper to taste
¼ teaspoon monosodium glutamate
2 teaspoons sesame oil
1 tablespoon chopped chives *or* scallions

1½ inch pieces. Cut the onion into thin slices, and the Szechuan pickled greens into strips. Soak the mushrooms in warm water for 30 minutes, remove the stalks, and cut into strips.

Cooking Place the greens and onion in a pan containing 5 cups of water. Bring to the boil, simmer for 3 minutes; then drain. Add all the other ingredients, except sesame oil. Bring to the boil and simmer gently for 15 minutes. Sprinkle with sesame oil, adjust the seasonings, and serve.

Sliced Pork (or Lamb) and Turnip Soup

Preparation Slice meat into thin slices, 1 × 2 inches in size. Rub with salt and cornstarch. Slice turnip and onion into 1½ inch wedge-shaped pieces. Boil in water for 5 minutes, and drain.

Cooking Bring stock to the boil in a heavy saucepan. Add the turnip and onion, and simmer for 15 minutes. Add meat together with all other ingredients except sherry and sesame oil, and simmer for a further 15 minutes. Adjust the seasonings. Sprinkle with sherry and sesame oil; then serve.

Sliced Pork and Mushroom Soup

Preparation Slice the bacon thinly into 1½ × 1 inch pieces. Rub with salt and cornstarch, discarding any excess cornstarch. Clean the mushrooms thoroughly and remove stalks. Cut the stalks into very thin slices

Cooking Bring stock to the boil in a saucepan. Add bacon and mushrooms. Simmer gently for 10 minutes. Add soy sauce, pepper, and monosodium glutamate. Simmer for a further 5–6 minutes. Adjust seasonings, and serve.

Sliced Pork and Egg-Flower Soup

Preparation Slice the bacon into 1½ × 1 inch thin slices. Beat the eggs lightly in a bowl for about 10 seconds. Rub pork with salt and cornstarch.

Cooking Bring the stock to the boil in a saucepan. Add the bacon, and simmer gently for 15 minutes. Trail the beaten egg into the soup in a fine stream along the prongs of a fork. Add soy sauce, pepper, and monosodium glutamate. Stir the soup gently, and pour it into a large soup bowl or tureen. Sprinkle with sesame oil and chives or scallions; then serve.

Sliced Pork and Bean Curd Soup

Preparation Treat the bacon in the same manner as in the recipe for Sliced Pork and Egg-Flower Soup: slice, then rub with salt and cornstarch. Cut each piece of bean curd cake into 14–16 pieces. Soak mushrooms in a cup of warm water for 20 minutes. Remove stalks and slice mushrooms into strips, retaining mushroom water.

Cooking Bring the stock to the boil in a saucepan. Add bacon, mushrooms, and mushroom water. Simmer gently for 15 minutes. Add the pieces of bean curd, soy sauce, and monosodium glutamate. Simmer for a further 10 minutes. Sprinkle with sherry, pepper, and sesame oil, and serve.

Bean curd has a soft custard-like texture. It has a great capacity for absorbing the flavors of other ingredients. The addition of dried mushrooms makes a very flavorsome and delicious soup, which is enhanced by the last-minute addition of the two aromatic ingredients, sherry and sesame oil.

Serves 4–6, with other dishes

$\frac{3}{4}$ lb slab bacon
2–3 cakes bean curd
5 cups good stock

$1\frac{1}{2}$ teaspoons salt
$1\frac{1}{2}$ tablespoons cornstarch
2 heaped tablespoons Chinese dried mushrooms
$2\frac{1}{2}$ tablespoons soy sauce
1 teaspoon monosodium glutamate *or* 1 chicken stock cube
2 tablespoons dry sherry
pepper to taste
2 teaspoons sesame oil

Tripe and Green Pea Soup

Preparation Cut sheet of tripe into four to six pieces. Chop the onion. Simmer the tripe in $2\frac{1}{2}$ cups water, together with the chopped onion and 2 teaspoons of the salt, for 30 minutes. Pour off onion and water, allow tripe to cool, and slice into very thin matchstick strips. Thaw the peas (if frozen) and cream them in a blender. Blend the cornstarch with 3 tablespoons water.

Cooking Heat 1 tablespoon fat in a saucepan. Add creamed peas and stir-fry gently over medium heat for 2 minutes. Add the remaining salt and stock, and bring to the boil. Add tripe and chopped chives, and simmer for 10 minutes. Add monosodium glutamate, cornstarch mixture, sherry, and chili sauce. Adjust the seasonings, simmer for a further 5 minutes; then serve.

The tripe adds to the smoothness of the texture of this rich soup.

Serves 4–6, with other dishes

$\frac{1}{2}$ lb pork tripe
$1\frac{1}{2}$ cups green peas
5 cups superior stock

1 medium-sized onion
1 tablespoon salt
$2\frac{1}{2}$ tablespoons cornstarch
$1\frac{1}{2}$ tablespoons chicken fat *or* lard
$1\frac{1}{2}$ tablespoons chopped chives *or* scallions
$\frac{1}{4}$ teaspoon monosodium glutamate *or* $\frac{1}{2}$ chicken stock cube
2 tablespoons dry sherry
$1\frac{1}{2}$ teaspoons chili sauce

Basic Beef Broth

It is the general belief in China that beef broth is extremely nutritious and excellent for convalescence. The traditional way of preparing it is as follows:

Take 2 lb lean beef (1 lb stewing and 1 lb shin). Cut beef into 1 inch square pieces. Clean and soak in 2 quarts cold water for 2 hours. Drain, and divide beef into three portions.

Place one portion of beef in 2 quarts water. Bring to the boil, skim away impurities, and simmer very gently for 2 hours (with the aid of an asbestos pad under the pan, or use double-boiler if available).

Place the second portion of beef in a saucepan with 2½ cups of water. Boil for 3 minutes and pour away the water. Add this portion of beef to the first, and continue to simmer for 30 minutes.

Repeat with the third portion of beef. After it has been added to the first two portions, continue to simmer for another 30 minutes, together with 3 slices of ginger root, and 1½ teaspoons of salt. The resultant beef broth will be suitable for various beef broth soups. The following are a selection.

Beef Broth and Mustard Green Soup

Serves 4–6, with other dishes

Remove the outer leaves of three mustard greens, using only the more tender stems and leaves. Cut each of these hearts into four pieces. Plunge them into boiling water for 3 minutes, and drain. Add them to 5 cups of beef broth. Simmer for 20 minutes. Add 1 teaspoon melted lard, 1½ teaspoons salt, and ¼ teaspoon monosodium glutamate. Stir, and serve.

Beef Broth and Turnip Soup

Serves 4–6, with other dishes

Clean and cut 12 oz turnip into approximately 1 inch wedge-shaped pieces. Plunge them in boiling water to simmer for 5 minutes, and drain. Add them to 1 quart of beef broth. Add 1 teaspoon melted lard, 1 teaspoon salt, 1 tablespoon soy sauce, ¼ teaspoon monosodium glutamate, and simmer gently together for 30 minutes. Sprinkle with pepper to taste, adjust other seasonings; then serve.

Beef Broth and Carrot Soup

Serves 4–6, with other dishes

Repeat the recipe for Beef Broth and Turnip Soup, using carrots instead of turnip. Cut them into the same wedge-shaped pieces, and simmer them for 30 minutes in the broth with the same seasoning ingredients.

In many cases the beef broth soups are made more interesting by the addition of a small amount of thinly sliced beef. In these cases the beef, sliced into razor-thin slices measuring 1 × ¾ inches, should be salted with ½ teaspoon salt, rubbed with 2 teaspoons cornstarch, and added to the soup only 2 minutes before serving. The purpose behind the addition of beef here is not so much to enhance the taste, but to increase interest and variety. The following are some of the recipes where sliced beef is added to beef broth.

Sliced Beef and Cucumber Soup

Serves 4–6, with other dishes

Preparation Scrape, but do not peel cucumber. Slice lengthwise into 1 × ½ inch thin pieces. Slice beef into pieces about the same size. Rub with salt and cornstarch, discarding any excess cornstarch.

Cooking Bring broth to the boil in a saucepan. Add beef and cucumber. When contents come to the boil again, simmer for 3 minutes. Add lard, soy sauce, and monosodium glutamate or stock cube. Add pepper to taste; then serve.

6 inch piece of a thick cucumber
¼ lb fillet of beef
6 cups beef broth
1½ teaspoons salt
1½ tablespoons cornstarch
2 teaspoons lard
1½ tablespoons soy sauce
¼ teaspoon monosodium glutamate
  or 1 chicken stock cube
pepper to taste

Sliced Beef and Szechuan Hot Pickled Greens Soup

Repeat the recipe for Sliced Beef and Cucumber Soup substituting 1–2 oz Szechuan hot pickled greens for cucumber. Two sliced, skinned tomatoes can be added if desired. To those to whom hotness in soups appeals, this is an interesting soup. The hotness somehow seems to bring out the flavor.

Note Szechuan pickled greens—often called cabbage greens—are usually available in cans from Chinese markets. They have a very hot tangy flavor and should be used sparingly by those who are unaccustomed to them.

Sliced Beef, Tomato, and Egg-Flower Soup

Serves 4–6, with other dishes

4–5 medium-sized tomatoes
⅓–½ lb fillet of beef
1 egg
5½ cups beef broth

1½ teaspoons salt
1½ tablespoons cornstarch
1 tablespoon soy sauce
pepper to taste
½ teaspoon monosodium glutamate
  or 1 chicken stock cube
1 teaspoon lard
¾ tablespoon chopped chives
  or scallions

Preparation Skin each tomato and cut into quarters. Cut beef into 1 × ½ inch thin slices. Rub with salt and cornstarch. Beat egg lightly in a bowl or cup for 10 seconds.

Cooking Bring the broth to the boil in a saucepan. Add tomatoes and soy sauce and simmer for 6–7 minutes. Add beef. After 3 minutes of further simmering, trail beaten egg into the soup in a thin stream along the prongs of a fork. Add pepper to taste, monosodium glutamate, and lard; adjust seasonings. Sprinkle with chopped chives or scallions, and serve.

With the yellow of the 'flower' contrasting with the red of the tomatoes and the brown meatiness of the beef, this is a colorful and appealing soup. (See illustration.)

Sliced Beef and Watercress Soup

Serves 4–6, with other dishes

⅓–½ lb fillet of beef
1 bunch watercress
1 quart beef broth

2 scallions
1½ teaspoons salt
1½ tablespoons cornstarch
1 tablespoon soy sauce
¼ teaspoon monosodium glutamate
  or 1 chicken stock cube
1 teaspoon lard
pepper to taste

Preparation Clean the watercress thoroughly; cut off and discard roots. Cut watercress into 1 inch lengths. Cut the scallions into pieces of similar length, including green parts. Slice beef into very thin slices, 1 × ½ inch in size. Rub with salt and cornstarch, discarding excess.

Cooking Bring broth to the boil in a saucepan. Add soy sauce, watercress, and beef. Simmer for 2 minutes, then add scallions, monosodium glutamate or stock cube, lard, and pepper. Simmer for 1 minute more; then serve.

Silver Ears in Crystal Syrup

Serves 6–8, with other dishes

3–4 tablespoons silver ears
1 egg white

8 oz rock sugar
¼ cup fresh orange juice

This sweet soup from Szechuan province is often used to end a party dinner; or sometimes to break the monotony of a series of savory dishes.

Preparation Soak the silver ears in warm water for 1 hour. Scrape and clean thoroughly, eliminating all impurities. Soak and clean in three changes of water Beat the egg white in 2 tablespoons water in a cup.

Cooking Boil rock sugar gently in 1 quart water. When all the sugar has melted, add orange juice; then add the beaten egg by trailing it into the sugar solution in a thin stream. Strain out the egg white which will carry with it all extraneous material, leaving the orange syrup mixture crystal clear. Place the liquid and the silver ears in an extra clean heatproof dish or casserole and steam for 1½ hours. Serve in a crystal or other glass bowl to emphasize its purity.

Shao Shing Soup

Serves 6–8, with other dishes

6 oz shrimp
½ cup bamboo shoots
½ cup cucumber
½ cup watercress
2 cups chicken stock
1 slice ginger root

From Kiangsu Province

Preparation Shell the shrimp. Chop the bamboo shoots and cucumber into small triangular axe-head shapes; clean the watercress thoroughly, and remove roots.

Cooking Bring stock to boil, and add bamboo shoots and ginger; then, after 2 minutes, add cucumber, watercress, salt, and shrimp. Simmer gently for 1 minute, then skim away any impurities. Pour in the melted lard, the wine or sherry, and the monosodium glutamate, and serve.

2 teaspoons salt
2 teaspoons melted lard
½ cup Shao Shing wine *or* 4–5 tablespoons dry sherry
½ teaspoon monosodium glutamate

Cream of Pork Tripe Soup

Preparation Place the tripe in boiling water and simmer for 5 minutes. Drain; then soak in fresh water for 30 minutes, and slice into matchstick strips. Break the broccoli into six to eight branches, place in boiling water and simmer for 3 minutes; then drain. Chop the onion into eight to ten slices, and chop the ham.

Cooking Fry the onion in the lard over medium heat for 3–4 minutes. Remove the onion and add the stock, cream, salt, bamboo shoots, broccoli, ham, tripe, and monosodium glutamate. Bring to the boil and simmer gently for 5–6 minutes, then add the cornstarch blended with 3 tablespoons water, and stir until the soup thickens.

The use of cream here is definitely a Western influence, but as mentioned elsewhere, Chinese cuisine is adventurous and always ready to borrow other culinary practices.

Serves 6–8, with other dishes

½ lb cooked pork tripe
1 quart white stock

¼ lb broccoli
1 large onion
4 small slices ham
1½ tablespoons lard
¾ cup heavy cream
2 teaspoons salt
¾ cup bamboo shoots
¼ teaspoon monosodium glutamate
2 tablespoons cornstarch

Crackling Cream of Fish Soup

From Peking

Preparation Dice the bread into ¼ inch cubes. Boil the fish, drain, and mince it to a paste. Soak the mushrooms in warm water for 30 minutes; then drain, discard the stems, and slice the caps into pieces the size of peas. Chop the tomatoes. Blend the melted chicken fat with the sesame oil.

Cooking Bring stock to boil in a saucepan. Add the minced fish, tomato, mushrooms, peas, wine, salt, and pepper, and simmer for 2 minutes; then add the cream, the cornstarch blended with 4–5 tablespoons of cold chicken stock, and the chicken fat/sesame oil mixture, and stir until the contents of the pan come to the boil. Turn the heat to low. Deep-fry the bread cubes in very hot oil until golden brown. Place the croutons, while still sizzling, at the bottom of a large, warmed, heat-proof bowl or tureen. Immediately pour in the soup which has been simmering gently, and the croutons will start to crackle. The soup should be served and eaten before the croutons become soft.

Serves 6–8, with other dishes

½ lb whitefish (cod, haddock, sole, carp, *or* bass)
1 quart white stock

1 slice bread *or* 1 Chinese steamed bun
3 medium-sized Chinese dried mushrooms
2 medium-sized tomatoes (peeled)
1½ teaspoons melted chicken fat
1½ teaspoons sesame oil
1 tablespoon green peas
3 tablespoons white wine
2 teaspoons salt
pepper to taste
¾ cup heavy cream
2 tablespoons cornstarch
6 tablespoons cold chicken stock
oil for deep-frying

Five Diced Ingredient Soup

From Peking

Serves 8–10, with other dishes

1 cup bêche de mer
½ cup Chinese dried mushrooms
½ cup Cantonese roast pork
½ cup roast chicken breast
½ cup bamboo shoots
5 cups good chicken stock

2 tablespoons coriander leaves
1½ teaspoons salt
2 tablespoons soy sauce
2 tablespoons vinegar
2 tablespoons dry sherry
¼ teaspoon monosodium glutamate
2 tablespoons cornstarch
pepper to taste
⅓ tablespoon chicken fat mixed with
⅓ tablespoon sesame oil

Preparation Soak the bêche de mer in water overnight; then boil for 30 minutes, and soak in cold water for 3–4 hours. Soak the mushrooms in warm water for 30 minutes; drain, and remove stalks. Dice the bêche de mer, mushroom caps, pork, chicken, and bamboo shoots into ¼ inch cubes. Chop the coriander leaves fine.

Cooking Heat the stock in a saucepan. Add all the diced ingredients, the salt, soy sauce, vinegar, sherry, and monosodium glutamate. Simmer for 5 minutes, then add the cornstarch mixed with ¼ cup water. Sprinkle with pepper and stir in the chicken fat/sesame oil mixture. Place the coriander at the bottom of a large soup bowl or tureen. Bring the soup back to the boil, pour into the tureen, and serve.

This soup appears elaborate, but once the bêche de mer has been soaked, the time taken in preparation and cooking is very short.

Serves 6–8, with other dishes

1 cup shrimp shells
1 cup leeks (sliced)
1 medium-sized onion
5 cups secondary stock

1½ teaspoons salt
pepper to taste
1½ teaspoons melted lard
2 tablespoons dry sherry
2 tablespoons soy sauce
¼ teaspoon monosodium glutamate

Shrimp Shells, Leek, and Onion Soup

This soup, which originated in Canton, developed from the Chinese sense of economy. It makes use of left-over shrimp shells, after the shrimp meat has been used for other dishes.

Preparation and Cooking Boil the shrimp shells in the stock for 20 minutes. Strain, and remove the shells. Slice the leeks and the onion thin; add to the stock with the salt, pepper, and lard. Simmer for 10 minutes, then add the sherry, soy sauce, and monosodium glutamate; stir and serve.

Chinese Seaweed Soup with Transparent Noodles

There are two varieties of seaweed in common use in China—one is commonly called purple vegetable seaweed, and is supplied in dry, paper-like sheets about 7–8 inches long, often tied in small bundles. The sheets need to be soaked in water and drained before use. Purple vegetable seaweed is most commonly used for soups, and is said to be highly nutritious. The second type is called hair vegetable seaweed, as it looks like bushy, coarse, black hair. It does not have any strong flavor, and is more often made into semi-soup than full soup. Purple vegetable seaweed is used in this recipe.

Preparation Soak the purple vegetable seaweed in water for 1 hour, changing the water twice. Drain. Soak the noodles in water for 10 minutes, and drain. Soak the scallops in warm water for 1 hour; then drain, and slice each piece into six. Chop the scallions into 2 inch segments; cut the red-in-snow pickled greens into strips, and cut the ham similarly.

Cooking Heat the lard in a large saucepan or casserole, and stir-fry the scallions, red-in-snow, and scallop for 2 minutes. Pour in the stock, add the salt, pepper, purple vegetable seaweed, and transparent noodles, and simmer gently for 20 minutes, stirring occasionally. Add the soy sauce, vinegar, and ham, adjust the seasonings, and serve in a large bowl or tureen.

Serves 8–10, with other dishes

1¼ cups (about ¼ lb) purple vegetable seaweed
1¼ cups (about ¼ lb) transparent noodles
6 cups good stock

3 tablespoons dried scallops
2 scallions
3 tablespoons red-in-snow pickled greens
2 slices cooked ham
1½ tablespoons lard
2 teaspoons salt
pepper to taste
1½ tablespoons soy sauce
1½ tablespoons vinegar

Chinese Seaweed Soup

This soup uses hair vegetable seaweed.

Preparation Soak the hair vegetable seaweed in water for 30 minutes, changing the water twice. Soak the bamboo shoots, bean curd skin, and lotus roots in warm water for 30 minutes, and slice into strips. Soak the mushrooms in a bowl of warm water for 30 minutes and drain, retaining 6 tablespoons of the water. Remove the stalks. Soak the tiger-lily buds and wood ears; drain, and clean them. Chop the celery into 2 inch pieces.

Cooking Heat 1½ tablespoons of the oil in a large saucepan, and stir-fry the bamboo shoots, bean curd skin, lotus roots, and mushrooms over a medium heat for 3 minutes. Pour in 1 cup of the stock, and the mushroom water; then add the bean curd cheese, and the hair vegetable seaweed, and stir into the soup. Bring to the boil, and add the celery, snow peas, transparent noodles, wood ears, and tiger-lily buds. Stir them together until most of the liquid has been absorbed, then add another cup of the stock and simmer gently for 10 minutes. Add the soy sauce, sherry, salt, and pepper; pour in the remaining stock, and simmer gently for a further 10 minutes. Sprinkle with the remaining sesame oil, and serve in a large tureen.

This is a semi-soup, with the emphasis on dried vegetables, the seaweed being one of them.

Serves 10–12, with other dishes

1 cup (¼ lb) hair vegetable seaweed
1 quart chicken stock
½ cup (¼ lb) dried bamboo shoots
½ cup (¼ lb) dried bean curd skin
2 pieces dried lotus roots
½ cup (⅛ lb) Chinese dried mushrooms
½ cup (⅛ lb) tiger-lily buds
2½ tablespoons wood ears
1 cup (¼ lb) celery
2 tablespoons sesame oil
2 tablespoons red bean curd cheese
1 cup (¼ lb) snow peas
1¼ cups (¼ lb) transparent noodles
2½ tablespoons soy sauce
3 tablespoons dry sherry
salt and pepper to taste

73

First Rank Hot Pot

Serves 10–12, with other dishes

1 cup (¼ lb) bêche de mer
1 medium-sized Chinese celery
  cabbage (about 1¼–1½ lb)
1 small cauliflower
1 piece ham (about ¾ lb)
1 piece pig's knuckle (about 2–3 lb)
6 medium-sized Chinese dried
  mushrooms
2 chicken breasts (about 1½ lb)
1 small duck (about 1½–2 lb)
2 slices ginger root
4 hard-boiled eggs
½ cup white wine
salt to taste

Preparation Soak the bêche de mer overnight, and drain. Discard the coarse outer leaves of the cabbage; clean and cut the heart into four pieces. Clean the cauliflower, and break into individual branches. Boil the ham and pork knuckle in water for 40 minutes; then drain. Soak the mushrooms in warm water for 30 minutes, remove the stalks, and drain. Chop the chicken and the duck into manageable pieces, place in a large pot with 3 quarts water and boil for 40 minutes. Remove the chicken and duck, place them in a large, heat-proof bowl, and strain and filter the stock until it is crystal clear.

Cooking Add the vegetables (cabbage, cauliflower, and mushrooms), the ginger, ham, pork knuckle, and bêche de mer to the chicken and duck. Place the bowl in a steamer, and steam for 30 minutes. Arrange all the solid materials, including the eggs, in layers in the moat of a charcoal burning hot pot. Pour in the stock and wine, and add the salt. Light the hot pot (by adding a few pieces of burning charcoal to the unburnt charcoal in the funnel), and fan until the soup starts to boil; then boil for 5–6 minutes.

Serving Bring the hot pot to the table; its arrival will be a heart-warming sight in winter.

Hot pots are available in many Chinese food stores and supermarkets.

Chrysanthemum Fish Hot Pot

Serves 8–12, with other dishes

1 lb whitefish (cod, sole, carp,
  bream, haddock *or* halibut)
1 large chrysanthemum bloom
2½ cups superior stock

¼ lb chicken
¼ lb lean pork
½ lb pork bones
2 slices ginger root
2 medium-sized onions
2 teaspoons salt
¼ cup transparent noodles
2 oz pork kidney
¼ cup chicken liver
¾ cup heart of mustard greens
¾ cup spinach
1 cup bean sprouts
2 tablespoons roasted peanuts
3 tablespoons wine
2 tablespoons coriander leaves *or*
  parsley

From Szechuan Province

Preparation Fillet the fish and slice as thin as possible; slice the meats similarly, and chop the onions. Prepare the stock by boiling the fish bones, heads, tails, pork bone, ginger, and onions in 5 cups of water for 45 minutes. Remove solids and discard. Strain, and add salt to taste. Soak the transparent noodles in water for 10 minutes, and drain. Boil the pork kidney and chicken liver for 10 minutes. Cut the heart of greens into six pieces and boil in water for 3 minutes; then drain. Clean the spinach and bean sprouts thoroughly.

Cooking and Serving Place the vegetables and noodles at the bottom of the hot pot. Arrange the slices of fish, chicken, pork, and kidneys on top, and sprinkle with the peanuts. Pour in the superior stock, 2½ cups of the prepared fish and meat stock, and the wine. Light the hot pot. When the soup has been simmering for 5–6 minutes, scatter the coriander leaves and chrysanthemum petals over it, and bring the hot pot to the table.

Bird's Nest Soup

Bird's nest itself has a faint subtle flavor, the appreciation of which is largely a cultivated taste. In the main, the total flavor of the soup is derived from the chicken and chicken stock—these must be first class if the soup is to be good. Birds' nests are generally available in small boxes from Chinese markets—they come in a porous and brittle form, ground down from the original pieces of birds' nests. They are not, by the way, the branches and twigs which make up an average bird's nest, but what is left by the birds in their nests, probably for their young ones, after eating or partly eating the fish and seaweed they live on. They are obtained from a species of sea swallow which inhabits the South Seas, and they also come in small nestlet shapes or as curved chips called Dragons' Teeth. The latter are rather rare and expensive.

Preparation Simmer bird's nest in 2½ cups water for 1 hour. Let it cool, and drain. (If Dragons' Teeth or nestlets are used, they must be soaked overnight first.) Cut the chicken meat into small pieces, and then mince. Beat the egg whites lightly with a fork.

Cooking and Serving Heat the chicken stock in a heavy pan, and add half of the minced chicken. After 10 minutes, add the bird's nest and the remaining chicken, and simmer for 15 minutes. Add the salt and monosodium glutamate, and thicken the soup with the water chestnut flour or cornstarch, blended with 3 tablespoons water. Slowly stream in the beaten egg whites along the prongs of a fork, trailing it evenly over the soup—thus producing a white cloud effect. Garnish the soup with the minced ham, and serve in a high quality ceramic bowl, worthy of the quality of the soup.

Serves 6–8, with other dishes

½ cup bird's nest
5 cups freshly prepared, high quality chicken stock

2 oz chicken breast meat
2 egg whites
1½ teaspoons salt
¼ teaspoon monosodium glutamate
1¼ tablespoons water chestnut flour *or* cornstarch
2½ tablespoons minced ham

Szechuan Oxtail Soup

Preparation Trim and chop the oxtail into sections through the joints; soak in water for 1 hour, and drain. Clean the chicken, remove claws, head, and innards, and joint it.

Cooking Place oxtail in 5 quarts water and bring to the boil. After 15 minutes, skim away fat and impurities; reduce heat and simmer gently in a heavy pan or iron pot for one hour. Add chicken, ginger, and peppercorns, and simmer for 2 hours; then remove and discard ginger and peppercorns, and skim away any fat or impurities. Insert an asbestos pad under the pan, and simmer for a further 2 hours; then add the salt,

Serves 8–10, with other dishes

5–6 lb oxtail

2–3 lb chicken
6 slices ginger root
1½ teaspoons peppercorns
3 teaspoons salt
¼ teaspoon monosodium glutamate *or* 1 chicken stock cube
2 teaspoons melted lard

monosodium glutamate, and melted lard. Adjust the seasonings, and serve.

This is an extremely rich soup, which can be called Beef-Chicken Tea.

Some Miscellaneous, Regional and Well-Known Soups

Hot and Sour Soup

Serves 8–12, with other dishes

¼ lb lean pork
6 medium-sized Chinese dried
  mushrooms
½ cup bamboo shoots
2 cakes bean curd
2 eggs
1 tablespoon dried shrimp *or* 2
  tablespoons peeled shrimp
5 cups superior stock
¼ teaspoon monosodium glutamate
  or 1 chicken stock cube
Hot and Sour Mixture
2 tablespoons soy sauce
3 tablespoons vinegar
2½ tablespoons cornstarch blended
  with 6 tablespoons cold stock
½ teaspoon black pepper

This is a thick soup, more popular in north China than in the south. It can actually be made almost ad lib from various bits and pieces of meat, fish, shrimp, or crab which are available. The classical version requires cooked, solidified chicken blood. A useful ingredient is bean curd, and Chinese dried mushrooms are essential. But first of all, you will need a good savory stock.

Preparation Shred pork into matchstick strips. Soak mushrooms in warm water for 30 minutes and drain, retaining 3 tablespoons mushroom water. Cut bamboo shoots into 1–2 inch segments, and bean curd into ½ inch cubes. Beat the eggs lightly for 10 seconds. Prepare the Hot and Sour mixture by blending the ingredients together until smooth.

Cooking Prepare the soup by simmering pork, shrimp, mushrooms, and bamboo shoots in the stock for 30 minutes. Add the bean curd, mushroom water, and monosodium glutamate, and simmer for a further 5 minutes. Now stream in the Hot and Sour mixture and stir—this should thicken the soup. Trail the beaten egg into the soup along the prongs of a fork—the egg will coagulate almost immediately—and the soup is ready to serve.

Because of its heat, and the solid ingredients used, this soup is very popular in winter. (See illustration.)

Whole Chicken Soup

Serves 10–12, with other dishes

5–6 lb capon

6 scallions
1 tablespoon salt
3 slices ginger root

Preparation Clean capon thoroughly. Cut the scallions into 2–3 inch pieces. Place capon and scallions in 4 quarts water in a heavy metal or earthenware pot and bring to the boil. After 7–8 minutes boiling, skim away all impurities, and pour away 1¼ cups of the top stock. Add the salt, ginger, and ham, and after a further 5 minutes simmering, skim away any further impurities, and remove the ham. Slice the cabbage into 1 inch slices, and the ham and abalone into thin slices; return the ham to the pot.

Cooking Insert an asbestos pad under the pot, reduce the heat, and simmer for 2 hours. Put the cabbage under the chicken, and continue to simmer for 30 minutes. Add the abalone and sherry, and simmer for 5 minutes more.

The soup should be both rich and refreshing (owing to the late addition of the cabbage), and it should now be possible to take most of the chicken apart with a pair of chopsticks. The dish can be the central point of a big home dinner, or a major course during a banquet.

¼ lb ham
1¼–1½ lb Chinese celery cabbage
¼ lb (about ½ cup) abalone
¼ cup dry sherry

Whole Duck Soup

This recipe is similar to the recipe for Whole Chicken Soup, but as ducks are usually fatter than chickens, they require longer boiling to remove the excess fat. No abalone is added, but a greater quantity of ham and onion is used.

Preparation Clean the duck thoroughly. Place in a heavy metal pot with 3½ quarts water and bring to the boil. After 10 minutes, skim away impurities; boil for 10 minutes more, and skim off any more impurities. Slice the bamboo shoots thin, and cut the scallions into 2–3 inch pieces. Stuff the duck with the bamboo shoots, scallions, and the ginger, and replace in the soup, with the salt. Cut the cabbage into 1 inch thick slices, and the mushrooms and ham into strips.

Cooking Insert an asbestos pad under the pot, reduce heat, and simmer for 2 hours. Put cabbage underneath duck in the pan, and place ham and mushrooms on top. Simmer for a further 30 minutes and serve in a very large tureen.

The large quantity of cabbage should absorb most of the fat in the duck and provide a final freshening. The black and red garnish of mushrooms and ham provides added interest. Because of the very slow cooking, the soup should be very rich and crystal clear.

Serves 10–12, with other dishes

4–5 lb duck

1 cup (⅓ lb) bamboo shoots
6 scallions
3 slices ginger root
1 tablespoon salt
1½ lb Chinese celery cabbage
6 medium-sized Chinese dried
  mushrooms
½ lb ham

Triple Shred Soup

Preparation Soak the mushrooms in ¾ cup warm water for 30 minutes; then remove the stems and shred the caps. Reserve the mushroom water. Shred the chicken and abalone fine, using a sharp knife.

Serves 6–8, with other dishes

4 medium-sized Chinese dried
  mushrooms

¼ lb cooked chicken breast
¼ cup abalone

4–5 cups chicken stock
salt and pepper to taste

Cooking Add the mushrooms, chicken, and abalone to the stock and mushroom water in a large pan; season with salt and pepper. Bring to the boil, and simmer for 10 seconds.

Serving Follow the instructions given for Painted Soup.

Painted Soup

This soup makes an occasional appearance on Chinese banquet tables, usually when the cook preparing the meal is a chef/artist, and likes to present something intriguing: however, Painted Soup does not involve actually painting the surface of a liquid! The preparation of a solid surface to place a design on is made simply by beating up 2–3 egg whites with a rotary or electric beater for 3 or more minutes (until quite stiff), then spreading the egg white thickly over the soup (usually the soup bowl or tureen is filled only up to two thirds full) and smoothing it carefully with a spatula or large spoon. When the surface of the egg white is smooth, all kinds of designs can be placed on it. The Chinese chef/artist usually creates a rural scene, where the brownish yellow strips of golden needles (tiger-lily buds) are used to illustrate branches or trunks of trees; any green vegetables thinly sliced or in leaves can be used to illustrate foliage or leaves, or a fresh carrot can be cut into a disc with thin strips radiating from all sides to simulate the sun. Tomato skins are cut into all shapes of bright red flowers. All these can be lightly pressed into the malleable surface of the egg white. The more ambitious chef/artist would create and add pictures of human beings and animals to further enliven the scene.

The actual soup used in the Painted Soup is usually Triple Shred Soup (see page 77), which is comparatively simple to prepare. When the soup is ready to serve, the host or hostess would break up the picture in the common tureen or soup-bowl, and ladle the soup and a part of the picture intact into each individual's soup bowl. (See illustration.)

RICE

Rice is the main bulk-food of China and is eaten just as bread and potatoes are eaten in the West. It is eaten with every meal: soft rice (or congee) for breakfast in the morning, and boiled or steamed rice for lunch as well as dinner. The only time when rice is not eaten is at a party dinner or banquet, for during such occasions so many courses are served that the customary bulk intake of rice might hinder the enjoyment and progress of the dozen or more dishes. Not infrequently, however, at the end of a banquet, four emphatically plain dishes with a soup or two and rice are served to settle the stomach.

So in China you just cannot get away from rice altogether. It gives unity to the multi-dish or multi-course meal. Its absorbent softness enables it to set off both dry, crackling foods as well as the stews and dishes with sauce. Its neutral blandness enables it to act as an ideal absorbent for all the spicy, savory, rich, and hot dishes which are often served to the diners at a Chinese dinner. For foods which are fresh, light, and refreshing, rice can act as an essential complement which helps to smooth their progress, thus giving more time for the palate to enjoy them. Rice, therefore, has an all-purpose function in the context of a Chinese meal, quite apart from such considerations as calorific value. For this reason we Chinese hardly ever have fried rice at a meal when numerous savory dishes are being served. (Fried rice is only eaten as a snack when not much is provided or expected to be provided on the table.) Some connoisseurs even enjoy eating rice on its own: this accounts for their nibbling at some plain rice with morsels of food, a practice which is often seen at the end of a meal.

In Chinese restaurants abroad one often sees Westerners emptying spoonfuls of soy sauce on their rice to make it tasty. This should never be done, as after such treatment rice loses its character and therefore its function at a Chinese meal. A Chinese meal should provide enough savory and spicy dishes with rich gravies and sauces to make the rice as tasty as one is ever likely to want it, without resorting to plain soy sauce. For the maximum enjoyment and appreciation rice is best served without adornment.

Although we often talk about rice existing as a complement to various dishes, it is in fact equally true that a great many dishes exist to complement rice. Without rice, much of their significance and appeal would be lost. There must be hundreds of Chinese dishes which belong to this category, but we Chinese tend to forget that rice is not merely a complement to other dishes simply because we are so used to eating it. An example of a rice-complementing dish is Red-Cooked Pigs' Knuckle. Indeed, if the diners are not used to eating large quantities of rice, some other bulk-food such as steamed buns or toasted pancakes could be provided as a substitute, since quantities of Red-Cooked Pigs' Knuckle would be too rich for people unaccustomed to rice.

Let us now turn our attention to the preparation of a range of Chinese rice dishes, the majority of which are comparatively simple. In China, rice is generally boiled or

79

steamed; it is very seldom prepared in the way European savory rice dishes such as paella are prepared; fried first, then stock or water added. Rice is usually cooked in quantity in China, and seldom for just one meal; what is left over can be used for fried rice, or fried in deep oil into crackling rice. It can be further boiled with quantities of water into soft rice (congee), or it can be easily re-heated as plain boiled rice for subsequent meals.

Since rice takes two or three times as long to steam as it does to boil, and since the end product is much the same (although the steamed variety is a little flakier), boiling is the most common way of cooking it for ordinary day to day requirements, particularly in the West.

Boiled Rice

The problem of cooking boiled rice is that one can so easily make it too watery; but on the other hand it is all too easy to use too little water and burn it. Great care is therefore necessary when boiling rice, as it should be dry, flaky, and well-cooked. There are many methods of achieving this result. The following is a method which I have found simple and foolproof, and which I have used many hundreds of times:

Quantity For Westerners a pound of rice should be sufficient for 6–8 persons. When cooking rice one should add to it $1\frac{1}{2}$ times its volume in water, *i.e.* for a cup or bowl of rice one should use $1\frac{1}{2}$ cups or $1\frac{1}{2}$ bowls of water as the case may be.

Washing Before cooking, rice must be washed and rinsed until the water runs clear. This has the effect of washing away the starch and helps to prevent the grains from sticking to one another, thus assuring the rice will be flaky when cooked.

Cooking Before beginning to cook the rice, boil a kettle of water and leave it simmering for later use. Place the rice in a saucepan, add the required quantity of water and bring to the boil. Leave to boil for 2 minutes. Reduce to a low heat and continue to boil very gently under cover for 7–8 minutes. By this time the surface of the rice will have become dry (if not, replace the lid and wait until it dries). Once the top layer of the rice is dry, pour in sufficient boiling water to cover the top of the rice by about $\frac{1}{4}$ inch. Replace the cover, insert an asbestos pad under the pan and leave the contents to simmer for another 5 minutes. Turn off the heat and leave the rice to stand in the pan to cook in its own heat and steam for the next 7–8 minutes (do not open the lid). By this time, after a total of just over 20 minutes cooking time, the rice should be ready; well-cooked and flaky, but not soggy.

Cooked, boiled rice which has not been used can be re-heated again when required, or it can be made into fried rice by frying with various other ingredients. It can also be made into soft rice by further boiling with additional water.

To keep left-over rice for further use it is best to loosen it from the pan and break up any large lumps so that they do not become hard and encrusted. Rice which has been loosened can best be prepared for use again simply by placing it in a fresh saucepan and heating it up again with a small quantity of water, approximately two tablespoons of water to every bowl of rice.

Steamed Rice

There are two traditional ways of steaming rice. In both cases the rice has to be boiled first in ample water for five minutes, then drained.

(a) Divide the partly-boiled rice into the number of portions required. Place each portion in a heat-proof bowl and cover with $\frac{1}{4}$ inch of hot or boiling water. (Leave space in each bowl for rice to double its size.) Place the bowl or bowls in a steamer and steam for 1 hour. Alternatively, place the bowls on a rack inside a large saucepan in which $1\frac{1}{2}$–2 inches of water has been brought to the boil. Boiling water should be added at intervals when required. Under the cover of the closed lid of the saucepan, the rice should be steamed and well-cooked in approximately 30–40 minutes. This method of steaming is often employed in restaurants as the heated bowls help to keep the rice very warm when served.

(b) The second method of steaming, which is more often employed at home, depends on the use of a flat, round, tray-like, bamboo steamer, which is placed on top of a cauldron of boiling water. There is a bamboo cover which fits over the top of the steamer. When the water in the cauldron boils, the rising steam passes through the steamer—frequently, there are several layers of steamer in use for one meal. A layer of cheesecloth is spread at the bottom of the steamer, and the drained boiled rice is spread on top to not more than 1 inch thickness. The rice is then pierced at numerous points with a pair of chopsticks to allow the steam to pass through. It should be cooked for just under one hour. Rice can also be steamed this way wrapped in a lotus leaf.

The advantage of steaming rice over boiling it is that steamed rice never gets burned, but it requires much more time and many more elaborate utensils. For cooking in the average Western kitchen boiling is much simpler, and recommended.

Soft Rice

There are two types or two degrees of soft rice in China.

(a) Thick porridgy soft rice, which is eaten by the poorer people, who add more water to the rice in order to increase its bulk. This is usually prepared by simply boiling or simmering the rice in twice the amount of water normally employed for cooking the same amount of boiled rice, and for two to three times as long, that is for 30–45 minutes instead of about 15–18 minutes.

Among those who cannot afford a full rice diet, the limited amount of rice available is often boiled up with a proportion of shredded, dried, sweet potato, which helps to give it greater bulk. Anybody who has seen the life of the poorer peasants of China must have seen this preparation.

(b) Watery Soft Rice (or Congee) on the other hand is eaten by all classes of people, both rich and poor. It is used mainly at breakfast time, or for late night supper, when it is eaten with strong-flavored foods such as salted eggs, Thousand Years Old Eggs, pickled vegetables, salted fish, fried salted peanuts, Chinese sausage, salted turnips, soy bean curd cheese, meats, and gizzards which have been simmered in Soy Herbal stock, etc.

The Watery Soft Rice is made simply by simmering rice, or left-over rice, in 8–10 times the normal quantity of water for a period of $1\frac{1}{2}$ hours to 2 hours, or until it forms a smooth creamy broth, or rice porridge. Apart from its being refreshing in the morning, it also has a heating or warming effect in the winter. In this way, it serves the same purpose as cups of hot tea or coffee at breakfast in the winter mornings.

Fried Rice

As rice is not an independent dish for eating on its own (as is the case of bread and potatoes), it is usually served to complement other dishes, and, therefore, in its native state (cooked of course). When it is cooked or cross-cooked with other foods and ingredients, it is usually as Fried Rice, which is regarded as a snack or is served when there are very few other items available on the dining table. It should never be served at a full dinner or a banquet. (Just as you do not serve hot dogs and beans at a State dinner.)

There are no rules as to what can be fried with rice. In fact, almost any fryable item can be fried with rice, and made into Fried Rice. However, there are a few traditional ones, which seem to bring out the best orchestration.

Some of the points to aim at in the frying or in this orchestration are:

(a) Aroma—hence some onion is always introduced in the earlier stages of frying.

(b) Tastiness—

(1) by providing some direct contrast to the blandness of rice, some chopped ham or bacon is often used.

(2) by providing savoriness as a contrast in texture and taste—hence chopped, cooked pork, chicken, beef, lobster, or shrimp are frequently used.

(c) A Variation in Texture and Color—this is achieved by the inclusion of chopped vegetables which are lightly cooked (fried), such as celery, cucumber, peas, or bamboo shoots.

(d) The unity and basic background tastiness in Fried Rice is provided by the beaten eggs, which should always be stir-fried and well-scrambled in the pan before the rice is introduced. The eggs have to be set before rice is added, otherwise a messiness will soon become apparent.

One of the fatal mistakes in frying rice is to make it messy and mushy, for one of the aims of Fried Rice is to maintain all the distinctiveness in flavor and texture of all the participating ingredients in spite of the general mix up and cross-cooking. As a dish it is meant to be a dry dish, and not a dish with gravy or sauce. Hence if any soy sauce is introduced it should be used only in very limited quantity.

Because it is a dry dish, it should be accompanied by a savory soup, even if eaten as a snack. (If ordered in a Chinese restaurant for a meal, it should be eaten with a savory dish, together with a soup.)

The following are a few of the more traditional Fried Rice Dishes.

Basic Fried Rice

Preparation Chop the onion fine. Slice the ham or bacon into small pieces. Dice the celery, cucumber, or greens into small pea-size pieces. Defrost the peas if the frozen variety is used. Beat the eggs lightly with ½ teaspoon of the salt.

Cooking Heat the oil in a frying-pan or saucepan. Add the onion, the bacon or ham, and remaining salt. Stir-fry over a high heat for 1½ minutes. Reduce the heat to low and pour in the egg. Allow the eggs to set and then scramble. Add the peas and celery. Continue to stir and scramble for 1 minute. Pour in the rice and continue to turn, mix, and stir for 2 minutes. Sprinkle with soy sauce. Turn and mix once more; then serve.

Fried rice should be eaten as soon as possible after it leaves the pan, otherwise it will no longer be aromatic and it might become greasy.

Serves 4

2–3 cups cooked rice
1 medium-sized onion
3 oz ham or bacon
6 tablespoons diced celery, cucumber *or* greens
6 tablespoons green peas
3 eggs
1½ teaspoons salt
6 tablespoons vegetable oil
1¼ tablespoons soy sauce

Chicken Fried Rice

This is one of the favorites among the fried rice dishes served in restaurants, probably because many parts of the chicken meat come in bits and pieces and this is one of the best ways of using them up.

Serves 4

The chicken used in this dish is usually cooked beforehand. The ingredients and method of preparation for this dish are the same as for Basic Fried Rice, with just two exceptions: 4–6 oz of chicken meat should be added to the pan 30 seconds after the onion, and an extra teaspoon of salt will be needed.

Shrimp or Lobster Fried Rice

Seafood such as shrimp and lobsters are favorites for frying with rice, mainly because of their savory flavor. When lobsters and shrimp are used, the meat should be diced to about the same size as peas. A clove or two of garlic (crushed and chopped) could be added to the pan, together with the chopped onion. This will make the dish even more aromatic. If ginger root is available, a thin slice or two, finely chopped, could also be added at the same time as the garlic and onion. This will reduce the fishy taste of the seafood. Otherwise, the procedure is precisely the same as in the previous recipes for fried rice.

Serves 4

Fancy Fried Rice

Cooked rice can be fried with any item of food suitable for quick-frying. The following are some of the items which are more frequently used.

Chinese dried mushrooms. They should be soaked for 20–30 minutes and diced into small cubes. Do not use the stalks, or the mushroom water, as they tend to color the dish.

Button mushrooms may be added. The small firm ones, sometimes available in cans, are best.

Scallions should be chopped into ¾ inch pieces and sprinkled into the frying-pan towards the end of the cooking.

Bamboo shoots should be diced into small cubes. They provide a crunchy contrast.

Carrots and cabbage should be diced into small pieces and added at an early stage of the stir-frying.

Almonds and walnuts, to be used only in small quantities, chopped.

Raisins, which are seldom used in China, but are popular with Westerners.

All these ingredients can be used singly or together in varying proportions, dictated only by one's taste or fancy.

Cooked Rice with Other Ingredients

Rice may be cooked with many types of ingredients, but this practice is more popular in Europe than in China. Spanish paellas and Italian risottos are examples of dishes in which the rice and savory ingredients are cooked together. In China, rice is most often used as an accompaniment to several other dishes, and the Chinese prefer making their own selection from these dishes to having the rice served already mixed with other ingredients. The following recipes are for a few Chinese dishes in which the rice is cooked along with the other ingredients.

Vegetable Rice

This is one of Shanghai's native dishes.

Preparation Clean the rice in two changes of water and drain. Discard the coarse outer leaves of the greens, and chop the rest into 1½ × 2 inch pieces.

Cooking Heat the lard and butter in a saucepan. Add the greens and salt. Stir-fry over a medium heat for 3 minutes. Add the rice and 1 quart of water. Bring quickly to the boil. Reduce heat to a minimum, and insert an asbestos pad under the pan. Simmer gently, covered, for 15 minutes. Turn the heat off altogether, keep covered, and allow the rice and greens to steam in their own heat for another 15 minutes before serving.

Serving Serve on a well-heated dish.

The rice should be well-cooked and impregnated with the fresh vegetable flavor of the greens after 30 minutes of cooking together. It should be eaten as an accompaniment to any savory dish or dishes, and is very often served with hot or cold red-cooked meat dishes.

Vegetable rice need not always be made with mustard greens. Various other cooked vegetables may be substituted.

Serves 6–8

2 cups rice
3 cups water
2 cups mustard greens

2½ tablespoons lard
1 tablespoon butter
2 teaspoons salt

Cooked Rice with Poached Eggs

The usual way of cooking this rice dish is to treat it in the same way as Steamed Rice (see page 80). As soon as the rice in the individual heatproof bowls has dried and is nearly ready, make an indentation in the middle and place 1–2 teaspoons of lard or butter in it, then break an egg on top. the bowl or bowls to the steamer for a further 3–4 minutes steaming. The short cooking will give a skin to the outside surface of the egg but will leave the yolk soft. When the bowls have been taken out of the steamer, sprinkle the top of each egg with a teaspoon of soy sauce, oyster sauce, or shrimp sauce; then serve immediately.

Serves 1 or more

Rice cooked in this manner is often served to the very young, the aged, or the infirm, or when there are only a few dishes to accompany the rice. It is the sort of rice dish which is seen only in the most Chinese of surroundings; for example, in Chinese villages.

Rice with Green Peas

Serves 6–8

1 cup green peas
2 cups rice
3 cups water

1–2 teaspoons salt
1 tablespoon lard
1 tablespoon butter

This dish is similar to vegetable rice. Mix 1 cup green peas with 2 cups of rice. Place in a saucepan with 1 quart of water, bring to the boil, and boil for 2 minutes. Add 1–2 teaspoons salt, 1 tablespoon lard, and 1 tablespoon butter; stir. Reduce the heat and simmer for 7–8 minutes. Add some boiling water and simmer for a further 3 minutes. Turn the heat off and allow the mixture to cook in its own heat for 7–8 minutes.

Like the previous recipe, this rice dish should be served with other dishes. The addition of peas makes the rice more colorful and also provides a fresh vegetable flavor, while the lard and butter give the rice a smooth texture.

Rice Cooked with Chinese Sausages

This is considered a somewhat more sophisticated dish than the recipe for Cooked Rice with Poached Eggs. It is often served in middle-class homes and even occasionally in restaurants. Chinese sausage has the appearance and flavor of salami: it is salty, spicy, and rich. As it is an ideal complement to the neutral blandness of rice, they are often eaten together and occasionally are cooked together. The usual point at which to add the sausages to the rice is when the surface of the steamed or boiled rice has dried during the cooking. Pieces of sausage are pushed into the rice and buried as deeply as possible, then allowed to steam in the pan with the rice for at least 15–20 minutes, to allow the characteristic flavor and aroma of the cooked sausage to impregnate the rice. The flavor and aroma have a peculiar Chinese quality, recognizable to all who have any experience of Chinese food. The sausage and rice mixture should be accompanied by all the other savory foods normally served with rice. As these sausages are pinkish-red in color, they contrast with the whiteness of the rice, giving the dish a colorful and attractive appearance.

Topped Rice, or Cooked Rice with Toppings

Topped rice is not often served in China as it is a dish most suitable for a person dining alone. Since a Chinese meal is a communal meal, all the dishes accompanying the rice are set on the table for the diners to share. This means that a far greater variety of dishes can be sampled than would be practical in preparing a meal for one person.

However, as people nowadays are more mobile than in the past, the practice of dining alone has increased. Furthermore, the mushrooming of Chinese restaurants abroad, where life is lived in a more individualistic manner than in China, has resulted in an increasing demand for portions of rice to be served along with portions of the savory foods which form the garnish, as a complete, self-contained dish.

It is probably true to say that plain cooked rice can be topped with almost any Chinese dish, especially those served with some sauce or gravy. A well-balanced dish of rice with topping should have two types of topping—meat and vegetable—and these, if possible, should be separate and distinct. They should not only present a contrast in color, but also a difference in type, texture, and flavor. As a rule, if the meat for the topping is 'dry', such as roast pork, chicken, or duck, the vegetable or vegetables should be fry-braised and sauce-covered, thus providing the necessary gravy.

For the less demanding, the topping for rice can be one of the many cross-cooked dishes where meat and vegetables are already blended in the cooking. There are countless cross-cooked Chinese dishes; the following list contains only a few.

Sliced Lamb Quick-Fried with Scallions (see page 188)
Shredded Lamb Quick-Fried with Ginger and Young Leeks (see page 188)

Quick-Fried Beef Ribbons with Celery (see page 179)
Quick-Fried Sliced Beef with Green and Red Peppers (see page 178)

Quick-Fried Beef Ribbons with Transparent Noodles and String Beans (see page 180)
Red-Cooked Beef with Tomato (see page 170)

Steamed Beef Balls with Oyster Sauce (see page 174)
Diced Chicken in Soy Jam (see page 212)

Sliced Chicken with Smoked and Salted Fish (see page 226)
Slivered Chicken with Asparagus (see page 230)

Sweet and Sour Pork (see page 133)
Braised Curried Fresh Ham with Potato (see page 137)

Sliced Pork Stir-Fried with Bamboo Shoots (see page 148)
Sliced Roast Pork Stir-Fried with Bean Curd (see page 150)

Ideally the rice for such a dish should be freshly cooked and scooped steaming out of the pan. The topping too should be freshly stir-fried or stir-braised and placed on the rice directly from the heat of the pan. An alternative method of preparation is to top the cooked rice with all the necessary savory foods and vegetables, and place the complete dish in a steamer to steam for 6–7 minutes before bringing to the table. It is essential for the dish to be served hot and steaming. As Topped Rice is not a traditional Chinese dish, it must not be served wrongly or its already limited Chinese quality will be completely lost.

Soft Rice or Congee

Soft rice is a traditional Chinese dish, unlike Topped Rice, as it is used throughout China for breakfast and midnight suppers, or for invalids and the aged. It is usually eaten as an accompaniment to cold, salty, pickled, or highly savory foods. Another dish often eaten with soft rice is Meat Wool (see page 90), together with soy sauce of the highest quality. Indeed, one of the tests for the quality of soy sauce is to take it with soft rice, the blandness of which provides a contrast with the mild, not too salty, savory flavor of good soy sauce. This unique savory flavor cannot be imitated by any chemical ingredient such as monosodium glutamate, which is not used in the original Chinese preparations.

Few Westerners have taken to soft rice at the first try. This is probably because there is no Western food with a corresponding function—it is as if one were asked to eat porridge with a cold savory dish! However, by persisting, the Westerner would almost certainly find that there is a particular pleasure to be derived from every method of preparing and serving Chinese food.

Savory soft rice is more readily appreciated than ordinary soft rice by the Westerner, as it has the appearance of a thick savory soup. To the Chinese, however, it is simply a variation of soft rice or congee which is eaten only at certain times of the day, and not at any meal.

Basic Soft Rice

Serves 10

1½ cups long-grain rice
½ cup glutinous rice

Cooking Wash the rice thoroughly in three changes of water. Place it in a deep saucepan and add 5 quarts of water. (Note: soft rice boils over very easily.) Bring to the boil, immediately reduce heat to the minimum, and insert an asbestos pad underneath the pan if available. Leave to cook for 1½ hours, stirring occasionally. If it becomes too thick, add a little boiling water. Continue to cook gently for approximately 30 minutes.

Soft rice or congee should be about half as thick as the usual rice pudding, although some prefer it thinner. At breakfast time it is valued for its refreshing quality and for its warmth. At supper time it has a settling effect on the digestive system and it provides warmth throughout the night, like an internal hot water bottle.

Almost any kind of meat can be added to cook with soft rice to produce savory soft rice. Often the meat is first of all marinated or previously cooked and added to the rice during the later stages of its cooking. Usually a drop or two of sesame oil is added to give it special appeal and flavor. The following recipes are a few of the more popular savory soft rice dishes, some of which are served in the Cantonese Chinese restaurants abroad.

Chicken Soft Rice

Preparation Chop 10 oz chicken through the bones into 1½–2 inch cubes. Many Americans may prefer the chicken to be boned, in which case 8 oz of chicken meat should be chopped into cubes. Marinate the chicken cubes for 1 hour in a mixture of salt, soy sauce, sherry, ginger root, scallions, pepper, and hoisin sauce.

Cooking Follow the instructions given in the Basic Soft Rice recipe for cooking the rice, using 5 quarts water. When the rice has simmered for 1¼ hours, the chicken and marinade should be stirred in, but the ginger root should be removed. Add a chicken stock cube to the saucepan. Simmer the rice and chicken together for 30–45 minutes. Add the sesame oil 3 minutes before serving.

Serving Divide the rice and chicken mixture among six to ten bowls as required. Ideally, this dish should be eaten with chopsticks. The pieces of chicken should either be dipped in high quality soy sauce or sprinkled with soy sauce. The savory flavor of the sauce and the contrasting blandness of the rice combine to form a most enjoyable dish.

Serves 6–10

1½ cups chopped chicken (see *Preparation*)
1½ cups long-grain rice
½ cup glutinous rice

1 teaspoon salt
2 tablespoons soy sauce
½ tablespoon dry sherry
2 slices chopped ginger root
2 scallions, chopped into ½ inch pieces
pepper to taste
1 tablespoon hoisin sauce
1 chicken stock cube
2 teaspoons sesame oil
soy sauce for dip

Pork Spare Rib Soft Rice

Repeat the recipe for Chicken Soft Rice, substituting about ¾–1 lb spare ribs, chopped into 1 inch long pieces, for the chicken. Pork bones are easier for Westerners to handle than chicken bones, therefore it should not be necessary to bone the spare ribs. The rice and spare ribs should be cooked together for 45 minutes.

Serves 6–10

Roast Duck or Roast Pork Soft Rice

As roast duck or Cantonese roast pork are two of the more readily available cooked foods in a Chinese kitchen, they are often added to soft rice.

Use the recipe for Basic Soft Rice (see page 88) as the basis of this dish. Chop about ¾–1 lb roast duck or pork into 1½ inch pieces and add to the rice 15–20 minutes before serving. At the same time add 2–3 scallions chopped into 1 inch pieces, 2 slices of ginger root, 2 teaspoons salt, and 1 teaspoon sesame oil. Remove the pieces of ginger when serving.

Serves 6–10

1 lb roast duck *or* roast pork
2–3 scallions
2 slices ginger root
2 teaspoons salt
1 teaspoon sesame oil

Beef Soft Rice

Serves 6–10

½–¾ lean beef
1 chicken stock cube
½ cup green peas

This is probably the most suitable dish for Westerners, as it contains no bones. Use ½–¾ lb lean beef (rump or fillet). Cut into 1½ × 1 inch very thin slices, and marinate in the same manner as the chicken in the Chicken Soft Rice recipe (page 99). Add a chicken stock cube and ½ cup raw green peas to the rice 30 minutes before serving. Add the beef to simmer in the rice for 10–12 minutes. Stir before serving.

Sampan Soft Rice

This is a typical Cantonese dish where various types of fish or seafood are added to the rice. Most types of fish can be used (except those which are too bony) and every type of shellfish. When fish is used, it should be marinated in soy sauce, hoisin sauce, salt, ginger, onion, garlic, and a small amount of lard or vegetable oil. The ginger (2–3 pieces) should be removed before serving. Sprinkle a tablespoon of chopped scallions or parsley and a teaspoon of sesame oil over the rice before serving.

Fish which has been sliced very thinly and marinated for one hour does not require much cooking. One practice is to place a few pieces of marinated fish at the bottom of the individual serving bowls and pour in the boiling hot soft rice until it almost reaches the rim of the bowl. Add 1 drop of sesame oil, 1 teaspoon chopped scallions, and 1 teaspoon best quality soy sauce. Allow the rice to stand for 5 minutes before eating. As boiling soft rice is hotter than boiling water, the fish or seafood ingredients will cook in its heat in 5 minutes.

Crackling Rice, or Sizzling Rice

Crackling rice is made from the rice crust or scrapings of the rice—the part which invariably sticks to the bottom of the pan, especially when a large quantity of it is being cooked. These pieces of rice should be collected and kept dry, and the larger ones broken down to square pieces, about 1½–2 inch. When they are required, they are placed in a fine-mesh wire basket and plunged into boiling oil to deep-fry for 2–3 minutes until golden brown. They should then be drained quickly and placed at the bottom of a well-heated serving bowl or dish. They start to crackle or sizzle when a dish of shrimp, diced meat, or chicken with sauce is poured over them.

Pieces of crackling rice can take the place of croutons in soups. They must be covered by a fish or meat dish with sauce as soon as possible after the oil has been drained off if full crackling effect is to be achieved. In Chinese restaurants abroad which specialize in Peking dishes, crackling rice is often served as a base for Shrimp in Tomato Sauce, or diced cubes of meat in Sweet and Sour Sauce.

NOODLES

After rice, noodles and steamed buns (known as Man Tou, or unstuffed steamed breads) rank as the most important bulk-foods of China. Steamed buns are eaten primarily in the north, while noodles are eaten both in the north and south at all times of the day and night except at breakfast. Noodles therefore seem to have beaten buns as a bulk-food by a short head.

It has been said that Italian pasta has its origin in Chinese noodles, which were first introduced to Europe in the fourteenth century by none other than Marco Polo, and which have now blossomed into all the familiar spaghettis, macaronis, and vermicellis. The main difference between Chinese noodles and Italian pasta does not lie in their shape or substance—there they are very similar—but in the way they are prepared and cooked. Because of the Chinese habits of cross-cooking, blending, and multi-phase heating, and because of the possibility of combining noodles with almost every variety of meat, fowl, seafood, or vegetable, there are probably many more Chinese noodle dishes than Italian pasta dishes. There is, in fact, an almost inexhaustible number of Chinese noodle dishes, and the majority of them are delicious and acceptable to the Western palate.

In the main, Chinese noodle dishes fall into the following categories:

1. Soup Noodles
2. Noodles in thickened sauce and gravies
3. Cooked Noodles
4. Fried Noodles: soft-fried and crisp-fried noodles
5. Tossed Noodles: hot-tossed and cold-tossed noodles
6. Transparent Bean-Thread Noodles

Soup noodles are generally served as an appetizer to commence a social occasion, often to precede an evening of dining and banqueting. They are often served in the hall or reception room soon after the guests arrive. In China when there is a wedding, anniversary, funeral, or memorial of any sort, noodles are usually served in clear chicken stock and garnished with a few strands of cooked chicken meat or shredded ham. This dish is designed to heighten interest and improve sociability, but not to hamper the great expectations of the banquet to come.

However, should the occasion be a birthday, the noodles will be served in a thickened gravy-sauce called Lu Mein. There is a good range of gravy-sauce noodles prepared with a variety of ingredients and garnishes, which are without exception highly delicious and appetizing. In all these cases, the gravy-sauce, garnish, and noodles are prepared and cooked separately, then combined together in the serving bowl.

When the noodles, sauce, and other ingredients are cooked together in a large pan and served in a large tureen, garnished in profusion, the dish is called Cooked Noodles or Wo Mein. Wo Mein is served mostly by restaurants where a wide range of ingredients is more easily available and where it is important to impress. The Cantonese often use seafood such as shrimp and crabs in the ingredients or as a garnish.

Fried noodles or Chow Mein are the best known Chinese noodles to Westerners. Chow Mein is a dish of soft-fried noodles, that is, boiled noodles which have been stir-fried in oil and gravy and then garnished with a good helping of shredded meats, vegetables, and seafood. In Canton there is a special version of fried noodles where the noodles and other ingredients are pressed down flat into the frying pan until they are slightly scorched, and then turned over like a pancake and pressed down again to fry until slightly scorched on the other side. Noodles cooked in this manner are generally fried with ample oil or fat (about 4–5 tablespoons) and are not popular in other parts of China. This type of noodle dish quite often makes an appearance abroad, as the majority of Chinese restaurants abroad are Cantonese.

Tossed Noodles, or Pan Mein, are boiled noodles which are served like a salad. They are boiled, drained, and placed in serving bowls. The diner helps himself to spoonfuls of soy jam (or soy jam and meat sauce), shredded cucumber, radishes, scallions, and bean sprouts which he mixes and tosses with the noodles. Vinegar and sesame oil are frequently added to this type of noodles. This method of serving noodles is probably the nearest Chinese version to the Italian spaghetti bolognese or milanese. A meat sauce prepared by stir-frying minced meat with soy jam in oil can be mixed with the noodles, making the dish very similar indeed to the Italian versions (except that the soy jam contributes an extra piquancy which the Italian dishes lack). But the use of crunchy vegetables, such as bean sprouts, cucumber, and radishes gives the Chinese sauce a texture which contrasts well with the softness of the noodles.

Another method of preparing Tossed Noodles is to add shredded meat—usually roast chicken or duck—seasoned with salt, pepper, mustard, soy sauce, and monosodium glutamate to cold cooked noodles. Selected shredded raw vegetables, sesame oil, and vinegar should then be mixed and tossed with the noodles and meat. This grand conglomeration of ingredients, all with very different flavors and characteristics, results in what the Westerner might call a salad. This salad can be further spiced with a small amount of chili oil. It is a useful dish to serve as a starter to a meal. As Chinese Cold Tossed Noodles form a salad with bulk, the dish should complement the lighter Western salads to make an interesting summer meal, especially if served outdoors.

The principal noodles used in China are wheat-flour noodles, egg noodles, rice-flour noodles (often called rice sticks) and transparent bean thread noodles. The latter are used primarily in soups, or to cook with and complement meats and vegetables. They are never eaten as a bulk ingredient in themselves. Rice-flour noodles, which often come in straight strands or sticks, from which the name rice sticks is derived, are popular in the south, where more rice is grown, and where rice is the principal diet. They are often cooked with seafood, and when cooked with oysters coupled with meats, their savoriness is devastating! Egg noodles usually come in small pads like the Western breakfast food Shredded Wheat; these have been partially pre-cooked by steaming. They generally require only a minimal amount of cooking (4–5 minutes of boiling and loosening in water). They can be made into various types of noodle dish in a very short time indeed.

Basic Noodles

All noodles have to be boiled or steamed before they are cooked in any other way. It is difficult to specify the exact length of time they should be boiled or steamed, as that depends partly upon the quality of the noodles themselves, and partly upon the length of time they are going to be subjected to further cooking with other ingredients in the later stages of preparation. The general rule is that noodles should never be cooked until they are soft, mushy, and on the point of breaking up. They should be cooked to a point where they are soft outside but still firm inside. This can be tested by taking out a strand and biting it, or pressing it between one's thumb and finger. The additional cooking in preparing the noodles as soup noodles, fried noodles, cooked noodles, or gravy noodles should provide sufficient further heating to cook them through.

Boiled Noodles

Cooking Heat 2 quarts of water in a pan until it boils. Add salt and noodles. Keep contents at a lively simmer until cooked, stirring and turning over now and then. If spaghetti is used, cook for about 18 minutes. If Chinese wheat-flour noodles are used, 12–14 minutes simmering is necessary. Test by biting or pressing. Drain the noodles in a colander. Rinse with fresh water, and leave to drain for a further 30 seconds. Add oil to the noodles, mix well to prevent sticking, and either spread out on a large plate or place in a bowl.

Fresh noodles usually take only half as long to cook as dried noodles. Chinese precooked egg noodles take an even shorter time, but test in each case.

Serves 8, with other dishes

1 lb wheat-flour noodles *or* spaghetti

2 teaspoons salt
2 teaspoons vegetable oil

Steamed Noodles

Cooking Boil the noodles in the same manner as in the recipe for Boiled Noodles, but for just 5 minutes. Drain, add oil, mix well, and spread the noodles out as much as possible in a large colander. Place the colander on top of a saucepan containing 3–4 inches of boiling water. Cover the top of colander and steam vigorously for 20 minutes.

Fresh noodles are best cooked by steaming. They require no parboiling, but need only to be tossed and rubbed with oil and placed in a colander to steam for 15 minutes. The advantages of steaming over boiling are that you do not overcook quite so quickly and the flavor of the noodles is better retained.

Serves 8, with other dishes

1 lb wheat-flour noodles

2 teaspoons vegetable oil

Soup Noodles

Although soup noodles are often used as 'Noodles of Occasion' (that is, when there is an occasion in the family and there is a crowd of guests and visitors to be entertained), they can also be eaten as between-meal snacks or as a full meal. The quantity of noodles and toppings or garnish used may be varied accordingly. After all, there are no limits to the size of the serving bowls which can be used or to the quantity of toppings added. It is always impressive to see people in China eating enormous soup bowls or tureens of soup noodles with great relish!

The soup served with soup noodles can be any meat or chicken broth, the traditional superior stock, or more cheaply, secondary stock. If secondary stock is used, it would be advisable to add $\frac{1}{4}$ teaspoon of monosodium glutamate to each bowl of soup to give it added flavor. Since the noodles are in themselves comparatively bland and tasteless, the soup has to be of reasonable strength in flavor and savoriness. In a Western kitchen a useful concoction for use as soup could be prepared by melting a chicken stock cube in 5 cups of any meat or chicken stock, or stock derived from simmering an assortment of bones and meat, such as necks and gizzards of chickens, etc.

The toppings or garnish, which are incorporated in considerable quantity in such Chinese dishes, consist of a mixture of sliced pork, beef, chicken, duck, or seafood, with sliced or shredded vegetables. Mushrooms (the dried variety, soaked before use) and wood ear fungi are also very often used. The dried mushrooms are an important ingredient because of the distinctive flavor they contribute to these savory dishes. The quantity of the toppings can be varied more or less according to your liking. The connoisseur prefers his soup noodles not be overloaded with toppings, as this prevents enjoyment and appreciation of the noodles themselves.

Soup Noodles with Cantonese Roast Pork and Spinach Topping

Serves 4 or 5

1 lb wheat-flour noodles
3 cups ($\frac{1}{2}$ lb) spinach
1 cup ($\frac{1}{2}$ lb) Cantonese roast pork

1 small onion
2 tablespoons vegetable oil
1 teaspoon sugar
1$\frac{1}{2}$ tablespoons soy sauce
1$\frac{1}{4}$ cups stock
$\frac{1}{2}$ teaspoon salt
$\frac{1}{4}$ teaspoon monosodium glutamate
2 tablespoons dry sherry

Preparation Parboil the noodles for 11–12 minutes, drain, and divide among four bowls. Wash the spinach thoroughly, drain, and remove coarser stems. Slice the roast pork and onion thin.

Cooking Heat the oil in a large frying-pan. Add the onion and spinach, and stir-fry over a high heat for 1 minute. Add sugar and soy sauce and stir-fry for another minute. Place the pork on top of the spinach and cook them together for 1 minute. Heat the stock in a saucepan. Add salt, monosodium glutamate, and sherry. When the mixture comes to the boil, stir, and pour over the noodles in the individual bowls.

Serving Top the noodles first with spinach and then with the pork. This is a simple but satisfying dish, which provides a balanced meal.

Chinese Chicken and Ham Soup Noodles

This is the usual style of light noodle snack served at receptions, social functions, and other occasions of that nature.

Preparation Parboil the noodles for 5–6 minutes if pre-cooked, and 12–14 minutes if uncooked. Drain and divide among four serving bowls. Slice the chicken meat and ham into very thin, thread-like strips. Sprinkle these chicken and ham strips evenly over the noodles in the bowls.

Cooking and Serving Heat the stock in a saucepan. Add the salt, monosodium glutamate, and ginger. Allow to simmer gently for 4–5 minutes. Stir, then pour the stock into the bowls containing the noodles. Place the bowls on a saucer or plate with a pair of chopsticks and serve.

Serves 4 or 5

½ lb (1 cup) egg noodles
¼ lb (½ cup) cooked chicken breast
¼ lb (½ cup) cooked ham

5 cups superior stock
1 teaspoon salt
¼ teaspoon monosodium glutamate
1 slice ginger root

Soup Noodles with Chicken and Vegetable Topping

Preparation Parboil the noodles for 11–12 minutes, drain, and divide among four bowls. Slice the chicken meat and bamboo shoots thinly. Soak the mushrooms and wood ears in warm water for 20 minutes. Drain the mushrooms and remove stalks. Keep aside ¼ cup mushroom water. Cut scallions and cabbage into 2 inch pieces.

Cooking Heat the oil in a frying pan. Add chicken, scallions, and bamboo shoots, and stir-fry together for 1 minute over medium heat. Add the mushrooms, wood ears, soy sauce, sugar, and pepper and continue to stir-fry for another minute. Add cabbage or celery and mushroom water. Cook, covered, for 3 minutes. Stir and turn the ingredients over. Heat the stock in a saucepan, adding salt, monosodium glutamate, and shrimp sauce. Bring to the boil and pour it over the noodles in the individual bowls.

Serving Top the noodles in each bowl with the contents of the frying pan, and serve. This is a much more substantial dish than Chinese Chicken and Ham Soup Noodles, and can be eaten as a snack meal.

Serves 4 or 5

1 lb wheat-flour noodles
¼ lb (½ cup) chicken meat
¼ cup bamboo shoots
4 large Chinese dried mushrooms
1½ tablespoons wood ears
2 scallions
1 cup Chinese celery cabbage *or* celery

1½ tablespoons vegetable oil
1 tablespoon soy sauce
1 teaspoon sugar
pepper to taste
5 cups superior stock *or* chicken stock
1 teaspoon salt
¼ teaspoon monosodium glutamate
½ tablespoon shrimp sauce

Soup Noodles with Red-Cooked Beef or Pork

Serves 4 or 5

Prepare noodles and stock as in the previous recipes for Soup Noodles. All red-cooked meats (pork, beef, lamb, etc.) can be used as toppings for soup noodles. These meats are often cut into large chunks, unlike the recipe for Soup Noodles with Cantonese Roast Pork and Spinach Topping, where the pork is sliced thin. To increase the appeal of the dish, and to provide a balanced meal, about 2 oz of vegetables for each bowl are usually cooked and added to the noodles along with the meat. The meat can be added cold or hot. The vegetables—spinach, mustard greens, cauliflower, leeks, pepper, celery, etc.—should be cut into 2 inch pieces, then stir-fried for a couple of minutes in $1\frac{1}{2}$–2 tablespoons of oil, with salt and pepper to taste. Then add 2–3 tablespoons of stock, a pinch of monosodium glutamate, and 2 tablespoons of the gravy from the red-cooked meat. Cook over a high heat for 2 minutes, gently stirring and turning over the contents of the pan, then place the vegetable toppings on the noodles in the bowls. The meats should now be placed on top of the vegetables to complete this attractive dish. Some Chinese rice wine or dry sherry may be sprinkled over the dish at the last moment to provide an appealing bouquet. Rice wine is widely used in this manner in China even among the peasantry, who also sometimes break an egg into the soup to provide variety, added appeal, and nourishment when there is no meat available.

Lu Mein (or Noodles in Sauce)

'Lu' is the general Chinese word for sauce or herbal sauce. Hence Lu Mein means 'sauce noodles'. The noodles served on birthdays are usually sauce noodles. Lu Mein is composed of approximately the same amounts of noodles and sauce served in the same bowl. The sauce can vary a good deal in thickness and flavor; even fish sauce, which can be extremely appetizing, can be used in preparing sauce noodles, and they are often topped with a chunk of red-cooked fish and a few strands of scallion tops or chives. The sauce or gravy used in preparing Lu Mein is usually thickened first with cornstarch or water chestnut flour. This appetizing dish of noodles, covered with plenty of thick sauce, is particularly suitable for serving in winter as it generates inner warmth.

Noodles in Meat Sauce

Serves 4–6

1 lb wheat-flour *or* egg noodles
8 oz slab bacon

Preparation Parboil and prepare the noodles in the same way as in the Soup Noodle recipes. Cut the bacon into thin lean and fat strips. Shred the ginger root and cut the scallions into 2 inch pieces. Soak the wood ears and mushrooms in warm

96

water, and remove the mushroom stalks. Reserve ¼ cup of the mushroom water. Cut the bamboo shoots into thin slices.

Cooking Heat 2½ cups stock in a saucepan. Add soy sauce, monosodium glutamate, sherry, and cornstarch blended with ¾ cup cold stock. Stir until the liquid thickens into a sauce. Heat the oil in a frying pan, add the pork and ginger, and stir-fry for 3–4 minutes over a high heat. Add mushrooms, wood ears, bamboo shoots, and scallions. Stir-fry them together for 2 minutes. Add the meat-gravy, salt, and mushroom water. Continue to stir-fry for 3 minutes.

Serving Serve by dividing noodles among four to six bowls. Pour a proportion of the thickened stock into each bowl, and top the noodles with the other ingredients fresh from the frying pan.

1 slice ginger root
2 scallions
1½ tablespoons wood ears
4½ tablespoons Chinese dried mushrooms
4½ tablespoons bamboo shoots
2½ cups chicken *or* superior stock
2 tablespoons soy sauce
¼ teaspoon monosodium glutamate
3 tablespoons dry sherry
3 tablespoons cornstarch
½ cup cold stock
2 tablespoons vegetable oil
6 tablespoons red-cooked meat gravy
½ teaspoon salt

Long Life Noodles in Egg Sauce

Preparation Parboil the noodles for 5–6 minutes. Drain, and divide among four or five bowls. Shred the ham and beat the eggs lightly for about 10 seconds.

Cooking Heat the stock in a saucepan. Add gravy, soy sauce, and sherry. Blend the monosodium glutamate and cornstarch with ¼ cup of water. Pour the mixture into the simmering stock and stir until it thickens into a sauce. Trail the egg along the prongs of a fork into the soup in as thin a stream as possible. When the egg coagulates, which is almost immediately, give the soup a stir or two. Add pepper to taste.

Serving Pour a proportion of the soup over the noodles in each of the bowls. Sprinkle with shredded ham, and serve.

In China, eggs are associated with long life. Here we have egg noodles in egg sauce; it is not surprising that this dish is called Long Life Noodles, and is usually served on birthdays.

Serves 4 or 5

2 cups (scant 1 lb) egg noodles
2 eggs

1½–2 tablespoons cooked ham
2½ cups superior stock
¾ cup red-cooked pork gravy
2 tablespoons soy sauce
3 tablespoons dry sherry
¼ teaspoon monosodium glutamate
3 tablespoons cornstarch
pepper to taste

Noodles in Shrimp Sauce

Preparation Parboil the noodles as in the recipe for Long Life Noodles in Egg Sauce Shred the pork and ham. Soak the mushrooms in a cup of water for 30 minutes, remove stalks and slice caps into matchstick strips. Reserve the mushroom water. Cut the scallions into ½ inch pieces. Crush and chop the garlic. Mix the monosodium glutamate and cornstarch with 6 tablespoons water.

Cooking Heat the oil in a large saucepan. Add garlic, ginger, pork, and salt. Stir-fry for 2 minutes over a high heat. Add the scallions and mushrooms and stir-fry for a further 2 min-

Serves 4–6

1½–2 cups (¾ lb) egg noodles
5 oz peeled shrimp
1 quart superior stock

5 oz (¾ cup) lean pork
3 oz (½ cup) cooked ham
½ cup Chinese dried mushrooms
3 scallions
1 clove garlic
¼ teaspoon monosodium glutamate

3 tablespoons cornstarch
2 tablespoons vegetable oil
2 slices ginger root
½ teaspoon salt
3 tablespoons soy sauce
3 tablespoons dry sherry

utes. Add shrimp, mushroom water, soy sauce, sherry, and finally the stock. Bring to the boil, reduce heat and simmer gently for 5 minutes. Pour the cornstarch mixture into the stock. Stir until stock thickens into a sauce.

Serving Divide the noodles among four to six bowls. Pour the prepared sauce over the noodles, dividing the ingredients evenly among the individual bowls. Sprinkle with shredded ham and serve.

Braised Noodles with Oysters

Serves 4–6

2 cups (scant 1 lb) wheat flour *or* rice stick noodles
10–12 oysters

2 tablespoons golden needles (tiger-lily buds)
6 Chinese dried mushrooms
1½ tablespoons wood ears
¼ lb (½ cup) lean pork
2 scallions
¼ lb leeks
½ teaspoon salt
3 tablespoons vegetable oil
2 slices ginger root
2½ cups superior stock
1 tablespoon soy sauce
2½ tablespoons dry sherry
2 tablespoons cornstarch
¼ teaspoon monosodium glutamate
1½ tablespoons sesame oil

Preparation Parboil the noodles for 10 minutes. Rinse in fresh water and put aside. Soak the golden needles for 30 minutes. Soak the mushrooms and wood ears separately for 20 minutes. Retain 6 tablespoons of the mushroom water. Slice the pork and mushroom caps into matchstick strips. Cut the scallions and golden needles into 1½ inch pieces. Slice the leeks into 1 inch pieces. Remove the oysters from their shells, reserving the oyster water. Sprinkle the oysters with salt.

Cooking Heat the vegetable oil in a saucepan. Add the scallions, ginger, and pork, and stir-fry together over medium heat for 2 minutes. Add the wood ears, golden needles, mushrooms, and leeks, and stir-fry for a further 2 minutes. Pour in half of the stock, and add soy sauce and oyster water. Bring to the boil and simmer for 5 minutes. Pour in the oysters and sherry, then simmer for 2 minutes. Meanwhile, blend the cornstarch and monosodium glutamate with the remaining stock and pour into the pan. Cook, stirring, for 3 minutes until the sauce thickens. Heat the sesame oil in a separate pan. Add the scallions and the noodles and turn them gently over a low heat for 2–3 minutes. Pour in all the soup from the other pan, together with half the solids. Leave to simmer and braise for 5 minutes. Heat the remaining solids in the first pan over a high heat and pour them on top of the noodles.

Serving Serve either by ladling the soup, noodles, and other ingredients into individual bowls, or serve all the ingredients together in a large soup bowl or tureen.

In China, such a dish is usually eaten as a big afternoon or midnight snack. In the south, it is usually prepared with rice stick noodles.

Chow Mein

Chow Mein is probably the best-known Chinese noodle dish in the West. It is also one of the fastest savory noodle dishes which a restaurant cook can slap out when time is pressing, yet at the same time it has the advantage of having been freshly cooked. Chow Mein illustrates the principal difference between Chinese noodles and Italian pasta: Chinese noodle dishes are usually made in two basic steps, the flavoring of the noodles by frying them in oil and meat-gravy, and garnishing the dish with a mixture of ingredients, thus providing additional variety of textures, tastes, and colors. In short, there is rather more blending and cross-cooking in the Chinese version.

The cooking of Chow Mein is therefore a two stage stir-frying process, apart from the parboiling of the noodles themselves. The ingredients for the topping are stir-fried together in rapid stages, and then removed from the pan and put aside. The cooked noodles are turned in the oil and gravy in the pan to achieve a savory flavor. By adding more oil or gravy you can make the noodles crisper or more savory. This early treatment gives the noodles a tasty flavor. Half of the topping is stir-fried into the noodles before they are placed on the serving dish. In the final phase the remainder of the topping is stir-fried, adjustments to the seasonings are made, and a spoonful or two of sherry and a pinch of monosodium glutamate may be added. Then the topping is added to the noodles.

Thus Chow Mein is the product of a two-stage stir-frying treatment, with a two-tier presentation. For an efficient chef, with all the ingredients at his finger tips, the whole operation need not take more than 3 minutes ($1\frac{1}{2}$ minutes for the first stir-frying of the topping, 1 minute for the stir-frying of the noodles, and 30 seconds for the second frying of the topping). However, in the recipes included here, it has been done at a much more leisurely pace.

Fried Noodles with Pork and Vegetable Topping

Preparation Parboil the noodles as in the instructions for Boiled Noodles (see page 93). Soak the mushrooms and golden needles separately in warm water for 30 minutes. Cut the golden needles and the scallions into 2 inch pieces. Slice the pork and mushrooms into matchstick strips.

Cooking Heat $1\frac{1}{2}$ tablespoons of the oil in a large frying pan. Add bacon, salt, and golden needles, and stir-fry together for 3 minutes over a high heat. Add mushrooms, scallions, and bean sprouts, and continue to stir-fry for $1\frac{1}{2}$ minutes. Add half of the soy sauce, sherry, sugar, and pepper, and stir-fry for a further $1\frac{1}{2}$ minutes. Remove vegetables with a spoon and keep hot. Add the remaining oil and soy sauce to the pan. Pour in the noodles and turn them over in the oil/soy gravy for $1\frac{1}{2}$ minutes over medium heat, to heat well through. Add a quarter of the fried topping to the noodles, blend and stir-fry together for $1\frac{1}{2}$ minutes and remove to a well-heated serving dish. Return the remainder of the topping to the pan, adding a small quantity of oil, soy sauce, or sherry at this point if necessary. Stir-fry over a high heat for 30 seconds, then arrange the topping on the noodles.

This is a fairly standard way of cooking Chow Mein. Other meat ingredients can be substituted for pork, and other sliced vegetables such as leeks, cabbage, broccoli, celery, or greens

Serves 5–6

1 lb wheat-flour noodles
6 Chinese dried mushrooms
3 tablespoons golden needles (tiger-lily buds)
3 scallions
$\frac{1}{2}$ lb (1 cup) slab bacon
6 tablespoons bean sprouts

$\frac{1}{4}$ cup vegetable oil
$\frac{1}{2}$ teaspoon salt
3 tablespoons soy sauce
$2\frac{1}{2}$ tablespoons dry sherry
1 teaspoon sugar
pepper to taste

can be substituted for bean sprouts, golden needles, etc. with equal success; however, dried mushrooms and scallions are always essential. (See illustration.)

Fried Noodles with Chicken and Vegetable Topping

Serves 4–6.

Repeat the recipe for Fried Noodles with Pork and Vegetable Topping, substituting 4–5 oz ($\frac{1}{2}$–$\frac{3}{4}$ cup) of chicken breast meat for the pork, and 2 oz (3 tablespoons) of wood ears (soaked in two changes of water for 30minutes) for the golden needles.

Fried Noodles with Shredded Roast Duck or Roast Chicken and Vegetables

Serves 4–6

In this case cooked meat is used, and therefore only a minimal amount of further cooking is required. Shred the meat, removing all bones. Since duck is a stronger-tasting meat than chicken, it should be combined with the same ingredients and supplementary material as beef (see Fried Noodles with Beef Ribbons and Vegetable Topping, below). If chicken meat is used, combine it with the same vegetables and other ingredients as in the pork recipe (see Fried Noodles with Pork and Vegetable Topping, page 99). In both cases the meat and vegetables can be stir-fried together; or indeed, the meat could be added after the vegetables have been stir-fried for a couple of minutes.

Note In all four preceding recipes an extra tablespoon of sherry and a teaspoon of sesame oil can be added into the final stir-frying of the topping to produce an extra aromatic effect, if desired.

Fried Noodles with Beef Ribbons and Vegetable Topping

Serves 4–6

$\frac{1}{2}$ cup celery
2 leeks

Repeat the recipe for Fried Noodles with Pork and Vegetable Topping, substituting the same quantity of beef (fillet, rump, etc.) for the pork, and about $\frac{1}{2}$ cup of celery and 2 stalks leeks for bean sprouts. Cut the leeks and celery into 1 inch pieces and stir-fry them with the meat and 1 slice of ginger root. Remove the ginger, and put the meat/leek/celery mixture aside. Add a quarter of the vegetable ingredients when stir-frying the noodles; the remainder should be retained for the final stir-frying process and then placed on top of the noodles.

Fried Noodles with Fresh Shrimp or Crabmeat and Vegetables

A feature of Chinese cooking is that seafood is often combined with meat. Although these two quite different materials are sometimes blended together (in some shrimp balls or fish balls), in the majority of cases they are usually prepared and cooked separately, and are combined only at a later stage of the cooking. This is because in the creation of Chinese dishes, one should always try to avoid making a mess and ingredients and flavors should remain recognizable and distinct.

This dish can be prepared by simply repeating any of the previous recipes, reducing the meat content to half, and adding an equal or slightly greater quantity of whatever seafood you have decided to use (shrimp, crab, and lobster are all suitable). The meat and seafood can be stir-fried together, but it is preferable to cook them separately. The same vegetables should be added to both; a slice or two of ginger root and a clove of crushed garlic should also be added to the seafood.

When meat and seafood have been stir-fried, a proportion of each can be stir-fried into the noodles. The balance is left to be stir-fried for use as a topping when the dish is almost ready to be served. Naturally some preparation of the seafood is needed; in the case of crab, the meat will have to be removed and flaked, and in the case of large shrimp or lobsters, the larger pieces of meat will have to be cut into three or four smaller bite-sized pieces before cooking.

Variations Many other types of vegetables can be introduced either as substitutes for, or in addition to, the vegetables used in the previous recipes. Spinach, green peas, string beans, sliced pole beans, snow peas, fresh mushrooms, cauliflower, broccoli, and carrots are very often used. The only difference in the treatment of these vegetables is that the harder vegetables will have to be introduced into the stir-frying earlier than the softer ones. Some of the still harder vegetables require a period of parboiling before frying. When vegetables are cooked with noodles they are always sliced into strips first. In those cases where a hard vegetable is not parboiled first before being stir-fried, the stir-frying process can be prolonged by a minute or two without burning, simply by introducing a small amount of stock or gravy into the frying pan: stock and gravy are always available in a Chinese kitchen.

It is not necessary that only one type of meat is used at a time. Both chicken and pork are very versatile, and they could be used in conjunction with ham, salt beef, kidney, liver, tripe, bacon, or seafood. To achieve a more piquant and tangy flavor, pickles and chutneys are frequently added to the frying pan. Soaked dried vegetables are often used with fresh vegetables to enhance the flavor. An inexhaustible variety of noodle dishes can be prepared using fresh, cooked, cured, or salted meat and fresh, dried, or pickled vegetables.

Fried Noodle Variations

Many other types of vegetables can be introduced, either as a substitute for, or in conjunction with the vegetables used in the previous recipes. Spinach, green peas, string beans, sliced pole beans, fresh mushrooms, cauliflower, broccoli, and tender young carrots are particularly successful. The harder vegetables will have to be introduced into the stir-frying earlier, and the softer ones at a later stage. Carrots, broccoli, cauliflower, and string beans especially will generally require a short period of parboiling before frying. However, if the hard vegetables are not parboiled before stir-frying, the latter process can be prolonged by a minute or two without burning, simply by introducing a small amount of stock or gravy into the frying. Whichever the case, any meat or vegetables cooked with noodles should be sliced or shredded into strips of similar size.

With regard to meat, it is not necessary that only one type of meat is used at a time. Chicken, and pork are very versatile, and may be used in conjunction with ham, kidney, liver, tripe, bacon, or one of the seafoods.

To give more piquancy and twang to the flavor, pickles and chutneys are frequently added to the frying, and many dried vegetables (after having first been soaked) may be used along with fresh vegetables to enhance the flavor.

With so many variations of meat (fresh, cooked, cured, or salted) and vegetables (fresh, dried, or pickled) available, the number of possible combinations for noodles is practically inexhaustible.

Hot Noodles with Soy Jam and Fresh Vegetables

Serves 4–6

1 lb wheat-flour noodles
¾ cup radishes
1 small cucumber
6 scallions
5½ tablespoons bean sprouts
6¼ tablespoons soy jam *or* paste
3 tablespoons soy sauce

3 tablespoons dry sherry
2 teaspoons sugar
¼ cup vegetable oil
¼ lb (½ cup) finely chopped pork
½ teaspoon salt
2 slice ginger root

Preparation Parboil the noodles for 12–14 minutes, drain, and keep hot. Peel the radishes and cucumber and cut them into matchstick strips. Cut the scallions into 2 inch pieces. Wash and blanch the bean sprouts and drain well. Place the different vegetables in separate serving dishes. Mix the soy jam with soy sauce, sherry, sugar, and 4 tablespoons water.

Cooking Heat the oil in a small frying pan. Add pork, salt, and ginger and stir-fry over a high heat for 2 minutes. Reduce heat to medium, remove ginger, and stir the soy jam mixture into the pork. Stir-fry for 2 minutes, and leave to cook for 2 minutes. Pour the meat/soy jam sauce into a bowl and place at the center of the dining table

Serving Divide the noodles among four to six bowls. Each diner mixes one or two spoonfuls of the sauce into his noodles, and adds a selection of the shredded vegetables provided. This is a very popular and simple way to serve noodles and is a favorite of the Chinese of the north. Frequently a couple of small dishes of pickles and chutneys are provided as additional side dishes for mixing with the noodles and raw vegetables. The final blending of flavors and ingredients with the noodles is left to the diner himself.

Hot Noodles with Sesame Paste or Peanut Butter and Vegetables

This is a variation of the recipe for Hot Noodles with Soy Jam and Fresh Vegetables using sesame paste or peanut butter instead of soy jam or paste. Sesame paste has a very nutty flavor, like peanut butter. As it is very dry, it must be blended with a certain amount of vegetable oil and other liquid ingredients to improve its smoothness when served with noodles. The following recipe can be used with the same quantity of noodles and sliced raw vegetables as the previous one.

Preparation and Serving Blend the ingredients together in a bowl and place it on the table for the diners to help themselves. The mixture should be added to the noodles, along with the raw shredded vegetables, the chutney, and the pickles.

This is a vegetarian dish and is favored by the poorer section of the population who are vegetarian-inclined both in north and south China.

Serves 4–6

3¼ tablespoons sesame paste *or* ¼ cup peanut butter
3 tablespoons vegetable oil
1 tablespoon hoisin sauce
3 tablespoons soy sauce
3 tablespoons dry sherry
¼ cup concentrated chicken stock
1 teaspoon chili sauce
1 teaspoon sugar

Transparent Bean-Thread Noodles with Stewed Meat and Vegetables

Transparent noodles are not served in the same way as other noodles. They are not used as a bulk food, but are usually cooked with savory foods in plenty of gravy, and eaten with rice. As transparent noodles have the unusual quality of never becoming soft and mushy through cooking, and since they are very useful as absorbers and conveyors of flavors, it is both traditional and convenient to cook them along with meats and other foods. To the connoisseurs they are a great boon as an aid to the consumption of rice; they serve almost as a savory lubricant when eating quantities of rice and provide one of the basic pleasures in the enjoyment of Chinese food.

Preparation Soak the noodles in warm water and drain. Clean the greens or broccoli, discarding outer leaves. Cut into 1½ inch pieces. Parboil for 2 minutes, then drain, Soak the mushrooms and dried shrimp in a bowl of warm water for 30 minutes. Drain, retaining the mushroom water. Discard the

Serves 6–8

¼ lb transparent bean-thread noodles
½ lb mustard greens *or* broccoli
½ lb (1 cup) red-cooked pork *or* beef (see Index)

2½ cups superior stock
6 Chinese dried mushrooms
3 tablespoons dried shrimp
¼ teaspoon monosodium glutamate
2 tablespoons soy sauce
3 tablespoons dry sherry

mushroom stalks, and slice the caps into matchstick shreds. Cut the pork or beef into 1 inch cubes.

Cooking Heat the stock in a saucepan. Add greens, mushrooms, shrimp, monosodium glutamate, soy sauce, and mushroom water. Simmer for 5–6 minutes. Add the noodles and mix with the vegetables. Continue to heat gently for another 7–8 minutes. Pour the mixture into a large ovenproof dish or casserole. Plac the red-cooked pork or beef on top, pour in any gravy from the meat, and then add the sherry. Place the dish or casserole in a steamer for 15 minutes, then serve.

Noodles in Lobster Sauce

Serves 4–6

¾ lb egg noodles
¾ cup lobster meat
1½ pints superior stock

¼ lb (¾ cup) lean pork
¼ lb (½ cup) cooked ham
½ cup Chinese dried mushrooms
3 scallions
1 clove garlic
¼ teaspoon monosodium glutamate
3 tablespoons cornstarch
2 tablespoons vegetable oil
2 slices ginger root
½ teaspoon salt
1½ tablespoons soy sauce
1½ tablespoons dry sherry

Preparation Prepare and parboil noodles as in recipe for Long Life Noodles in Egg Sauce. Slice pork and ham into matchstick strips. Soak mushrooms in a cupful of warm water for 30 minutes, remove the stems, and slice caps into matchstick strips. Reserve the mushroom water. Cut the scallions into ½ inch segments. Crush and chop the garlic. Combine the monosodium glutamate and cornstarch with 6 tablespoons water.

Cooking and Serving Heat the oil in a large saucepan. Add the garlic, ginger, pork, and salt, and stir-fry for 2 minutes. Add the scallions and mushrooms, stir-fry for a further 2 minutes, then add lobster meat, mushroom water, soy sauce, sherry, and finally the stock. Bring to the boil, and simmer gently for 5 minutes; then pour the cornstarch mixture into the pan and stir until it thickens into a sauce. Divide the noodles among four to six bowls. Pour the lobster sauce over the noodles, sprinkle with shredded ham, and serve.

Ten Variety Hot Pot

Serves 10–12, with other dishes

¼ lb (½ cup) cooked ham
6 oz (¾ cup) red-cooked roast duck
  (see Index)
6 oz (¾ cup) Cantonese roast pork
  (see Index)
6 oz (¾ cup) red-cooked chicken
  (see Index)

¼ cup bêche de mer
½ cup Chinese dried mushrooms
1½ tablespoons golden needles
  (tiger-lily buds)

In contrast to Transparent Bean Thread Noodles with Stewed Meat and Vegetables, this is a much heavier, meaty dish.

Preparation Soak the bêche de mer overnight, and cut into 1 inch pieces. Chop the ham, duck, pork, and chicken into 1½ × 1 inch pieces. Soak mushrooms for 30 minutes and remove stalks. Cut each of the golden needles into three pieces. Cut the vegetables and meats into pieces the same size. Slice the pea pods diagonally into ½ inch wide strips. Boil the vegetables in water for 2 minutes and drain. Cut the bean curd into ½ inch cubes, deep-fry in hot oil for 3 minutes, then drain.

Select a very large heat-proof metal pot or casserole, and arrange the ingredients in orderly layers, starting with the celery at the bottom, followed by transparent noodles, bamboo shoots, broccoli, cauliflower, golden needles, and snow peas, with the chicken, duck, bêche de mer, and mushrooms at the top.

Cooking and Serving Add salt, monosodium glutamate, and sherry to the stock in a saucepan and bring to the boil. Pour the stock gently over the materials in the hot pot. Bring the contents to the boil, and simmer gently for 20 minutes. Light the heater under the hot pot or fondue pot and bring it to the table. Although the dish is called Ten Variety, there is no need to stick to ten ingredients.

½ cup snow peas
1 cake bean curd
oil for deep-frying
½ cup celery
½ cup bean thread transparent
   noodles
¼ cup bamboo shoots
¼ cup broccoli
¼ cup cauliflower
2 teaspoons salt
¼ teaspoon monosodium glutamate
6 tablespoons dry sherry
5 cups superior stock

Wo Mein (Pot-Cooked Noodles)

Wo Mein (or Pot-Cooked Noodles) is really a variation of Noodles in Sauce. But because it is cooked in a pot, rather than having sauce poured over it in the serving bowl, it comes to be called 'cooked noodles' or 'pot-cooked noodles' (Wo being the Cantonese word for pot; hence pot-cooked). These noodles are frequently served in restaurants, where many different materials for toppings and garnishes are usually available. Very often these noodles are served in a large tureen and brought to the table with quantities of garnish piled on top. The dish is rather more elaborate than Lu Mein. The soup or sauce in Wo Mein is likely to be thinner than in Lu Mein (sauce noodles), but since the noodles and soup have been cooked together with the various ingredients and a proportion of the garnish, it tends to be a more highly savory dish. In Cantonese restaurants, a selection of seafood, such as fresh shrimp, crabs, or lobsters are bound to have been added. Wo Mein is a larger dish with a greater variety of added ingredients than Lu Mein, and therefore gives the impression of being more sumptuous.

VEGETABLE
AND VEGETARIAN DISHES

There are three background factors in Chinese vegetable and vegetarian cooking which give them strength, tradition, and variety.

The first of these is the widespread use of soy beans and their by-products which, as we have already seen, add a great deal of flavoring power to Chinese meat cooking, as well as the cooking of other foods. One must also recognize that the use of bean curds is of great importance—for sheer versatility they have few equals in the whole realm of food materials.

Vegetable and vegetarian dishes derive their tradition principally from Buddhist monastery and temple cooking. As many of these monasteries and temples are large communities of people with well-developed traditions and hierarchy like the Papal Court which go back to antiquity or at least to medieval times, their kitchens were often institutions of their own, carrying within them traditions and methods of which many palace kitchens would be proud. It was in these kitchens that a great array of vegetarian dishes were invented and developed (much in the same manner as the Benedictine Monks developed their liqueur).

The variety in Chinese vegetable and vegetarian cookery is, of course, derived from the practice of cross-cooking ingredients and the cross-blending of flavors. Many readers may have already noticed that long before reaching this chapter on vegetables, we have dealt with a very large number of dishes which were concerned with vegetables. This is because practically all the meat, poultry, and fish dishes use vegetables as flavoring or supplementary ingredients or, in some cases, as the bulk material of dishes on which the meats act to impart their taste and flavor. In fact, in describing and dealing with these dishes in the previous chapters we have, perhaps inadvertently, described the cooking of a great number of vegetable dishes, although they were not 'pure vegetable' dishes.

Making these cross-cooked dishes composed of meats and vegetables is largely a question of orientation: when the dish is meant to be a vegetable dish the orientation will be towards vegetables, the purpose of this being to bring out the qualities and characteristics of the vegetables in the dish. In these latter cases, it is likely that a greater variety of vegetables would be used, and probably greater and more stringent care would be exercised in their selection and preparation.

Therefore, in dealing with Chinese vegetable dishes, it should be noted that they differ from meat dishes not wholly in kind, but rather in degree. The frontier here becomes even more blurred because in Chinese cooking so much reliance is placed on the use of meat stocks—such as chicken stock and superior stock—as flavoring agents. In addition, when we consider the use of soy beans and their by-products (soy sauce, soy paste, soy cheese, soy bean curd, fermented salted soy beans) which act as a common denominator between meat and vegetable dishes, together with the ingrained Chinese habit of using meat gravies and fish gravies on almost everything for the cross-blending of flavors, the intermingling of meats and vegetables becomes more than ever basic and inextricable.

In the case of the cross-blending of flavors, one must always be aware of the Chinese practice of blending the taste of salted, pickled, and dried materials with that of the young and fresh. As a great many vegetables can be obtained in salted, dried, or pickled form, there exists a host of natural flavorers with which the fresh vegetables may be strengthened and blended, even without resorting to the use of meats and meat ingredients.

Stir-frying is the most frequent and popular method by which vegetables are cooked. The usual practice is to stir-fry the stronger vegetables first (the garlic, ginger, onions, etc.), and thus impregnate the oil with their flavors before it is used to cook the fresh vegetables. This practice of frying with impregnated oil, often with a small quantity of salt which has the salutary effect of making green vegetables greener, usually acts as the first-line of flavoring, and this is frequently followed and supplemented by other phases of further seasoning and flavoring. Furthermore, by taking advantage of the interplay of textures which results partly from the Chinese practice of blending the cooked with the uncooked (or fresh), and partly from the throwing together of foods of widely different substance and texture, the 'tapestry of texture' in cooking, if one might invent an expression, is in this way brought to a new height in Chinese vegetarian cooking.

For these reasons, and probably for others, Chinese vegetable and vegetarian dishes can often be eaten on their own, as interesting savory dishes. Once vegetable dishes were considered to be able to stand in their own right, more time and competence naturally came to be devoted to their cooking and preparation—resulting in their attaining a high degree of excellence and distinction.

In the past, it was not uncommon in China to find bloated connoisseurs of foods drifting quietly away from their normal haunts and fleshpots to the seclusion of the ancient trees and temple bells of the monastery, in order to savor the joy of contemplation and the purity of vegetarian dishes. So when the great critics start to praise the undeniable excellence of vegetarian dishes and monkish creations, who is there to dispute?

When assessing Chinese vegetable foods, one must make a clear distinction between ordinary vegetable dishes, the majority of which have meat contents, and the pure vegetarian dishes. Since in the earlier chapters of this book we have already come across in some detail a good many ordinary vegetable dishes, we shall now give greater emphasis to the pure vegetarian dishes.

In this chapter it seems appropriate to deal first of all with Chinese vegetarian stock—that very important ingredient which is used constantly in the preparation of vegetarian meals.

Basic Vegetarian Stock

¼ lb fresh mushrooms
¼ cup dried mushrooms
¼ lb dried mushroom stalks
1 lb fresh mushroom stalks
1½ lb yellow beans
¼ teaspoon monosodium glutamate

Cooking Boil the fresh and dried mushrooms, the mushroom stalks, and the yellow beans in 10 quarts of water for 3 hours. Keep the quantity of liquids constant by adding small amounts of water whenever the level of the stock falls visibly. Add the monosodium glutamate 5 minutes before the stock is ready. This stock is used in the same way as superior stock is used in normal cooking.

Pao T'Sai (White Hot Pickle)

Makes 2 quarts

1 medium-sized white cabbage
2 young carrots
1 turnip
¼ cup radishes
¼ cup salt
¼ cup gin *or* Pai Kan liqueur
2 dried red chili peppers

This plain pickle is used extensively in China to accompany soft rice; it is also used with other vegetables in Chinese salads.

Preparation Clean the cabbage thoroughly, breaking it up into individual leaves and discarding the coarse outer leaves. Cut the leaves into 1½–2 inch pieces. Shake off any lingering water and put the cabbage leaves in a colander. Leave them in an airy place to dry for 1 day. Peel the carrots and turnip and cut them into thin slices. Remove the tops and roots from the radishes, quarter them, and wash and dry them. Dissolve the salt in 2 quarts of boiling water. When cold, add the gin and all the vegetables. Put the mixture in a screw-top jar, close it firmly, and place it in a warm room for 1 week. The resultant pickles will be slightly hot, salty, and very crunchy.

Three Fairies Salad

Serves 4–6, with other dishes

1 large Chinese celery cabbage *or* cabbage
¼ cup radishes
2 teaspoons salt
2 tablespoons watercress *or* 1 tablespoon coriander
2 onions
2 fresh chili peppers
¼ cup vegetable oil
2½ tablespoons Pao T'Sai pickle (above)
1 teaspoon sesame oil

Preparation Clean the cabbage or lettuce and cut the leaves into 2 × 1 inch pieces. Shred the radishes, and mix with the cabbage or lettuce in a bowl. Add the salt and rub it into the vegetables. Leave to stand for 4 hours in a large colander. Clean the watercress thoroughly, discarding the roots, and cut the onions into thin slices. Chop the chili peppers and discard the seeds.

Cooking Stir-fry the onion and chili in the vegetable oil for 3 minutes; then remove from pan.

Serving Put the cabbage and radishes into a salad bowl, add the watercress and pickle, and pour in the onion/chili-impregnated oil. Sprinkle with sesame oil. Toss and mix well; then serve.

Mustard Cabbage

Preparation Break the cabbage into individual leaves, discarding the coarser ones. Shred each leaf into 12 pieces by cutting crosswise downwards.

Cooking Plunge the cabbage into a pan of boiling water. Bring it to the boil again and boil for 20 seconds; then drain. While still hot, add all the other ingredients and mix well. Place the cabbage mixture in a saucepan and heat over a medium heat for 45 seconds. Allow the mixture to cool for 2 hours; then serve as an hors d'œuvre or use for cooking with meat and other ingredients.

Serves 4–8, with other dishes

1 large Chinese celery cabbage, about 1½–2 lb, *or* Savoy caggage

2 tablespoons mustard powder mixed with 3 tablespoons water
3 tablespoons soy sauce
1 teaspoon salt
1½ tablespoons wine vinegar

Chinese Celery Cabbage with Shrimp and Green Pepper

This is a non-vegetarian dish.

Preparation Cut away the cabbage stalk, and remove the coarse outer leaves. Split the cabbage in half, horizontally, and then quarter each half. Soak the dried shrimp in warm water for 1 hour; drain. Cut the pepper into two, removing the seeds. Blend the cornstarch and milk in a bowl.

Cooking Heat the oil in a large saucepan, add the ginger and pepper, and stir-fry over medium heat for 1 minute. Discard the ginger and pepper, then add the cabbage pieces and turn them in the oil for 3 minutes until they are thoroughly coated. Pour in the stock, then add the salt, soaked dried shrimp, and the monosodium glutamate. Bring to the boil, then cover and simmer for 12 minutes, gently turning the cabbage over once or twice. Pour in the milk and cornstarch mixture, stir gently, and bring to the boil. Simmer for 3 minutes.

Serving Lift out the still intact cabbage pieces with a perforated spoon; arrange them neatly in a deep dish, partly reconstructing the cabbage if possible. Garnish with chopped ham.

Serves 4–8, with other dishes

2½–3 lb Chinese celery cabbage (if not available, use Savoy cabbage)

1 tablespoon dried shrimp
1 green pepper
1 tablespoon cornstarch
¾ cup milk
3 tablespoons vegetable oil
1 slice ginger root
2 cups superior stock (or chicken stock)
1½ teaspoons salt
¼ teaspoon monosodium glutamate
1 tablespoon chopped smoked ham

Chinese Carrot Salad

Preparation Scrape and clean the carrots; then slice them thinly by cutting downwards in a slanting, crosswise fashion. Soak in water for 15 minutes; then drain. Sprinkle with salt and pepper, and rub the seasonings into the carrots. Set them

Serves 6–8

12 young carrots
1 heaping teaspoon salt
dash of pepper

3 tablespoons vinegar
1½ tablespoons sugar
2 tablespoons soy sauce
3¾ teaspoons sesame oil
2½ tablespoons dry sherry

aside for 2 hours; then drain away all the liquid extracted from the carrots at the end of this time. Add the vinegar, sugar, soy sauce, sesame oil, and sherry. Toss and serve.

Eight Precious Hot Salad

Serves 6–8

4 golden needles (tiger-lily buds)
2 tablespoons wood ears
¼ cup bean curd skin
4 large Chinese dried mushrooms
¼ cup carrots
¼ cup turnip
¼ cup bamboo shoots
½ cup celery
½ cup bean sprouts
6 tablespoons vegetable oil
2 teaspoons salt
¼ cup vegetarian stock (see Index)
3 tablespoons sesame oil
2 tablespoons soy sauce
1½ tablespoons vinegar
¼ teaspoon monosodium glutamate

This salad can also be served cold.

Preparation Soak the golden needles for 1 hour in warm water; then cut them into 2 inch segments. Soak the wood ears for 1 hour and rinse in two changes of water. Soak the bean curd skin for 1 hour in warm water and cut it into 2 inch segments. Soak the mushrooms for 30 minutes, discard the stalks and shred the caps. Shred the carrots, turnip, bamboo shoots, and celery.

Cooking Stir-fry the carrots, turnip, and bean sprouts in 2 tablespoons of vegetable oil for 2 minutes over a high heat; then for 2 minutes more over a low heat, adding 1 teaspoon of salt. Stir-fry the mushrooms, wood ears, celery, bean curd skin, and bamboo shoots in the remaining vegetable oil and salt over a medium heat for 3 minutes. Combine the two lots of vegetables and add the vegetarian stock, sesame oil, soy sauce, vinegar, and monosodium glutamate. Toss and 'assemble' over a high heat for 1½ minutes; then serve.

The Lo-Han Grand Vegetarian Ensemble

Serves 6–8 with other vegetarian dishes

1 cup transparent noodles
¼ cup dried bamboo shoots
2 cups vegetarian stock (see Index)
1½ tablespoons soy sauce
¼ teaspoon monosodium glutamate
3 tablespoons dry sherry

The 'Lo-Hans' are the minor gods who sit in arrays in the Buddhist temples. As they exist in great numbers, the dish for them has to be a large one.

Preparation and Cooking Repeat the previous recipe for Eight Precious Hot Salad, and prepare the following ingredients to add to it. Soak the noodles and bamboo shoots in warm water for 20 minutes; then drain. Put the stock in a large saucepan with the noodles and bamboo shoots, and add the soy sauce, monosodium glutamate, and sherry. Simmer for 10 minutes. Add the hot salad, prepared according to the previous recipe, and cook for 3 minutes. Serve hot in a large bowl, befitting the monastic scale and appearance of this dish.

Vegetarian Cold Salad

Preparation Shred the cabbage, lettuce, carrots, and radishes; skin and quarter the tomatoes. Chop the scallions into 1 inch segments. Slice the onion, and crush the cloves of garlic.

Cooking Heat the vegetable oil in a saucepan. Add the scallions, onion, ginger, and garlic. Stir-fry over a medium heat for 3 minutes, discard the onions, ginger, and garlic, and allow the oil to cool. Clean and blanch the bean sprouts, drain them, and allow to cool.

Serving Place the shredded cabbage, lettuce, carrots, and radishes, the tomato quarters, and the bean sprouts in a large salad bowl. Add the impregnated oil with the salt, soy sauce, vinegar, and chili oil. Toss well. Sprinkle with monosodium glutamate, sesame oil, chives, and coriander; then serve.

Serves 6–8 with other vegetarian dishes

½ cup Savoy cabbage
½ cup Cos lettuce
3 young carrots
¼ cup radishes
3 medium tomatoes
3 scallions
1 large onion
2 cloves garlic
6 tablespoons vegetable oil
2 slices ginger root
½ cup bean sprouts
1 teaspoon salt
3 tablespoons soy sauce
3 tablespoons wine vinegar
¾ teaspoon chili oil
¼ teaspoon monosodium glutamate
1 tablespoon sesame oil
1½ tablespoons chopped chives
1½ tablespoons chopped coriander

Plain-Fried Spinach with Vegetarian Stock

Preparation Wash the spinach thoroughly, discarding all the coarse leaves and stems. Slice the onions thin, and crush and chop the garlic.

Cooking Heat the oil in a large frying pan. Add the ginger, garlic, and onion, and stir-fry together for 2 minutes over a high heat. Remove the ginger, garlic, and onion. Add the spinach and stir-fry over a high heat for 2 minutes until it has been well-coated with oil. Add the salt, soy sauce, and vegetarian stock and stir-fry for a further minute. Sprinkle with sesame oil, sherry and monosodium glutamate. Continue to stir-fry for another 30 seconds; serve and eat immediately.

Throughout the cooking, a high heat should be maintained. The glistening green of the resulting dish is one of the most appealing sights of Chinese vegetable cuisine.

Serves 6–8, with other vegetarian dishes

1½ lb spinach
¼ cup vegetarian stock (see Index)

2 medium-sized onions
2 cloves garlic
6 tablespoons vegetable oil
2 slices ginger root
½ teaspoon salt
2 tablespoons soy sauce
1 tablespoon sesame oil
1½ tablespoons dry sherry
¼ teaspoon monosodium glutamate

Stir-Fried Spinach with Chicken and Ham

This is a non-vegetarian dish.

Preparation Repeat the recipe for Plain-Fried Spinach with Vegetarian Stock, adding 2 oz (¼ cup) shredded chicken, and ¼ cup shredded smoked ham to the pan along with the ginger, garlic, and onion.

Serves 4–6, with other dishes

Splash-Fried Bean Sprouts

Serves 4–6, with other dishes

1 cup bean sprouts

2 tablespoons chives
oil for splash-frying
1 teaspoon salt
2 teaspoons sesame oil

This salad should be served hot. One of the best-known qualities of bean sprouts is their crunchiness. Splash-frying is said to enhance this, but be very careful when using this method.

Preparation Select white bean sprouts, all of about the same length. Lay them to an even depth, like a bed, on a wire basket. Clean and dry the chives thoroughly, and use a pair of scissors to cut them to about the same regular length as the bean sprouts. Lay them down evenly on top of the bed of sprouts.

Cooking Hold the wire basket over a pan of boiling oil, and use a large ladle to spoon the oil over the vegetables in the basket. Take your time when pouring the oil over; let it drain and drip through slowly. Spoon about 18 ladles of oil over the vegetables. After the last of the oil has drained through, pour the vegetables into a large, heat-proof glass or china bowl. Sprinkle with salt and sesame oil; then toss. This dish should be eaten while still very hot.

The interlacing of the green chives with the white bean sprouts makes a most attractive color combination.

Double-Fried Vegetarian Bamboo Shoots

Serves 6–8

1½ lb fresh bamboo shoots (choose small ones

3 tablespoons vegetarian stock (see Index)
¼ cup red-in-snow
10 tablespoons oil
2 teaspoons brown sugar
1½ tablespoons dry sherry
3 tablespoons soy sauce
¼ teaspoon monosodium glutamate

This recipe uses red-in-snow, which is a type of Chinese pickle.

Preparation Clean the bamboo shoots and cut them slant-wise into thin 1 inch pieces, using only the inner, more tender parts. Chop the red-in-snow coarsely. Rinse them in hot water, and drain.

Cooking Heat 2 tablespoons oil in a frying pan, add the red-in-snow and stir-fry over a high heat for 2½–3 minutes until crispy. Remove the red-in-snow, drain, and put aside. Heat the remaining oil in a frying pan, add the bamboo shoots, and stir-fry gently over a medium heat for 2 minutes, until all the shoots are well-covered in hot oil. Simmer for a further 5 minutes, turning them over occasionally, until the shoots have turned golden-brown. Drain away all the oil, or as much of it as possible. Return the red-in-snow to the pan, with the brown sugar, sherry, soy sauce, monosodium glutamate, and vegetarian stock. Turn the heat up to maximum, stir-fry quickly for 1 minute; then serve.

This is a connoisseur's dish which should be served in a plain, but artistic bowl, such as a Sung piece (or imitation), rather than one from the Ming or Ching dynasties.

Red-Cooked Szechuan-Style Bamboo Shoots

This is a non-vegetarian dish.

Preparation Soak the mushrooms for 30 minutes, remove the stalks and shred the tops. Remove the skin and excess fat from the bacon and chop it very finely. Chop the scallions and the bean sprouts into fine pieces. Cut off the root end of the bamboo shoots and remove the outer leaves. Use only the more tender spears. Slice them slantwise into segments 1¼–1½ inches long.

Cooking Heat the lard in a frying pan until it is quite hot. Add the bamboo shoots and stir-fry gently for 4 minutes. Drain away all the fat. Remove the shoots from the pan and put them aside. Replace the pan over the heat. Add the bacon and stir-fry vigorously over a high heat for 1 minute. Add the scallions, bean sprouts, and mushrooms, and stir-fry for 30 seconds. Return the bamboo shoots to the pan, add the soy sauce, chili sauce, sugar, and meat gravy, and continue to stir-fry gently over a medium heat for another 3 minutes. Blend the cornstarch and stock smoothly and pour the mixture into the pan. Turn and simmer for 3 minutes; then serve.

Serves 6–8, with other dishes

1½ lb bamboo shoots

4 Chinese dried mushrooms
¼ lb slab bacon
2 scallions
½ cup bean sprouts
6 tablespoons lard
1½ tablespoons soy sauce
2 teaspoons chili sauce
2 teaspoons sugar
¼ cup red-cooked meat gravy (see Index)
1½ tablespoons cornstarch
6 tablespoons chicken stock

Sweet and Sour Chinese Celery Cabbage

This is a vegetarian dish.

Preparation Remove the root and outer leaves from the cabbage. Cut the inner leaves crosswise into 1½ inch pieces. Cut the pepper in two and discard the seeds. Mix the vinegar, soy sauce, sherry, sugar, monosodium glutamate, and orange juice in a bowl. Blend the cornstarch with 3 tablespoons water and add to the mixture in the bowl.

Cooking Fry the pepper in the oil for 1 minute; then discard the pepper. Pour in the cabbage and stir-fry over a high heat for 2 minutes. Add the stock and salt. Reduce the heat to low and simmer for 5 minutes. Pour in the vinegar mixture. Stir-fry gently for 1–2 minutes, and serve in a deep dish or bowl.

Because of its sweet and sour quality, this is a good dish to serve with other rich foods. It is a favorite in Peking.

Serves 4–6, with other dishes

1½ lb Chinese celery cabbage *or* Savory cabbage

1 dried chili pepper
2½ tablespoons vinegar
1½ tablespoons soy sauce
2½ tablespoons dry sherry
2 tablespoons sugar
½ teaspoon monosodium glutamate
¼ cup orange juice
1½ tablespoons cornstarch
¼ cup vegetable oil
6 tablespoons vegetarian stock (see Index)
½ teaspoon salt

Red-Cooked Chinese Celery Cabbage

Serves 4–10, with other vegetarian
dishes

2½–3 lb Chinese celery cabbage *or*
Savoy cabbage

3 Chinese dried mushrooms
3¼ teaspoons soy sauce
2½ teaspoons sugar
½ teaspoon salt
¼ cup dry sherry
¼ teaspoon monosodium glutamate
6 tablespoons vegetarian stock (see
Index)
1 dried chili pepper
2 scallions
6 tablespoons vegetable oil

This is a vegetarian dish. Although cabbage is a common vegetable, this dish, made by the common people, is one of the most highly prized home-cooked dishes from Peking.

Preparation Soak the dried mushrooms; then shred them. Remove the coarser outer leaves from the cabbage. Cut the inner leaves crosswise into 1½ inch pieces. Wash, drain, and dry well. Mix the soy sauce, sugar, salt, and sherry in a bowl. In another bowl, blend the monosodium glutamate with the vegetarian stock. Chop the chili pepper into four pieces, removing the seeds. Chop the scallions into 1 inch pieces.

Cooking Put the oil in a large frying pan over a medium heat. Stir-fry the pepper and onions in it for 1½ minutes, then discard the pepper. Add the cabbage and mushrooms, and stir-fry over a medium heat for 5 minutes. Pour in the soy sauce mixture and stir-fry gently for 1 minute. Reduce the heat, and simmer gently for 10 minutes, turning the cabbage over a couple of times. Add the vegetarian stock mixture. Stir and turn over a few times more, allowing the gravy to thicken. Serve in a large bowl.

This is a dish which one does not tire of eating day after day.

White Braised Chinese Celery Cabbage

Serves 4–10, with other dishes

2½–3 lb Chinese celery cabbage *or*
Savoy cabbage

6 tablespoons vegetable oil
2 slices ginger root
¾ cup chicken stock
2 teaspoons salt
2 teaspoons sugar
1½ tablespoons shrimp
¼ cup white wine
¼ teaspoon monosodium glutamate
1 heaping tablespoon cornstarch
¾ cup milk
pepper to taste

This is a non-vegetarian dish.

Preparation Remove the root of the cabbage and cut away the outer leaves. Select the whiter leaves and cut them horizontally into two; then quarter each piece.

Cooking Heat the oil in a large saucepan. Add the ginger and cabbage, and turn them gently in the oil for 4 minutes. Discard the ginger. Add the stock, salt, sugar, the shrimp, wine, and monosodium glutamate. Bring to the boil and simmer, covered, over a low heat for 10 minutes. Take off the lid, turn the cabbage over a few times, replace the lid and simmer for a further 5 minutes. Blend the cornstarch and milk and pour the mixture into the pan. Bring to the boil, turn the ingredients over until the sauce thickens, and sprinkle with pepper. Serve in a bowl or tureen.

Coral Cabbage

This is another version of Sweet and Sour Cabbage, this time from the province of Shantung, where the people are very fond of piquant foods.

Preparation Remove the outer leaves from the cabbage. Cut the heart vertically into quarters, then slice into pieces 1½–2 inches long. Slice the bamboo shoots and sweet pepper into matchstick strips. Cut the chili pepper into four and remove the seeds.

Cooking Heat 2 quarts of water, add the salt, and bring to the boil. Plunge the cabbage into the boiling water for 5 minutes. Drain well, and arrange the cabbage in a nice, orderly pattern on a large serving dish. Heat the vegetable oil in a large frying pan. Add the chili pepper, sweet pepper, and bamboo shoots, and stir-fry over a high heat for 2 minutes. Add the soy sauce, sugar, vinegar, and tomato puree. Stir-fry over a medium heat and simmer for 2 minutes. Blend the cornstarch with ¼ cup water and add this mixture to the pan. Stir-fry until the liquid thickens. Scramble over a high heat for 2 seconds. Add the sesame oil, then pour the mixture over the cabbage as a hot dressing, and serve. This dish is best served immediately.

Serves 4–8

2 lb Chinese celery cabbage *or* Savoy cabbage

¼ cup bamboo shoots
1 red sweet pepper
1 dried chili pepper
1½ tablespoons salt
2½ tablespoons vegetable oil
2½ tablespoons soy sauce
2 tablespoons sugar
2½ tablespoons vinegar
2½ tablespoons tomato puree
2 teaspoons cornstarch
2½ teaspoons sesame oil

Braised Triple White

This is a popular, non-vegetarian dish from Chinese-Moslem cooking. Because of its color and lightness, it is often served to follow a red-cooked dish to provide contrast.

Preparation Cut the chicken meat into 1½ × ¼ inch strips. Dredge in ½ tablespoon cornstarch. Remove the coarser outer leaves of the cabbage and slice the asparagus lengthwise into two pieces. Then cut the asparagus into strips about 1½–2 inches long. Place the three ingredients on a plate, in separate piles. Slice the onion.

Cooking Heat the oil in a large frying pan. Stir-fry the ginger and onion over a high heat for 1 minute; then discard them. Put the asparagus into the pan and stir-fry quickly for 2 minutes. Push it to one side and add the cabbage and chicken, keeping them separate. Fry them over a medium heat for 1 minute; then turn them over to cook on the other side for the same length of time. Sprinkle with salt and pour in the stock. Bring to the boil; then simmer for 5 minutes. Blend the remaining cornstarch with the wine, milk, and monosodium glutamate. Pour the mixture evenly over the contents of the pan. Mix gently, and simmer for 1 minute.

Serves 4–8

3 oz (¼ cup) chicken breast meat
1 cup Chinese celery cabbage heart *or* celery
1 cup white asparagus

1½ tablespoons cornstarch
1 medium-sized onion
¼ cup vegetable oil
2 slices ginger root
1 teaspoon salt
¾ cup superior stock
2½ tablespoons white wine
½ cup milk
¼ teaspoon monosodium glutamate
dash of pepper
1½ tablespoons chicken fat

Lift the chicken, asparagus, and cabbage separately onto a wide, flat dish and put them in piles, close to each other. Sprinkle with pepper. Add the chicken fat to the sauce in the pan, heat quickly, and pour the sauce over the meat and vegetables. Serve immediately.

Silk-Thread Bamboo Shoots in Cream of Chicken

Serves 4–8, with other dishes

1½ lb fresh bamboo shoots *or* canned shoots
¼ cup chicken breast meat
1 cup chicken stock

1 oz (2 tablespoons) ham
1 oz (2 tablespoons) pork fat
2 egg whites
1½ tablespoons cornstarch
¼ teaspoon monosodium glutamate
1½ teaspoons salt
1½ tablespoons lard

This is a non-vegetarian dish.

Preparation Remove the outer leaves and coarser parts of the bamboo shoots. Using only the more tender parts, slice them into very fine matchstick strips. Chop the ham into fine pieces. Finely chop the chicken meat and pork fat together twice. Beat the egg whites in a bowl for 15 seconds. Add the cornstarch, monosodium glutamate, half of the salt, and half of the stock. Beat together for 15 seconds. Add the chopped chicken and pork to the egg and cornstarch mixture. Stir and beat until thoroughly blended.

Cooking Heat the remainder of the chicken stock in a saucepan. Add the bamboo shoots and cook over a medium heat until practically dry. Immediately add the lard and the remaining salt, and stir-fry gently for 1½ minutes, until all the strips of bamboo shoot are well-covered with oil. Pour the egg and minced meat mixture into the saucepan. Stir-fry gently for 2½ minutes. Serve on a well-heated plate, garnished with chopped ham or Fukien meat wool, if available.

Fu-Yung Cauliflower

This is a non-vegetarian dish. When minced chicken, egg white, and cornstarch are mixed together, the resulting highly savory, white, creamy mixture is called 'Fu-Yung' in north China. It is used extensively for cooking with various vegetables, including cauliflower.

Preparation Remove the root of the cauliflower and break it into small individual branches. Blanch them by dipping into boiling water for 5 minutes, drain, and put aside. Finely chop the chicken meat and mix it in a bowl with the egg whites, cornstarch, monosodium glutamate, half of the salt, and the chicken stock. Blend together into a smooth mixture.

Cooking Heat the oil in a frying pan. Add the pieces of cauliflower and sprinkle with the remaining salt, stir-fry gently for 2 minutes and remove from the pan. Pour the chopped chicken and egg white mixture into the pan. Mix and stir-fry for 2–3 minutes over a medium heat. As soon as the liquid thickens into a white sauce, return the cauliflower to the pan and stir-fry gently for a further 2 minutes. Serve on a well heated dish, garnished with chopped ham.

Serves 4–8, with other dishes

1 medium cauliflower

¼ lb chicken breast meat
2 egg whites
1½ tablespoons cornstarch
¼ teaspoon monosodium glutamate
¾ cup chicken stock
2 teaspoons salt
2½ tablespoons vegetable oil

Fu-Yung Heart of Mustard Greens

Preparation Remove the roots and outer leaves of the mustard greens. Quarter and slice the hearts and blanch them by dipping them in boiling water for 4 minutes. Finely chop the chicken meat and mix it in a bowl with the egg whites, cornstarch, monosodium glutamate, half of the salt, and the chicken stock. Blend together into a smooth mixture.

Cooking Heat the oil in a frying pan. Add the greens and sprinkle with the remaining salt. Stir-fry gently over a medium heat for 3 minutes and remove from the pan; then add chicken mixture and stir-fry gently for 30 seconds. Return the greens to the pan and stir-fry for 2½ minutes. Serve on a well-heated dish. Heat the chicken fat in a small saucepan and sprinkle it over the greens with a dash of pepper.

Serves 6–8, with other dishes

2 lb mustard greens

¼ lb chicken breast meat
2 egg whites
1½ tablespoons cornstarch
¼ teaspoon monosodium glutamate
2 teaspoons salt
¾ cup chicken stock
¼ cup vegetable oil
2 tablespoons chicken fat
dash of pepper

Sliced Sole in Braised Heart of Mustard Greens

This is a non-vegetarian dish. It is seldom that fish are cooked with greens, but here they are cooked together, resulting in a very successful combination.

Preparation Cut the fish into 2 × 1 inch pieces. Mix the salt with the cornstarch, self-rising flour, and egg whites, and beat into a batter. Dip the pieces of fish into the batter. Remove the roots and outer leaves of the greens. Slice each heart into quarters, and then into 2 inch lengths.

Serves 4–8, with other dishes

1½ lb fillet of sole
2 lb mustard greens to provide
    1–1¼ lb of hearts

1 teaspoon salt
1 tablespoon cornstarch
½ tablespoon self-rising flour
2 egg whites

2 tablespoons lard
1 slice ginger root
6 tablespoons chicken stock
2 teaspoons soy sauce
1 tablespoon white wine
¼ teaspoon monosodium glutamate
dash of pepper

Cooking Heat half of the lard in a frying pan and stir-fry the ginger for 1 minute. Add the stock and pan-fry (or poach) the slices of fish in it for 1 minute on either side. Remove the fish and drain. Add the remaining lard to the pan and stir-fry the greens for 2 minutes. Add the soy sauce and wine. Simmer for 1 minute over a moderate heat. Turn the greens over and simmer for another minute; then place them on a heat-proof dish and arrange the fish slices on top. Sprinkle with monosodium glutamate and pepper. Place the dish in a steamer and steam for 3–4 minutes; then serve.

Spinach Balls

Serves 4–8, with other dishes

1 lb fresh spinach

8 Chinese dried mushrooms
¾ lb bean curd
1 egg
1 teaspoon salt
¼ teaspoon monosodium glutamate
3 tablespoons cornstarch
½ cup bamboo shoots
1 tablespoon sesame oil
6 tablespoons vegetarian stock (see Index)
1½ teaspoons soy sauce
2½ tablespoons dry sherry
1½ tablespoons vegetable oil

This is a vegetarian dish.

Preparation Soak the mushrooms for 30 minutes, remove the stalks and chop the tops very fine. Beat the egg lightly. Mash the bean curd. Mix together the mashed bean curd, mushrooms, beaten egg, salt, monosodium glutamate, and cornstarch (2 tablespoons). Form the mixture into walnut-sized balls. Blanch the bamboo shoots for 3 minutes and the spinach for 30 seconds. Drain them thoroughly, and slice into strips about half the size of matchsticks. Spread the strips on a tray and roll the bean curd balls over the tray to pick up the strips.

Cooking Place the spinach-and-bamboo-shoot-covered balls on a heat-proof dish and steam vigorously for 10 minutes. Meanwhile, mix the sesame oil with the vegetarian stock, soy sauce, vegetable oil, sherry, and remaining cornstarch, blending well. Heat in a small pan for 2 minutes. As the mixture thickens and comes to the boil, pour it over the spinach balls, and serve immediately.

Dish of Harmony

Serves 4–8, with other dishes

1 cup corn, mashed
1 lb green peas, mashed
2½ cups chicken stock
2 teaspoons salt
pepper to taste
¼ teaspoon monosodium glutamate
1½ tablespoons chicken fat
1½ tablespoons butter
2½ tablespoons cornstarch

This is a non-vegetarian dish.

Cooking Place the corn and green peas in separate pans. Divide the chicken stock, salt, pepper, monosodium glutamate, chicken fat, and butter equally between the two pans. Bring to the boil and simmer over a medium heat for 5 minutes; then stir the peas and corn, and turn over a few times. Blend the cornstarch with ¼ cup water. Pour half of the cornstarch mixture into each pan and stir until the liquid thickens.

Serving Select a round, deep dish. Bend a sheet of aluminum foil, folded into three thicknesses, into an 'S' shape, to act as a partition across the middle of the dish. Pour the peas into one half of the dish and the corn into the other. Remove the partition and serve.

The 'S' line drawn across a perfect circle is the Chinese symbol for perfect harmony, hence the name of the dish. Peas and corn cooked in this manner are a useful complement to rice.

Vegetarian Toasted 'Shrimp'

Preparation Mash the bean curd; beat the egg. Blend the bean curd, egg, cornstarch, salt, monosodium glutamate, bean curd cheese, and sesame oil into a paste. Cut the crusts off the bread. Spread the mashed bean curd paste over the bread and sprinkle each piece with sesame seeds.

Cooking Heat some oil in a deep frying pan. When it is very hot, lower two pieces of bread at a time into the oil to fry for 3 minutes. Drain well after frying. While still very hot, use a sharp knife to slice each piece of bread into six. Arrange them on a well-heated dish and serve. If desired, decorate each piece of toasted 'shrimp' with a sprig of parsley.

Serves 4–6, with other dishes

2 cakes bean curd
1 egg
1½ tablespoons cornstarch
1 teaspoon salt
¼ teaspoon monosodium glutamate
1 teaspoon bean curd cheese
2 teaspoons sesame oil
4 slices bread
2½ tablespoons sesame seeds
vegetable oil for deep-frying

Vegetarian Spring Rolls

Make the Vegetarian Spring Roll skins according to the instructions given in the recipes for egg roll or spring roll skins (see Index). Alternatively, they can usually be bought nowadays from Chinese markets. The instructions given below are for the filling.

Preparation Soak the wood ears for 1 hour and rinse them in two changes of water. Soak the dried mushrooms for 30 minutes; then remove the stalks and shred the tops. Chop the bean curd into small pieces. Mash together the bean curd, bean curd cheese, salt, hoisin sauce, mushrooms, bamboo shoots, and wood ears. Use this mixture as a filling for the spring roll skins, rolling and sealing them in the manner described in the recipe.

Cooking When the spring rolls are sealed, place them in a wire basket and deep fry for 2 minutes over a high heat, followed by 2 minutes over a medium heat. They are usually served as snacks.

Serves 6

2 tablespoons wood ears
4 Chinese dried mushrooms
2 cakes bean curd
1 teaspoon bean curd cheese
½ teaspoon salt
2 teaspoons hoisin sauce
¼ cup bamboo shoots

Braised Mushrooms with Crackling Rice

Serves 4–8, with other dishes

12 large Chinese dried mushrooms
1 lb crackling rice

2 tablespoons bamboo shoots
2½ tablespoons sesame oil
2½ tablespoons soy sauce
1½ tablespoons vinegar
1 teaspoon sugar
1½ tablespoons dry sherry
1½ tablespoons hoisin sauce
2 teaspoons cornstarch
oil for deep-frying

This is a vegetarian dish.

Preparation Soak the mushrooms, remove the stalks, and shred the tops. Reserve ¼ cup of mushroom water. Shred the bamboo shoots. Crackling rice is generally obtained by scraping off the dried patches of rice which become stuck to the bottom of pans when large quantities of rice are cooked. These pieces of rice are then deep-fried until they turn brown. The same result can be achieved in a hot oven.

Cooking Heat the sesame oil in a frying pan. Add the bamboo shoots and mushrooms and stir-fry for 2 minutes over a medium heat. Add the soy sauce, vinegar, sugar, sherry, hoisin sauce, and mushroom water. When the mixture has simmered for 2 minutes, add the cornstarch, blended with 2 tablespoons water. Stir until the liquid thickens. Place the browned crackling rice in a wire basket and lower it into very hot oil to deep-fry for 1½ minutes. Drain quickly, and lay the crackling rice on a large, very well-heated dish. Bring the dish to the table and pour the braised mushrooms and sauce over the rice. The rice will crackle appealingly.

Sweet and Sour Lotus Roots

Serves 4–6, with other dishes

2 medium-sized fresh lotus roots

1½ tablespoons vegetable oil
2½ tablespoons sugar
1½ tablespoons soy sauce
¼ cup pineapple syrup (from a can)
2½ tablespoons vinegar
¾ tablespoon cornstarch

This is a vegetarian dish.

Preparation Clean the lotus roots thoroughly, by rubbing and scrubbing in three changes of water. Peel them, and cut them into ¼ inch thick slices. Blanch by dipping them in boiling water for 2 minutes. Drain well, then overlap the slices on a serving plate.

Cooking Heat the oil in a saucepan. Add the sugar, soy sauce, pineapple, syrup, vinegar, and cornstarch, blended with 3 tablespoons water. Stir until the liquid becomes a thick sauce; then pour it over the lotus root slices and serve.

Pan-Fried Pasted Tomatoes

Serves 6

6 firm medium-sized tomatoes

Preparation Finely chop the chicken, bacon, and shrimp and mix them together in a bowl. Add the salt, egg whites, and 1 tablespoon cornstarch, and blend into a smooth paste. Slice each tomato into four pieces horizontally, discarding the thinner top and bottom pieces. Spread a thick layer of the paste on top of the two middle slices from each tomato.

Cooking Heat the oil in a frying pan; then place the pieces of tomato, paste-side down, in the pan. Fry over a medium heat for 4 minutes. Turn the pieces over with a spatula and fry for 1 minute on the other side. Lift the pieces of tomato from the pan and arrange them on a flat, well-heated dish. Blend the remaining cornstarch with ¼ cup water, then mix in all the other ingredients. Pour this mixture into the frying pan and stir over a low heat until the liquid thickens into a thick sauce. Pour the sauce over the tomatoes, and serve.

2 oz (¼ cup) chicken breast meat
2 oz (¼ lb) slab bacon
2 oz (¼ cup) peeled shrimp
½ teaspoon salt
2 egg whites
2 tablespoons cornstarch
¼ cup vegetable oil
1½ tablespoons sugar
1½ tablespoons vinegar
1½ tablespoons soy sauce
1½ tablespoons dry sherry
2½ tablespoons orange juice

Pan-Fried Stuffed Cucumber

This is a type of treatment very similar to that described in the previous recipe, except that the cucumber segments are cut much more thickly and are actually stuffed with the paste. The sauce used here, however, is savory rather than sweet and sour.

Preparation Cut the ends of the cucumber, and slice the middle part into 1 inch segments. Scoop out ½ inch of each segment. Finely chop the bacon, chicken, and shrimp, and mix them in a bowl with 1 teaspoon salt, egg white, white wine, and 1½ teaspoons cornstarch. Blend into a smooth paste. Stuff 1 tablespoon of the paste into the excavated part of each piece of cucumber.

Cooking Heat the oil in a large, flat frying pan, ensuring that it is spread evenly over the surface. When it is hot, place all the pieces of cucumber, paste-side down, in the pan and fry for 4 minutes over a medium heat. Turn them over and fry the other side for 1 minute. Use a spatula to remove the pieces of stuffed cucumber from the pan. Arrange them on a well-heated serving plate. Heat the chicken stock in a small saucepan. Add the remaining salt, the remaining cornstarch, blended with the milk, and the monosodium glutamate. Stir until the liquid boils and thickens into a sauce. Pour this white sauce over the stuffed cucumbers, and serve.

Serves 4–6, with other dishes

1 large cucumber

3 oz (¼ lb) slab bacon
3 oz (¼ cup) chicken breast meat
2 oz (¼ cup) peeled shrimp
2 teaspoons salt
2 egg white
1½ tablespoons white wine
2 tablespoons cornstarch
6 tablespoons vegetable oil
1 cup chicken stock
6 tablespoons heavy cream
¼ teaspoon monosdium glutamate

Sweet and Sour Pickled Cucumber

Cut cucumber into ⅕ × 2½ inch strips. Combine vinegar, sugar, and soy sauce. Marinate cucumber strips in this mixture for 1 hour, then drain and serve.

Serves 4–6

1½ cups cucumber, unpeeled

2½ tablespoons vinegar
2½ tablespoons sugar
1½ tablespoons soy sauce

PORK

Pork is even more important to the Chinese than beef is to Americans. This is principally because of the greater versatility of pork—there is an almost inexhaustible number of ways in which it can be prepared in China.

Hence, while all other types of meat have to have the name of the animal affixed to them—such as bullock-meat (beef), sheep-meat (lamb or mutton), goat-meat, and deer-meat (venison)—pork is often just referred to as 'meat'. The amount of pork eaten in China probably outweighs all other meats several times over.

The Chinese feeling for pork probably differs somewhat from the average Western idea. The Westerner sometimes feels a certain aversion to the fat; we Chinese feel no such aversion. Perhaps because of the Chinese treatment of pork, the fat and skin are regarded almost as a kind of highly savory jelly, which is of great appeal when eaten with quantities of rice. Hence a good proportion of pork dishes are either long-simmered and lengthily steamed, or else pot-cooked (casseroled) over a low heat for several hours at a time. All these 'time-cooking' methods (as in time-exposure in photography) differ from instantaneous cooking such as stir-frying, because they are aimed at rendering the pork into a state of jelly-like tenderness.

On the other hand, because of the neutrality in the taste and flavor of pork, which is not unlike chicken (as opposed to the much stronger taste of lamb, beef, and venison), it can be successfully combined with an almost unlimited range of other materials and foodstuffs, whether they be vegetables, seafood, other meats, or various salted or pickled ingredients. Hence, apart from being cooked whole, pork is often cooked diced into cubes, cut into thin slices, shredded into threads, or chopped fine and made into cakes or balls. In all these latter forms (except the cakes and balls) the meat is usually cooked instantaneously by stir-frying—a process which is economical both in time and fuel consumption. With our Chinese propensity towards cross-cooking and cross-blending, and our natural sense of economy, the avenues which are opened to us here are many and inviting indeed.

Because of the comparative shortage of supply, it has always been an inherent necessity in China to combine meat with less expensive foodstuffs in order to produce the necessary bulk of dishes to go with the enormous quantity of rice which we consume. For it is only through cross-cooking and cross-blending that we are able to use just a small amount of meat to feed a large number of mouths, and yet provide each person with the feeling that he has consumed mouthful after mouthful of meaty food. Perhaps it was necessity that was, as usual, at the root of the Chinese inventiveness and variety.

At the other end of the scale, because of the considerable tradition of Chinese cooking derived from the Imperial kitchen, official entertainments, and the households of the rich, there are also many dishes which reach extremes of elaboration, and in the preparation of which neither the cost in time nor in materials used is counted. Some regard such dishes with reverence. To others, these are dishes more to talk about than to eat; they derive as much or more satisfaction in eating the simplest dishes. There are dishes of both types amongst the recipes which follow, but they are in the main pork dishes which are well-known and popular throughout China, although many of them vary considerably from one part of the country to another because of the differences in regional interpretation and emphasis.

Red-Cooked Fresh Ham

Red-cooking usually means stewing with soy sauce at a slow simmer, with the addition of such ingredients and flavorers as sugar, ginger, sherry, and star anise. It is one of the simplest as well as one of the most effective ways of cooking meat, with almost foolproof results. So long as the heat is kept low during the slow-simmering (the placing of an asbestos pad underneath the pan is recommended), one can hardly go wrong. There are so many ways and so many parts of the pig which can be red-cooked.

Preparation Score the skin of the ham by cutting several slashes along both sides.

Cooking Choose a heavy saucepan, heat-proof casserole, or iron pot. Pour in 3–4 quarts of water and bring to the boil. Place the ham in the water and boil for 7–8 minutes; then pour away all of the water. Sprinkle the ham with salt, half of the soy sauce, and half of the sherry. Pour in $\frac{3}{4}$ cup water, down the side of the pan. Insert an asbestos pad under the pan, or put the casserole into an oven preheated to 350°F. Keep the liquid at a slow simmer for 1 hour. Turn the ham over once and baste it with the liquid at the bottom of the pan.

Sprinkle the ham with the remainder of the soy sauce and sherry; then add the sugar, with 6 tablespoons water, and continue to cook at a low simmer. Turn the meat over after 15 minutes, and then twice, each time after a 30 minute interval. Baste the ham with the gravy in the pan every time it is turned over.

Serves 8–10, with other dishes

4–5 lb fresh uncured ham

$1\frac{1}{4}$ teaspoons salt
$\frac{1}{2}$ cup soy sauce
$\frac{1}{2}$ cup dry sherry
$1\frac{1}{2}$ tablespoons sugar

Serving Carve and serve in thick oblong slices, 1½ × 2 inches. Alternatively, carve and serve in large, thin slices measuring 2 × 3 inches. In each case, leave the skin attached to the slices of ham.

Ham cooked in this manner is usually extremely tender and rich. Although the meat is white, the skin and outside of the pork should be brownish red, and almost jelly-like in tenderness. The gravy from ham cooked in this way is almost the tastiest thing in the whole repertoire of Chinese cooking, and is absolutely heavenly to eat with rice.

Red-Cooked Pork in Pieces

Serves 6–8

3–3½ lb slab bacon

2 scallions
2 slices ginger root
¾ teaspoon salt
6 tablespoons soy sauce
6 tablespoons dry sherry
2 teaspoons sugar

Preparation Slice the bacon through the skin into 2–3 inch long pieces, making sure that each piece has about 1 square inch of skin attached on the top, and that each piece is composed of alternate layers of lean and fat. Cut the scallions into 1 inch segments, and shred the ginger. Rub the bacon with salt and 2 tablespoons of the soy sauce. Place in a heavy pan or casserole, skin side down, then pour in 6–8 tablespoons of water and half of the sherry. Sprinkle with the ginger and scallions.

Cooking Bring the contents of the pan to the boil, insert an asbestos pad beneath the pan, and reduce the heat to a low simmer. Simmer for 45 minutes, turning the pieces of pork once. Add another 6–8 tablespoons water. Sprinkle the bacon with the remainder of the sherry, sugar, and finally the soy sauce. Cover and allow the pork to simmer for a further hour, turning the pieces of meat over every 20 minutes.

Serving After a total of 1¾ hours cooking, the bacon and skin should be sufficiently tender to serve in a bowl or deep dish. It should be served skin side up. This is a favorite dish for a family meal.

Red-Stewed Pork

Serves 6–8

3 lb slab bacon, with skin attached

1 large onion
¼ cup vegetable oil
1¼ cups secondary stock
2 cloves star anise

This recipe from Peking is very similar to Red-Cooked Pork in Pieces, except that it involves frying before stewing, which is closer in concept to an American stew.

Preparation Cut the bacon through the lean and fat into 1 × 2 inch oblong pieces, leaving the skin attached at the top of each piece. Slice the onion thin.

Cooking Heat the oil in a heavy saucepan or heat-proof casserole. Add the bacon and onion, and stir-fry over a high heat for 5 minutes. Add the stock and all the other ingredients. When the liquid comes to the boil, reduce the heat to a minimum and put an asbestos pad under the pan. Alternatively, place the casserole in an oven preheated to 350°F. Cook at a very low simmer for 1½ hours, turning the meat over every 30 minutes.

Serving Serve the pork and gravy in a large bowl or deep dish. This is another favorite home-made dish.

1 piece Chinese dried tangerine peel
6 tablespoons soy sauce
¼ cup dry sherry
2½ teaspoons sugar

Pork of Original Preciousness

Preparation Boil the bacon in water for 15 minutes. Drain away the water; then paint both sides of the piece of bacon with a mixture of salt, soy paste, and 1 tablespoon of the soy sauce. Blend together the remainder of the soy sauce, the sherry, bean cheese, and sugar. Shred the ginger, and slice the onions very thin.

Cooking Heat the oil until it is about to smoke. Fry the bacon in it for 5–6 minutes. Remove from the oil and leave to cool. When cool, cut into fairly thick slices, 1 × 2 inch, each with some skin attached. Arrange the bacon in a heat-proof dish, skin side down. Spoon half of the soy/sherry mixture over the pork, scatter the onion and ginger over, and then sprinkle with the remaining soy mixture. Cover the dish securely with the lid or aluminum foil; then place in a steamer and steam for 1¼ hours. While the bacon is steaming, hard-boil the eggs, shell them, and simmer them in ¾ cup soy sauce for 5 minutes. They will take on a brown coloring. Five minutes before serving, cut the eggs in half and arrange them on the slices of pork in the heat-proof dish. Steam for a further 3 minutes; then serve from the heat-proof dish.

Serves 6–8

3 lb slab bacon, with skin attached

¾ teaspoon salt
1½ tablespoons soy paste
6 tablespoons soy sauce
¼ cup dry sherry
1½ teaspoons red bean cheese
¾ teaspoon brown sugar
2 slices ginger root
2 large onions
vegetable oil for deep-frying
3 eggs
¾ cup soy sauce

Pork of Original Preciousness with Noodles and Vegetables

This is a variation of the previous recipe. Use half the amount of pork and cook it the same way, with the same amount of ingredients, plus ¼ cup of water (to be added during the steaming). When the pork is almost ready, soak 8 oz (about 2 cups) transparent noodles in warm water for 5 minutes, and shred 1½ cups celery. Drain the noodles, and place them at the bottom of a heat-proof dish, then add the celery. Spoon the gravy from the pork over, and arrange the pieces of meat and egg on top. Place the dish in a steamer and steam for 10 minutes. Serve in the heat-proof dish.

Serves 6–8

Red-Steamed Pork

Serves 6–8

3 lb slab bacon, with skin attached

4 scallions
6 tablespoons soy sauce
1½ tablespoons soy paste
6 tablespoons dry sherry
1½ tablespoons sugar

Although the treatment of the pork in this dish from Soochow is somewhat different from the method used for Pork of Original Preciousness, the end result is fairly similar.

Preparation Cut the bacon through the lean and fat into 1 × 1½ × 2 inch pieces, leaving a piece of skin attached to each slice. Cut the scallions into 2 inch segments. Mix the soy sauce with the soy paste, sherry, and sugar until well-blended. Rub the pieces of bacon with the mixture and leave to marinate for 2 hours.

Cooking Arrange the bacon skin side down in a heat-proof dish. Pour in remaining marinade, and scatter the scallion segments on top. Place the dish in a steamer and steam for 2½ hours. Remove the scallions, and serve from the heat-proof dish.

Red-Cooked Round Pigs' Knuckle with Spinach

Serves 6–8, with other dishes

3 lb large pigs' knuckle with skin
1 lb fresh spinach

¾ teaspoon salt
6 tablespoons soy sauce
3 scallions
2 cloves garlic
2 slices ginger root
1½ teaspoons soy bean cheese
6 tablespoons vegetable oil
2½ tablespoons dry sherry
1½ tablespoons sugar

Preparation Clean the skin of the knuckle and remove any hairs. Cut the knuckle-end open half-way lengthwise and remove the bone. Rub the pork with salt and 2 tablespoons of the soy sauce. Cut the scallions into 1 inch segments. Crush the garlic, and shred the ginger. Mix them in a bowl with the soy bean cheese. Wash the spinach thoroughly, and drain.

Cooking Heat the oil in a frying pan. Turn and fry the knuckle in it for 5–6 minutes, until brown; then stuff the cavity with scallions and the garlic/ginger mixture. Sit the knuckle vertically in a round pot or deep heat-proof dish or casserole. Add the remaining soy sauce, sherry, sugar, and whatever is left of the sauce at the bottom of the frying pan. Pour in sufficient boiling water to cover the meat. Cover the dish securely with a lid or aluminum foil and place in an oven preheated to 400°F for 15 minutes. Reduce the heat to 350°F and simmer very gently for 3 hours, turning the knuckle over four times. It should finish with the smaller end pointing up. Five minutes before serving, pour 6–8 tablespoons of oil and gravy from the heat-proof dish into a large saucepan. Turn the heat up to full and when the liquid boils vigorously, add the spinach. Stir-fry for 4–5 minutes until well-cooked and glistening.

Serving Place the knuckle in a serving bowl or deep dish and arrange the spinach around it. Pour the remaining gravy over the knuckle. This small, brown mountain of glistening pork surrounded by a field of dark green is always one of the most appealing sights on a Chinese dinner table. (See illustration.)

Red-Cooked Pork with Chestnuts

Preparation Repeat the recipe for Red-Cooked Pork in Pieces (see page 124), but with the addition of about 1 lb shelled chestnuts. Skin the chestnuts and boil them for 15 minutes. Add them to the pan during the last 45 minutes of the simmering, with an additional 2½ tablespoons of soy sauce. Use the chestnuts as a base or bed for the pork when serving.

Serves 6–8

Red-Cooked Pork with Bamboo Shoots

Preparation Repeat the recipe for Red-Cooked Pork in Pieces (see page 124), but with the addition of about 1½ cups of bamboo shoots. If you use canned bamboo shoots, drain away all the liquid. Cut the bamboo shoots into triangular wedges, similar in size to the pieces of pork, and add them to the pan during the last 45 minutes of simmering.

Serves 6–8

Red-Cooked Pork with Carrots

Preparation Repeat the recipe for Red-Cooked Pork in Pieces (see page 124) with the addition of 1½ cups of well-scrubbed carrots, cut slantwise into triangular wedges about 1½ inches long. Add them to the pan during the last hour of simmering.

Serves 6–8

Red-Cooked Pork with Dried Squid and Golden Needles

Dried squid is used widely in Chinese cooking, particularly in red-cooked dishes, to flavor meat. It has a half-cheesy, half-smoked flavor. Golden needles are also a very typical Chinese dried vegetable ingredient, and are used in a wide number of dishes—both meat and vegetable. Appreciation of their taste, which can only be described as moldy, is entirely acquired, and they generally have no appeal to the Western palate. They are regarded by the Chinese as an essential and traditional ingredient for many dishes.

Serves 6–8

Preparation Both golden needles and dried salted squid should be soaked in warm water for 45 minutes before being added to the pork for the last 45 minutes simmering. Repeat the recipe for Red-Cooked Pork in Pieces (see page 124), with ½ cup of golden needles, and about ½ cup dried squid. They will produce a flavor and savoriness which are unique, and which are capable of inducing near-addiction if indulged in for any period of time, especially when eaten with quantities of rice and gravy.

Red-Cooked Pork with Abalone

Serves 6–8

Abalone (or awabi) is a rubbery textured seafood with a strong savory taste. It enhances the savoriness of meat dishes, and is therefore very useful in flavoring soups and stews. It is normally available either dried or canned, and is sold in most Chinese shops, usually shaved into thin slices. It will only need to be soaked if it is to be combined with other foods in quick-fried cooking. For dishes with gravy or soup which are cooked for a longer time, the abalone should be added either in the last stages or at the very beginning (like beef, abalone has the tendency to quickly become hard when cooked, unless it is cooked for a very long period of time).

Preparation Use one small can of abalone and repeat the recipe for Red-Cooked Pork in Pieces (see page 124). When adding the sugar, remainder of the sherry, and the soy sauce for the last 45 minutes simmering, also add half of the abalone water from the can, and 2–3 minutes before serving, add the abalone, which should be cut into very thin 1½ × 1 inch slices.

The flavor of the abalone has the same strong savory appeal as that of dried squid, albeit probably stronger. This meat/fish or meat/seafood combination is particularly popular among the inhabitants of the coastal areas south of the Yangtze River.

White-Cooked Pork with Anchovy

In contrast to red-cooked pork, seafoods and salted fish can also be cooked with white-cooked meat, without the use of soy sauce.

Preparation Cut the bacon through the skin into $2\frac{1}{2} \times 1\frac{1}{2} \times 1$ inch oblong pieces, leaving skin attached at one end of each piece. Sprinkle and rub with salt. Shred the ginger and sprinkle over the bacon. Cut the scallions into 1 inch segments.

Cooking Arrange the bacon, skin side down, in a heavy pan, and add $1\frac{1}{4}$ cups water. Bring to a gentle boil, insert an asbestos pad under the pan, and allow the contents to simmer gently for 45 minutes. Remove the bacon from the pan and re-arrange in a heat-proof dish, skin side up. Scatter the anchovy and scallions evenly over the pork, and pour any remaining stock from the pan over the meat. Cover the dish with the lid or aluminum foil, and steam for 1 hour.

Serving Bring the heat-proof dish to the table and serve with rice.

This dish has unique appeal to those who are accustomed to the taste of fish-impregnated meat.

Serves 8–10, with other dishes

3 lb slab bacon
2 tablespoons canned anchovy

$2\frac{1}{2}$ teaspoons salt
2 slices ginger root
3 scallions

Singed Simmered Fresh Ham

This dish appears to have been of Chinese Moslem origin, derived from the great grasslands of northwest China. It is very popular in Peking, but little known in the south.

Preparation Clean and skewer the ham.

Cooking Turn it over a large, brisk, charcoal fire for 8–10 minutes, until the outer skin starts to blister and turn golden-brown, even burned in some places. Plunge the ham into cold water for 10 minutes; then drain, and scrape off the burned parts. Heat 4 quarts water in a large pan. When it starts to boil, put the pork into the pan and simmer gently for 1 hour; then strain, and let it cool for 2–3 hours. Slice the meat thin into 2 × 3 inch lean and fat pieces.

Serving Arrange the ham slices in overlapping layers on a large dish. Serve the following condiments to enable diners to prepare their own dips and mixes:

    Soy sauce, soy paste, mustard powder, chili oil, sesame oil, chopped chives (or scallions), shredded ginger root, crushed and chopped garlic, vinegar, and sherry.

Note One of the distinctive features of Chinese Moslem cooking, originating from the vast plains and plateaus of the north-west, is that most meats are cooked plain, and all the flavoring is done at the table by the diners themselves.

Serves 10–12, with other dishes

5–6 lb fresh uncured ham, with
    skin attached

15 cups water

Steamed Fresh Ham

Serves 6–10, with other dishes

2–3 lb fresh uncured ham

2½ tablespoons sugar
6 tablespoons dry sherry

Sugar and sherry are added to give even ordinary ham a sweetened flavor.

Preparation and Cooking Place ham in a heat-proof dish and steam for 1 hour; then brush with a mixture of sherry and sugar, and steam for 30 minutes. Turn over, and brush again with the sherry-sugar mixture, and steam for a further 30 minutes. Pour the remaining sherry-sugar mixture over the ham, and steam for a final 30 minutes.

Serving Cut the ham into fairly thick slices, and then cut these into double Mah-jong-size pieces.

White-Cooked Sliced Pork

Serves 8–10

3 lb slab bacon *or* ham

1½ tablespoons salt
4 slices ginger root

This dish is fairly similar to Singed Simmered Fresh Ham, but is a simpler and more widely used version, popular throughout China.

Cooking Bring 10 cups of water to the boil in a heavy sauce-pan or casserole. Place the bacon in the boiling water; add the salt and ginger. Cover the pan, insert an asbestos pad under it, and simmer gently for 45 minutes. Remove the bacon from the pan (reserve the stock for other uses) and cool for 2–3 hours. When cold, cut the meat into thin slices measuring 2 × 3 inches.

Serving Arrange the slices in overlapping rows, and serve with various table dips:
> Soy sauce, soy paste, mustard powder, chili oil, sesame oil, chopped chives (or scallions), shredded ginger root, crushed and chopped garlic, vinegar, and sherry.

Barbecued Pork (Cantonese Roast Pork)

Serves 10–12, with other dishes

4 lb lean pork

This dish is easily cooked, and should appeal to Americans.

Preparation Slice the pork along the grain into 5 × 2 inch strips. Sprinkle and rub with salt, pepper, and five spice powder; season for 2 hours.

Cooking Mix the oil, soy sauce, hoisin sauce, sherry, honey, and monosodium glutamate until well-blended, and heat in a frying pan. Add the strips of pork and turn in the sauce until they take on a thick, glossy brown coating. Preheat the oven to 400°F. Place the strips of pork on a rack, and roast for 12 minutes, then turn meat once more in marinade. Lower the heat to 350°F and roast for a further 20 minutes.

Serving Slice the pork across the grain (that is, across the strips into $\frac{1}{4}$–$\frac{1}{3}$ inch thick slices and arrange in four rows on a serving dish.

Although often called Barbecued Pork, it is in fact the Cantonese version of roast pork, and is more popular in Canton than anywhere else. In Chinese restaurants abroad, it is often served with a sauce which rather spoils the effect of the tender roast pork inside a rich brown savory crust.

$2\frac{1}{2}$ teaspoons salt
$\frac{1}{2}$ teaspoon freshly ground pepper
$\frac{1}{2}$ teaspoon five spice powder
$\frac{1}{4}$ cup vegetable oil
$2\frac{1}{2}$ tablespoons soy sauce
$1\frac{1}{2}$ tablespoons hoisin sauce
$2\frac{1}{2}$ tablespoons dry sherry
$1\frac{1}{2}$ tablespoons honey
$\frac{1}{4}$ teaspoon monosodium glutamate

Tip Out Steamed Pork

Tip Out Steamed Pork is one of the basic ways in which pork is cooked in China. It is very similar to the way in which many English puddings are made—prepared and cooked in a greased casserole, and then tipped out into a dish before being covered with custard or syrup. In this case bacon is cut with the skin attached, and steamed, skin side down, in a heat-proof casserole, with a number of supplementary and flavoring ingredients. When ready, the bacon is tipped out like a pudding with the skin side facing up. The jelly-like skin is delicious to eat, and is the major attraction of the dish. The bacon is usually boiled and fried shortly before being packed into the dish for steaming. There are many variations of this method. The following recipe is one of the most basic. In Szechuan, the dish is made hotter by some chili pepper or oil during the steaming.

Preparation Boil the bacon in one piece in boiling water for 15 minutes. Drain, and rub with salt and 2 tablespoons of the soy sauce; then heat the oil in a pan, and fry the bacon, turning it over, for 6–8 minutes over medium heat. Drain; cool; then cut the bacon into 2 × 1 inch chunks, making sure that each piece has some skin attached. Slice the onions thin, and shred the picked greens.

Cooking Arrange the bacon, skin side down, at the bottom of a heat-proof dish. Add the sugar, hoisin sauce, sherry, pickled greens, onion, monosodium glutamate, and remaining soy sauce to the stock, and heat, stirring until well-blended. Pour the mixture evenly over the bacon in the dish, then place the

Serves 10–12, with other dishes

4 lb slab bacon

$1\frac{1}{2}$ teaspoons salt
6 tablespoons soy sauce
oil for semi deep-fry
1 large onion
$\frac{1}{4}$ cup red-in-snow pickled greens
2 teaspoons sugar
$1\frac{1}{2}$ tablespoons hoisin sauce
$\frac{1}{4}$ cup dry sherry
$\frac{1}{4}$ teaspoon monosodium glutamate
$\frac{3}{4}$ cup superior stock

dish in a steamer and steam for 1¼ hours. Turn the dish over into a deep serving dish, so that the meat will stand like a small meat pudding with the skin side on top. It is for this reason the dish came to be called 'tip out meat'.

Note In China, it is often the practice to place potato, turnip, bean curd cakes, transparent noodles, and chopped, salted vegetables on top of the meat during steaming. When the contents are tipped out, these materials become the base of the pork, and help to absorb the gravy.

Kweichow 'Salt and Sour' Tip Out Pork

Serves 8–10, with other dishes

3½–4 lb slab bacon

2 slices ginger root
3 tablespoons hot Szechuan pickled greens
2½ tablespoons sweet chutney
oil for deep-frying
2½ tablespoons soy sauce
2½ tablespoons vinegar
1½ tablespoons sugar
2½ tablespoons dry sherry
2½ teaspoons salt

This dish is a variation of Tip Out Steamed Pork. Kweichow is a western province, where dishes are often hot, salty, and sour—straightforward basic qualities of food for the poor, which nowadays often appeal to jaded and sophisticated palates.

Preparation Shred ginger and chop Szechuan pickled greens and chutney into small pieces.

Cooking Boil the piece of bacon in water for 5–6 minutes; drain. Deep-fry for 5–6 minutes; then drain and cut with a sharp knife into 2 × 1½ × 1 inch pieces, each with skin attached. Place ginger in a bowl with soy sauce, vinegar, half of the sugar, and sherry. Place the Szechuan pickle and chutney in a separate bowl. Pack the pieces of bacon, skin side down, in a heat-proof dish. Sprinkle with salt and the remaining sugar, and pour the soy/vinegar/sherry mixture evenly over the bacon. Arrange the chutney and pickle on top of the pork. Place the dish in a steamer, cover with aluminum foil, and steam for 1½ hours. Tip out, and serve as Tip Out Steamed Pork.

Diced Pork Cubes Quick-Fried with Soy Paste

The texture and quality of pork meat are not unlike those of chicken. Consequently, it is often cooked in the same way—in this case, with soy paste. The only difference is that the time taken for cooking pork must be longer. This dish, which is very economical both in ingredients and fuel, makes a highly savory meal.

Preparation Soak the pork in water and refrigerate for 30 minutes; then cut into ½ inch cubes. Beat half of the egg in a bowl, add the pork cubes, mix with the egg, then sprinkle with cornstarch. Shred the ginger, and chop the onion.

Cooking Heat the oil in a frying pan. When it is very hot, add the pork cubes, stir-fry for 4–5 minutes; then drain. Heat 2 tablespoons oil in a separate frying pan over medium heat. Add the ginger and onion, and stir-fry for 1½ minutes at the center of the pan. Add the soy paste and stir it with the oil, ginger, and onion for 1 minute before adding the sugar and sherry. Stir them together with the other ingredients for 8–10 seconds, pour in the pork cubes, turn the heat to high, and scramble the pork with the other ingredients for 1½ minutes before serving in a well-heated dish.

Note If soy jam is unavailable, mix ¼ cup soy sauce with 1 tablespoon tomato pureé, 1 tablespoon blackcurrant jam, and 1 tablespoon apple sauce. Heat and stir over a gentle heat until the mixture is reduced by about one third.

Serves 6–8, with other dishes

2 lb boneless pork
3 tablespoons soy paste
1 egg
2 tablespoons cornstarch
2 slices ginger root
1 small onion
½ cup oil for frying
2½ teaspoons sugar
1½ tablespoons dry sherry

Sweet and Sour Pork

This is a favorite southern Cantonese dish, and as most Chinese restaurants in America are Cantonese, it is likely that more Sweet and Sour Pork is cooked and eaten in America today than in Canton itself. For some unknown reason, the Western palate seems to take more readily to this Chinese dish than to any other.

Preparation Remove the skin from the bacon and dice into ¾ inch cubes; then sprinkle and rub with salt. Beat the egg lightly and add to the bacon. When the meat is thoroughly wet, dredge with flour. Slice the onion very thin; cut the sweet pepper into thick slices, and then cut these slantwise into approximately 1 × ½ inch pieces. Mix the soy paste with the soy sauce. For the sauce, blend the cornstarch with half of the water, then mix in rest of ingredients.

Cooking Either deep-fry the bacon or use 6 tablespoons oil and semi-deep fry it in a frying pan for 5–6 minutes, by stir-frying it over a high heat. Drain thoroughly and place the meat in a

Serves 6–8, with other dishes

2–2½ lb slab bacon

1½ teaspoons salt
1 egg
2 tablespoons cornstarch
1 medium-sized onion
1 medium-sized green or red sweet pepper
2 tablespoons soy paste
1 tablespoon soy sauce
oil for deep frying

Sauce

1½ tablespoons cornstarch
5–6 tablespoons water
1½ tablespoons sweet chutney
2 tablespoons sugar
2 tablespoons vinegar
2 tablespoons soy sauce
1½ tablespoons tomato puree
2 tablespoons orange juice
2 tablespoons dry sherry

bowl. Add the soy sauce/paste mixture; mix and marinate the pork for a few minutes. Drain the excess oil from the frying pan, and use the remaining oil to stir-fry the onion for 1 minute over medium heat; then add the sliced sweet pepper and stir-fry for another minute. Add the bacon, and stir and toss for 2 minutes. Pour in the sauce mixture; then turn bacon and pepper in the sauce gently until the liquid thickens (this should take 10–15 seconds) and gives a translucent, glistening coating to the pieces of pork.

The contrast between the sweet and sour coating and the salty savoriness of the pork inside gives the dish its special appeal.

Twice-Cooked Pork

Serves 6–8, with other dishes

3 lb slab bacon

3 cloves garlic
2 slices ginger root
1½ tablespoons salted black beans
3 scallions
2 tablespoons soy sauce
2 tablespoons soy paste
2 tablespoons tomato puree
2½ teaspoons sugar
2½ tablespoons dry sherry
1½ teaspoons chili oil (or 2½ teaspoons Tabasco sauce)
¼ cup vegetable oil

Although this dish comes from the western province of Szechuan, it is popular throughout China.

Preparation Crush and chop the garlic, shred the ginger, and soak the black beans in water for 25 minutes, then drain. Cut the scallions into 1 inch segments. Mix the soy sauce, soy paste, tomato puree, sugar, sherry, and chili oil until well-blended.

Cooking Place the bacon in boiling water and simmer for 35 minutes. Drain thoroughly. When cool, cut it across the lean and fat into pieces ¼ inch thick, 2 inches broad, and 2 inches long. Heat the oil in a frying pan for 1 minute. Add the black beans; stir-fry for ½ minute. Add the soy/tomato/sherry/sugar/chili mixture, and mix well with the oil and other ingredients into a sauce-paste. Finally, add the pieces of bacon and the scallions. Turn the pork in the saucepan for 2–3 minutes until every piece is covered, and serve on a well-heated dish.

Pork of Four Happiness

This is another fairly simple way of cooking pork. It is derived from east China, and carries with it its local flavor—an inclination to use sugar with savoriness.

Preparation Cut the onion into thin slices, and crush the garlic.

Cooking Cut the bacon into six pieces of approximately the same size. Place them in a saucepan, add the salt, and just cover with water. Bring to the boil and simmer for 20 minutes. Remove and drain the bacon, and skim the liquid of all impurities and oil. When cool, cut the bacon through the skin into thin 2 × 1½ inch slices. Place the ginger, tangerine peel, onion, and garlic in a thick-bottomed, heavy saucepan or casserole. Lay the pieces of pork on top, add the soy paste, soy sauce, and sugar, and pour in half of the skimmed stock. Bring to the boil, put an asbestos pad under the pan, and simmer gently for 1½ hours.

Serving The pork should be served in a bowl or tureen, or in the casserole in which it was cooked. Being well-spiced, and of jelly-like tenderness (especially the skin and fat), and having ample gravy, it is popular with rice eaters.

Serves 6–8, with other dishes

3½ lb slab bacon, with skin attached

1 large onion
2 cloves garlic
1½ teaspoons salt
5 slices ginger root
1 piece Chinese dried tangerine peel
1½ tablespoons soy paste
¼ cup soy sauce
2 tablespoons sugar

Tung-Po Pork

This recipe is attributed to the Chinese classical romantic poet, Soo Tung-Po. Although it is not very different from other red-cooked dishes, it deserves a separate mention because of its fame and universal popularity.

Preparation Boil the bacon for 10 minutes, and cut it through the skin into four pieces of equal size. Marinate the meat in a mixture of soy sauce, sugar, and sherry for 2 hours, turning the pieces over four times. Cut the onions into thick slices.

Cooking Arrange the pieces of bacon in a casserole, skin side down. Pour any remaining marinade over the meat, place the ginger and onion on top, then add the stock. Cover, and place the casserole in an oven preheated to 400°F and cook for 15 minutes; then reduce the temperature to 350°F and cook the pork for 2 hours. Open the lid of the casserole, and transfer the pork to a heat-proof dish. Arrange three pieces at the bottom of the dish, skin side down, and the fourth piece on top with the skin side up. Remove the ginger and onion, skim the excess fat from the gravy and pour it over the pork. Cover securely with the lid or a sheet of aluminum foil, and steam the bacon vigorously for 10–15 minutes before bringing the dish to the table to serve.

The enjoyment of this dish lies in the appreciation of the jelly-like texture of the skin and fat, and the tenderness of the lean meat. This is perhaps a connoisseur's taste, but essential to the full enjoyment of a Chinese meal with rice.

Serves 6–8, with other dishes

3½ lb slab bacon with at least 3 layers of lean and fat, and skin

6 tablespoons soy sauce
2 tablespoons brown sugar
6 tablespoons dry sherry
3 medium-sized onions
½ cup superior stock

Chinese Pork Scallop

Serves 6–8, with other dishes

3 lb slab bacon with at least 3
layers of lean and fat, and skin

6 tablespoons soy sauce
¼ cup dry sherry
2 tablespoons brown sugar
1 tablespoon bay leaves
½ cup carrots
½ cup radishes
1 tablespoon salt
1½ tablespoons sugar
2 tablespoons vinegar
1½ tablespoons sesame oil
2 duck eggs
½ cup breadcrumbs
oil for deep frying

From Amoy

In the province of Fukien where Amoy is situated, there is a well-known feast called the Whole Pig Banquet, in which a whole pig is used to make 108 dishes. This is one of them.

Preparation Boil the bacon for 7–8 minutes; then drain. Cut through the skin into strips of approximately 3 oz each, making sure that each has lean, fat, and skin. Marinate strips in a mixture of soy sauce, sherry, brown sugar, and bay leaves for 1½ hours, turning the meat over three times. Shred the carrots and radishes into a colander and rub salt into them. After 10 minutes, rinse them in running water. Drain, then dry on paper towels, and place in a bowl. Sprinkle with sugar, vinegar, and sesame oil, and toss them together as a salad.

Cooking Place the bowl of marinated bacon in a steamer and steam for 45 minutes. Remove and cool. When the pork is quite cold and solid, break the eggs into a bowl, beat lightly, and then wet each piece of pork with the beaten egg. Dredge the pieces of meat in breadcrumbs until completely covered. Heat the oil in a deep-fryer and deep-fry the bacon—three or four pieces at a time—for about 3½ minutes each, until golden brown. Cut each piece of bacon vertically down through the skin into three slices (each piece a little bigger than a Mahjong piece).

Serving Pile the shredded vegetables in the middle of a round dish, and surround them with the breadcrumb-encrusted pieces of pork.

Red-Simmered Fresh Ham with Bean Curd Cheese

Serves 6–8, with other dishes

1½ lb lean fresh uncured ham
1½ lb slab bacon
2 tablespoons red bean curd cheese

2 cloves garlic
¼ cup dry sherry
1½ tablespoons soy sauce
1½ tablespoons sugar
6 tablespoons vegetable oil
1¼ cup superior *or* secondary stock
1 tablespoon sesame oil
¼ teaspoon monosodium glutamate

Preparation Cut the ham and bacon into 1½ inch cubes. Crush the garlic; mash the cheese and blend with the sherry, soy sauce, and sugar.

Cooking Heat the oil in a heavy saucepan or casserole. Add the garlic, and stir-fry for 15 seconds. Add the bacon, turn the heat to maximum, and stir-fry the meat for 4–5 minutes until it starts to brown. Pour out any excess fat, and pour in the cheese/sherry/soy/sugar mixture. Stir the pieces of bacon in this for 1½ minutes and pour in the stock. When it comes to the boil, cover, place an asbestos pad under the pan, and simmer very gently for 1½ hours. Stir sesame oil and monosodium glutamate into the gravy; then serve.

This is another dish suitable for serving with rice. It derives its distinction from the special flavor of the bean curd cheese.

Red-Cooked Pork Chops

This attractive dish can be quickly and easily prepared.

Preparation Heat oil in a large frying pan. Fry three chops in it at a time, for 2 minutes on either side. Remove and drain, but keep the remaining oil in the pan to fry the spinach. Wash the spinach thoroughly, and remove all tough stems. Crush the garlic.

Cooking Place the ginger at the bottom of a heavy pan or casserole, arrange the pork chops in a single layer on top, sprinkle them with sherry and soy sauce, and add the stock, pouring it into the pan from both sides. Bring to the boil, then place the casserole in an oven preheated to 375°F and simmer gently for 30 minutes. Turn the chops, and simmer for a further 30 minutes. Five minutes before the chops are cooked, heat the oil which was used for frying them. When it is very hot, add the garlic and then the spinach, sprinkle with salt, and turn in the oil until well-lubricated and somewhat softened. Stir-fry for another 3 minutes.

Serving Line a well-heated serving dish with the spinach. Arrange the chops on top. Heat the remaining gravy in the casserole, with the sesame oil and monosodium glutamate, stir for 30 seconds, and pour over the chops.

Serves 6

6 pork chops

½ cup vegetable oil
1 lb spinach
2 cloves garlic
2 slices ginger root
6 tablespoons dry sherry
6 tablespoons soy sauce
¾ cup superior *or* secondary stock
1½ teaspoons salt
2½ teaspoons sesame oil
¼ teaspoon monsodium glutamate

Braised Curried Fresh Ham with Potato

Preparation Cut ham into ¾ inch cubes. Peel the potatoes and chop them into pieces of about the same size. Slice the onion thin. Heat the oil, deep-fry the pork for 6–7 minutes; then put aside to drain. Deep-fry the potatoes for 3–4 minutes and set aside to drain.

Cooking Heat 3 tablespoons oil in a saucepan. Stir-fry the ginger, onion, and salt for 2 minutes. Remove the ginger and discard. Add the curry powder and stir-fry for another 2 minutes. Add the pieces of pork, and stir-fry them with the curried ingredients for 2 minutes. Pour in the stock and soy sauce, add the potato, and bring to the boil. Turn the contents over a few times, reduce the heat to low and simmer gently for 30 minutes.

Although curry is not of Chinese origin, it has great appeal as an accompaniment to rice.

Serves 6–8, with other dishes

2 lb fresh uncured ham
2 lb potatoes
2 tablespoons curry powder

1 medium-sized onion
oil for deep-frying
2 slices ginger root
2½ teaspoons salt
1½ cups secondary stock
2½ tablespoons soy sauce

Red-Braised Pork Chops

Serves 6–8

6 pork chops

2 medium-sized onions
3 scallions
2 cloves garlic
3 slices ginger root
6 tablespoons soy sauce
¼ cup dry sherry
1 heaping tablespoon sugar
pepper to taste
½ cup vegetable oil
½ cup superior *or* secondary stock
2 tablespoons hoisin sauce

The principal differences between this dish and Red-Cooked Pork Chops are that the cooking time is much shorter, and more ingredients are used in the marinating and cooking.

Preparation Slice the onions thin and cut the scallions into 2 inch segments. Crush the garlic and shred the ginger. Cut the bones out of the chops, and cut the meat into pieces 1½ inches square. Sprinkle with garlic, ginger, onion, soy sauce, sherry, sugar, and pepper. Rub them into the pork, and leave to marinate for 1 hour, turning the meat over twice. Pour the remaining marinade into a bowl.

Cooking Heat the oil in a frying pan with a lid over a high heat. Fry the pieces of pork for approximately 3½–4 minutes on either side, until they begin to brown. Pour away any excess oil. Add all the marinating ingredients, the remaining marinade, and the ½ cup of stock; place the lid securely on the pan, and simmer for 15 minutes, turning the meat pieces over a few times—the liquid should be reduced to less than half. Scatter the scallion segments over the pork, pour in the hoisin sauce, turn the heat to high, and stir-fry quickly for 1 minute more.

This dish should be served very hot on a bed of rice.

Toasted Gold Coin Fresh Ham

Serves 6–8, with other dishes

1½ lb round piece fresh uncured ham
8 oz pork fat

2 tablespoons sugar
¼ cup dry sherry
8 Chinese steamed buns (or Man Tou buns)
2½ tablespoons lard

Preparation and Cooking Mix the sugar with the sherry into a smooth blend. Brush ham with the mixture. Steam for 30 minutes, turn meat over, brush and steam again for 30 minutes, and then repeat. Steam the buns for 10 minutes. Cut each piece into slices as thick as a very thin slice of bread; slice the ham similarly, and cut the fat into slices about a quarter as thick. Place a piece of fat on each piece of ham, brush with the sugar-sherry mixture, then with melted lard, and then skewer them through the center like a kebab. Put five or six ham/fat combinations on each skewer, and either toast under the broiler, or bake on a rack in an oven pre-heated to 400°F for 10–12 minutes. Grill the sliced buns until well-toasted.

Serving As soon as they are ready, pull the ham and fat combinations off the skewers, and arrange them, one on top of each other, with ham and fat alternating, until they rise like a tower of gold coins. The toasted buns should be arranged in four smaller piles around the Gold Coins. Eat in sandwich fashion, by placing a piece of ham and fat between two pieces of toasted bun. Plum Sauce, Sweet and Sour Sauce, hoisin sauce, and mustard can all be brushed on the ham to enhance piquancy and flavor if desired.

Drunken Fresh Ham

Like chicken, pork can be prepared 'drunken'. It makes a very good cold hors d'œuvre.

Preparation Cut ham into six pieces. Crush the garlic, and cut the scallions into 1 inch segments.

Cooking Heat 5 cups (generous liter) water in a saucepan. Add the pork, scallions, garlic, ginger, salt, and pepper. Bring to the boil and simmer gently for 35 minutes; then allow to cool for several hours. When cold, drain the ham (reserve the stock for other uses), and refrigerate overnight. Cut each piece of ham into four. Place them in a jar and cover with dry sherry. Cover tightly and place in the refrigerator for 2–5 days.

Serving When ready to use, drain each piece of pork and slice into ⅛ inch thick slices. Arrange in overlapping rows on a serving dish, and accompany with salted radishes and pickled cucumbers.

Serves 6–8, with other dishes

3 lb fresh uncured ham

3 cloves garlic
4 scallions
3 slices ginger root
2½ tablespoons salt
½ teaspoon freshly ground black
  pepper
dry sherry

Herbal-Master-Stock-Simmered Fresh Ham

Preparation and Cooking Plunge the ham into a saucepan of boiling water to simmer for 7–8 minutes; then drain. Heat stock in a heavy pot or casserole. Add ham and bring to boil; then set asbestos pad under the pan and simmer gently for 1 hour. Add eggs during the last 30 minutes' simmering. Leave for 1½ hours to cool.

Serving Drain the ham (keep stock for other uses) and eggs. Cut the eggs into quarters and slice the pork thin (approximately ⅛ inch thick). Arrange the pork in overlapping slices surrounded by egg wedges.

Note If soy-herbal-master stock is not readily available, use 2½ cups soy sauce, 2½ cups dry sherry, 6 slices ginger, 4 cloves garlic (crushed), 3 cloves star anise, ½ teaspoon five spice powder, 1 teaspoon peppercorns, ¼ cup brown sugar, 2 medium-sized onions (chopped). Mix together, and simmer very gently for 40 minutes.

Serves 8–10

4 lb ham
10 cups (generous 2 liters) soy-
  herbal master stock
6 hard-boiled eggs

Roast Pork

Serves 8

3–4 lb shoulder of pork

2 cloves garlic
6 tablespoons soy sauce
1 teaspoon salt
6 tablespoons dry sherry
1½ tablespoons brown sugar
1 medium onion

In China, roast pork (or roast suckling pig) is usually marinated first before roasting—or it can be brushed with marinade a few times during roasting. The marinade used can be blended from a large choice of ingredients, but the most popular and easily made marinade is a simple mixture of soy sauce, sherry, and brown sugar.

Preparation Crush and chop the garlic. Chop the onion fine. Mix 2 tablespoons of the soy sauce with the garlic, onion, salt, and 2 tablespoons of the sherry to make marinade 'A'. Mix the remaining soy sauce with sugar, the remaining sherry, and 2 tablespoons of water to make marinade 'B'. Rub the pork first with marinade 'A' and let it season for 2 hours, turning it over every 30 minutes; baste it with excess marinade.

Cooking Preheat the oven to 425°F. Place pork on a rack in a roasting pan, and roast for 30 minutes. Remove the pork from the oven and brush with marinade 'B'. Reduce the heat to 375°F, and roast for a further hour. Turn the meat over a couple of times and baste each time with some of the meat drippings which have collected in the roasting pan.

Serving Allow the meat to cool slightly, then slice through the skin into oblong pieces 2½ × 1½ inches, or slice into thin slices ¼ × 3 × 2 inches.

In China, roast pork is not only eaten on its own but is used for cooking with other materials, such as vegetables, bean curd cakes, and as a garnish on rice or noodles.

Crispy Skin Roast Pork

Serves 6–8

3 lb shoulder of pork, with skin attached

1 tablespoon salt
½ teaspoon five spice powder
1½ tablespoons soy sauce
1½ tablespoons honey

Crispy Skin Roast Pork and Cantonese Barbecued Roast Pork (or Cha Shao Roast Pork) are the two most popular roast pork dishes available in Chinese restaurants abroad. The most distinctive quality of Crispy Skin Roast Pork is the unusually crispy skin. With an oven in every modern kitchen, it is more convenient to roast meat in American kitchens than in China, where ovens are found in only the largest restaurants and much technique has to go into the building and control of the fire, which is usually fueled with firewood or charcoal. Pork with crackling skin is particularly appealing to rice eaters who are sensitive to the blending in the mouth of the soft blandness of the rice with the rich, crackling, aromatic qualities of the pork and its skin. These characteristics should be equally attractive to Americans.

Preparation Score the skin crosswise at 1 inch intervals with a sharp knife. Pierce the meat side (as opposed to the skin side) with a fork, also at 1 inch intervals. Mix the salt with the five spice powder and rub evenly into the meat and skin. Allow the pork to stand for 2 hours. Mix the soy sauce, honey, and 1 tablespoon warm water until well-blended.

Cooking Preheat the oven to 450°F. Place pork in a roasting pan, meat side up, with skin side sitting in about ¾ inch water. Roast for 30 minutes, then remove from oven and dry the skin of the pork thoroughly with paper toweling. Allow to stand and dry for 30 minutes, then rub the skin with the soy/honey mixture. Lower the oven temperature to 375°F and roast for 1 hour, starting with the skin side up and turning the meat over twice.

Note Skin may be rubbed or brushed with 2 teaspoons sesame oil after the first 30 minutes' roasting.

Spare Ribs

In China, spare ribs have been cooked since time immemorial. But there is a difference between the spare ribs cooked and served in China and those which have become so popular in the West. In China, spare ribs are normally chopped into 1 inch lengths, so that the cooked pieces can be put directly into the mouth and the meat stripped from the bone by a skilled manipulation of the tongue and teeth in an almost unconscious action—an involuntary movement which all Chinese acquire from infancy even before they have lost their milk teeth. Since this skill is lacking in the West, we often find the so-called spare ribs are full length bones which are not chopped at all and have to be eaten with the aid of fingers.

What we Chinese call 'spare ribs' are the rib bones from the rib back of the flank (i.e. the backing to the belly of the pork). In China, ribs are generally fried or steamed, and so they are chopped through the bone into 1 inch long pieces, with as much meat left on them as possible. Because the individual pieces are much smaller than the spare ribs in the West, they can be quite easily stir-fried and steamed.

Basic Spare Ribs (Simplest Version)

Preparation Cut the onions into thin slices, crush the garlic, and shred the ginger.

Cooking Place the ribs in a large saucepan; cover with 1 quart water. Bring to the boil over a high heat, and boil briskly for 5 minutes. Skim away all impurities, and drain off three quarters of the water. Reduce heat to low, and simmer for 15 minutes, turning the ribs over two or three times. Add the oil and all other ingredients, and raise the heat temporarily to maximum. Stir and turn briskly for 5–6 minutes until the ribs are brown. Reduce the heat to low, cover, and simmer for 30 minutes or until the liquid is reduced to one fifth, and serve on an attractive dish.

Serves 8–10, with other dishes

3–3½ spare ribs, cut into individual strips

2 medium-sized onions
2 cloves garlic
2 slices ginger root
2½ tablespoons vegetable oil
6 tablespoons soy sauce
1 chicken stock cube
1½ tablespoons sugar
salt and pepper to taste

If drier ribs are required, after the final stirring and turning, the ribs can be placed in a roasting pan and put into an oven preheated to 400°F for 8–10 minutes.

Braised Spare Ribs with Peppers

Preparation Use the recipe for Basic Spare Ribs (see above), adding one red or green sweet pepper, cut into strips, when the ribs are cooked. Toss and turn ribs and pepper strips for an additional 3–4 minutes just before serving. The presence of the pepper makes this dish more colorful, and adds to the flavor, particularly for those who appreciate the taste of pepper. (See illustration.)

Spare Ribs with Black Beans (Chinese Style)

Serves 8–10, with other dishes

3½ lb spare ribs
2 tablespoons fermented black beans

1½ teaspoons salt
pepper to taste
3 slices ginger root
3 cloves garlic
1 large onion
¼ cup soy sauce
½ cup vegetable oil
¾ cup secondary stock
1 chicken stock cube
4 teaspoons sugar
¼ cup dry sherry
¼ teaspoon monosodium glutamate
1½ tablespoons cornstarch

Preparation Cut spare ribs into individual bones, and chop each into 1–1½ inch long pieces. Crush the garlic, shred the ginger, and chop the onions. Soak the black beans in water for 30 minutes; then drain and mix with the garlic, ginger, onions, sherry, soy sauce, and 3 tablespoons of water. Mix cornstarch with sugar, monosodium glutamate, and 3 tablespoons water.

Cooking Heat oil in a saucepan over high heat. Add the spare ribs and stir fry for 4–5 minutes until they begin to brown. Drain away excess oil, and add black bean/soy sauce mixture. Continue to stir-fry for ½ minute; then cover and cook over low heat for 8–10 minutes. Remove lid, and add cornstarch mixture. Turn heat up to maximum, stir-fry for 1 minute; then serve.

Spare Ribs with Black Beans (Overseas Chinese Style)

Serves 6–8

2½ lb spare ribs
2 tablespoons fermented black beans

3 cloves garlic
3 slices ginger root
3 scallions
¼ cup dry sherry

Preparation Mix salt and pepper, and rub both sides of the rib cage with the mixture. Shred the ginger, crush the garlic, and chop the scallions. Soak the black beans in water for 30 minutes, drain and mash; then mix with the ginger, garlic, scallions, and soy sauce. Cut the ribs into individual slices.

Cooking Heat the oil in a heavy saucepan over high heat. Turn the ribs in the hot oil for 7–8 minutes until they begin to brown. Drain away excess oil, and add the black bean mixture to the pan, then reduce the heat to medium and turn the contents over for 4–5 minutes. Pour in the stock, sprinkle with the monosodium glutamate, the sugar, and sherry. Stir around and turn a few more times. Cover the saucepan and cook gently for 30 minutes. By this time, the liquid should have been reduced to less than half. Lift the spare ribs out onto a roasting pan, and place in an oven preheated to 400°F for 10 minutes.

Note The spare ribs can be served dry by arranging them on a well-heated serving dish. However if some sauce or garnish is desired, blend 1 tablespoon cornstarch with 3 tablespoons water, and mix with the sauce at the bottom of the saucepan. Add 2 tablespoons sherry, heat and stir for 1 minute, and pour the sauce over the spare ribs on the serving dish. Garnish with 2 tablespoons of chopped scallions or parsley if desired.

2½ tablespoons soy sauce
1 tablespoon cornstarch
4 teaspoons sugar
¼ teaspoon monosodium glutamate
½ cup vegetable oil
½ cup secondary stock
pepper to taste

Sweet and Sour Spare Ribs

This dish is a popular starter to a Chinese meal.

Preparation Cut spare ribs into individual ribs. Slice the onion and pepper thin. Crush the garlic, and shred the ginger. Mix the sauce ingredients until well-blended.

Cooking Place the spare ribs in a saucepan, and cover with water. Bring to the boil and simmer for 15 minutes; then drain off the water. Add the onion, garlic, ginger, salt, soy sauce, hoisin sauce, and oil to the spare ribs, and stir together until well-mixed. Simmer over a low heat for 25 minutes, stirring occasionally; then arrange in a deep heat-proof dish, and place in an oven preheated to 375°F. Heat the oil in frying pan, add the sliced pepper, and stir-fry over medium heat for 2 minutes. Pour the sauce mixture over the pepper and stir until it thickens into a translucent sauce. Take the spare ribs out of the oven, pour the sauce over, and serve.

Serves 8–10, with other dishes

3–3½ lb spare ribs

1 large onion
1 sweet pepper
2 cloves garlic
2 slices ginger root
1½ teaspoons salt
¼ cup soy sauce
1½ tablespoons hoisin sauce
2½ tablespoons vegetable oil

Sauce
2 tablespoons cornstarch
6 tablespoons water
2½ tablespoons vegetable oil
3 tablespoons sugar
3 tablespoons vinegar
2½ tablespoons tomato puree
2½ tablespoons orange juice
2½ tablespoons soy sauce
2½ tablespoons dry sherry

Spare Ribs with Red Bean Curd Cheese

Preparation Ask the butcher to cut spare ribs into individual strips, and to chop ribs into 1½ inch long pieces. Crush and chop the garlic, slice the onions thin. Cut scallions into 1 inch segments. Blend cornstarch with sherry and 3 tablespoons water.

Serves 8–10, with other dishes

2½ lb spare ribs
2 tablespoons red bean curd cheese

2 cloves garlic
2 medium-sized onions
2 scallions
1½ tablespoons cornstarch
2½ tablespoons dry sherry
6 tablespoons vegetable oil
2½ tablespoons soy sauce
2½ teaspoons sugar

Cooking Heat oil in a heavy saucepan over high heat. Add spare ribs and stir-fry for 4 minutes. Add the garlic and onions, and stir-fry for a further 4 minutes. Now add the bean curd cheese, soy sauce, and sugar. Mix and stir for 2 minutes, then pour in ¾ cup water. Bring to boil and simmer gently for 25–30 minutes, turning the ribs over occasionally until the liquid has been reduced enough to appear quite thick. Add the cornstarch/sherry mixture, and turn the heat to high. Sprinkle with chopped scallions, stir-fry for 2 minutes, and serve.

Deep-Fried Spare Ribs

Serves 6–8, with other dishes

2 lb spare ribs

1 large onion
2 cloves garlic
2 slices ginger root
¾ teaspoon salt
¼ cup soy sauce
1½ tablespoons hoisin sauce
6 tablespoons dry sherry
1½ tablespoons sugar
2 tablespoons flour
oil for deep-frying

This is prepared by the straight-forward method of combining long marinating with short deep-frying.

Preparation Chop spare ribs into 1 inch pieces. Slice the onion and chop fine, crush and chop the garlic, and shred the ginger. Place the chopped spare ribs in a bowl and add all ingredients. Mix well together and leave to marinate for several hours or overnight. Turn the ribs occasionally.

Cooking When ready to cook, drain the ribs and sprinkle and dredge them with flour. Heat the oil in a deep-fryer. Divide the ribs into two batches and deep-fry them twice—that is, fry one batch for 3–4 minutes and put aside to drain and keep hot. Fry the second batch in the same way. Finally, combine and deep-fry together for another 3–4 minutes. Serve immediately.

Good dips to accompany deep-fried spare ribs are: Soy-Mustard Dip, Salt and Pepper Mix, Soy-Chili Dip, and Plum Sauce (see Index).

Salt and Pepper Deep-Fried Spare Ribs

Serves 8–10, with other dishes

3 lb spare ribs
1½ tablespoons salt
1½ teaspoons freshly ground black pepper

2½ tablespoons cornstarch
1 egg
oil for deep-frying

Preparation Mix salt with pepper and stir-fry together in a small dry frying pan over medium heat for 2–3 minutes, until a distinct bouquet arises. Cut the spare ribs into individual bones and rub them lightly with this mixture. Leave to season for 1–2 hours. Blend the cornstarch and egg into a batter.

Cooking Place the spare ribs in a steamer and steam vigorously for 25 minutes. Batter them with the egg/cornstarch mixture. Heat the oil in a deep-fryer; place the ribs in a wire basket and deep-fry for 3–4 minutes. When slightly cool, chop them into 2 inch long pieces, place the pieces in the wire basket, and deep-fry again for 3–4 minutes.

Smoked Spare Ribs

This recipe originated in the province of Szechuan.

Preparation Trim and cut the ribs apart until there are only three bones to each piece. Boil in 5 cups of water with salt and pepper for 20 minutes. Drain. Cut the ribs into individual bones, and chop each bone into 1½ inch segments. Shred the ginger, and chop the scallions into 1 inch segments.

Cooking Place the ribs, ginger, scallions, soy sauce, hoisin sauce, sherry, sugar, and oil in a saucepan, and stir-fry over low heat for 10 minutes until the ribs have become fairly dry. Transfer the ribs to a wire basket. Place a large lump of smoldering charcoal at the bottom of a large heavy saucepan, and sprinkle it with very dry pine needles. Suspend the wire basket just below the top of the saucepan, and when the needles start to blaze, cover it. Place the saucepan over medium heat (to encourage combustion) and smoke for 10–12 minutes. The pine needles are said to give an interesting aroma to the ribs.

Serves 8–10, with other dishes

3 lb spare ribs

1½ tablespoons salt
1½ teaspoons pepper
2 slices ginger root
3 scallions
2½ tablespoons soy sauce
1½ tablespoons hoisin sauce
2½ tablespoons dry sherry
1½ tablespoons sugar
6 tablespoons sesame oil
1 lb pine needles

Stir-Fried Sliced Pork Dishes

When pork is stir-fried it is always cut into thin slices or matchstick strips, or else shredded, and it is usually stir-fried with other materials—mostly vegetables—which have been cut or shredded into similar sizes or shapes.

Stir-frying has three advantages over other forms of cooking—firstly, it is economical of time (cooking seldom exceeds a few minutes); secondly, by cross-cooking with other, usually cheaper materials, a large quantity of savory and appealing food can be produced from only a limited quantity of meat (for example 1 lb meat can serve 6–7 people); thirdly, by combining pork with other materials which differ in texture, color, and flavor, a large number of dishes can be easily created. As stir-frying invariably involves quick cooking at a high temperature, finger-tip timing and fire control are crucial. Hence quick stir-frying requires more experience to achieve perfection than other methods of cooking.

The rendering of other materials, apart from pork or the main material itself, into the correct size and shape also requires considerable practice and patience. However, once all the materials, ingredients, and flavorings are prepared and laid out (often in numerous small plates and bowls), the cooking is quick, continuous, and pressed on enthusiastically to its final conclusion.

This is a form of cooking which I might even compare to modern action painting giving full reign to man's artistic instincts. Many a Chinese chef has shown his hand and staked his reputation on his mastery of this form of cooking alone. Here his performance and the excellence of the eventual dish are physically and visibly linked.

Often the different materials used and combined in the dishes require different lengths of cooking. They are often cooked separately in the same pan and put aside, and when all the individual materials have been cooked or semi-cooked, they are finally combined together in one last sizzling assembly, generally over high heat. This final assembly or sealing process has the effect of rising to a crescendo as if things original and unique, like heaven and earth, are being created! There is something godlike in creation, and the master chefs seem to know it. Hence they have to perform with dignity, or not at all.

The following are some of the more easily created dishes which can be prepared very rapidly and cooked quickly from everyday materials. Nonetheless, when well-cooked, they are highly appealing, and respected by even the connoisseurs. Pork used for stir-frying is usually lean pork, pork chop, tenderloin, lean shoulder, lean leg (ham), and the leaner parts of the belly, or the meatier parts of the spare ribs.

Sliced Pork Stir-Fried with Cabbage

Serves 6–8, with other dishes

1 lb lean pork
½ medium-sized Chinese cabbage *or* Savoy cabbage

1½ teaspoons salt
pepper to taste
1 clove garlic
6 tablespoons vegetable oil
2½ tablespoons soy sauce
6 tablespoons stock (chicken *or* superior stock)
2½ teaspoons sugar
¾ teaspoon monosodium glutamate *or* ½ chicken stock cube

This dish goes particularly well with rice.

Preparation Cut the pork against the grain into very thin 1 × 2 inch slices; rub well with salt and pepper. Cut the cabbage into 1 inch pieces; crush the garlic.

Cooking Heat 3 tablespoons of the oil in a large frying pan over a high heat. Add the garlic and stir once or twice. Spread the pork slices over the pan and stir-fry them vigorously for 3 minutes; then lift out with a perforated spoon, drain, and keep hot. Pour the remaining oil into the pan and add the cabbage; turn in the oil until all the pieces are well-coated. Stir-fry for 2–3 minutes until they begin to heat through; then pour in the soy sauce, stock, and sugar, and sprinkle with the monosodium glutamate or crushed stock cube. Turn the cabbage in the sauce for 2–2½ minutes, then replace the pork in the pan and stir-fry for a further 2–2½ minutes.

Note It is optional in stir-frying of this sort whether or not to dredge and rub the meat with flour or cornstarch. By doing so, the surface of the meat is given a feeling of smoothness, and there is no detraction from the flavor so long as only a small quantity of flour or cornstarch is used.

Sliced Pork Stir-Fried with Cauliflower

Serves 6–8, with other dishes

Repeat the recipe for Sliced Pork Stir-Fried with Cabbage, but substitute a medium-sized cauliflower for the cabbage. Cut the cauliflower flowerets into very thin slices (⅛ inch in thickness), and cut away the thicker, coarser stems. After stir-frying the meat, stir-fry the cauliflower gently in oil for 2–3 minutes, coating the pieces with oil. Six tablespoons of stock (chicken, superior, or secondary) should be used, and the cauliflower should be cooked for a few minutes longer than the cabbage—a total of 4 minutes. Cover the pan during this time. Several tablespoons sherry, and 1 teaspoon sesame oil added during the last stage of cooking, give added zest to the dish.

Sliced Pork Stir-Fried with Cucumber

Repeat the recipe for Sliced Pork Stir-Fried with Cabbage using a medium-sized cucumber instead of cabbage. Slice the cucumber thin, either crosswise or lengthwise, but do not peel. Cook it for the same length of time as the cabbage, and serve with rice.

Serves 6–8, with other dishes

Sliced Pork Stir-Fried with Mushrooms

Repeat the previous recipe, using 1 cup fresh mushrooms and $\frac{1}{2}$ cup Chinese dried mushrooms. In China, we use dried mushrooms much more frequently than fresh ones—they seem to have more 'bite,' as well as more flavor. Dried mushrooms must be soaked for 30 minutes before use, and the tough stems discarded. Always retain some mushroom water—3–4 tablespoons—to add to the frying with some sherry, sesame oil, and monosodium glutamate, during the final stages of cooking. This will add to the flavor of the dish.

Serves 6–8, with other dishes

Repeat the recipe for Sliced Pork Stir-Fried with Cabbage, using 4 oz fresh mushrooms and 2 oz dried mushrooms, which have been previously soaked. As mushrooms are very absorbent, it is best to add them directly to the pork in the frying pan, after the latter has first been stir-fried with garlic and ginger, and then with soy sauce, sugar, stock, and mushroom water. The mushrooms will absorb this tasty sauce. If added earlier, they will only absorb the oil of the stir-frying. An ounce or two of butter mixed with the sauce mixture just before the mushrooms are added should appeal to Western taste.

In such a dish both dried and fresh mushrooms can be used. Add them at the same time. The fresh provide the main bulk, and the soaked, dried mushrooms provide the flavor.

In the final stages, the sherry, sesame oil, and monosodium glutamate mixture, mixed with $\frac{1}{2}$ tablespoon cornstarch blended with 2 tablespoons water, can be added to advantage—if cornstarch has not previously been rubbed into the pork.

Sliced Pork Stir-Fried
with Bamboo Shoots

Serves 6–8, with other dishes

In the West, bamboo shoots are most easily available in cans. Since they are eaten for their crunchy texture rather than their over-subtle flavor which is appreciated only by the well-cultivated connoisseur, the timing of their cooking need not be precise, since a few minutes more or less cooking will neither increase nor reduce the crunchiness. Repeat the recipe for Sliced Pork Stir-Fried with Cabbage (page 146), substituting bamboo shoots for cabbage. Sliced thin, they can be fried for 1, 2, or 3 minutes and then added to the sliced pork which has had its 2-stage stir-frying—2 minutes in oil, garlic, and ginger, followed by 2 minutes with soy sauce, sugar, and stock.

Fresh bamboo shoots have to be treated more carefully as they can be quite tough. They are best cooked in the same way as cauliflower—2–3 minutes of lubricating and frying in hot oil impregnated with garlic, ginger, and meat, followed by 4 minutes cooking in stock and soy sauce, before the final stir-frying with the pork.

Sliced Pork Stir-Fried with Young Leeks

Serves 6–8, with other dishes

Young leeks can be treated in the same way as cabbage. Repeat the recipe for Sliced Pork Stir-Fried with Cabbage (page 146). The leeks should be sliced into pieces about the same size as the pork (use all the green part), and added to the pan immediately the pork has been stir-fried. Use an extra ¾ teaspoon salt instead of 1 tablespoon soy sauce—i.e. reduce the soy sauce by 1 tablespoon in the later stage of flavoring. The salt will make the leeks greener than ever. To balance the comparatively strong taste of leeks, 1 tablespoon hoisin sauce may be used to advantage during the initial frying of the pork. It will give an extra brownness and piquancy to the meat, combining well with the glistening greenness of the leeks, and thus making the dish an extremely attractive one, both in flavor and appearance.

Sliced Pork Stir-Fried with Lettuce

Serves 6–8, with other dishes

Repeat the recipe for Sliced Pork Stir-Fried with Cabbage. However, as lettuce does not need as much cooking as cabbage—indeed it barely requires any cooking at all—a turn in the frying pan immediately after the pork has been stir-fried, followed by some sprinkling with soy sauce, sugar, stock, and monosodium glutamate, and a further turn or two should suffice until the final assembly and stir-fry with the pork.

Sliced Pork Stir-Fried with Golden Needles and Transparent Noodles

Transparent noodles and golden needles are typical Chinese cooking materials. Although transparent bean thread noodles are in themselves tasteless, they are great absorbers and conveyors of other tastes and flavors. Golden needles have an earthy, woody taste, which might have emanated from autumn leaves—appreciation of the taste is very much acquired. To Chinese people living abroad, both these ingredients are extremely evocative of the Good Earth of China: however, to make any dish using these materials interesting, it is essential to use both Chinese dried mushrooms (during the middle stage of cooking) and scallions and sesame oil during the concluding stage.

Preparation Soak the mushrooms, golden needles, and transparent noodles separately in warm water for 30 minutes. Retain 5–6 tablespoons mushroom water, remove the stems of the mushrooms and discard, and cut the caps into four. Cut the golden needles into 2–3 inch long segments, and leave soaking until required. Cut the scallions into 2 inch segments, and slice the pork against the grain into 1½ inch long and ½ inch wide pieces. Shred the ginger.

Cooking Heat the oil in a large frying pan or saucepan. Add the ginger, salt, and pork, and stir-fry over high heat for 3 minutes; then add 1 tablespoon of the soy sauce and the sugar, and continue to stir-fry for 1 minute. Pour in the stock, mushrooms, mushroom water, and golden needles, bring to the boil and boil for 2 minutes. Add the noodles, remainder of the soy sauce, the sherry, and monosodium glutamate; stir several times and simmer gently for 5–6 minutes. Sprinkle with the scallions and the sesame oil, and cook for a further minute. Serve in a deep dish.

Serves 4–8, with other dishes

¾ lb lean pork
½ cup golden needles (tiger-lily buds)
1 cup transparent noodles

6 large Chinese dried mushrooms
3 scallions
2 slices ginger root
2½ tablespoons vegetable oil
¾ teaspoon salt
¼ cup soy sauce
1½ teaspoons sugar
¾ cup superior stock
¼ cup dry sherry
¼ teaspoon monosodium glutamate
1 tablespoon sesame oil

149

Sliced Roast Pork Stir-Fried with Bean Curd

Serves 4–6, with other dishes

½ lb Cantonese roast pork
2 cakes bean curd

4 Chinese dried mushrooms
2½ tablespoons wood ears
2½ tablespoons dried shrimp
2 scallions
6 tablespoons vegetable oil
2 slices ginger root
¾ teaspoon salt
¼ cup soy sauce
1½ teaspoons sugar
½ cup stock (superior *or* secondary)
1½ tablespoons oyster sauce
¾ teaspoon monosodium glutamate

Bean curd is another typical Chinese ingredient. Like the transparent noodles, it is comparatively tasteless, but a great absorber and conveyor of other tastes and flavors. In texture, it is like a fairly firm, but slightly spongy custard, and it usually comes in cakes about one sixth of the size of an ordinary loaf of bread. In fact, it is one of the most widely used food materials in China, and is stocked by most Chinese markets abroad.

Preparation Soak the mushrooms, wood ears, and dried shrimp separately for 30 minutes. Retain ¼ cup of the mushroom water, and discard the stems. Drain the wood ears and the shrimp. Chop the scallions. Slice the Cantonese pork thin. Slice each bean curd cake into six pieces.

Cooking Heat 2 tablespoons of the oil in a frying pan. Add the shrimp, pork, ginger, and salt, and stir-fry for 2 minutes over a high heat; then remove pork with a slotted spoon and keep hot. Pour the remaining oil into the frying pan, and add the pieces of bean curd. Turn them over gently in the oil, and when all sides have been briefly fried, add the mushrooms, wood ears, soy sauce, scallions, mushroom water, sugar, stock, oyster sauce, and monosodium glutamate. Turn the bean curd over in the sauce, and cook gently for three minutes. Finally return the pork, stir-fry it gently in the sauce for several minutes, and serve. By this time, the bean curd should have become as rich in flavor as the meat.

Sliced Pork Stir-Fried with Szechuan Pickle

Serves 8–10, with other dishes

1½ lb lean pork
¼ cup Szechuan pickle

¼ cup vegetable oil
1½ tablespoons soy sauce
2 teaspoons sugar
¼ cup superior stock

Szechuan Pickle (often called cabbage) is usually available in cans from Chinese markets. Its hot pungent saltiness has the effect of doubling the strength of the principal food with which it is cooked. It should be used sparingly by those who have never tried it before, as the dish may easily become too hot or salty for the average taste. One quarter of an 8 oz can should be quite sufficient for 1½–2 lb pork.

Preparation Slice pork against grain into 1 × ¾ inch thin pieces. Slice the pickles similarly.

Cooking Heat oil in a frying pan over a high heat. Stir-fry the pork for 6–7 minutes; add the soy sauce, sugar, and stock, and continue to stir-fry for 1 minute more. Add the sliced pickles, stir-fry for a further 2 minutes, and serve.

Sliced Pork Stir-Fried with Oyster Sauce

This dish is very similar to the better known Beef in Oyster Sauce, which is a Cantonese favorite. Many people think that pork prepared in this way is just as good.

Preparation Slice the pork against the grain into 1½ × 1 inch very thin pieces. Rub with salt, and dredge and rub with cornstarch. Discard any excess flour, and use this to mix with the monosodium glutamate, sugar, sherry, and stock. Shred the ginger.

Cooking Heat the oil in a frying pan over a high heat. Add the pork and ginger, and stir-fry for 5 minutes. Pour in the oyster sauce and soy sauce, stir-fry for another 2 minutes, and then add the cornstarch mixture. Turn and stir for 1½ minutes, then serve.

Serves 8–10, with other dishes

1½ lb lean pork
2½ tablespoons oyster sauce

¾ teaspoon salt
2½ tablespoons cornstarch
¼ teaspoon monosodium glutamate
1½ teaspoons sugar
2½ tablespoons dry sherry
6 tablespoons superior stock
2 slices ginger root
6 tablespoons vegetable oil
2½ tablespoons soy sauce

Quick-Fried Sliced Pork

This is a dish where the flavoring of the pork is left to the diners, who can choose from the condiments arranged on the table. It is most important to offer Salt and Pepper Mix (which must be heated, and gives off a bouquet), and others such as Soy-Tomato Dip, Soy-Chili Dip, and Plum Sauce (see Index).

Preparation Slice pork against the grain into very thin pieces, 2 × 1 inch. Flatten each piece by pounding it several times with the side of a heavy Chinese cleaver or a wooden mallet. Sprinkle salt and monosodium glutamate as evenly as possible over the pork, and rub them in thoroughly. Shred the ginger and add to the pork. Leave to season for 1 hour. Beat the egg whites with a fork for 15–20 seconds. Add the cornstarch and mix into a consistent batter. Discard the ginger which has been seasoning the pork, and give the meat an even coating of the batter.

Serves 8–10, with other dishes

1½ lb lean pork

1½ teaspoons salt
¼ teaspoon monosodium glutamate
2 slices ginger root
2 egg whites
2 tablespoons cornstarch
scant ½ cup vegetable oil
1 lemon

Cooking Heat the oil in a large frying pan. When it is hot, turn the heat to medium and spread the pieces of pork evenly in the pan. Press them down with a spatula and shake the pan over the heat for about 3 minutes; then turn them and cook the other side for approximately the same length of time. As the pork is very thin and well spread out, it should be cooked in that time.

Serving Serve on a flat, well-heated dish. Squeeze lemon juice over the pork, and stack lemon wedges on one side.

Quick-Fried Shredded Pork Dishes

Almost all sliced pork dishes can be cooked as shredded pork dishes simply by cutting the pork, and any other ingredients, into thread-like shreds. However, there are some materials which are more suitable than others for shredding into threads; others already exist in threads or shredded form, so the pork is shredded to cross-cook and stir-fry with them. The cooking method for quick-fried shredded pork is very similar to that used for sliced pork—the participating ingredients are stir-fried separately and finally combined in a quick crescendo of a last hot sizzling assembly. The choice of meat for shredding is very much the same as that used for slicing—pork chop, tenderloin, leg, lean parts of shoulder and belly, and the meatier parts of spare ribs. As the cooking time for shredded meat can be even shorter than that for sliced meat, and as there is greater surface area exposed to the heat of the pan and oil, it is often seasoned or marinated before the actual cooking.

Shredded Pork Stir-Fried with Bean Sprouts

Serves 4–6, with other dishes

¾ lb lean pork
1 lb bean sprouts

1 medium-sized onion
2 cloves garlic
2 slices ginger root
2 scallions
2 teaspoons salt
1½ tablespoons cornstarch
6 tablespoons vegetable oil
2½ tablespoons soy sauce
2 teaspoons sugar
¼ teaspoon monosodium glutamate
2½ tablespoons dry sherry

Preparation Slice the onion thin. Crush the garlic, shred the ginger, and cut the scallions into 2 inch segments. Shred the pork into matchstick shreds, sprinkle with salt and cornstarch, and rub these into the meat.

Cooking Heat 3 tablespoons of the oil in a large frying pan or saucepan. Add the onion, garlic, and ginger, and stir-fry together over a high heat for 1 minute. Add the pork, spread it out over the pan, and stir-fry together with the other ingredients for 4 minutes. Remove with a slotted spoon and put aside to keep hot. Add the remaining oil and, after a moment, the bean sprouts. Turn them in the oil, and stir-fry over a high heat for 2 minutes. Sprinkle the bean sprouts with soy sauce, sugar, monosodium glutamate, and sherry, and continue to stir-fry for 2 minutes. Replace the pork in the pan, and stir together with the bean sprouts. Add the scallions, stir-fry for 2 minutes; then serve.

Shredded Pork Stir-Fried with Onions and Scallions

Repeat the recipe for Shredded Pork Stir-Fried with Bean Sprouts, using 2 large onions and 3 scallions. The idea is to use onions as a basic ingredient with the pork; the scallions, which are almost a garnish, are added only during the last minute of stir-frying together. Onion requires longer cooking than bean sprouts, and should be stir-fried first of all in oil for 2–3 minutes before adding the pork. Stir-fry them together for a further 3–4 minutes before the scallion segments are added. As onion is a strong-tasting vegetable, it will not be over-powered by the extra tablespoon of soy sauce and the teaspoon of sugar which should be added. If a slightly hotter dish is required, 1 tablespoon hoisin sauce may be added with the soy sauce, sugar, and sherry. The dish can be served after the scallions have been stir-fried with the pork and onion for 1 minute.

Serves 4–6, with other dishes

Shredded Pork Stir-Fried with Celery

Repeat the recipe for Shredded Pork Stir-Fried with Bean Sprouts, using celery instead of bean sprouts. The celery should be shredded into matchstick strips, and given an extra minute of stir-frying with the pork, after the meat has been replaced in the pan.

Serves 4–6, with other dishes

Shredded Pork with Asparagus Tips

Use 1 lb asparagus. Remove the tough parts, and slice the stalks lengthwise into double matchstick-size strips. Blanch the asparagus by simmering it in boiling water for 2 minutes, then drain thoroughly. Repeat the recipe for Shredded Pork Stir-Fried with Celery.

Serves 6–8

Shredded Pork with Sweet Pepper

The combination of red and green pepper with the brown pork strips presents an attractive dish.

Serves 6–8

Use 1 large green pepper and 1 red pepper to 1 lb pork. Unlike asparagus, pepper needs no blanching, but it must not be fried on its own for more than 2 minutes or it will burn—it is better to cook it over a medium heat. When it is stir-fried with shredded pork, it should be sliced into double matchstick-size strips and stir-fried for 2 minutes in 2 extra tablespoons of oil, after the shredded pork has been stir-fried. A teaspoon of chili sauce may be added during the final last assembly frying with the pork, thus giving the dish added hotness and pungency.

Curried Shredded Pork Stir-Fried with Scallions

Serves 4–6, with other dishes

1 lb lean pork
2½ tablespoons curry powder
6 scallions

1 green pepper
2½ teaspoons salt
1½ tablespoons cornstarch
6 tablespoons vegetable oil
1½ tablespoons soy sauce
6 tablespoons secondary stock

This dish can be prepared quickly if unexpected guests arrive.

Preparation Shred pork and green pepper. Sprinkle the salt and cornstarch over the pork, and rub in. Cut the scallions into 2 inch segments—use all of the green part.

Cooking Heat 3 tablespoons of the oil in a large frying pan. When it is very hot, add the pork and stir-fry for 2 minutes over a high heat, then sprinkle the pork with curry powder, add the green pepper to the pan, and continue to stir-fry for 5 minutes. Add the remaining oil, the soy sauce, and stock, stir-fry for 1 minute, then add the scallions; turn and toss for another minute, and serve.

Shredded Pork Quick-Fried with Leeks and Szechuan Pickles

Serves 4–6, with other dishes

Only 1–2 tablespoons of Szechuan Pickles need to be added to give extra strength of flavor to the pork. The pickles must be shredded to the same matchstick strips as the pork, added to the meat, and stir-fried with it. The leeks too should be shredded to double matchstick size, but they should be stir-fried separately for a couple of minutes, before they are all combined in the final assembly stir-frying.

Shredded Pork Stir-Fried with Transparent Bean-Thread Noodles

Transparent bean-thread noodles are available from Chinese markets and are usually quite inexpensive. They increase

154

several times in size and weight when soaked, and as they are already the same shape as shredded pork, the two can be cooked together very effectively and conveniently.

Preparation Shred the pork and soak the noodles. Soak the golden needles and dried mushrooms separately for 30 minutes; then drain, reserving 3 tablespoons of mushroom water. Cut the needles into 2 inch segments, and shred the mushroom caps. Discard the stems. Shred the ginger, crush and chop the garlic, and clean the spinach thoroughly, removing all the tougher parts.

Cooking Heat 3 tablespoons oil in a large frying pan. Add the golden needles and the ginger, then add the pork. Sprinkle with salt and monosodium glutamate, and stir-fry together over a high heat for 5 minutes; then add the mushrooms, mushroom water, 1 tablespoon of the soy sauce, and the stock. Bring to the boil, and add the noodles. Stir together, and simmer for 5 minutes. Meanwhile, heat the remaining oil in a saucepan. Stir-fry the garlic in it for 30 seconds, add the spinach and stir-fry over a high heat for 3 minutes; then add the remaining soy sauce. Combine the spinach and the pork and noodles. Stir and turn together for 2 minutes; then serve.

Serves 4–6, with other dishes

1 lb lean pork
1 cup transparent bean-thread
  noodles

3 golden needles (tiger-lily buds)
3 large Chinese dried mushrooms
2 slices ginger root
2 cloves garlic
1 cup spinach
6 tablespoons vegetable oil
½ teaspoon salt
¼ teaspoon monosodium glutamate
¼ cup soy sauce
¾ cup superior stock

Shredded Pork Stir-Fried with Shredded Carrots and Bamboo Shoots

Preparation Shred the pork, slice the onion thin, and cut the carrots and bamboo shoots into approximately double-matchstick-size strips.

Cooking Heat 3 tablespoons of the oil in a large frying pan. Add the onion and stir-fry for 1 minute. Add the pork, sprinkle with salt and monosodium glutamate, and stir-fry over a high heat for 3 minutes. Add the bamboo shoots, sprinkle with 1 tablespoon of the soy sauce, stir with the pork and leave to cook gently for 4–5 minutes over low heat. Heat the remainder of the oil in a small saucepan, and stir-fry the carrots over high heat for 3 minutes. Pour in the remaining soy sauce, the sugar, stock, and sherry and simmer gently over low heat for 10 minutes, until nearly dry. Add the contents of the saucepan to the pork in the frying pan, sprinkle with sesame oil, and stir-fry together for 1½ minutes over high heat.

The comparative crunchiness of the bamboo shoots, and the sweet richness of the carrots, combine to set off the savory meatiness of the pork, making this dish a most interesting one.

Serves 4–6, with other dishes

1 lb lean pork
1 cup carrots
1 cup bamboo shoots

1 large onion
6 tablespoons vegetable oil
2 teaspoons salt
¼ teaspoon monosodium glutamate
¼ cup soy sauce
1½ teaspoons sugar
6 tablespoons superior stock
2½ tablespoons dry sherry
2½ teaspoons sesame oil

Shredded Pork with Bean Curd Skin and Broccoli

Serves 4–6, with other dishes

1 lb lean pork
½ cup bean curd skin
8 oz broccoli

1½ teaspoons salt
1½ tablespoons cornstarch
2 large Chinese dried mushrooms
6 tablespoons vegetable oil
¼ cup soy sauce
10 tablespoons superior stock
2½ tablespoons dry sherry
¼ teaspoon monosodium glutamate
2½ teaspoons sesame oil

Preparation Shred the pork and sprinkle with salt and cornstarch. Soak the bean curd skin and mushrooms separately for 30 minutes; then drain. Discard mushroom stems and cut skin and caps into thin strips. Cut the broccoli into thin branches.

Cooking Heat 3 tablespoons oil in a large frying pan. Stir-fry the pork over high heat for 3 minutes; then add the skin, mushrooms, half of the soy sauce, and half of the stock, and continue to stir and turn for a further 3 minutes. Cover and simmer gently over low heat for 5 minutes. Heat the remaining oil in a suacepan and stir-fry the broccoli for 2 minutes. Pour in ¼ cup stock, the remaining soy sauce, and the sherry; stir several times, then cover and leave to cook for 5 minutes over a low heat. Combine the broccoli and its sauce with the pork and other ingredients in the frying pan. Sprinkle with monosodium glutamate and sesame oil, and stir-fry over a medium heat for 2 minutes.

Ground Pork Dishes

In China meat is not ground by putting it through a meat grinder but by the drumbeat action of a pair of choppers held in both hands, with the meat placed on a chopping board 6 inches thick. The connoisseurs say that this way prevents the loss of much valuable meat juice, which is squeezed out by a grinder. In the West, it is much easier to obtain ground meat by using a grinder or by asking the butcher to grind it.

Steamed Ground Pork with Cauliflower

Serves 6–8

½ lb slab bacon
½ lb lean pork
1 medium-sized cauliflower

2½ teaspoons salt
2½ tablespoons soy sauce
1½ tablespoons cornstarch
1 egg
2 cloves garlic
2 slices ginger root
pepper to taste

Preparation Grind the bacon, mixing the fat through the lean. Add half of the salt, half of the soy sauce, and the cornstarch. Lightly beat the egg, crush and chop the garlic and ginger, and add to the bacon, mixing well. Clean the cauliflower and break into individual flowerets, discarding the coarse stem. Arrange the flowerets in the bottom of a large bowl, sprinkle with the remaining salt and soy sauce, add the pepper, then spread the pork mixture in a thick layer over the top, until the cauliflower is completely covered.

Cooking Place the bowl in a steamer and steam for 1 hour. Serve in the bowl.

This is very much a home-cooked dish, popular with both young and old.

Steamed Ground Pork Cake

Serves 4–6

Preparation Chop onion and water chestnuts fine, shred and chop ginger, crush and chop garlic. Add them all to the ground pork, together with the egg, salt, sugar, soy sauce, and pepper. Mix well. Spread the mixture out like a thick pancake on a large, round, greased, heat-proof dish. Slice the sausage slantwise into ¼ inch thick slices, and stud them into the pork at regular intervals.

Cooking Place the heat-proof dish in a steamer and steam for 40 minutes. Serve from this dish.

1 lb ground pork

1 large onion
2 water chestnuts
1 slice ginger root
1 clove garlic
1 egg, lightly beaten
1½ teaspoons salt
1 teaspoon sugar
2 tablespoons soy sauce
pepper to taste
2 Chinese sausages

Deep-Fried Meatballs

Makes approximately 24

Preparation Chop the water chestnuts coarse. Chop and mince the onion, garlic, and ginger; and beat the egg lightly. Mix them with the ground pork, cornstarch, salt, and soy sauce until well-blended, and form into balls about the size of walnuts.

Cooking Heat oil in deep-fryer. Fry the meatballs six at a time by lowering them into the oil in a wire basket. Deep-fry each batch for about 3 minutes at a time, and put aside in a well-heated dish to keep hot. Finally, put all the meatballs together in the wire basket and give them a final deep-fry for 1½ minutes. Drain thoroughly, and serve.

These meatballs can be served plain to be eaten dipped in Salt and Pepper Mix, or they can be covered in Sweet and Sour Sauce (see Index).

1 lb ground pork

2 water chestnuts
1 onion
1 clove garlic
1 slice ginger root
1 egg
2½ tablespoons cornstarch
2½ teaspoons salt
1½ tablespoons soy sauce
oil for deep-frying

Meatballs with Spinach

Serves 4–6

This is an attractive and highly palatable dish suitable for serving at a party at home.

Repeat the recipe for Deep-Fried Meatballs up to the end of the first frying. Stir-fry ½ lb spinach in 3 tablespoons of vegetable oil, adding 1 chopped clove garlic, 1½ tablespoons soy sauce, and 1 teaspoon sugar. Place this mixture in a large heat-proof dish as a bed, and arrange the meatballs on top of the spinach. Place the dish in a steamer, and steam vigorously for 5 minutes.

1½ cups spinach
¼ cup vegetable oil
1 chopped clove garlic
2 tablespoons soy sauce
1½ teaspoons sugar

Lions' Heads

Serves 8–12

A
1½ lb lean pork
¼ lb pork fat
4 water chestnuts
2 medium-sized onions
4 Chinese dried mushrooms
2½ tablespoons cornstarch
1 teaspoon salt
1¾ tablespoons soy sauce
1½ teaspoons sugar
pepper to taste

B
½ cup superior stock
1½ tablespoons soy sauce
2½ tablespoons dry sherry
¼ teaspoon monosodium glutamate
2 teaspoons cornstarch

1 cup spinach
1 clove garlic
1 cup transparent bean-thread
  noodles
2½ tablespoons oil for deep-frying
2½ tablespoons vegetable oil
2 tablespoons soy sauce

Preparation Grind the pork and finely chop the water chestnuts and the onion. Soak the mushrooms for 30 minutes, drain and discard the stems, and finely chop the caps. Combine these ingredients with all the others in list A, and make four large meatballs. Heat the oil for deep-frying. Mix all the ingredients in list B into a well-blended sauce. Clean the spinach thoroughly, removing all the coarse tough parts. Crush the garlic; soak the noodles for 20 minutes, and then drain.

Cooking Place two meatballs at a time in a wire basket and deep-fry for 5–6 minutes until golden brown. Drain on paper toweling. Cook the other two similarly. Stir-fry the garlic and spinach in a large frying pan. After 1 minute, when the spinach is well-coated, add the soy sauce. Stir-fry for a further 2 minutes, then pour in the noodles, and toss gently with the spinach for 3 minutes. Transfer the spinach and noodles to a large earthenware pot or casserole. Place the meatballs on top of the spinach and noodles, and cover with a lid or aluminum foil. Steam for 30 minutes, or bake in an oven preheated to 375°F for 25 minutes. Meanwhile, heat the sauce mixture B in a small saucepan for 2–3 minutes until it thickens.

Serving Pour the sauce over the 'Lions' Heads' in the casserole, and serve.

This is a dish which is usually served at parties.

The Chiang Kiang Lions' Heads

Serves 8–12

½ cup crabmeat
2 oz (¼ cup) peeled shrimp
2 slices ginger root

Ching Kiang is a Yangtze river port where fish and seafood are abundant. The main difference between the Ching Kiang version, which is well-known in China, and the usual North China Lions' Heads (the previous recipe) is that in Ching Kiang, ½ cup of crabmeat, ¼ cup peeled shrimp, and 2 slices ginger root (finely chopped) are added to the ground pork mixture from which the meatballs are made. A further difference is that the spinach and noodles not only make a bed in the dish, but are also draped heavily over the Lions' Heads, thus providing them with manes. The host should use his chopsticks to lift the spinach and noodles to reveal the meatballs when he is serving. The Ching Kiang Lions' Heads are very flavorsome with the crab and shrimp mixed into the pork, but the dish must be eaten hot, and immediately: it is not suitable for keeping until the next day.

Pork Specialties

Pigs' Feet with Gravied Eggs

Preparation Clean the pigs' feet thoroughly, boil them in water for 25 minutes, and drain. Slice the onions thin, crush and chop the garlic, and hard-boil the eggs.

Cooking Place the pigs' feet in a casserole with the onion and garlic, and sprinkle with ¼ cup of the soy sauce, ½ tablespoon of the sugar, 3 tablespoons of the sherry, and the superior stock. Place the casserole in an oven preheated to 350°F and cook for 1½ hours, turning the pigs' feet over every 30 minutes. Add the hard-boiled eggs to the casserole, sprinkle with the remaining soy sauce and sherry, and cook for a further 40 minutes at the same temperature, turning the eggs and pigs' feet every 20 minutes.

Serving Just before serving, cut each egg into quarters and arrange the pieces around the pigs' feet in a deep dish. Pour in the gravy from the casserole. If there is insufficient gravy add a small quantity of superior stock, together with ½ tablespoon soy sauce and ½ tablespoon sherry, and heat until sizzling. Stir, and pour over the pigs' feet. The meat and skin of the pigs' feet should be glistening brown and jellylike, set off by the yellow yolks of the eggs surrounding them.

Serves 8–10

3 lb pigs' feet
4 eggs

2 medium-sized onions
2 cloves garlic
½ cup soy sauce
1½ tablespoons sugar
½ cup dry sherry
10 tablespoons superior stock

Sweet and Sour Pigs' Feet

Another favorite method of cooking pigs' feet is the sweet and sour version. This is prepared by repeating the recipe for Pigs' Feet with Gravied Eggs, without adding the eggs. Just before serving, heat the sweet and sour sauce mixture and pour over the pigs' feet.

Cooking Heat oil in saucepan, and stir-fry mixed pickle for 1 minute. Blend cornstarch with 3 tablespoons water, and mix with all other ingredients until well-blended; pour into saucepan over medium heat. Stir until sauce starts to thicken and becomes translucent.

Serving Pour evenly over pigs' feet and serve.

This dish can be partly cooked beforehand.

Serves 8–10

1½ tablespoons vegetable oil
1½ tablespoons mixed pickle, chopped
1½ tablespoons cornstarch
2½ tablespoons sugar
2½ tablespoons vinegar
2 tablespoons soy sauce
2½ tablespoons dry sherry
2½ tablespoons fresh orange juice
2 tablespoons tomato puree
2½ tablespoons good stock

Quick-Fried Pork Kidney
with Celery and Wood Ears

Serves 4–6, with other dishes

¾ lb pork kidneys
1 cup celery
2 tablespoons wood ears
2 cloves garlic
3 scallions
6 tablespoons vegetable oil
2 slices ginger root
1½ teaspoons salt

Marinade
2½ tablespoons soy sauce
2½ tablespoons dry sherry
pepper to taste

Sauce
2½ teaspoons cornstarch
¼ teaspoon monosodium glutamate
2½ teaspoons sugar
2½ teaspoons vinegar
1½ tablespoons soy sauce
¼ cup chicken stock

This kidney dish is considered a speciality mainly because it is cooked in a very short time.

Preparation Remove membrane from kidneys, cut each into halves, and score or slice each piece crosswise halfway through at ¼ inch intervals, until each piece is covered with a network of cuts. Cut each piece into 1 inch wide strips. Place in a bowl, add the well-blended marinade ingredients and marinate for 30 minutes. Crush the garlic, cut the scallions into 1 inch segments, and slice the celery into ½ inch pieces. Soak the wood ears in warm water for 30 minutes, rinse under running water, and drain. Blend the sauce ingredients well.

Cooking Heat 2 tablespoons of the oil in a frying pan, add the garlic and ginger, and stir-fry over high heat for 1 minute; then remove. Add celery, wood ears, and salt; stir-fry for 3 minutes, then remove and put aside. Pour the remaining oil into the center of the pan; when it is hot, add the kidneys and stir-fry quickly for 1 minute. Add the scallions, the celery, and wood ears to the kidney. Pour in the sauce mixture, and any left-over marinade. Stir-fry for a further minute; serve in a well-heated dish and eat immediately.

Kung-Po Hot Fried Kidneys

Serves 4–6, with other dishes

¾ lb pork kidneys

¾ teaspoon salt
2½ tablespoons soy sauce
chili pepper to taste
1 medium-sized onion
2 cloves garlic
½ cup leeks
6 tablespoons vegetable oil
2 slices ginger root

Sauce
1½ tablespoons soy sauce
¼ cup chicken stock
1½ teaspoons chili oil
2½ teaspoons tomato puree
¼ teaspoon monosodium glutamate
2½ tablespoons dry sherry

This is a dish from Szechuan in west China—a province where dishes are noted for hotness. The dish is usually reddish in color because of the chili oil, but in the West, where tastes are not accustomed to large amounts of chili oil, a small amount of tomato puree may be used instead. Connoisseurs of hot food think that the kidneys should be eaten almost immediately from the pan, so that the hotness in the flavor is reinforced by the heat in the food, giving that double-strength appeal.

Preparation Remove membrane from kidneys, and cut each into two. Score each piece crosswise halfway through at ¼ inch intervals, until each piece is covered in a network of cuts. Cut each piece into 1 inch wide strips. Rub with salt, and marinate in soy sauce and chili pepper for 30 minutes. Slice the onion thin, crush the garlic, and slice the leeks slantwise at 1 inch intervals. Mix the sauce ingredients until well-blended.

Cooking Heat 2 tablespoons of the oil in a frying pan. Add the ginger and garlic, stir-fry for ½ minute and remove. Then add the leeks, stir and turn in the oil for 1½ minutes, and push to the sides of the pan. Pour the remaining oil into the center of the pan and when it is very hot, add the kidneys; turn and stir them in the oil for 1 minute, pour in the sauce mixture and stir-fry for 1 minute more. Throughout the cooking, the stir-frying is done over high heat.

2½ teaspoons cornstarch
2½ teaspoons sesame oil

Whole Happy Family

This is a grand assembly of animal and vegetable items from both land and sea, all gathered together as if in one 'whole happy family'.

Preparation Soak and simmer bêche de mer in water overnight, and cut into ½ inch segments. Soak mushrooms in water for 30 minutes, remove the stems, and dice the caps into ¼ inch pieces. Cut the roast pork into ½ inch cubes. Heat the chicken breast in boiling water, dice into ¼ inch pieces, and cut the ham similarly. Chop the bamboo shoots and broccoli into ½ inch cubes. Soak the dried shrimp in water for 1 hour, and drain. Blend the cornstarch with 3 tablespoons water, and add the soy sauce, sherry, monosodium glutamate, sugar, and half of the cold chicken stock.

Cooking Heat the oil in a saucepan and add the meatballs. Stir-fry for 4 minutes; then push to the sides. Add the bêche de mer, roast pork, and salt; stir-fry for 3 minutes; then pour in the remaining stock, and add the chicken, ham, bamboo shoots, broccoli, dried shrimp, shrimp, and peas. Simmer for 30 minutes over low heat; then add the cornstarch/sherry mixture, and heat gently for a further 10 minutes.

Serves 4–6, with other dishes

¼ cup bêche de mer
4 Chinese dried mushrooms
½ cup Cantonese roast pork
1 chicken breast
¼ cup smoked ham
½ cup bamboo shoots
½ cup broccoli *or* heart of mustard
  or dandelion greens
1½ tablespoons dried shrimp
1½ tablespoons cornstarch
2½ tablespoons soy sauce
¼ cup dry sherry
¼ teaspoon monosodium glutamate
2½ teaspoons sugar
1¼ cups chicken stock
¼ cup vegetable oil
6 small meatballs (see page 157)
1½ teaspoons salt
¼ cup fresh peeled shrimp
⅓ cup green peas

Quick-Fried Pork Liver

Preparation Slice onion and bamboo shoots thin; soak the mushrooms for 30 minutes, remove the stems, and cut the caps into quarters. Slice the liver into thin 2 × 1 inch wide pieces. Place these pieces in a large bowl, and pour in half a kettle of boiling water, stir two or three times, and drain away the water. Sprinkle the liver with cornstarch, and marinate in the soy sauce, salt, sugar, and sherry.

Serves 4–6, with other dishes

1 lb pork liver

1 medium-sized onion
½ cup bamboo shoots
6 large Chinese dried mushrooms
1 tablespoon cornstarch

161

2½ tablespoons soy sauce
¾ teaspoon salt
1½ teaspoons sugar
1½ tablespoons dry sherry
2½ tablespoons vegetable oil
½ cup lard

Cooking Heat the oil in a frying pan. Add the onion, bamboo shoots, and mushrooms; then stir-fry over a medium heat for 2 minutes and set aside. Add the lard, heat, and when it is very hot, pour in the liver. Spread out over the pan and stir-fry over high heat for 2 minutes. Pour away excess fat, put the onion, bamboo shoots, and mushrooms back into the pan, and stir-fry with the liver for 1 minute. Serve from a well-heated dish.

Steamed Ground Liver

Serves 4–6, with other dishes

1 lb pork liver

2 teaspoons salt
2½ tablespoons dry sherry
pepper to taste
3 egg whites
¾ cup chicken stock
2 teaspoons light soy sauce
¼ teaspoon monosodium glutamate

Preparation Cut each piece of liver into two or three pieces. Grind twice until very fine; then force through a sieve into a deep bowl. Add the salt, sherry, and pepper, and blend well. Beat the egg whites separately, and when they become stiff, fold gently but thoroughly into the liver. Mix the chicken stock with the light soy sauce and monosodium glutamate in a small saucepan.

Cooking and Serving Place the bowl containing the liver/egg white mixture in a steamer, and steam for 30 minutes. Heat the stock-soy sauce mixture in the saucepan until it starts to boil (it should be a clear consomme). Pour over the steamed liver and bring the dish to the table in the original bowl.

This dish is considered a delicacy in Szechuan. It is enjoyed mainly by rice-eaters, who are inclined towards pure, uncomplicated, yet distinctive dishes.

Fukien Meat Wool

Serves 10–12

4 lbs lean pork

½ cup soy sauce
1½ teaspoons salt
2 tablespoons sugar
1½ tablespoons tomato puree
2½ tablespoons red wine-sediment
    paste
½ cup lard

Nothing reminds a Chinese more of home than meat wool, which is eaten mostly at breakfast time and for supper. In the West, it can be used for garnishing vegetables, omelets, soups, or for canapés or an extravagant sandwich. Indeed, it can be added to almost any savory dish. The only thing this 'wool' cannot be used for is knitting! After it has been prepared, it should be kept in a sealed jar for use when required.

Preparation Clean the pork and carefully remove every bit of fat and gristle. Slice against the grain into 1½ inch thick pieces, then cut along grain into 1½ × ½ × ¼ inch strips.

Cooking Place pork in a heavy casserole, add one quart water, soy sauce, salt, sugar, tomato puree, and wine-sediment paste, and bring to a gentle boil. Reduce heat to low, insert asbestos pad under the casserole, and simmer gently for 2 hours, turning the pork over every 30 minutes. Place the casserole in an oven preheated to 300°F and cook for another hour, stirring every 30 minutes. Heat 2 tablespoons of the lard in a large, heavy frying pan. When it has melted, add the pork, insert an asbestos pad under the pan, and stir and turn the pork continually for 1 hour with a wooden spoon, breaking up the fibers of the meat, until they are all loose and crisp. When the pork has become completely dried, continue to stir-fry slowly and gently, adding 1 tablespoon lard every 10 minutes until all the lard has been used. It is important that every piece of the pork should be turned and stirred every few seconds to prevent burning. The purpose here is to stir-fry as long as possible over low to medium heat, evenly spread over the whole surface of the frying pan by the asbestos pad and the heavy bottom of the pan, until all the water has been evaporated from the meat. The result is extremely tasty dried meat which just seems to melt in the mouth.

Serving Meat wool is traditionally served in China with plain soft rice (or congee) at breakfast or a midnight supper. It is usually placed on the table in saucer-sized dishes from which it can be helped onto the rice with chopsticks or a spoon. It is served cold, but its warm savoriness has a comforting impact on the mouth. (See illustration.)

Lychee Pork

Lychees are abundant in the province of Fukien, from which this dish originates. It came to be called Lychee Pork, I think, partly because it is cooked with lychees, and partly because the pork is cut crosswise like the skin of a ripened lychee which is rough and deep red, in contrast to the white flesh underneath.

Preparation Slice the pork into ⅛ inch thick slices; cut the surface of each piece crisscross at ⅛ inch intervals (in imitation of lychee skin), and then cut again into 1½ × 1 inch slices. Dredge each piece with salt and half of the cornstarch, and rub in. Slice onion thin. Remove seeds from lychee meat.

Cooking Heat oil in large frying pan; when very hot add pork and stir-fry for 3–4 minutes. Then place pieces of pork cut side down and fry steadily for two minutes. Remove and put aside. Pour away excess oil. Stir-fry onion for 2 minutes; add stock, soy sauce, sugar, vinegar, sesame oil, sherry, and remaining cornstarch blended with 3 tablespoons water. When the sauce thickens and boils add the lychee and pork. Stir together gently for 2 minutes; then serve.

This is very much a local dish, but likely to be readily acceptable to Americans already familiar with the delicate flavor of the lychee fruit.

Serves 4–6, with other dishes

½ lb fresh lychees
¾ lb lean pork

¾ teaspoon salt
1½ tablespoons cornstarch
1 large onion
½ cup vegetable oil
6 tablespoons superior stock
1½ tablespoons light-colored soy
  sauce
4 teaspoons sugar
2½ teaspoons vinegar
2½ teaspoons sesame oil
2½ tablespoons dry sherry

Paper-Wrapped Spare Ribs

Serves 6–8, with other dishes

2 lb meaty spare ribs
parchment paper

2 cloves garlic
2 slices ginger root
1½ teaspoons salt
6 tablespoons soy sauce
2½ tablespoons dry sherry
1 heaping tablespoon sugar
¼ teaspoon monosodium glutamate
1½ tablespoons hoisin sauce
3 scallions
oil for deep-frying

The spare ribs in this dish are naturally cooked and served in Chinese style, chopped into segments measuring 1–1½ inches.

Preparation Boil spare ribs in water for 20 minutes. Drain and cool. Cut into individual strips of bone, and chop into 1½ inch lengths. Place in bowl. Crush and chop garlic, shred ginger, and add them to the spare ribs together with the salt, soy sauce, sherry, sugar, monosodium glutamate, and hoisin sauce. Mix well and leave to marinate for 30 minutes. Cut the scallions into 2 inch segments. Cut the parchment paper into 5 inch squares. Wrap each piece of spare rib with a segment of scallion in a paper square, as if in an envelope— fold up the lower corner of the paper over the meat, turn in the two sides, and tuck down the top corner as the tongue. Tuck in firmly and tightly—if necessary, place a plate on top for a while to flatten them. Make 24–36 envelopes.

Cooking Heat oil in deep-fryer. Place six envelopes at a time in the wire basket, and deep-fry each lot for 3½ minutes. Place them in an oven preheated to 350°F, and keep hot. Repeat until all ribs have been fried. Finally, place all the envelopes in the wire basket, and fry together for 2½ minutes. Drain.

Serving Arrange the envelopes in fish scale fashion on a large, well-heated, serving dish. The diners will open the packets with a pair of chopsticks on the side dish provided for them in front of their rice bowls. The rush of heat, when the packets are opened, is fascinating; the dish must of course be eaten as soon as it arrives on the table.

Naturally, other ingredients can be added to the envelope according to one's taste, thus adding interest to the 'letter'.

Red-Cooked Pork Tripe

Serves 4–6, with other dishes

2 lbs pork tripe

1½ tablespoons salt
2 slices ginger root
2 large onions
6 large Chinese dried mushrooms
2 tablespoons chopped parsley
¼ cup lard
6 tablespoons soy sauce

Tripe appears to be more extensively used in Chinese than in Western cooking, although in some parts of Western Europe it is extremely popular. In China, some pigs are specially bred for their tripes, which are exceptionally thick (about 1 inch) and meaty. This is one of the many ways in which tripe can be prepared.

Preparation Wash tripe thoroughly. Dissolve salt in 5 cups boiling water, add tripe, and boil for 20 minutes; then drain, discarding water. Cut tripe into 2 inch triangles. Shred ginger, and slice onions thin. Soak mushrooms in warm water for 30 minutes, remove stems and cut caps into thin strips. Chop the parsley.

Cooking Heat lard in flame-proof casserole, and stir-fry onions and ginger for 2 minutes. Push to sides, and stir-fry tripe for 3 minutes over medium heat. Add mushrooms and all other ingredients. As soon as the contents of the casserole come to the boil, remove from the heat and place in oven preheated to 350°F for 1½ hours.

Serving Sprinkle with parsley, bring to table, and serve.

¼ cup dry sherry
1½ tablespoons vinegar
2½ teaspoons sugar
¾ cup superior stock

Cured Ham Dishes

Cured ham is not used as often as pork or fresh ham in China, although shredded smoked ham is frequently used as a garnish for egg dishes, and quick- or stir-fried dishes. Here is a selection of the most popular ham dishes.

Honey Pear Ham

This is a very well-known south-west China dish, which has a high reputation throughout the country. It developed in Kunming, where the Yunnan ham originated. Unlike sweet and sour, sweet and savory is a flavor much more frequently found in China than in the West.

Preparation Slice the ham into thin slices, 2 inches long, 1 inch wide. Use it to line the bottom of a flat heat-proof dish. Peel the pears, cut each into six slices, and deep-fry them for 30 seconds in hot oil. Place them on top of the ham. Mix the sauce ingredients into a smooth blend.

Cooking Sprinkle the pears and ham with rock sugar, place them in a steamer, and steam for 25 minutes. Heat the sauce mixture until it starts to boil and thicken. Pour over the ham and pears, after first tipping the latter from the heat-proof dish into a large serving dish.

Serves 4, with other dishes

4 large pears
½ lb Yunnan or cooked Smithfield ham

½ cup rock sugar
oil for deep-frying

Sauce
3 tablespoons cornstarch
2 tablespoons sugar
2 tablespoons honey
¾ cup water

Sliced Ham Stir-Fried with Celery

0Like pork, ham can be stir-fried with a wide variety of vegetables. However, as ham is stronger tasting and saltier than pork, a smaller amount is used with the same quantity of other ingredients.

Serves 4–6, with other dishes

1 cup cooked ham (steamed *or* baked)
1½ cups celery

1 clove garlic
1 slice ginger root
¼ teaspoon monosodium glutamate
2 teaspoons cornstarch
¼ cup secondary stock
6 tablespoons vegetable oil
2 teaspoons sugar
2 tablespoons light soy sauce

Preparation Slice ham into 1½ × 1 inch thin pieces. Clean celery and cut into 1 inch segments. Crush and chop garlic, and shred ginger. Parboil celery for 2 minutes and drain. Blend monosodium glutamate, cornstarch, and stock until smooth.

Cooking Heat oil in frying pan, and stir-fry garlic and ginger over medium heat for 30 seconds. Add ham, turn in oil for 1 minute, remove and keep hot. Pour in celery, turn heat to high, and stir in oil for 3 minutes. Add sugar and soy sauce, replace ham in pan, and stir-fry with celery for 2 minutes. Stir in monosodium glutamate/cornstarch mixture, and turn the contents of the frying pan over a few times.

Sliced Ham Stir-Fried with Cauliflower

Serves 4–6, with other dishes

Repeat the recipe for Sliced Ham Stir-Fried with Celery, but use cauliflower instead of celery. As cauliflower has a texture fairly similar to that of celery, it needs the same 2–3 minutes parboiling before it is stir-fried with the ham. Both need the garlic and ginger to set off their flavor, and as they are both white in color, they both contrast well with the pink ham in the finished dish. As they are not complicated to prepare, both can be produced at a moment's notice for unexpected guests, if the ham is available.

Sliced Ham Stir-Fried with Spinach

Serves 4–6, with other dishes

½ lb cooked ham (steamed *or* baked)
¾ lb fresh spinach

1 clove garlic
1 slice ginger root
¼ teaspoon monosodium glutamate
2 teaspoons cornstarch
¼ cup secondary stock
3½ tablespoons vegetable oil
2 teaspoons sugar
2 tablespoons light soy sauce

Spinach is a different kind of vegetable from celery and cauliflower: it does not need to be parboiled before the stir-frying with the ham; indeed, it will lose all its luster if it is parboiled. As spinach loses its water quickly when fried, an additional 1 or 2 tablespoonfuls of oil should be poured into the pan after the ham has been stir-fried, and before the spinach is added. An additional clove of garlic and a slice of ginger root can be placed in the pan, and the spinach should be turned quickly in the oil for 2 minutes. Use about ¾ lb spinach, and trim off all the coarse and tough parts. The glistening green spinach will contrast well with the ham when the latter is added for the final stir-fry. Since the two main ingredients are dark in color (dark green and dark pink), there is no need to use light-colored soy sauce—ordinary or dark soy sauce should do very well.

Sliced Ham Quick-Fried with Scallions

This is a dish from the south-western province of Yunnan, where ham is widely used. It is the blend of sweetness with saltiness in the one dish which gives it its distinction. It is truly *quick*-fried, as the total cooking time is less than 1 minute.

Preparation Slice the ham into 2 × 1 × ⅛ inch thick pieces. Cut the scallions into 2 inch segments.

Cooking Heat half of the lard in a frying pan, and stir-fry the ham, sugar, and sherry over a high heat for 20 seconds. Put aside. Put the remaining lard in the pan, add the scallions, sprinkle with salt, and stir-fry for 20 seconds. Return the ham to the pan, add the stock, and stir-fry the ham and the scallions still over high heat, for 10 seconds. Serve and eat immediately.

Serves 4–6, with other dishes

½ lb (1 cup) Yunnan *or* cooked Smithfield ham
8 scallions

¼ cup lard
2½ teaspoons sugar
2½ tablespoons dry sherry
1½ teaspoons salt
2½ tablespoons superior stock

Chinese Sausages

To Western eyes, Chinese sausages are not sausages but miniature salamis. They are often used in flavoring, or cooked in steamed rice, but they can be cross-cooked with other materials, in the same way as ham.

The Chinese sausage is usually about the same length as a Western sausage, but only half as thick in diameter. When used alone, it is generally sliced diagonally into ¼ inch thick pieces, fried in a little oil for 2–3 minutes over gentle heat, and served in a small dish or saucer as a side-dish.

The sausages are often used to garnish vegetables, having been lightly fried first, then arranged on top of the vegetables, and the whole steamed for a few minutes. Being red or reddish-brown in color with patches of transparent fat, they lend color, as well as flavor, to vegetable dishes. Chinese sausages are often seen strung together in pairs in the windows of Chinese markets or restaurants where Chinese congregate. Because of their similarity to salamis, they are easily acceptable to Westerners; and like their Western counterpart, they are usually bought in shops, rather than produced at home. (See illustration.)

BEEF

牛 肉

Beef is not so widely used in Chinese as in Western cooking, being less popular than pork. Nevertheless, it is an important item of meat, and should be available from all good butchers and in restaurants of any standard.

There are beef dishes from every region of China, but they are mainly eaten by Chinese Moslems, who have a somewhat kosher outlook, and think that pork is unclean. There is also a good range of beef dishes from the western province of Szechuan, where a great many oxen are employed for haulage in the salt-mines. A proportion of them, as would be expected, eventually end up on the table. In the other parts of China there is probably only one beef dish for every ten pork dishes. Taken in the main, the majority of Chinese regard the ox and cow more as the source of muscular power than as a source of flesh. Unlike the pig, which we Chinese regard as existing primarily for its total edibility (besides, hog's hair is valuable for exporting for the production of good brushes and tooth-brushes), we Chinese keep cows and oxen more or less as people in the West nowadays keep cars—in ones, twos, or threes. They are there to work—pulling the plough, doing some haulage, or grinding the corn. It is only in the great grassland regions of western Manchuria, and Inner Mongolia, stretching westwards to distant Sinkiang (Chinese Turkestan) that great herds of cattle exist. This is the region where the Chinese Moslems roam. It is of little wonder that they are the originators of many of the Chinese beef dishes.

In the rest of China, not only are there no herds of cattle, but there are no dairies as such. The Chinese as a rule do not drink milk, and there is no butter or cheese made from milk. These items are, however, becoming better known in China, as a result of Western influence during the past half century. The Western impact has, perhaps imperceptibly, increased the Chinese interest in beef, and in fact some of the best beefsteaks I have ever eaten, I had in Tientsin and Shanghai.

Practically all Chinese pork dishes can be made with beef, by substituting beef for pork in the recipes. To achieve this change successfully, one has to remember that beef, unlike pork, is not suitable for medium-length cooking (5 to 25 minutes): to be tender, it has either to be cooked very quickly, in under 2–3 minutes (it is therefore suitable for quick stir-frying), or for a much longer time than 25 minutes, preferably 1 hour and upwards.

Another difference between pork and beef is in the stronger and more definite taste of the latter. Because of this, beef is generally cross-cooked with the stronger-tasting vegetables, such as onion, leek, ginger, garlic, and turnip. It is usually stewed with turnips, and stir-fried with onions and leeks. Ginger is often added to eliminate its 'rawness'.

168

Unlike pork and chicken, beef is never diced into small cubes and cooked—rather it is cut in thin slices, or in shreds and strips.

As with the other meat chapters, we start with Red-Cooking, which can also be called the Chinese version of the 'Eternal Stew'. However, if well-cooked, it can be excellent and most delectable—one of the best dishes ever created.

Red-Cooked Beef

Preparation Slice the onions thin. Shred the ginger and crush the garlic. Soak the tangerine peel in water for 20 minutes; then drain.

Cooking Boil the beef for 10 minutes, then cut it into 1–1½ inch cubes. Heat the oil in a heavy pan, add the meat cubes, and stir-fry over a high heat for 5–6 minutes. Remove the beef and put aside. Add the onions, ginger, and garlic to the remaining oil in the pan, and stir-fry over a medium heat for 3–4 minutes. Add 1 quart water, salt, and 2 tablespoons of the soy sauce. Bring to the boil, add the beef and tangerine peel, and return to the boil. Reduce the heat to minimum, cover, and simmer very gently for 1 hour. Add the remaining soy sauce, sugar, and sherry. Insert an asbestos pad under the pan and continue cooking over a very low heat for another 2 hours, turning the beef every 30 minutes. Alternatively, if the beef is cooked in a casserole, it can be cooked in the oven at 300°F for 2½ hours.

Serving This is a very tasty dish to eat with rice. It is best cooked in an iron pot or casserole so that the container can be brought to the table for serving.

Because of the long cooking, all the tendons in the muscles of the shin beef turn into delicious jelly. This makes the texture more interesting than if it were simply lean beef. Shin is a fairly inexpensive cut of meat.

Serves 6–8, with other dishes

3–4 lb boneless shin beef

2 large onions
2 slices ginger root
2 cloves garlic
1 piece (about 2 tablespoons) Chinese dried tangerine peel
¼ cup vegetable oil
1 teaspoon salt
5 tablespoons soy sauce
1 tablespoon sugar
6 tablespoons dry sherry

Red-Cooked Beef with Yellow Turnip

Use the recipe for Red-Cooked Beef with Tomatoes, substituting 1 medium-sized turnip for the tomatoes. Cut the turnip into 1½ inch triangular shape pieces and add to the pan at least 1 hour before serving. They appear golden and transparent when cooked. A tablespoon of chopped chives or scallions is sometimes sprinkled over the meat before serving.

The taste of beef with turnips is a very traditional Chinese one.

Serves 6–8

Red-Cooked Beef with Tomato

Serves 6–8

In north China, beef is often cooked with tomatoes, which are readily available.

Preparation The dish can be prepared simply by adding 1 lb skinned tomatoes to the recipe for Red-Cooked Beef during the last hour of cooking. An extra teaspoon of salt or 1½ tablespoons of soy sauce must also be added. If ordinary stewing beef is used, the total cooking time can be reduced by 1½ hours. 1 lb peeled tomatoes, each sliced into four, can be added during the last 45 minutes of cooking, with some salt or soy sauce, plus ½ tablespoon of hoisin sauce. A tablespoon of chopped chives or scallions is sometimes sprinkled over the meat before serving.

Braised Marinated Beef with Star Anise

Serves 8–10, with other dishes

4–5 lb boneless stewing beef

5 tablespoons soy sauce
2 tablespoons hoisin sauce
6 tablespoons dry sherry
1 tablespoon sugar
1 teaspoon salt
1 tablespoon vinegar
pepper to taste
2 tablespoons flour
2 cloves garlic
2 slices ginger root
4 tablespoons vegetable oil
2 cloves star anise

Preparation Pound the beef evenly with a wooden hammer or the back of a heavy Chinese cleaver. Prick it in about a dozen places with a fork; then place it in a deep dish to marinate for 2 hours in a mixture of soy sauce, hoisin sauce, sherry, sugar, salt, vinegar, and pepper. Turn it over every 30 minutes. Drain, and keep the remainder of the marinade for later use. Dredge the beef with flour, crush the garlic, and shred the ginger.

Cooking Heat the oil in a heavy frying pan. Add the garlic, ginger, and star anise. Stir-fry gently over a medium heat for 1 minute, then add the beef, and brown it on both sides by frying it over a medium heat for 6–7 minutes. Lower the heat to minimum and insert an asbestos pad beneath the pan. Add ¼ cup water to the remaining marinade, blend well, and pour over the beef. Cover and cook very gently for 45 minutes, turning the meat twice, and basting it every 15 minutes with the liquid at the bottom of the pan. Check to make sure that the liquid has not run dry: if it has, mix together 1 tablespoon soy sauce, 1 tablespoon sherry, and 2 tablespoons stock, and continue to baste the beef with this mixture, cooking the meat for a further 45 minutes. Keep only a small amount of liquid in the pan, but never allow it to run dry.

Serving When cooked, allow the beef to stand for 1 minute, then slice it into thin slices, about 1½ × 2 inches. Beef prepared in this manner can be eaten hot or cold, dipped in Soy-Mustard Dip (see Index).

Red-Simmered Beef

Preparation Cut the beef into 1½ inch cubes. Slice the onions thin.

Cooking Heat the oil in a heavy pan. Stir-fry the onions and ginger for 2 minutes, then pour in the soy sauce, sherry, sugar, salt, and stock. As soon as the mixture comes to the boil, add the beef. Cover and cook over a medium heat for 30 minutes, turning the beef every 10 minutes. Add 1¼ cups of water, and as soon as the contents come to the boil again, reduce the heat to a minimum, insert an asbestos pad under the pan, and leave to cook for 45 minutes, turning the beef every 15 minutes. Then add another 1¼ cups of water and cook for 45 minutes more.

Serving The beef should be served in a deep dish, accompanied by hoisin sauce, Soy-Sherry Dip, or Soy-Mustard Dip (see Index). Pour the gravy over plain, boiled rice.

Serves 8–10, with other dishes

4–5 lb lean boneless beef

2 medium-sized onions
3 tablespoons vegetable oil
2 slices ginger root
½ cup soy sauce
6 tablespoons dry sherry
1 tablespoons sugar
½ teaspoon salt
6 tablespoons superior stock

Red-Simmered Spiced Beef

Repeat the recipe for Red-Simmered Beef, adding 2 cloves star anise, ¼ teaspoon five spice powder, and ½ teaspoon chili powder at the beginning of the cooking. Add 2 tablespoons chopped scallions or chives just before serving.

Variations Add 1 lb turnips or carrots during the last hour of cooking, and use ½ cup soy sauce, ½ cup dry sherry, and 4 teaspoons sugar.

Serves 8–10, with other dishes

Moslem Long-Simmered Beef

The following recipe, which comes from the Yu I-Sung Moslem restaurant in Peking, shows that there is no absolute rule in Chinese cooking. For the beef is long-simmered, after first being stir-fried and then cooked quickly in water before the cooking proper commences. This is an unusual procedure.

Preparation Soak the tangerine peel in water for 20 minutes; then drain. Slice the onions thin and cut the beef into 1½ inch cubes.

Serves 6–10, with other dishes

4–5 lb boneless shin beef

1 piece (about 2 tablespoons)
    Chinese dried tangerine peel
2 large onions
6 tablespoons vegetable oil

½ cup soy sauce
¼ cup dry sherry
1½ tablespoons sugar
3 slices ginger root

Cooking Heat the oil in a large pan over a high heat. Stir-fry the beef cubes for 6–7 minutes, then drain and discard the excess oil. Pour the beef into a large pan of boiling water, and boil vigorously for 3 minutes. Drain the beef, and place it in a heavy pot or casserole. Just cover the meat with fresh water and add all the other ingredients. Bring to the boil, cover, and turn the heat down to minimum. Insert an asbestos pad under the pan. Keep tightly closed and cook for 4 hours, turning the beef over once every hour. The beef may also be cooked in a casserole in the oven—the temperature should then be kept at 280°F after the initial boil. If the liquid in the pan or casserole runs short after 3–3½ hours cooking, add a cup of water and turn the beef over.

The tendons in shin beef have a jelly-like quality which adds variation and interest to the texture of the meat, and a special succulence to the dish.

Steamed Beef

Since the ingredients of a dish are normally static during steaming (in contrast to stir-frying where all the ingredients are in rapid and continual movement, and seasonings and flavorers are thrown in and adjusted as required), practically all the preparations—such as marinating, flavoring, precooking, or arrangement and presentation of the food in the serving dish—are made beforehand. This gives the advantage of enabling one to see the finished dish before it is cooked.

Steaming can be either a short, sharp blast of steam which lasts for no more than 10–20 minutes (as is frequently used for cooking fish), or it may be a long, drawn out process which gives a result similar to long-simmering. Indeed, much Chinese long-simmering is done by steaming. In such cases, the food is steamed closed—that is, a lid is placed over the food so that it doesn't get too watery. But in vigorous steaming, the food is usually uncovered.

Meat which is to be short-steamed is cut into very thin slices and well-marinated, so that it can be cooked through in 10–12 minutes and at the same time not lose its flavorings through the action of the steam and water. Steaming has the advantage over other forms of cooking for a long period in that the temperature of the food during the cooking remains the same, in contrast to the concentration of heat at the bottom of the pan when the cooking is done on top of a stove.

Steamed Sliced Beef

Serves 4–8, with other dishes

3 lb lean boneless beef

1 teaspoon salt
3 tablespoons soy sauce
2 tablespoons dry sherry

Preparation Mix the salt, soy sauce, sherry, hoisin sauce, ginger, and cornstarch together. Add to the beef to marinate for 30 minutes. Soak the dried mushrooms in ½ cup warm water for 20 minutes; then drain, and retain ¼ cup of the mushroom water. Slice the bamboo shoots thin. Cut the scallions into 2½ inch segments, and chop the parsley fine.

Cooking Rub the slices of beef with vegetable oil, and arrange them on a shallow heat-proof dish, interwoven with bamboo shoot slices. Place the mushrooms on top of the beef. Pour the remainder of the marinade, and the mushroom water, over them. Scatter scallions over the beef and bamboo shoots. Place the dish in a steamer and steam vigorously for 20 minutes.

Serving Sprinkle with chopped parsley and sesame oil, and bring the dish to the table to serve.

1 tablespoon hoisin sauce
2 slices ginger root
1 tablespoon cornstarch
6 medium-sized Chinese dried
  mushrooms
¾ cup bamboo shoots
3 scallions
3 sprigs parsley
2 tablespoons vegetable oil
2 teaspoons sesame oil

Long-Steamed Beef

Preparation Use the same ingredients as in the recipe for Steamed Sliced Beef, but cut the beef into 1½ inch cubes, and after marinating, pack them into a heat-proof bowl on top of a base of bamboo shoots, also cut into cubes. Place the mushrooms and the scallions on top of the beef cubes, after pouring the mushroom water over.

Cooking The steaming can be done in a large saucepan or stockpot, with the heat-proof bowl containing the beef placed on top of an inverted plate, and the pot filled with 2½ inches water (up to about one third of the depth of the heat-proof dish). During the cooking period, the water should be kept at a gentle boil and at a constant level—replenish it by adding boiling water occasionally. Cover the bowl with a lid or aluminum foil so that the food will not collect too much water in the long process of steaming. Steam for 2 hours.

Serving When ready, sprinkle the contents of the bowl with chopped parsley and sesame oil just before bringing to the table.

Serves 4–8, with other dishes

Steamed Ribs of Beef

This dish combines the processes of braising and steaming, and the combination makes this type of beef much more tender than normal.

Preparation Chop the ribs into 2–2½ inch sections. Rub with salt, and sprinkle with soy sauce, sherry, and pepper. Leave to marinate for 1 hour. Soak the black beans in water for 30 minutes and drain. Crush the garlic, shred the ginger, and cut the scallions into 1½ inch segments (include the green parts).

Serves 4–8, with other dishes

4 lb short ribs of beef

2 teaspoons salt
3 tablespoons soy sauce
2 tablespoons dry sherry
pepper to taste
2 tablespoons fermented salted
  black beans
2 cloves garlic

2 slices ginger root
3 scallions
¼ cup vegetable oil
1½ cups superior stock
1½ tablespoons chopped parsley
2 teaspoons sesame oil

Cooking Heat the oil in a heavy pan over a medium heat. Add the garlic, ginger, black beans, and half the scallions. Stir-fry for 2 minutes and add the ribs. Continue to stir-fry over high heat for 5 minutes. Add 3 tablespoons stock at 3 minute intervals, and stir-fry for a further 9 minutes. Pour the contents of the frying pan into a heat-proof bowl; then cover, and place in a steamer, or steam in a stockpot (as in the recipe for Long-Steamed Beef) for 1½ hours.

Serving When ready, sprinkle the contents with the remaining chopped scallions and the sesame oil, and serve in the heat-proof bowl.

Steamed Beef Balls with Oyster Sauce

Serves 4–8, with other dishes

1½ lb lean ground beef

3 water chestnuts
2 medium-sized onions
1 egg
1 teaspoon salt
2 tablespoons flour
2 tablespoons cornstarch
oil for deep-frying
2 tablespoons oyster sauce
2 teaspoons shrimp sauce
1 tablespoon soy sauce
1½ teaspoons dry sherry
3 tablespoons water
½ teaspoon chili sauce
2 teaspoons cornstarch
1 tablespoon chopped parsley

Preparation Chop the water chestnuts and the onions fine. Mix with the egg, salt, and flour, and shape into balls the size of walnuts. Dredge with the cornstarch.

Cooking Place the beef balls in a wire basket and fry them in very hot oil in 3–4 lots for 3 minutes each. Place the balls in a bowl in a, and steam vigorously for 10 minutes. Meanwhile prepare the sauce by mixing the remaining ingredients together (except for the parsley) until they have blended into a smooth mixture; then heat until it thickens. Pour this over the balls after removing them from the steamer. Sprinkle them with chopped parsley and serve.

When oysters are in season, there is no reason why four large oysters should not be chopped up and added to the sauce. In this case, double the sherry used, and increase the heating time by 30 seconds. Sauce made with fresh oysters is invariably more interesting than sauce made with oyster sauce. In fact, sauce made with fresh oysters is one of the most exciting sauces used in Chinese noodle cooking in the coastal areas of China.

Steamed Beef Balls with Sweet and Sour Sauce

Serves 4–8, with other dishes

Preparation Repeat the recipe for Steamed Beef Balls with Oyster Sauce, using sweet and sour sauce (see Index) instead of oyster sauce.

Beef Balls with Sweet and Sour Sauce or Oyster Sauce can also be served just deep-fried, without steaming. Then it is usual to give the beef balls a double-fry before serving with the respective sauces—i.e. to fry the beef balls for 2½ minutes first, and then to place them in a wire basket and give them all a final 1½ minutes' frying together before putting them on a serving dish and pouring one or other of the sauces over them.

Steamed Beef Balls with Szechuan Cabbage

Preparation Repeat the recipe for Steamed Beef Balls with Oyster Sauce, but omit the ingredients for the sauce. Instead, use 1 medium-sized cauliflower, and ¼ lb (about 1 cup) pickled Szechuan cabbage.

Serves 4–8, with other dishes

The cauliflower should be broken up into individual branches—about 1½ × 2 inch pieces—and used to pack the bottom of a heat-proof dish or bow. Cover this with a layer of all the pre-fried balls, and then a layer of sliced Szechuan pickled cabbage. Leave the dish uncovered, and steam at full strength for 20 minutes. The moisture which seeps through the hot-spiced pickles down to the beef balls and cauliflower below will enrich and give extra spice to them.

Quick Stir-Fried Shredded Beef and Beef Slices

Except in a few instances, shredded beef and beef slices are always cooked with one or two other ingredients cut or sliced into similar shapes and sizes as the beef itself. These materials are generally vegetables—occasionally dried vegetables are used with fresh vegetables.

Most vegetables which are cooked with shredded beef can usually also be stir-fried with beef slices. The only adjustment which needs to be made is in the cutting of the meat. To avoid repetition, I have included both types of beef in the same section.

Quick Dry-Fried Beef Ribbons

This is one of the few instances where beef is fried almost entirely on its own, with the addition of seasonings and two pieces of chili pepper, to make it extremely hot and spicy.

Serves 4–8, with other dishes

1¼ lb flank steak

3 tablespoons soy sauce
2 teaspoons sugar
1 tablespoon dry sherry
2 chili peppers
¼ cup vegetable oil

Preparation Slice the beef with a sharp knife into matchstick strips. Add the soy sauce, sugar, and sherry; mix well and marinate for 1 hour. Cut the peppers into similar size strips, discarding the seeds.

Cooking Heat the oil in a frying pan until it is very hot. Add the peppers and stir-fry quickly for 20 seconds. Add the beef and stir-fry over a high heat for 3 minutes. Reduce heat to medium and continue to stir-fry until nearly all the liquid has evaporated or appears to have been absorbed into the meat; about 3–4 minutes. Reduce heat to very low and continue to stir-fry for 2 more minutes so that the beef becomes completely dried. Quick stir-frying has to be maintained throughout these last stages to prevent burning.

Serving When this dish is successful, there is a feeling that all the tasty-savoriness has gone into the beef. It should be served in a flat, very well-heated serving dish. The beef should by then be in brown crispy shreds and is highly savory and an excellent accompaniment to drinks.

In Western kitchens, the last stage of cooking can be done under a broiler.

Quick-Fried Spiced Steak in Oyster Sauce

Serves 4–8, with other dishes

1½ lb flank steak
3 tablespoons oyster sauce

1 tablespoon soy sauce
1 tablespoons hoisin sauce
2 tablespoons dry sherry
1¾ tablespoons cornstarch
5 tablespoons vegetable oil
¼ cup superior stock
2 scallions
2 slices ginger root

This is a favorite dish in Canton, where cooking meat and seafoods together is widely practiced.

Preparation Cut the beef (against the grain) into 1½ × 2 inch very thin slices. Marinate in a bowl for 30 minutes with soy sauce, hoisin sauce, and half of the sherry. Dust with half of the cornstarch. Finally add 1 tablespoon of the oil and work it into the beef with the fingers. In another bowl, mix the oyster sauce, the stock, and the remaining cornstarch. Cut the scallions into 1 inch segments.

Cooking Heat the oil in a large frying pan over a high heat. When it is very hot, pour in the marinated beef, spread it out in the pan and stir-fry quickly for 1 minute. Pour away any excess oil and drain the beef. Place the pan over the heat again, and use the oil left in it to stir-fry the ginger and scallions together for 30 seconds. Return the beef to the pan and pour in the remainder of the sherry. Stir and turn the beef round a few times, and spread it out in the pan. Pour the oyster/stock mixture evenly over the beef. Stir and scramble for 20 seconds over a high heat, and dish out immediately onto a well-heated serving plate.

Ideally, the steak should be eaten the moment it is served. It is a great dish, and being comparatively quick and easy to prepare, it is often seen and used in domestic cooking as well as at parties.

Quick-Fried Sliced Steak with Tomatoes

Preparation Slice the beef very thin against the grain into 1½ × 2 inch slices. Marinate with half of the salt, the soy sauce, and the sherry for 15 minutes. Peel the tomatoes, cut each one into quarters, and sprinkle with the remaining salt, and pepper to taste. Cut the scallions into 2 inch segments. Crush the garlic. Blend the cornstarch with 3 parts stock.

Cooking Heat the oil in a large frying pan. Add half of the scallions and garlic and stir-fry for 15 seconds. Add the beef and stir-fry over a high heat for 1 minute. Stir in the remainder of the stock and continue to stir-fry and scramble for 15 seconds. Add the cornstarch mixture. Stir until the liquid in the pan thickens, then add the tomato wedges, spreading them evenly over the pan. Allow these to heat through for 30 seconds. Sprinkle with the remainder of the scallions, and serve.

Serves 4–8, with other dishes

1¾ lb flank steak
4–5 firm medium-sized tomatoes

1 teaspoon salt
2 tablespoons soy sauce
1 tablespoon dry sherry
pepper
2 scallions
1 clove garlic
¾ tablespoon cornstarch
6 tablespoons stock
¼ cup vegetable oil

Quick-Fried Steak with Triple Winter

'Triple Winter' originally meant winter bamboo shoots, winter mushrooms, and winter Chinese cabbage. Apparently these vegetables are particularly tender and flavorsome in the winter as compared with the coarse, lush growth of the spring and summer. However, as these may not always be available in the West, Savoy cabbage or thinly sliced celery can be used instead; instead of winter mushrooms, one can use the usual Chinese dried mushrooms, and for winter bamboo shoots, use canned bamboo shoots. This would not satisfy connoisseurs, but how many of us have the opportunity of being so spoiled these days?

Triple Winter is a well known combination, and this recipe illustrates the way beef and vegetables are generally cooked together: the beef is stir-fried very quickly first— about 30 seconds for ½ lb—and then removed, thus leaving

Serves 4–6, with other dishes

1½ lb flank steak
½ cup bamboo shoots
¼ cup winter mushrooms *or* Chinese
  dried mushrooms
1 cup Chinese celery cabbage *or*
  Savoy cabbage, *or* celery

1 teaspoon salt
2 tablespoons soy sauce
pepper to taste
2 tablespoons dry sherry
1 clove garlic
1 slice ginger root
2 scallions
5 tablespoons vegetable oil
3 tablespoons superior stock

some savoriness and gravy in the oil, which is then used to fry the vegetables for a longer period—about 1–2 minutes. After a period of oiling and frying, a small amount of stock (2–3 tablespoons) is added to give the vegetables a further period (1–2 minutes) of quick sizzle-braising. When the liquid in the pan is about to dry up, the beef is returned to the pan for a final quick-frying. At this point, a small amount of wine or sherry and monosodium glutamate might be added to heighten the taste at the last moment (these are optional). All such dishes are meant to be eaten as soon as possible after they leave the pan.

Preparation Slice the beef against the grain into very thin 1½ × 2 inch pieces. Sprinkle with salt, soy sauce, pepper to taste, and half of the sherry. Mix and marinate for 30 minutes, turning the beef once or twice. Cut the bamboo shoots into the same size and thickness as the beef. Cut the cabbage or celery into similar pieces. Crush the garlic, shred the ginger, and cut the scallions into 1 inch segments. Soak the mushrooms for 30 minutes, drain, and remove the stalks.

Cooking Heat the oil in a large frying pan. Add the garlic and ginger, and stir-fry together for 10–15 seconds. Add the marinated beef and continue to stir-fry over a high heat for 1 minute. Remove the meat and put aside. Add the bamboo shoots, cabbage, and mushrooms to the remaining oil in the pan. Stir-fry for 1½ minutes. Add the stock and continue to stir-fry for 1½ minutes. Return the beef to the pan, add the remaining sherry, adjust the seasonings, and stir-fry quickly for 30 seconds over a high heat. Dish out onto a well-heated plate and serve immediately

Quick-Fried Sliced Beef with Green and Red Peppers

Serves 4–8, with other dishes

Preparation Repeat the recipe for Quick-Fried Sliced Beef with Cauliflower, using 1 red and 2 green peppers (medium-sized) instead of cauliflower. Remove the seeds from the peppers, and slice them into ½ inch wide pieces.

Cooking Stir-fry the peppers first in half of the oil for 1½ minutes, then put them aside. Add the remaining oil to the pan, and stir-fry the beef in it for 1 minute. Return the peppers to the pan, add the stock, stir-fry the beef and pepper together for 1 minute over a high heat, and serve.

Quick-Fried Sliced Beef with Cauliflower

Preparation Repeat the recipe for Quick-Fried Steak with Triple Winter (see opposite), using ¾ lb (about 2½ cups) young cauliflower instead of the three vegetables. After the initial frying, add more stock (6 tablespoons instead of 4½), cover the pan, and cook the cauliflower for a full 2½ minutes over a high heat. Return the beef to the pan for a final stir-frying; then serve.

Serves 4–8, with other dishes

Quick-Fried Beef Ribbons with Onion

This is one of the most commonly seen beef dishes, and one of the most easily successful.

Preparation Slice the beef against the grain into matchstick strips. Cut the onions into similar strips. Mix the soy sauce, hoisin sauce, half of the sherry, the sugar, and the pepper; add to the beef, and marinate together for 15 minutes. Dust the beef with cornstarch.

Cooking Heat 2 tablespoons of the oil in a frying pan. Add the onion and some salt, and stir-fry over a high heat for 3 minutes. Push the onion to the sides of the pan. Pour the remaining oil into the pan, and when it is hot, add the beef and any remaining marinade. Stir-fry quickly for 1 minute, then bring in the onions from the side of the pan and stir-fry together with the beef for 1 minute. Add the remaining sherry, stir-fry for a further 30 seconds, and serve.

This dish is a good accompaniment to rice, and should be served piping hot.

Serves 4–8, with other dishes

1½ lb flank steak
4 medium-sized onions

3 tablespoons soy sauce
1 tablespoon hoisin sauce
2 tablespoons dry sherry
1 teaspoon sugar
½ teaspoon salt
pepper to taste
½ tablespoon cornstarch
4½ tablespoons vegetable oil

Quick-Fried Beef Ribbons with Celery

Preparation Repeat the recipe for Quick-Fried Beef Ribbons with Onion, using ½ lb (about 3 cups) celery, sliced into matchstick shreds, instead of onions.

Serves 4–8, with other dishes

179

Hot Spiced Beef Ribbons Quick-Fried with Shredded Sweet Peppers and Chili Peppers

Serves 4–8, with other dishes

Preparation Repeat the recipe for Quick-Fried Beef Ribbons with Scallions using 1 large green pepper, 1 large red pepper, 2 chili peppers, and ⅛ teaspoon of five spice powder instead of the scallions. Remove the seeds from both peppers and slice them into matchstick shreds. Remove the seeds from the chili peppers and chop each into four pieces.

Cooking Heat half of the oil in a frying pan, and stir-fry the chili pepper over a high heat for 40 seconds. Use a slotted spoon to remove most of the scorched chili pepper. Stir-fry the red and green peppers for 1 minute, then push them to the sides of the pan. Add the remaining oil and beef to the center of the pan and stir-fry for 30 seconds. Sprinkle the beef with the five spice powder and stir-fry for another 30 seconds. Bring in the peppers from the sides of the pan and stir-fry them with the beef for 1 minute. Sprinkle the remaining sherry over the beef and peppers. Turn and toss several times; then serve.

This is a dish from Szechuan in west China and is therefore very hot—a boon to those who like hot spicy foods.

Quick-Fried Beef Ribbons with Transparent Noodles and String Beans

Serves 4–8, with other dishes

1½ lb flank steak
1 cup transparent bean-thread noodles
½ lb string beans

1 slice ginger root
2 tablespoons soy sauce
2 tablespoons dry sherry
2 teaspoons sugar
pepper to taste
5 tablespoons vegetable oil
1 teaspoon salt
6 tablespoons chicken stock
¼ teaspoon monosodium glutamate

The crunchiness of the beans contrasts well with the tenderness of the beef and noodles.

Preparation Shred the ginger. Slice the beef against the grain into matchstick shreds. Add soy sauce, half of the sherry, the sugar, pepper, and ginger; marinate the beef for 15 minutes. Soak the noodles in warm water for 15 minutes; then drain. Trim the string beans, then parboil them for 5 minutes.

Cooking Heat 2 tablespoons of the oil in a large frying pan. Pour in the beef and the marinade. Stir-fry over a high heat for 1 minute, then push to the sides of the pan. Pour the remaining oil into the center of the pan. Add the beans and sprinkle with salt. Stir-fry over a high heat for 1½ minutes, then add half of the stock and continue to stir-fry for a minute over medium heat. Remove the beef and beans separately with a perforated spoon and keep hot. Keep them separate. Add the noodles to the pan with the remaining stock and sprinkle with monosodium glutamate. Turn the noodles in the gravy a few times, and when they have heated through, lift them out with a slotted spoon and lay them as a bed on a serving dish. Pour the remaining sherry into the pan, and return the beef and beans to the pan for 15 seconds frying over a high heat. Keep them separate.

Serving Pile the beef on the noodles, and encircle it with the glistening string beans. Pour any remaining gravy over.

Quick-Fried Beef Ribbons with Young Leeks

Preparation Repeat the recipe for Quick-Fried Beef Ribbons with Onion, using ½ lb (about 3 cups) young leeks instead of the onions.

Serves 4–8, with other dishes

This is a particularly attractive dish; there is a striking contrast in color between the rich brown of the beef and the glistening green of the well-oiled leeks. The strong flavors of both ingredients appear to blend well together over high heat. (See illustration.)

Quick-Fried Beef Ribbons with Scallions and Shredded Carrots

Carrots and scallions combine to give this dish color appeal.

Serves 4–8, with other dishes

Repeat the recipe for Quick-Fried Beef Ribbons with Onion using ¼ lb scallions and 2 small, young carrots instead of the onions. Clean the scallions and chop them into 2 inch segments (include the green parts), and slice the carrots into matchstick strips. Stir-fry the carrots for 1 minute before adding the beef, and add the scallions to the pan only during the last minute's stir-frying over a high heat, together with the beef and other ingredients. An additional tablespoon of oil will probably be required during the stir-frying. (See illustration.)

181

Deep-Fried Shredded Beef Ribbons with Shredded Carrots and Peppers

Serves 4–8, with other dishes

Repeat the previous recipe, using the same ingredients but adding 1 medium sweet pepper, sliced into matchstick strips, and 1½ teaspoons chili sauce. Toss the beef and shredded vegetables in the sauce and seasonings, and leave to marinate for 2 hours; then, instead of quick-frying, place in a wire basket and deep-fry in hot oil for 5–6 minutes until almost scorched. Drain thoroughly, and serve on a well-heated dish.

This dish is rather different from the previous one in that the meat ribbons and shredded vegetables become crispy and chewy rather than tender, after being deep-fried. Eaten hot, they make a very tasty cocktail snack.

Stock 'Crackled' Sliced Beef

Serves 4–8, with other dishes

1½ lb flank steak

1 tablespoon black fermented salted beans
1 egg
½ teaspoon salt
2 tablespoons soy sauce
1 tablespoon dry sherry
1 tablespoon cornstarch
3 pieces dried chili pepper
5 tablespoons vegetable oil
2 cloves garlic
2 slices ginger root
3 young leeks
1 cup bamboo shoots
3 tablespoons white wine
1¼ cups superior stock
1 tablespoon light soy sauce
¼ teaspoon monosodium glutamate

Quick-frying is a common method of cooking in China. Quick 'crackled' or 'sizzled' in very hot stock is much less common, but it is sometimes used to excellent effect in some Chinese regional cooking. The following recipe, which is derived from the Restaurant of the Nationalities, in Chungking in west China, is an example.

Preparation Soak the black beans in water for 20 minutes. Drain and mash. Cut the beef with a sharp knife into paper-thin 1½ × 2 inch slices. Break the egg into a bowl, and add salt, soy sauce, sherry, and cornstarch. Blend into a smooth batter, then add the mixture to the beef and work it evenly over the meat, using your fingers. Chop each chili pepper into four and discard the seeds. Fry them in 2 tablespoons of the oil for 1 minute and remove from heat. Crush the garlic, shred the ginger, and cut the leeks into 1½ inch segments. Slice the bamboo shoots into thin 1 × 1½ inch slices.

Cooking Heat the remaining oil in a large frying pan. Add the leeks, ginger, garlic, bamboo shoots, and black beans. Stir-fry over high heat for 2 minutes. Add the white wine, stock, light soy sauce, and monosodium glutamate. Turn the heat up to full, and when the contents of the pan come to the boil, pour in the marinated, coated beef, and spread it out evenly over the pan. After 40 seconds of quick stir-crackling in the boiling stock over the highest heat, pour out onto a deep serving dish. Meanwhile, quickly heat up the dried chili pepper in oil and pour over the beef.

This dish produces perspiration, even on a winter's evening; it is a great favorite of all 'hot-food' lovers in west China. The pouring of heated oil over the beef is optional (the strength and heat of the oil can of course be varied by increasing or decreasing the number of chili peppers used), but it is the usual practice in the western provinces of China.

Stock 'Crackled' Sliced Beef with Kidney

Repeat the previous recipe, adding 2 lamb kidneys, sliced about the same size as the beef, and 1 more tablespoon of soy sauce. Because of the short cooking time, the beef will be tender and the kidneys crispy and crunchy, and this contrast of textures increases the interest of the dish.

Serves 4–8, with other dishes

The distinctive flavor of kidneys combined with the savoriness of the other ingredients, produces a dish of unique appeal.

Beef Barbecue

Beef Barbecue is one of the Chinese modern dishes (originating probably from the great grasslands of the north west) which is a great favorite in Peking. Thinly sliced beef, either marinated or unmarinated, is grilled over wire-mesh grates fitted over the top of an earthenware pot charcoal brazier with a diameter across the top of about 18–24 inches. An American version of this dish might be to use a Japanese hibachi, and serve it at an outdoor barbecue.

If unmarinated, diners should dip the slices of beef into one or several of the following dips on the table: Salt and Pepper Mix, Hot Mustard Sauce, Soy-Oil-Garlic Dip, Soy-Mustard Dip, Soy-Sherry Dip, Soy-Chili-Oil Dip, and hoisin sauce (see Index). The barbecued beef should then be eaten with ordinary Man Tou (steamed buns), Flower Roll Steamed Buns, or Silver Thread Steamed Buns, or it can be eaten with ordinary toasted rolls.

If the beef is to be marinated before being barbecued, the following recipe can be used.

Serves 6, with other dishes

3 lb flank steak

5 tablespoons soy sauce
2 tablespoons dry sherry
1½ tablespoons vinegar
1 teaspoon sugar
pepper to taste
2 cloves garlic
2 slices ginger root
6 scallions
6 eggs

Preparation Cut the beef against the grain into 1 × 2 inch very thin pieces. Add the soy sauce, sherry, vinegar, sugar, and pepper. Crush the garlic, shred the ginger, and add them to the beef with the other seasoning ingredients. Leave the meat to marinate for 30 minutes. Slice each scallion into two. Give each a bash with the side of a cleaver, and cut into 2½ inch segments. Tie each segment into a knot. Arrange them in three or four small saucer-size plates, and place them strategically around the table for the use of diners. Beat an egg in each of six bowls, one for each diner.

Cooking and Serving When the charcoal in the brazier is fully ablaze, and most or all of the smokiness has dissipated, bring it to the dinner table. Place it on a large metal tray. When the meal commences, each diner will pick up a piece of beef and a segment of scallion with a pair of extra long wooden or bamboo chopsticks, and place them on top of the grate or grill to barbecue for 1–1¼ minutes. He should then pick them up again quickly and dip them into the beaten egg (both to cool and to coat) and then into the dips and mixes, before eating them with his steamed or toasted buns or rolls.

To repair to the East Market in Peking to eat this dish after a freezing day out in the open was one of the relieving features of the great student demonstrations of the 1930s.

Red-Cooked Oxtail

Serves 6–8, with other dishes

5–6 lb oxtail, chopped into its natural segments

2 cloves garlic
3 slices ginger root
1½ teaspoons salt
6 tablespoons soy sauce
2 tablespoons hoisin sauce
¼ cup dry sherry
¾ cup superior stock
1 tablespoon sugar

Like all meats, oxtail can be red-cooked, and there seems to be no better way of preparing it.

Preparation Crush the garlic. Clean the oxtail and boil the segments for 3–4 minutes in boiling water. Place them in a heavy pot or casserole with the garlic, ginger, salt, soy sauce, and hoisin sauce. Add 1 quart water.

Cooking Bring contents of pan to the boil. Put an asbestos pad under the pan and leave to simmer over the lowest heat for 1½ hours. Turn the contents over once every 30 minutes. Add the sherry, stock, and sugar, and continue to simmer over the lowest heat for another hour, turning the contents over after 30 minutes. If cooked in a casserole in the oven, cook at 300°F for 3 hours.

Serving Oxtail so cooked should be served in a bowl or deep dish. Eat it with plain boiled rice, and ample gravy.

Smoked Beef

This is a useful dish for Chinese hors d'œuvre.

Preparation Shred the ginger. Cut the beef along the grain into pieces about 1–1½ inches wide, 1½–2 inches thick, and 3–4 inches long. Add the soy sauce, sherry, sugar, shredded ginger, and five spice powder, and marinate for 1 hour, turning beef over after 30 minutes. Mix the remaining ingredients together, and scatter the mixture evenly over the center of a large sheet of aluminum foil.

Cooking Heat the oil in a large frying pan. Add the beef and marinade, and stir-fry together over a medium heat for 7–8 minutes, when the meat will have nearly dried. Transfer the beef to a small roasting pan. Place the pan on top of the mixture on the aluminum foil, and fold the foil loosely over the pan and its contents, sealing it securely. Place the parcel in a very large heavy casserole over a medium heat. Heat until the sugar starts to smoke (this can be seen by poking a pin hole at the top of the foil through which the smoke can rise). When this happens, seal the pin hole and turn off the heat, leaving the parcel to stand for 20 minutes. Unwrap the parcel outdoors. Remove the strips of beef from the roasting pan, and place them on a chopping board. Slice each strip of beef against the grain into thin slices.

Serving Arrange the slices on a dish in overlapping slices and serve.

Serves 6–10, with other dishes

3 lb flank steak

2 slices ginger root
6 tablespoons soy sauce
¼ cup dry sherry
2 teaspoons sugar
¼ teaspoon five spice powder
pepper to taste
¼ cup brown sugar
2 teaspoons cinnamon
2 teaspoons ground anise
2 teaspoons ground cloves
¼ cup vegetable oil

Hot Spiced Chinese Peppered Steak

Preparation Shred the ginger. Cut the beef along the grain into pieces 3–4 inches long, 1 inch thick, and 2 inches wide. Sprinkle them with soy sauce, sherry, sugar, salt, hoisin sauce, shredded ginger, pepper, and chili pepper; rub in well. Allow the beef to marinate for 1 hour. Rub with 1½ tablespoons of the oil, and continue to marinate for another 30 minutes.

Cooking and Serving Heat the remaining oil in a large frying pan. Add the beef strips and marinade, and gently stir-fry over a medium heat for 9–10 minutes, turning the strips over as they fry. Remove the strips of beef from the pan, place them on a chopping board, and slice them against the grain into ⅕ inch slices. Arrange them on a serving dish in overlapping slices and serve.

Serves 6–10, with other dishes

3½ lb flank steak

2 slices ginger root
5 tablespoons soy sauce
¼ cup dry sherry
2 teaspoons sugar
½ teaspoon salt
1 tablespoon hoisin sauce
¼–½ teaspoon freshly ground black pepper
½ teaspoon red chili pepper
6 tablespoons vegetable oil

LAMB AND MUTTON

We Chinese do not make a distinction between lamb and mutton: sheep's meat is sheep's meat, regardless of the age of the animal. In fact, we even call goats mountain sheep (San Yang); and indeed, in many hilly and mountainous southern provinces, goat meat is eaten more often than lamb or mutton. It is in the north, in the provinces which border Mongolia, in Inner Mongolia, and Sinkiang, that lamb and mutton come into their own. They form the principal meat diet of the Chinese Moslems. Owing to the proximity of Peking to Inner Mongolia, and the large number of Chinese Moslem restaurants which have been established in the capital, mutton and lamb have become the favorite meats eaten in Peking. Yet there are not a great many lamb dishes. The best known are probably Mongolian Hot Pot, Mongolian Brazier-Grilled Lamb, and Thrice-Cooked Lamb of Lung Fu Ssi (from the east end of Peking), which have all become special features and attractions of that city.

However, we shall start from the easier and more practical lamb dishes and graduate towards those which are practised on a larger national scale.

Red-Cooked Lamb

Serves 10–12

5–6 lb boneless leg of lamb

6 scallions
1 teaspoon salt
½ cup soy sauce
1 tablespoon hoisin sauce
3 slices ginger root

Preparation Chop the lamb into 2 × 1 inch pieces. Wash in fresh water, and drain. Cut the scallions into 1½ inch segments.

Cooking Place the pieces of lamb in a large casserole or heavy frying pan. Add salt, soy sauce, hoisin sauce, ginger, half of the scallions, and 5 cups of water. Bring to the boil, then insert an asbestos pad under the pot, and simmer very gently for 2½ hours, turning the meat over once every 30 minutes. Sprinkle with the remaining scallions 5 minutes before serving.

Serving Serve either in a large serving bowl or tureen, or else in the casserole in which the meat was cooked.

Tung-Po Red-Cooked Lamb

Tung-Po, the great Chinese poet of the Sung Dynasty, is said to have created a great many Chinese dishes during his banishment from Court. However, it is doubtful whether he created this dish, as he was banished not to the north or west, but to the south, where people mostly ate goat. Nevertheless the dish is called by his name. It is taken from the Yu I-Sung, which is a well-known Moslem restaurant in Peking.

Preparation Slice the lamb into large thin pieces, about ¼ inch thick, and then cut again crosswise into triangular 1½ inch pieces. Peel the potatoes and carrots, and cut them into similar triangular pieces. Slice the onions thin, crush the garlic, and chop the pepper into four pieces, removing the seeds.

Cooking Pour the oil into a large frying pan over a high heat. When very hot, add the pieces of lamb and stir-fry for 4–5 minutes. Drain and set aside. Place the potato and carrot in the remaining oil. Stir-fry together for 5–6 minutes; then drain and put to one side. Place the lamb at the bottom of a heavy pan or casserole over a low heat, and add sufficient water to cover. Add the salt, soy sauce, garlic, ginger, pepper, and brown sugar. When the contents start to boil, cover the pan and insert an asbestos pad underneath it. Leave to cook gently for 2 hours, turning the meat every 30 minutes; then add the fried carrots, potato, and sherry, and cook for a further 15 minutes.

Serving When serving, lift the contents of the casserole into a large serving bowl or deep dish, so that the carrots and potato will be arranged at the bottom of the dish, and the lamb on top.

Note The same dish can also, of course, be cooked in the oven by simmering it at 300°F for 2½ hours, and adding the carrots, potato, and sherry during the last 30 minutes.

Serves 6

3 lb saddle of lamb

¼ lb potatoes
¼ lb carrots
2 medium-sized onions
2 cloves garlic
1 dried chili pepper
1 cup vegetable oil
½ teaspoon salt
5 tablespoons soy sauce
1 slice ginger root
1 tablespoon brown sugar
5 tablespoons dry sherry

Steamed Lamb

Repeat the recipe for Tun-Po Red-Cooked Lamb without adding any water to the pan with the lamb. Cook for 2 hours: leave the pan uncovered, and steam vigorously for the first 30 minutes; then cover and steam gently for the next 1½ hours, or until the meat is tender.

Serves 6

187

Sliced Lamb Quick-Fried with Scallions

Serves 6, with other dishes

1½ lb boneless leg of lamb
6 scallions

2 cloves garlic
2 slices ginger root
2 tablespoons soy sauce
½ teaspoon salt
1 tablespoon dry sherry
¼ cup vegetable oil

Preparation Slice the lamb thin into 2 × 1 inch slices. Crush the garlic and shred the ginger. Add the garlic, ginger, soy sauce, salt, and sherry to the lamb and marinate for 30 minutes. Cut the scallions into 2 inch segments (include all the green parts).

Cooking Heat the oil in a large frying pan. When very hot, pour in the marinated lamb, and stir-fry quickly over a high heat for 1½ minutes. Add the scallions and continue to stir-fry for 1½ minutes. Dish out onto a well-heated serving plate; serve and eat immediately.

This is a highly savory and aromatic dish, which is both quick to prepare and universally appealing.

Shredded Lamb Quick-Fried with Ginger and Young Leeks

Serves 6, with other dishes

2 lb boneless leg of lamb
½ lb young leeks
4 slices ginger root

1 chili pepper
3 tablespoons soy sauce
3 tablespoons dry sherry
5 tablespoons vegetable oil
1 teaspoon salt

Preparation Slice the lamb against the grain into matchstick strips. Cut the leeks, ginger, and pepper into similar shreds. Combine soy sauce and sherry, and marinate the lamb in the soy mixture for 20 minutes.

Cooking Heat 2½ tablespoons of the oil in a frying pan. Add the pepper and ginger, and stir-fry them together for 30 seconds. Pour in the marinated lamb, spread the shredded meat out evenly over the pan, and stir-fry quickly for 1½ minutes over a high heat. Remove with a slotted spoon and put aside. Add the remainder of the oil to the pan; then add the leeks and salt and stir-fry for 1 minute. Return the lamb to the pan. Toss and mix well; then stir-fry together for 1½ minutes. Dish out onto a well-heated serving plate, and serve.

Long-Simmered Lamb of Lung Fu Ssi

This recipe comes from the well-known Pai Kwei Chinese Moslem restaurant of Lung Fu Ssi, in Peking. The lamb is cooked very simply. The important thing is that the pieces of meat must be dipped in a specially mixed dip served at the table.

Preparation Chop the lamb into $1\frac{1}{2} \times 1 \times \frac{1}{2}$ inch pieces. Rinse in fresh water, and drain. Heat 5 cups of water in a saucepan. When it boils, add the lamb pieces. Boil for 30 seconds, then pour away all the water and scum. Cut the onions into slices and crush the garlic.

Cooking Place the pieces of lamb in a heavy frying pan or saucepan, or in a heat-proof casserole. Just cover them with water. Add the salt, onion, 2 slices of the ginger, and 2 cloves of garlic. Bring to the boil, then lower the heat to a minimum. Insert an asbestos pad underneath the pan, and leave to simmer gently for $2\frac{1}{2}$ hours, turning the lamb over every 45 minutes. The pot should be kept securely covered all the time.

Serving Shred the remaining ginger, crush and chop the 3 remaining garlic cloves and chop the chili pepper fine. Mix these three ingredients with all the other unused ingredients and then divide the mixture among three or four bowls. Place these strategically around the table.

If the lamb is cooked in either an earthenware or iron pot, or in a casserole, it should be brought to the table in its container. Each diner may then dip the plain-cooked lamb in the dip sauce before eating it.

Serves 6–8

3 lb boneless leg of lamb

2 medium-sized onions
5 cloves garlic
2 teaspoons salt
5 slices ginger root
1 chili pepper
$\frac{1}{2}$ cup soy sauce
$\frac{1}{4}$ teaspoon freshly ground pepper
1 tablespoon chopped coriander *or* parsley
$1\frac{1}{2}$ tablespoons chopped chives
3 tablespoons dry sherry
1 tablespoon vinegar

Jellied Lamb

This is another favorite northern dish. Cut into pieces and served cold, it is often used as an accompaniment to hot soft rice (congee).

Serves 10–12

Preparation This is a variation of the first lamb recipe, Red-Cooked Lamb. Add 3 lb lamb bones, and an extra cup of water to the pan with the lamb pieces. Use only 1 tablespoon soy sauce. Bring to the boil, insert an asbestos pad under the pan or casserole, and reduce the heat to a minimum. Simmer gently for $2\frac{1}{2}$ hours, turning the meat and bones over once every 45 minutes. When the lamb is cooked, remove and discard the bones, spread the meat evenly over the pan and press down so that it is covered by the gravy. Leave to cool for 1 hour; then place in the refrigerator. After 2 hours the dish will have jellied. Scrape the fat from the top, reheat, then add $\frac{1}{4}$ teaspoon of monosodium glutamate and $\frac{1}{4}$ cup of dry sherry. Give the meat a stir, and remove the pan from the heat. Transfer the meat to a deep dish. When cool, place it in the refrigerator overnight. The jelly and lamb will then be quite clear.

Serving Cut the lamb and jelly into 2 × 1 × ½ inch pieces. This is an excellent dish to go with wine, or quantities of hot food such as hot rice or noodles.

Curried Lamb

Serves 6

3 lb boneless leg *or* shoulder of lamb

4 medium-sized onions
2 cloves garlic
2 slices ginger root
2 tablespoons soy sauce
1½ tablespoons dry sherry
1 tablespoon cornstarch
6 tablespoons vegetable oil
2 teaspoons salt
3 tablespoons curry powder
1 cup secondary stock

Preparation Cut the lamb meat into approximately 1½ inch cubes. Cut the onions into thin slices, crush the garlic, and shred the ginger. Mix the garlic, ginger, soy sauce, sherry, and 2 tablespoons water in a bowl. Blend the cornstarch with ¼ cup of water.

Cooking Heat 3 tablespoons of the oil in a heavy saucepan and add the pieces of lamb. Stir-fry over a high heat for 6–7 minutes; then remove the meat, drain it, and put aside. Pour the remaining oil into the pan, then add the onion, salt, and curry powder. Stir-fry over a high heat for 3 minutes. Return the lamb to the pan, and stir-fry for a further 3 minutes. Add the garlic/ginger/soy/sherry mixture and stir until boiling; then pour in the stock. When the mixture comes to the boil again, cover and simmer gently for 45 minutes, inserting an asbestos pad under the pan. Stir in the cornstarch and water, and when the contents thicken, pour the mixture into a deep dish and serve.

Although curry powder is an adopted ingredient in Chinese cooking, it is fast becoming an established one since curry dishes go so well with rice.

Quick-Fried Triple Lamb

Serves 6

1 lb boneless leg of lamb
¾ lb lamb's liver
3 lamb's kidneys
2 scallions
2 slices ginger root
2 cloves garlic
4½ tablespoons soy sauce
3 tablespoons dry sherry
5 tablespoons vegetable oil
2 tablespoons sesame oil

Preparation Cut the lamb into thin 2 × 1 inch slices; clean and remove any gristle from the liver and kidneys. Cut the liver into slices similar to the lamb meat. Cut each kidney into three flat slices, give each several crosswise cuts halfway through, and then cut each slice into three pieces. Chop the scallions into ¼ inch segments, shred the ginger, and crush and chop the garlic. Marinate the lamb slices in 1½ tablespoons of the soy sauce, 1 tablespoon of the sherry, and the scallions. Marinate the liver in 1½ tablespoons of the soy sauce, 1 tablespoon of the sherry, and the shredded ginger; and marinate the kidneys in 1½ tablespoons of the soy sauce, 1 tablespoon of the sherry, and the garlic. All three items should be marinated for 30 minutes.

Cooking Heat 3 tablespoons of the vegetable oil in a large frying pan. When the oil is very hot, pour in the marinated lamb meat, and stir-fry for 1½ minutes over a high heat. Remove, and set aside to keep hot. Add 1 tablespoon of vegetable oil to the pan. Pour in the marinated liver. Stir-fry quickly for 1 minute, then put aside and keep hot. Add the remaining vegetable oil to the pan, then add the kidneys, and stir-fry quickly for 30 seconds. Add the sesame oil. Return the lamb and liver to the pan. Stir-fry the contents over high heat for 45 seconds, then remove to a well-heated dish, and serve.

The three different types of lamb, with their three quite different textures, tastes, and marinades, give the dish quite a distinctive character. Eat with freshly cooked boiled or steamed rice.

Peking Mongolian Sliced Lamb Hot Pot

This dish is called Peking Mongolian, as it originated in Mongolia and later achieved fame and recognition in Peking. Thinly sliced lamb, cooked at the table by the diners themselves, in a funnelled charcoal-burning hot pot, was first introduced to Peking in 1855, in the reign of Emperor Shanfeng of the Manchu Dynasty. It has been gaining in popularity ever since, and is now recognized as one of the gastronomic features of Peking. The best-known establishment for this do-it-yourself hot pot is the Tung Lai Sung Restaurant in the East Market, where over twenty meat-slicing specialist chefs work full-time. A half-pound chunk of meat would usually be cut into 30 thin slices, and the average slicing speed of a specialist is from 12–16 slices per minute. In the West, the slicing can be done with an electric knife, or you can partially freeze the meat and then slice with a sharp knife. To achieve reasonable results is probably easier than one would at first imagine, since it is not essential that the slices of meat are of an absolutely regular shape or thickness, just so long as they are not thick.

Serves 6–8

5 lb boneless leg *or* shoulder of lamb

2½ cups secondary stock
1 quart superior stock *or* chicken stock
1 lb Chinese celery cabbage *or* a mixture of Savoy cabbage and celery
½ lb spinach
1½ cups transparent bean-thread noodles, soaked and drained
1½ teaspoons salt.

Table Dips Provide a selection of the following ingredients for the diners to use when mixing table dips: soy sauce, hoisin sauce, chili sauce, mustard, tomato sauce, vinegar, sesame paste, chopped ginger, chopped garlic, chopped scallions, and chopped coriander. These items can be placed in individual sauce dishes, or in some cases, two or more items, such as ginger and vinegar, or chili sauce and soy sauce, can be combined. Usually the mixing is done by the diners themselves according to their individual taste. (See illustration.)

191

Cooking Utensil The traditional Peking hot pot is different from many southern hot pots in that it has a large squat funnel which rises from the center of the cooking pot, and the foods are cooked in the 'moat' surrounding the funnel. The moat is approximately 5 inches deep and 3–4 inches wide at the top, as it should be able to hold at least 2½–3 quarts food and liquid. The base must be firm so that there will be little chance of the pot tipping over.

At the Tung Lai Sung in Peking the funnel is exceptionally squat, measuring about 5–6 inches in diameter at the base, and tapering to 3–4 inches at the top. As it is nearly 12 inches high, it holds a good stack of charcoal inside, ensuring the steady heat which is essential to this type of cooking and eating. The usual way of starting such a burner is to place a few pieces of burning charcoal at the bottom of the funnel, then stack more charcoal on top of this. After a short period of fanning through the side-opening at the base of the funnel, the smoldering will soon develop into burning, and within a few minutes there will be a beautiful blaze. The moat outside the funnel should be filled with stock before the first charcoal is introduced.

Because the average American home lacks such equipment, any heavy saucepan or large casserole placed on top of an alcohol- or gas-burning stand will do. However, Peking hot pots are becoming more easily available from Chinese markets.

Cooking and Eating As soon as the stock starts to boil furiously, about a quarter of the vegetables and noodles should be put into the pot, along with the salt. Within 1–2 minutes, the contents will be boiling again. At this point, the diners begin to put their own slices of meat into the cauldron. These should be pushed underneath and submerged in the boiling stock with the aid of bamboo chopsticks. Plastic ones should not be used.

Meanwhile, the diners can start to mix their own dips from any of the ingredients provided on the table. They can mix one or two types of dip ingredient together or experiment with several.

The slices of meat should cook in the stock within 1½ minutes. They should then be lifted out with a pair of chopsticks and dipped into one or more of the dips before eating.

As the meal progresses, the stock becomes tastier and tastier—until finally all the remaining meat, vegetables, and noodles on the table are added to the moat for a final boiling. This is done by placing a lid over the moat, thus allowing the centers to boil or simmer for 3–4 minutes. These are then divided among the individual bowls of the diners for a grand finale.

The point about this type of cooking-while-you-eat is the simplicity in the choice of materials, the freshness due to instant cooking, and the variety and livening effect of the quick dip in the various piquant sauces before consumption.

Peking Mongolian Barbecued or Brazier-Grilled Sliced Lamb

When winter comes around in Peking, another favorite feature of cook-at-the-table eating is the Mongolian Barbecue of Sliced Lamb. The lamb is cut into slices similar in size to those in the previous recipe, but the cooking method is different in that the lamb is brazier-grilled on the table. The brazier consists of an earthen pot with fine-mesh wire grills fitted over the top, on which the slices of lamb are cooked. The fire is fanned to a full blaze outside in the open, and then brought in and placed on the dining table on a metal tray, although as often as not, the cooking and eating are done in the courtyard.

This dish was first introduced to Peking by visiting Mongolian dignitaries in 1644 in the reign of Emperor Tun Chi. It is now one of the features of the Tung Lai Sung Restaurant in the East Market, but the two best-known places for this dish are the Barbecue Wan of the South City, which has been operating for one hundred years, and the Barbecue Chi of the North City which has been operating for nearly two hundred years.

The only vegetable used with this type of lamb dish is sliced onion or scallions. The wire grills are first of all rubbed with fat or oil, and tested with a drop of water. If the water sizzles, the grill is hot enough to commence the barbecue.

Each diner can mix his own selection of dips in his dip-bowl (empty bowls are given to each diner for this purpose). Provide the same dip ingredients as in the previous recipe, but the diners may beat an egg in another bowl and use that as an additional dip. Usually when a slice of lamb and a slice of onion have been grilled for about 1 minute, the diner plunges them into the beaten egg to cool and coat them before dipping them into one or more of the dips before eating. The lamb can be eaten on its own or with Chinese steamed buns, either the plain ones called Man Tou, or with the fancier ones called Lotus Leaf Buns (Ho Yeh Pao). It can also be accompanied by Toasted Cake (Shao Pin). The joy of eating lamb which is hot, tender, and aromatic is soul-consuming!

Such a meal is best staged outdoors in the West, as most ceilings are low in modern buildings. The Japanese hibachi stove, which is a derivation of the Peking-Mongolian brazier is, of course, excellent for the job, so long as it is a large one.

The approximate calculation for meat is ¾–1 lb of lamb per diner (although some student colleagues of my younger days have been known to consume 25 dishes, or about 5 lb!). When eaten in small thin slices one at a time, the total quantity eaten is often not realized.

Pai Kwei Thrice-Cooked Lamb
of Lung Fu Ssi

This dish or recipe is included here for reading rather than practice in the average kitchen: by reading one might get a feel for some of the larger Chinese dishes. For the whole concept of Chinese Moslem cooking was based on a background radically different from today's urban situation—the great plains of Central Asia. When the beast was slaughtered for food, it was necessary to cook all that was available from the animal at once. Thus, in its original conception and calculation the cooking was on an immense scale, since up to 100 lb of meat had to be cooked at once. Even today, in many Peking restaurants, where this lamb dish is served, the preparation is on the same immense scale.

The restaurant referred to here was first established in the 45the year of the reign of Emperor Chien Lung (1736–1795). Pai Kwei, who was the original proprietor, is said to have been exiled to Sinkiang for telling risqué stories at Court. But the restaurant still stands on the original site. Thrice-Cooked Lamb is the best-known dish of the establishment but the following is a very much contracted version of the recipe, to make it practicable for modern situations.

Preparation Cut the lamb meat into 6 × 4 × 2½ inch chunks. Parboil the meat and neck for 12 minutes in a large pot of boiling water. Parboil the tail, heart, liver, kidneys, and tripe for the same length of time. Drain and put aside to cool. Soak the mushrooms for 20 minutes, and drain. Select a very large, thick-bottomed, heavy metal pot, with a heavy wooden lid, which will fit inside it. In fact, it must be one clear size too small for the pot as it will be used to press the meat down after the pot has been properly packed.

Arrange the lamb bones and neck at the bottom of the pot, leaving a well in the center. Soak the tangerine peel for 30 minutes; then slice the onions into quarters, and crush the garlic. Scatter or drop these into the well, with the ginger, rosemary, star anise, sugar, pepper, and parsley; fill up the well with the tripe, liver, heart, and kidneys, and cover over with lamb meat and mushrooms.

Cooking Pour in 2 quarts water and 10 cups of the Soy Herbal Stock until nearly all the meats and materials are covered. Now place the lid on top of the contents and press down with a 20–25 lb weight. Bring the contents of the cauldron to a high boil for 30 minutes, then add 2½ cups of stock. Repeat the process twice over during a total of 1½ hours, with the total addition of 10 cups of stock.

Following this initial vigorous cooking over a high heat, simmer the pot over minimal heat for 2 hours. At the beginning of this period of simmering, 2½ cups of strong mushroom broth (made by simmering another ½ lb of dried mushrooms in 1 quart of water for 30 minutes) should be added. After this cooking and simmering, the meat and other pieces of lamb should be lifted out to drain and dry for 15 minutes before frying. The larger chunks of meat should then be cut to more manageable sizes (about two thirds of the size of a matchbox).

The various meats are not all fried at once; they are fried as they are required, when they are almost ready to be served. Twelve pieces are deep-fried and brought to the table at a time. The deep-frying should be done with sesame oil, and should be carried out not too far from the dining table, to ensure that the meat will be sizzling hot when eaten. Fry the meat for 3–4 minutes, or until it is beginning to turn golden-brown.

Serving Lamb prepared in this manner is usually eaten with Toasted Hot Cakes, aromated by being sprinkled with sesame seeds on top, and washed down with ample wine. Or a cupful of rich, hot lamb gravy could be poured over and mixed with a bowl of cooked noodles and eaten as an accompaniment to half a dozen pieces of lamb (fried or unfried). All the customary dips and mixes should be placed on the table for the lamb to be dipped in before eating.

Although this is a very much contracted version (the original required 100 lb of meat, 24 other ingredients, and 13 types of Chinese semi-medicinal herbs!), I can still recommend Borodin's *On the Steppes of Central Asia* as background music when this lamb dish is being eaten!

Serves 12–15

8–10 lb boneless leg of lamb	3 cups Chinese dried mushrooms
2–3 lb neck of lamb	¼ cup Chinese dried tangerine peel
1½–2 lb tail of lamb	3 large onions
1½–2 lb lamb's heart	4 cloves garlic
1½–2 lb lamb's liver	4 slices ginger root
1–1½ lb lamb's kidneys	1½ tablespoons rosemary
1½ lb lamb's tripe *or* intestines	1½ tablespoons star anise
3 lb lamb's rib bones	¼ cup rock sugar
	1 teaspoon freshly ground black pepper
	5 tablespoons chopped parsley
	1 gallon Soy Herbal Master Stock
	sesame oil for deep-frying

CHICKEN

Chicken is one of the most versatile items of food in China; it is also one of the most convenient because of its widespread availability. Every village in China is roused by the crowing cock, and every farmyard or peasant holding in the land is alive with the sound of clucking chickens. A chicken dish on the table is associated with a feeling of occasion or festivity, and it is invariably augmented by a wide selection of side dishes and condiments. When extra food is needed on the unexpected arrival of guests or relatives, or when there is a celebration in the family, a chicken can always be killed to provide a special meat.

In many dishes produced in China, chicken and pork are often interchangeable because of their many similarities. They are both white and, unlike beef, they do not become so tough after being cooked for a short period as to need very prolonged cooking before they are tenderized again. Chickens come in convenient unit sizes, and the meat is always ready for cooking, unlike the larger animals which cannot be killed and prepared for a meal with the same speed. Hence, although chicken is rather more of a delicacy than pork on the Chinese dinner table, it is nearly as extensively used.

Chicken can be combined with almost every known vegetable by stir-frying and can also be cross-cooked with most meats, fish, and seafood. In China, chicken bones and chicken meat are the basic ingredients of high quality stocks (broths) such as superior stock, clear stock, or chicken stock, which are used in the preparation of numerous dishes, soups, and sauces. Like pork, chicken can be lightly boiled and served white-cut, or it can be prepared red-cooked (with soy sauce) or clear-simmered, steamed, or fry-braised. The breast meat can be chopped and combined with other materials to produce a variety of chicken "velveteen" dishes or chicken dumplings. The liver and giblets, lightly cooked, are valued for their crunchiness, whether stir-fried or served in soups. They are considered a delicacy when long-simmered in herbal stock. In this form, they are often served for midnight suppers, or with congee (soft rice) at breakfast. Chicken blood, cooked and solidified, is a traditional ingredient in Hot and Sour Soup or Chicken Blood Soup. Typical of the Chinese sense of economy and variety, we frequently use one chicken to prepare two or three dishes; hence such dishes as Chicken in Three Flavors. For lightly cooked chicken dishes, such as Crystal Chicken or White-Cut Chicken, which are prepared without the addition of any sauce or other highly flavored ingredients, the delicate flavor has to be derived from the chicken meat itself. In such cases, it is important to use free-range birds from the farmyards, rather than frozen, mass-produced chickens which do not have nearly such a good flavor. Certainly, whenever possible it is best to use fresh-killed chicken. On the other hand, it doesn't really matter what kind of bird is used for Red-Cooked Chicken, or in the recipes for chicken cooked with numerous supplementary ingredients and flavorings; although for long-simmered or long-steamed dishes older birds are preferable, as the length of the cooking time should tenderize any kind of meat, and the mature fowls generally have more flavor.

As with the majority of other foods in Chinese cooking, chicken can be cooked either whole or chopped through the bone into square or oblong pieces. To enjoy chicken served in this way we Chinese have learned to become experts in disengaging and stripping the meat from the bone; this is done with dexterity within the mouth. The breast meat can be cut into thin slices and stir-fried with other ingredients; or the meat can be chopped, mixed with other ingredients and formed into balls or cakes, or else served as "velveteen" chicken. Sometimes chicken meat is shredded into matchstick strips for quick-frying with other ingredients, such as pimento or mushrooms, which are also cut or shredded into similar strips. In this form, chicken is used very extensively with noodles, which are similar in shape to chicken strips, and prepared by frying or cold-tossing or even used with ham as a garnish.

The total number of dishes which can be produced from chicken, including all the possible combinations and regional variations, certainly runs into many hundreds. The recipes included in this chapter are only a selection.

Red-Cooked Chicken

Serves 4–6, with other dishes

A 4–5 lb chicken or capon

2 medium-sized onions
3 scallions
½ cup soy sauce
3 slices ginger root
2½ teaspoons sugar
½ teaspoon salt
¼ cup dry sherry

This is really a form of Chinese stewing and it is one of the most popular and common ways of cooking chicken in China because of its simplicity. Red-cooking mainly differs from Western stews in that ginger, soy sauce, and sugar are used. These three ingredients have a marked contribution to the end product: the ginger eliminates any rankness and untoward taste in the bird, the soy sauce enhances its savoriness, and sugar helps to enrich it. Most meats can be red-cooked, and Red-Cooked Chicken is one of the favorite dishes on a Chinese dinner table at home.

Preparation Wash the chicken thoroughly, inside and out; then place it in a heavy pot with 1 quart of water. Bring to the boil and continue boiling for 5 minutes, turning the bird over a few times. Pour away all the water and impurities. Meanwhile, slice the onions thin and cut the scallions into 2 inch pieces.

Cooking Put the chicken into a heat-proof casserole, pour over ¾ cup of fresh water, then add the soy sauce, ginger, onions, sugar, and salt. Bring the liquid to the boil, then put the casserole in an oven preheated to 375°F. Cook in the oven for 1¼ hours, turning the bird over two or three times. Remove the casserole from the oven and sprinkle the scallions and the sherry over the chicken. Return the casserole to the oven for a further 30 minutes.

Serving Serve the chicken from the casserole or in a large bowl or tureen. It should be sufficiently tender to take apart with a pair of chopsticks but fingers may be used discreetly. Although the cooking here is simple, the chicken should be delicious.

Note Instead of cooking the chicken in a casserole, it could also be cooked in a pot over a very low heat, with an asbestos pad inserted under the pot, if necessary.

Chinese Roast Chicken

For the best flavor, use a fresh-killed chicken.

Preparation Wash and dry the chicken, inside and out. Leave it in an airy place for 1 hour to dry out. Crush the garlic, shred the ginger, and chop both very fine. Combine the garlic and ginger with the soy sauce, salt, and vegetable oil, and blend thoroughly. Rub the chicken all over with this mixture and allow the seasoning to sink in for 30 minutes before cooking.

Serves 4–6, with other dishes

A 3–4 lb chicken

1 clove garlic
2 slices ginger root
2 tablespoons soy sauce
1½ teaspoons salt
1½ tablespoons vegetable oil

Cooking Roast the chicken for 1 hour in an oven preheated to 400°F.

Serving The chicken can either be served carved in the Western style or else chopped into pieces or Chinese double-Mahjong pieces. It should have a better flavor than the average roast chicken, without the dull and sometimes unpleasant taste often present in a mass-produced chicken.

Crispy-Skin Pepper Chicken

This is a good way of cooking mass-produced chicken, as the meat becomes richer in flavor.

Serves 4–6, with other dishes

A 3–4 lb chicken

2 tablespoons salt
1½ teaspoons freshly-ground black
  pepper
3 slices ginger root
2½ tablespoons soy sauce
2½ tablespoons vegetable oil

Preparation Wash and dry the chicken thoroughly; then leave it in an airy spot for 1 hour to dry further. Mix the salt and pepper in a very dry saucepan and heat over a low heat for 2 minutes until a distinct peppery 'bouquet' arises from the mixture. Shred the ginger and chop it very fine. Rub the bird with the ginger and then with the salt and pepper mixture, inside and out. Repeat. Retain the remainder of the salt and pepper mixture for further rubbing. Leave the chicken in a refrigerator overnight. Repeat the rubbing process the next day and again refrigerate the chicken overnight. The rubbing process may be repeated once more, if desired. Before roasting the chicken, mix the soy sauce and oil in a bowl by beating them together for 15 seconds, then rub bird with this mixture.

Cooking Place the chicken in an oven preheated to 300°F for 2 hours. Increase the heat to 400°F for 10 minutes. The skin of the chicken should be evenly browned and crispy and the meat should have a delicious flavor by this time.

Serving The chicken can be served either carved in the normal Western style or chopped into pieces or Chinese double-Mah-jong pieces.

White-Cut Chicken

Serves 4–6, with other dishes

A 2–3 lb broiler chicken

3 slices ginger root
1½ tablespoons salt
2½ tablespoons soy sauce
2½ teaspoons sesame oil

This is a basic chicken dish. Its interest is greatly increased by the variety of dips and mixes into which the pieces of chicken can be dipped when served at the table (for the chapter on Table Condiments, see Index). The quality of the chicken meat is also of prime importance here; it must be juicy and tender and rich in flavor. Hence free-range chickens are preferable to mass-produced birds for this dish. Fresh-killed birds will also be very satisfactory.

Preparation Wash and dry the chicken thoroughly inside and out.

Cooking Bring 2 to 2½ quarts of water to the boil in a heavy saucepan. Add the ginger and salt, and immerse the chicken in the boiling water. Reduce the heat to a simmer and insert an asbestos pad under the pan. Simmer for 30 minutes; then leave the chicken to cool in the stock (which can be used for other purposes).

Serving When the chicken is cool, place it on a heavy chopping-board and chop it into 2 × 1 inch double-Mah-jong pieces. Reassemble these pieces in a serving dish, roughly in the shape of a chicken. Pour over the soy sauce and sesame oil, mixed together. Serve with a variety of table condiments, dips, and mixes. (See illustration.)

Steamed Chicken with Southern Snake

The Cantonese use an eel instead of a snake to prepare this dish.

Preparation Cut the ham into slices, about 2 × 1 inch. Chop the eel into 2–3 inch pieces. Boil the pieces of eel in 1 quart of water with 1 tablespoon of salt for 5 minutes. Discard the water, add 2½ cups of fresh water and 2 slices of the ginger root; then simmer for 20 minutes. Discard the ginger, but retain the stock. Cut the meat from the bones of the eel and fry it in the lard and sherry until the meat has absorbed almost all of the liquid. Boil the chicken in water for 5 minutes. Discard the water and place the chicken in a casserole. Pour in the superior stock and 1 cup of the eel stock with a little salt and the remaining ginger root.

Cooking Place the casserole in a steamer, or put its contents into a double-boiler, and simmer for 2 hours. Remove the larger bones from the chicken and return the meat to the casserole. Add the sliced ham, lychee fruit, and pieces of eel and cook for a further 30 minutes.

Serving Just before serving, squeeze the lemon juice over the chicken and eel, and decorate with the petals of a large chrysanthemum bloom.

Serves 4–6, with other dishes

1½–2 lb eel
A 3–4 lb chicken

2 oz smoked ham
salt
4 slices ginger root
1½ tablespoons lard
2½ tablespoons dry sherry
1¼ cups superior stock
1 cup lychee fruit
2 tablespoons fresh lemon juice
1 large chrysanthemum bloom

Steamed Chicken with Chinese Cabbage

Preparation Clean chicken thoroughly, and plunge it into a large pan of boiling water. Boil for 10 minutes, then drain. Stuff the bird with ginger and scallions, and sprinkle with the salt.

Cooking Place chicken in a heat-proof dish or casserole, cover with 2½ cups water, and steam in an open steamer, then break the cabbage into individual leaves and place under and around the bird in the casserole. Sprinkle all over with monosodium glutamate, seasonings, and sherry. Cover with a lid or aluminum foil, steam for a further 40 minutes, then serve. (See illustration.)

Serves 4–6, with other dishes

A 3 lb chicken
1½–2 lb Chinese celery cabbage

2 slices ginger root
6 scallions
3½ teaspoons salt
¼ teaspoon monosodium glutamate
salt and pepper to taste
½ cup dry sherry

Wind-Cured Chicken

Serves 4–6, with other dishes

A 4–5 lb chicken

2½ tablespoons salt
1½ teaspoons freshly ground black
  pepper
1½ tablespoons lard

A freshly-killed chicken is normally used for this dish in China, together with Szechuan pepper. Since such chicken and the Szechuan pepper berry are sometimes hard to obtain, we have to compromise in the ingredients, as well as in the length of hanging time. In China, the bird is usually hung for 10 days: here in America, I doubt if it would be advisable to hang it longer than about five days.

Preparation Clean and rub the chicken dry, inside and out. Mix the salt and pepper and heat the mixture in a dry pan over a low heat for about 2 minutes, until a distinct peppery 'bouquet' arises. Rub the chicken twice with this salt and pepper mixture; then hang it up in a cool, airy place overnight, away from the sun and other vagaries of climate. Mix the remainder of the salt and pepper mixture with lard, blending well. On the next day, rub the chicken with this impregnated lard and hang it up in an airy spot. After 4–5 days of hanging the chicken should be cured and ready for cooking.

Cooking The chicken is normally cooked either by boiling vigorously for 25 minutes or by 35 minutes vigorous steaming. In the West, it can best be cooked by steaming for 10 minutes, followed by 40 minutes roasting at 400°F.

Serving Chop the bird into serving pieces or Mah-jong-size pieces and pile them up on a serving dish. If the chicken has been boiled, the stock is a useful by-product. Wind-Cured Chicken has a taste and quality of its own; the stock, too, is extremely rich in flavor.

Note It is best not to try Wind-Cured Chicken in the summer as it might turn into something quite different.

Salt-Buried Chicken

Serves 4–6, with other dishes

A 2–3 lb chicken
6–7 lb coarse (kosher) salt

Preparation Clean the chicken thoroughly and hang it up to dry overnight. Heat the salt in a heat-proof casserole.

Cooking When the salt is quite hot, make a hole in it and bury the chicken completely. Put the lid on the casserole and place it over a low heat for 10 minutes. Put the casserole in an oven preheated to 375°F for 1 hour.

Serving Excavate the chicken. Chop it into serving pieces or double-Mah-jong pieces, and pile them on a well-heated serving dish. (See illustration.)

Note The salt may be used again.

Cantonese Salt-Buried Chicken

Preparation Clean the chicken thoroughly and hang it up to dry overnight. Heat the salt in a heat-proof casserole. Cut the scallions into 3 inch segments; then shred the ginger root and mix both ingredients with the tangerine peel. Pour over the soy sauce and the brandy. Stuff the chicken with this mixture.

Cooking When the salt is quite hot, make a hole in it and bury the chicken completely. Put the lid on the casserole and place it over a low heat for 10 minutes. Then put the casserole in an oven preheated to 375°F for 1 hour.

Serving Excavate the chicken. Chop it into serving pieces or double-Mah-jong pieces and pile them on a well-heated serving dish.

An interesting feature of salt-buried chicken is that at the end of the cooking time, the chicken skin has become quite brown and contrasts well with the whiteness of the salt. When the white salt is brushed or shaken away from the top of the chicken, it gives the appearance of snow melting from a mountain top, but instead of earth or rock, warm, brown, tanned skin is exposed. The brownness of the bird is probably caused by the moisture on its skin being absorbed by the salt during its period of hot burial.

Note The salt may be used again with the addition of some fresh salt.

Serves 4–6, with other dishes

A 2–3 lb chicken
6–7 lb coarse (kosher) salt

10 scallions
3 slices ginger root
2 tablespoons Chinese dried tangerine peel
2 tablespoons soy sauce
2 tablespoons brandy

Tramp's Chicken

From the province of Kiangsi

This dish is said to have been derived from Chu Yuan Chang, First Emperor of the Ming Dynasty, who went to the south, and, while traveling incognito through the province of Kiangsi, learned this recipe.

Preparation Slice the onion thin, chop the leek into 1 inch segments, shred the ginger root, and crush and chop the garlic fine.

Serves 4–6, with other dishes

A 3–4 lb chicken

1 large onion
1 leek
2 slices ginger root
2 cloves garlic
2 teaspoons salt

201

pepper to taste
2 tablespoons lard
1½ tablespoons soy sauce
2½ teaspoons sesame oil

Cooking Heat a large pan of water and boil the chicken in it for 40 minutes. Clean the chicken giblets thoroughly; then slice the kidney, liver, and heart thin. Dip these parts of the chicken into boiling water, boil for 1 minute; then drain. Chop the chicken, through the bone, into large serving pieces or double-Mah-jong pieces. Arrange them in a serving dish or bowl and sprinkle with salt and pepper. Heat the lard in a frying pan. Add the onion, leek, ginger, and garlic. Stir-fry over a high heat for 1½ minutes. Add the giblets and stir-fry them with the vegetables for 3 minutes. Add the soy sauce and sesame oil and continue to stir-fry for a further 3 minutes.

Serving Pour the contents of the frying pan over the pieces of chicken, and serve.

Aromatic Crispy Chicken (1)

Serves 4–6, with other dishes

A 3–4 lb chicken

1 tablespoon salt
3 slices ginger root
2½ tablespoons chopped coriander
2½ tablespoons soy sauce
dash of five spice powder
2½ tablespoons dry sherry
oil for deep-frying
mustard greens
tomatoes

Preparation Clean the chicken. Rub it thoroughly with the salt, inside and out, and leave to dry overnight. Shred the ginger and mix it with the chopped coriander leaves, soy sauce, five spice powder, and sherry. Rub the chicken with this mixture twice during a period of 2 hours, and leave to dry in an airy place.

Cooking Roast the chicken in an oven preheated to 300°F for 1½ hours. Drain the bird and place it in a wire basket then deep-fry in hot oil for 6–7 minutes, by which time the skin should have become quite crispy.

Serving Chop the chicken into 24 pieces through the bone. Assemble these pieces on a well-heated serving dish in the shape of a chicken. Garnish with greens and tomatoes.

Aromatic Crispy Chicken (2)

Serves 4–6, with other dishes

A 3–4 lb chicken

1 gallon Herbal Master Stock
oil for deep-frying
mustard greens
tomatoes

The end result of this recipe is much the same as the previous recipe, but the preparation is somewhat different. Instead of rubbing seasonings on the bird to marinate it, in this recipe the chicken is hot-marinated in herbal master stock before it is deep-fried.

Preparation Clean the chicken thoroughly. Submerge it in a pan of boiling water, boil for 5–6 minutes, then drain.

Cooking Bring the herbal master stock to the boil in a large heavy saucepan, then lower the chicken into the stock and simmer for 35 minutes, until it turns brownish-red. Remove the chicken from the stock and drain for 20 minutes. When well-drained, deep-fry the chicken for 10 minutes until the skin is crispy and aromatic.

Serving Chop the chicken into 24 pieces through the bone. Reassemble these pieces in the shape of a chicken on a well-heated serving dish. Garnish with greens and tomatoes.

Onion-Stuffed Chicken

From the province of Shangtung

Preparation Clean the chicken thoroughly and rub with 1 tablespoon of salt both inside and out. Crush the thicker end of the scallions, remove the roots, and chop the stalks into 2 inch lengths. Crush and chop the cloves of garlic. Add the Kaoliang liqueur or brandy to the pieces of scallions and garlic. Mix them together well. Stuff the chicken with the mixture and secure the opening with skewers or by sewing. Shred the slices of ginger root.

Cooking Place the chicken in a deep heat-proof dish. Put the dish in a steamer and steam for 1¼ hours. At the end of the cooking time, pour the chicken gravy from the heat-proof dish into a small saucepan. Add the shredded ginger and salt to taste to the gravy. Heat until the liquid boils. Sprinkle with sesame oil and pour the gravy into two dishes for use as a dip for the chicken.

Serving Serve the chicken whole. It should be tender enough to take apart with chopsticks. Dip the pieces of chicken in gravy before eating them.

Serves 4–6, with other dishes

A 4–5 lb chicken
¾ lb scallions

3 cloves garlic
2 tablespoons Kaoliang liqueur *or* brandy
2 slices ginger root
1½ tablespoons sesame oil

Cold Crystal Chicken

From Canton

Preparation Clean the chicken thoroughly and boil it in 1 quart of water for 35 minutes. Remove the chicken from this stock and drain well. Skim the fat from the stock and retain 1 cup of stock for later use. Chop the chicken into 20–24 pieces and cut the ham into thin slices. Arrange the pieces of chicken and ham alternately in a deep dish, placing the chicken pieces skin-side down.

Serves 4–6, with other dishes

A 3–4 lb broiler chicken
¼ lb smoked ham

1½ tablespoons gelatin
2 cups superior stock
1½ tablespoons cornstarch
¼ teaspoon monosodium glutamate
2½ teaspoons salt
6 tablespoons dry sherry *or* white wine

Cooking Blend the gelatin with the superior stock, cornstarch, monosodium glutamate, salt, and sherry or wine. Add the reserved chicken stock and heat until the liquid begins to thicken. Pour this mixture over the chicken and ham pieces, and place the dish in a refrigerator for 3–4 hours.

Serving When the sauce has turned to jelly, turn the Cold Crystal Chicken on to a large serving plate. This is a summer dish, and the jellied meat is often garnished with colorful vegetables and fruits. Cherries, lychees, strawberries, lettuce, spinach, and even flowers may be used.

Royal Concubine Chicken

Serves 4–6, with other dishes

A 3–4 lb chicken

oil for deep-frying
2½ tablespoons soy sauce
¼ lb slab bacon
2 medium-sized onions
2 slices ginger root
2 cloves garlic
2 tablespoons lard
2½ teaspoons salt
1¼ cups superior stock
1½ cups Chinese rice wine *or* red wine *or* dry sherry

or the Chinese Coq au vin

Preparation Clean and dry the chicken thoroughly. Deep-fry it in hot oil for 7–8 minutes, until evenly browned. Remove the bird from the oil and dip it into a pan of boiling water to remove excess oil. Rub it thoroughly with soy sauce. Chop the bacon, cut the onions into thin slices, shred the ginger, and crush the cloves of garlic.

Cooking Place the chicken in a heat-proof casserole. Heat the lard in a frying pan. Add the bacon, onions, ginger, and garlic. Stir-fry for 6–7 minutes; then add the mixture to the casserole containing the chicken. Add the salt, and pour in the superior stock and wine or sherry. Bring the sauce to the boil, then cook in the oven for approximately 1 hour at 375°F.

Note It is best to use a fresh-killed bird in this recipe.

Double-Fried and Marinated Chicken

Serves 4–6, with other dishes

A 3–4 lb fryer chicken

2 medium-sized onions
4 slices ginger root
½ cup soy sauce
½ cup dry sherry
1½ teaspoons chili sauce *or* ¾ teaspoon chili oil
oil for deep-frying

The interesting thing about this recipe, which is popular in Peking, is the process of double-marinating and double-frying.

Preparation Slice the onions thin and boil with the ginger in ¾ cup of water for 15 minutes. Remove the ginger and onions, and mix the liquid with the soy sauce, sherry, and chili sauce or oil until well-blended. Clean the chicken and marinate it in this mixture for 3 hours, turning the bird over every 30 minutes.

Cooking Remove the chicken from the marinade and let it dry for 15 minutes in an airy place; then deep-fry in hot oil for 8–10 minutes. Drain the chicken thoroughly for 10 minutes; then replace it in the marinade for a further 10 minutes. Drain off the marinade from the bird. Heat ¾ cup of oil in a frying pan and turn the chicken in the oil for about 10 minutes. Pour away all the oil and add the remainder of the marinade to the chicken. Add the sugar, monosodium glutamate, and pepper. Cook over medium heat, turning the chicken in the marinade, until the liquid has thickened.

Serving Remove the chicken from the pan and chop it through the bone into serving pieces or double-Mah-jong pieces. Serve on a well-heated dish.

1½ teaspoons sugar
¼ teaspoon monosodium glutamate
pepper to taste

Distilled Chicken

From the province of Yunnan

Serves 4–6, with other dishes

The traditional Chinese method of preparing Distilled Chicken involves the use of a special casserole with a funnel running through the center. Steam passes through this funnel, and on coming into contact with the lid of the casserole it condenses and drops on to the ingredients in the casserole. When the cooking process is completed, the pieces of meat and other ingredients are immersed in a crystal-clear stock. Since the specialized type of casserole used by the Chinese is not available in America, a little ingenuity is necessary to cook this dish successfully. Put the meat and other ingredients in a heat-proof casserole. Place a pair of chopsticks across the dish and cover it with a lid, preferably one which is rather larger than the casserole. The rising steam will be caught by this lid and, as it condenses, it will drop into the casserole. The casserole should be placed inside a large boiler on a trivet and steamed for 3–4 hours.

A 3–4 lb chicken

4 Chinese dried mushrooms
½ cup bamboo shoots
¼ lb ham
2 slices ginger root
2½ teaspoons salt
5 tablespoons dry sherry
¼ teaspoon monosodium glutamate

Preparation Soak the mushrooms for 30 minutes. Clean the chicken thoroughly and chop it into about 20 pieces. Place the pieces of chicken in the casserole, then add the ginger, salt, and sherry. Cut the bamboo shoots into slices, approximately 1½ × 1 inch, and mix with the chicken pieces. Cut the ham into pieces in the same way as the bamboo shoots and place on top of the other ingredients. Remove the stalks from the mushrooms and mix the mushroom caps with the ham.

Cooking Place the casserole on a trivet in a boiler containing 1–2 inches of water. Keep the water boiling gently for 3–4 hours, adding more when necessary.

Serving At the end of the cooking time, sprinkle the monosodium glutamate into the casserole and serve immediately.

The aim of the dish is to achieve pristine purity, which all the polite diners will pretend to marvel at and appreciate. In the end, they will convince themselves that the dish is extraordinarily nourishing and good for their delicate health.

Drunken Chicken

Serves 4–6, with other dishes

A 3 lb broiler chicken

2 tablespoons salt
2 medium-sized onions
4 slices ginger root
2½ cups dry sherry *or* Chinese rice wine

This is an unfailingly successful dish for use as an hors d'œuvre or as a canapé at a cocktail party.

Preparation and Cooking Clean and truss the chicken. Bring 6 cups of water to the boil in a pan and add the salt, onions, and ginger. Boil for 5 minutes; then add the chicken and simmer for 15 minutes. Turn off the heat. Let the bird cool in the liquid for 3 hours; then drain it and put the chicken into a large container. Pour the sherry or wine over the chicken and turn it several times to ensure that it is completely immersed. Let the chicken soak in the sherry for at least 48 hours, turning it every 12 hours.

Serving Drain and untruss the chicken. Chop it through the bone into serving pieces or double-Mah-jong pieces. Arrange the pieces in the center of a large dish of hors d'œuvres, or divide them among several saucer-sized dishes to pass around during a cocktail party. Eat with the fingers, or speared with cocktail picks.

Wrapped Roast Stuffed Chicken

Serves 4–6, with other dishes

A 3–4 lb chicken

2 slices ginger root
6 Chinese dried mushrooms
3 scallions
2½ tablespoons soy sauce
¾ teaspoon salt
2 teaspoons hoisin sauce
1½ teaspoons sugar
2 tablespoons dry sherry
½ lb lean boneless pork
½ lb chestnut meat
2½ tablespoons lard
1 large piece of pork suet, about ¾ lb

Preparation Shred the ginger. Soak the mushrooms for 30 minutes, remove the stalks, and cut the caps into thin strips. Cut the scallions into 2 inch pieces. Mix together the ginger, soy sauce, salt, hoisin sauce, sugar, sherry, and ginger. Rub the chicken inside and out with this mixture. Chop the pork and chestnuts and mix them with the remainder of the mixture used to rub the chicken; then add the mushrooms, scallion, and sugar. Melt the lard in a frying pan and stir-fry this mixture for 5–6 minutes. Stuff the chicken with the fried mixture; then sew it up securely and wrap in the piece of suet. Secure with skewers.

Cooking Put the chicken in an oven preheated to 400°F and roast for 1 hour, turning over every 20 minutes; then unwrap it, and roast it for a further 10 minutes.

Serving Chop the chicken through the stuffing into 12 pieces.

Lay the piece of suet on a large well heated serving-dish. Pile the stuffing in the center of the piece of suet and arrange the chicken pieces on top.

Cantonese Crackling Chicken

Preparation Clean the chicken inside and out. Immerse it in a pan of boiling water for 3 seconds. Dry it with paper towels and hang it up to dry out for 3 hours; then rub with salt and leave it in an airy spot overnight. Mix the honey, sherry, and cornstarch into a paste and rub the chicken with the mixture, inside and out. Leave it to dry for a few hours or overnight.

Cooking The chicken should be placed in a wire basket suspended above a deep frying pan containing hot oil. Pour hot oil continually over the chicken with a large ladle until it is evenly browned and crispy. This method is known as 'splash-frying'.

Serving Chop the chicken into serving pieces or double-Mahjong pieces and serve on a well-heated dish. Alternatively slice off the crackling skin and serve it like Peking Duck in thin pancakes, accompanied by scallions, cucumber, and Plum Sauce (see Index).

Serves 4–6, with other dishes

A 3–4 lb fryer chicken

1 tablespoon salt
2½ tablespoons honey
2½ tablespoons dry sherry
1 tablespoon cornstarch
oil for frying

The People's Coq au Vin

From Nanchang, the province of Kiangsi

This recipe originated in China during the Cultural Revolution, hence its total simplicity. It is also known in China as 3-Cup Chicken, as only three glasses of ingredients are used: one large glass of sherry or red wine, one glass of oil or fat, and one glass of soy sauce.

Preparating and Cooking Clean chicken and quarter it. Heat oil or fat in a heat-proof casserole and stir-fry chicken quarters for 6–7 minutes; then pour away excess oil. Add sherry or red wine, and soy sauce. Turn the chicken in this mixture for 2–3 minutes. Put the lid on the casserole and place it in an oven preheated to 350°F for 1 hour, turning the chicken pieces every 15 minutes. Serve from the casserole or any deep dish or bowl.

This is a very simple dish which can be made more elaborate in two ways. Firstly, when stir-frying the chicken quarters, a chopped onion and 1 teaspoon each of crushed garlic and chopped ginger may be added. Secondly, a teaspoon of sesame oil may be sprinkled over the chicken just before serving.

Serves 4–6, with other dishes

A 3–4 lb chicken

glass of oil *or* fat
large glass of dry sherry *or* red wine
glass of soy sauce

Melon Chicken

Serves 4–6, with other dishes

A 2–3 lb broiler chicken
1 melon

2 large Chinese dried mushrooms
½ cup bamboo shoots
¼ lb ham
2½ tablespoons oil
1 slice ginger root
1 cup button mushrooms *or*
    Chinese grass mushrooms
salt and pepper

This makes an attractive party dish.

Preparation Soak the dried mushrooms for 30 minutes, remove the stalks, and cut each mushroom cap into six pieces. Chop the bamboo shoots and ham into pieces about the size of small sugar lumps.

Cooking Steam the chicken for 1 hour. Remove all the bones; then chop the chicken meat into pieces about the same size as the cubes of ham. Heat the oil in a frying pan; then add the ginger, bamboo shoots, and both sorts of mushrooms. Fry for 3 minutes. Add the ham and chicken; stir-fry gently for 3 minutes. Season to taste with salt and pepper. Slice off the top quarter of the melon, and keep it aside to use as a lid. Scoop out all the soft flesh from the inside, and mix it with the fried chicken and other ingredients. Pack the cavity in the melon with this mixture, secure the lid with toothpicks; then put it into a heat-proof bowl with a close-fitting lid, and steam for 25 minutes.

Serving Bring the melon to the table in the bowl and serve by opening the lid and leaving it against the melon, as if the contents were a natural part of the fruit.

A large honeydew melon is the best type to use with this dish.

Beaten Chicken

Serves 4–6, with other dishes

A 3–4 lb chicken

1½ tablespoons sesame oil
2½ tablespoons sesame paste *or* peanut butter
2½ tablespoons soy sauce
1½ tablespoons roasted sesame seeds

From the province of Szechuan

This is a cold chicken dish and each piece is beaten with a rolling pin before serving. It is fairly unusual and is seldom seen in other parts of China.

Preparation and Cooking Clean the chicken and place it in a saucepan with 10 cups of water. Bring the water to the boil. After it has boiled for 2 minutes, add 1 cup of cold water and bring to the boil once more. Let it boil for 2 minutes, then add another cup of water. Continue this process for about 30 minutes; then leave the chicken in the water to cool for 3 hours.

Serving Remove the chicken from the water and drain well. Chop it through the bone into about 12 pieces. Place these pieces on a chopping board and give each a heavy bash with a rolling pin. Mix the sesame oil, sesame paste or peanut butter, and soy sauce into a paste. Brush each piece of chicken with this paste, sprinkle with the roasted sesame seeds, and serve on a large platter, garnished with parsley sprigs or fresh coriander leaves if desired.

Tsinan Red-Cooked Chicken

From Tsinan, Shantung

It is usual in China to steam, simmer, or stew the chicken first before frying it to make it crisp. The interesting and distinctive thing about this dish is that the process is reversed; it is fried first and steamed last!

Preparation Shred the ginger and chop the scallions as fine as possible. Mix the ginger, scallions, sugar, salt, soy sauce, sherry, pepper, and five spice powder in a bowl. Rub the chicken with this mixture, inside and out, and leave to let the seasoning sink in for 2 hours. Then rub the chicken with the mixture once more and leave it to season for a further 2 hours.

Cooking As soon as the marinating ingredients have dried on the bird, place it in a wire basket and deep-fry it in hot oil for 8–10 minutes until golden-brown. Drain the chicken and stuff it with the remainder of the marinade. Place it in a heat-proof dish and steam for approximately 40 minutes, or until the meat is tender.

Serving Serve the chicken whole. It should be tender enough to take apart with chopsticks. Serve with cooked rice or a variety of dips.

Serves 4–6, with other dishes

A 2–3 lb broiler chicken

3 slices ginger root
6 scallions
1½ teaspoons sugar
¾ teaspoon salt
¼ cup soy sauce
1½ tablespoons dry sherry
½ teaspoon freshly ground black pepper
¼ teaspoon five spice powder
oil for deep-frying

Wine-Sediment Paste Chicken

From Foochow

This chicken is redder in color than any other Chinese chicken dish, as it is prepared not with ordinary soy sauce, but with a bright, deep red wine-sediment paste, which is processed from fermented ground rice and wine lees or sediment. It is available from many well-stocked Chinese markets, especially if the proprietor is from the province of Fukien.

Serves 4–6, with other dishes

A 3–4 lb young chicken

2½ teaspoons salt
¾ teaspoon freshly ground black
   pepper
2 tablespoons Kaoliang (Chinese
   liqueur) *or* brandy
¼ cup wine-sediment paste
2½ teaspoons sugar
¼ teaspoon monosodium glutamate
½ teaspoon five spice powder
2½ tablespoons soy sauce
1½ tablespoons dry sherry

Preparation and Cooking Clean the chicken thoroughly and boil it for 25 minutes in a large pan of water. Let the chicken cool in the water for 2 hours; then drain it and hang it up in an airy spot to dry out.

Marinading Blend the salt, black pepper, and Kaoliang or brandy together and rub the bird with this mixture, inside and out. When marinade has dried on the chicken rub it with the remaining mixture and leave it to dry. Blend the remaining ingredients together and rub the chicken with the mixture until it is completely covered. Place in a sealed container and leave it in a cool place overnight, or for several days.

Serving Chop the chicken through the bone into 15–20 pieces. Pile the pieces in the center of a serving dish and surround them with radishes prepared according to the method described below.

Serve as part of an elaborate hors d'œuvre or as a main course.

Prepared Radishes for Wine-Sediment Paste Chicken

Serves 4–6, with other dishes

6 large radishes

2 dried chili peppers, chopped and
   deseeded
1 tablespoon salt
2½ teaspoons sugar
2½ tablespoons vinegar

Serve radishes prepared in this way with Wine-Sediment Paste Chicken (see page 209).

Preparation Cut each radish into quarters and place in a bowl. Chop the chili peppers and remove the seeds. Sprinkle the radishes with the salt, sugar, chili peppers, and vinegar. Work these ingredients into the radishes. Add 8 tablespoons water and leave to marinate for 2 hours.

Serving Drain the radishes thoroughly and arrange them round the pile of chicken pieces.

Eight-Precious Steamed Chicken

Serves 4–6, with other dishes

A 4–5 lb chicken *or* capon

2 oz chestnuts
4 large Chinese dried mushrooms
½ cup glutinous rice
¼ cup bamboo shoots
2 oz smoked ham

Shanghai style

Duck is more frequently used in this recipe than chicken, but if it is not available, chicken makes just as appealing and succulent a dish.

Preparation Dip the chicken in boiling water for 3 minutes; then drain. Discard the heart, but retain the kidney and liver and slice them thin. Slash the chestnut shells and cook them in boiling water for 25 minutes. Remove the shell and skin and chop each chestnut into four pieces. Soak the mushrooms for 20 minutes, remove the stalks, and cut the caps into six pieces. Steam the glutinous rice for 20 minutes. Chop the bamboo shoots and ham into ⅛ inch cubes. Simmer the lotus seeds and golden needles in water for 5 minutes; then drain. Chop the golden needles into 1 inch pieces. Mix all these ingredients in a bowl with the peeled shrimp, salt, sugar, and 1 tablespoon of the sherry. Stuff the chicken with the mixture and secure with skewers or by sewing with thick thread.

Cooking Place the chicken in a heat-proof bowl and steam for 3–3½ hours. At the end of the cooking time, pour the liquid that has collected in the steaming bowl into a small saucepan. Add all the remaining ingredients, blend well, and cook over a medium heat, stirring constantly, until the gravy thickens and has a glossy appearance.

Serving Cut the chicken into six to eight pieces and carefully remove the main bones. Spread the stuffing on a well-heated serving dish; then place the chicken pieces on top and pour over the gravy. Steam for 5 minutes, and serve.

2 tablespoons lotus seeds
2 golden needles (tiger-lily buds)
¼ cup peeled shrimp
1½ teaspoons salt
2½ teaspoons sugar
2½ tablespoons dry sherry
1½ tablespoons soy sauce
¾ tablespoon cornstarch
¼ teaspoon monosodium glutamate
1¼ cups superior stock
¾ tablespoon lard

Diced Chicken

Chicken meat diced into cubes about half the size of sugar lumps is a very popular and traditional form of cooking chicken in China. When cooked and served in this manner, the chicken is usually stir-fried with additional sauces and seasonings, but without the use of the supplementary ingredients which are usually added to dishes where the chicken is chopped and cooked in larger pieces. Breast meat is usually used for diced chicken dishes. As chicken prepared in this manner is boneless, it is very acceptable and appealing to Westerners.

Vinegar-Tossed Chicken Cubes

A favorite dish in Peking

Preparation Cut the chicken and bamboo shoots into small cubes. Rub them with salt and 1 tablespoon cornstarch. Chop the chili pepper as fine as possible, discarding the seeds. Chop the onion, ginger, and garlic as fine as possible and mix together well. Blend the 2½ teaspoons of cornstarch with the stock, sherry, and vinegar.

Serves 4–6, with other dishes

10 oz (1½ cups) chicken breast meat
2½ tablespoons vinegar

¼ cup bamboo shoots
¾ teaspoon salt

1 tablespoon cornstarch
1 dried chili pepper
1 medium-sized onion
1 slice ginger root
1 clove garlic
2½ teaspoons cornstarch
¼ cup superior stock
1½ tablespoons dry sherry
2½ tablespoons lard
1½ tablespoons vegetable oil

Cooking Melt the lard in a frying pan over a high heat. Add the chicken and bamboo shoot cubes and the chili pepper. Stir-fry for 2 minutes; then remove from the pan and keep hot. Stir-fry the onion, ginger, and garlic mixture with the oil over a high heat for 2 minutes. Pour in the cornstarch, stock, sherry, and vinegar mixture and stir until the mixture thickens. Return the chicken and bamboo shoots to the pan, stir-fry them with the sauce for 1½ minutes, and serve immediately.

This is a fairly spicy dish. Serve with boiled rice.

Kung-Po Chicken Cubes

From the province of Szechuan

Serves 4–6, with other dishes

10 oz (1½ cups) chicken breast meat

1 teaspoon salt
4 teaspoons cornstarch
2 dried red chili peppers
3 tablespoons superior stock
2 teaspoons vinegar
2 teaspoons tomato puree
1 teaspoon sugar
1 small onion
2 tablespoons lard
1½ tablespoons vegetable oil
1 teaspoon red chili oil

Preparation Dice the chicken into small cubes and rub them with salt and 2 teaspoons of the cornstarch. Chop the peppers and discard the seeds. Mix the remaining cornstarch with the stock, vinegar, tomato puree, 2 tablespoons water, and the sugar. Chop the onion as fine as possible.

Cooking Melt the lard in a frying pan over a high heat. Add the chicken cubes and stir-fry for 2 minutes; then remove them from the pan and keep hot. Pour the vegetable oil into the center of the pan. Add the onion and chili peppers and stir-fry for 2 minutes. Add the chili oil and the cornstarch mixture, and stir until the mixture thickens. Return the chicken cubes to the pan, stir-fry for 1½ minutes, and serve on a well-heated dish.

Note This is a very hot dish and is particularly appealing to those who like really spicy food. However it is a good idea to serve a large dish of rice with the Kung-Po Chicken Cubes to dampen the fire—should it be necessary!

Diced Chicken in Soy Jam

Serves 4–6, with other dishes

8–10 oz (1½ cups) chicken breast meat
2½ tablespoons soy jam *or* paste

1½ egg whites
1 tablespoon cornstarch
1½ tablespoons ginger water
1½ teaspoons sugar

Preparation Dice the chicken meat into ⅓ inch cubes. Blend the egg whites, cornstarch, and 2 teaspoons water into a batter, and use it to coat the chicken cubes. Mix the soy jam, 2 teaspoons ginger water, sherry, and sugar into a smooth paste.

Cooking Melt 1½ tablespoons of the lard in the center of a small frying pan, add the chicken cubes, and stir-fry over a high heat for 1 minute. Remove the chicken and keep it hot.

Add the remaining lard to the pan and stir in the soy jam with a spoon for about 30 seconds, until most of the moisture has evaporated. Return the chicken cubes to the pan and stir-fry for 1 minute with the soy paste until they turn brown and glistening. Serve immediately on a well-heated dish.

Note Ginger water may be prepared by soaking shredded ginger in ¼ cup of water, then discarding the ginger.

1½ tablespoons dry sherry
2½ tablespoons lard

Chicken Cubes with Ground Peanuts
From the province of Szechuan

Preparation Dice the chicken neatly into small cubes and rub them with salt and cornstarch. Chop the chili pepper as fine as possible and discard the seeds. Combine the onion, 1½ tablespoons of the vegetable oil, sugar, vinegar, chicken stock, and soy sauce to form s smooth sauce. Fry or roast the peanuts until aromatic; then grind them.

Cooking Melt the lard in a frying pan over a high heat; then add the chili pepper. Stir once or twice before adding the chicken cubes. Stir-fry for 2 minutes; then remove them from the pan. Heat the remaining vegetable oil in another frying pan, and add the ground peanuts. Stir-fry for 1 minute. Return the chicken to the pan, pour in the sauce and sherry, stir-fry for 1–2 minutes; then serve.

Serves 4–6, with other dishes

10 oz (1½ cups) chicken breast meat

1½ teaspoons salt
4 teaspoons cornstarch
1 dried chili pepper
1½ tablespoons finely chopped onion
4½ tablespoons vegetable oil
2 teaspoons sugar
2 teaspoons vinegar
2½ tablespoons chicken stock
1½ tablespoons soy sauce
½ cup peanuts
2½ tablespoons lard
1½ tablespoons dry sherry

Chicken Cubes Quick-Fried
with Giblets

Preparation Dice the chicken meat and giblets into small cubes. Rub them first with salt; then with 1 tablespoon of the cornstarch. Shred the ginger; crush and chop the garlic. Combine the soy sauce, sherry, superior stock, monosodium glutamate, vinegar, pepper, and remaining cornstarch in a bowl, until smoothly blended.

Cooking Heat 2 tablespoons of the oil in a frying pan, add the chicken meat and quick-fry over a high heat for 1½ minutes. Remove the chicken cubes and keep hot. Add the remaining oil, the onion, ginger, and garlic; stir-fry for 30 seconds. Add the giblets and stir-fry for 2 minutes. Pour in the sauce mixture and return the chicken to the pan. Mix the chicken meat and giblets in the sauce for about 1 minute, until the sauce thickens. Serve immediately.

Serves 4–6, with other dishes

6 oz (¾ cup) chicken breast meat
6 oz (¾ cup) chicken giblets (kidney and liver)

2 teaspoons salt
1¾ tablespoons cornstarch
2 slices ginger root
2 cloves garlic
2 tablespoons soy sauce
2½ tablespoons dry sherry
¼ cup superior stock
¼ teaspoon monosodium glutamate
2½ teaspoons vinegar
dash of pepper
¼ cup vegetable oil
2½ tablespoons finely chopped onion

This is an extremely savory dish. Its distinctive quality lies in the contrast between the texture of the chicken cubes, which should be really tender and melting, and the texture of the giblets, which should be bouncy and lively like a ball. Giblets must not be over-cooked as they easily become hard and relatively uninteresting to the taste.

Chopped Chicken

Apart from cooking it whole or diced into cubes, another way of cooking chicken is to chop it into eight to twenty pieces through the bone. Chopped chicken is sometimes cooked along with other ingredients, but frequently it is cooked on its own.

Deep-Fried Eight Piece Chicken

Serves 4–6, with other dishes

A 3–4 lb fryer chicken

2 slices ginger root
2½ teaspoons salt
1 egg
2½ tablespoons flour
1¼ cups oil

In China, what we call deep-frying is often not actually deep-frying in the Western sense. Usually no more than ¾–1½ cups of oil is used. The food to be fried—such as meatballs, chopped pieces of chicken, or meat—is turned in the oil with a pair of bamboo chopsticks, a metal spoon, or else a spatula.

Preparation Clean the chicken and chop it through the bone into eight pieces (or more if you like). Shred the ginger and chop it very fine. Mix it with the salt. Rub the chicken pieces with this mixture. Beat the egg lightly, blend it with the flour to a smooth batter; then coat the chicken.

Cooking Heat the oil in a frying pan. When it is very hot, drop in three or four pieces of chicken and stir them around with bamboo chopsticks or a metal spoon. Cook in this way for 3–4 minutes until each piece is evenly fried. Remove the chicken pieces and keep them hot in the oven. Continue deep frying until all the pieces have been cooked.

Serving Chicken cooked in this manner is best eaten with dips and mixes (see section on Table Condiments). The best accompaniment of all is Salt and Pepper Mix.

Deep-Fried Marinated Chicken

The principal difference between this dish and the previous one is that here the chicken is marinated at some length before cooking. Because of the marinating, it is not essential that the pieces of chicken be dipped in mixes before being eaten.

Preparation Chop the chicken into 12–15 serving pieces or double-Mah-jong pieces and sprinkle them with salt. Chop the onion as fine as possible. Shred the ginger and chop it in the same way as the onion. Mix the onion and ginger with the soy sauce, soy paste, hoisin sauce, sugar, and sherry. Rub the pieces of chicken with this mixture and leave to marinate for at least 2 hours; then dust the chicken pieces with cornstarch, discarding any excess.

Cooking Deep-fry in hot oil for 2–4 minutes, and drain before serving.

Serving Although chicken cooked in this way need not be dipped before eating, some sauces, such as plum sauce or tomato sauce, could be placed on the table to give people a choice. However, the Salt and Pepper Mix mentioned in the previous recipe should not be used, as the chicken pieces should be salty enough as they are.

Serves 4–6, with other dishes

A 3–4 lb chicken

1½ teaspoons salt
1 large onion
2 slices ginger root
2½ tablespoons soy sauce
1 tablespoon soy jam or paste
1 tablespoon hoisin sauce
2½ teaspoons sugar
1½ tablespoons dry sherry
2½ tablespoons cornstarch
oil for deep-frying

Chicken in Breadcrumbs

In China, in the past, breadcrumbs had always to be made at home by hand. Since in America they can be easily made in a blender or purchased, this is an easy and convenient dish to prepare.

Preparation Repeat the instructions given in the previous recipe. After marinating the chicken pieces, dip them in lightly beaten egg and dredge them with breadcrumbs. Deep-fry for 3–4 minutes.

Serves 4–6, with other dishes

Hot Ginger-Gravy Chicken

From the province of Szechuan

Preparation Chop the chicken through the bone into 12–15 pieces, and rub them with salt. Chop the ginger, garlic, and onions as fine as possible. Mix the superior stock, sugar, soy sauce, vinegar, sherry, monosodium glutamate, and cornstarch in a bowl.

Cooking Melt the lard in a large frying pan over a medium heat. Add the onions, ginger, and garlic; stir-fry for 2 minutes. Add all the chicken pieces and stir-fry briskly over a high heat for 4–5 minutes. Reduce the heat to low and continue cooking for a further 4–5 minutes. Pour in the sauce mixture, turn the chicken pieces in the sauce for 2–3 minutes, then serve on a well-heated dish.

Serves 4–6, with other dishes

A 3–4 lb fryer chicken

2 teaspoons salt
6 slices ginger root
4 cloves garlic
2 medium-sized onions
5 tablespoons superior stock
2½ teaspoons sugar
2½ tablespoons soy sauce
1½ tablespoons vinegar
2½ tablespoons dry sherry
¼ teaspoon monosodium glutamate
1 tablespoon cornstarch
¼ cup lard

This is a dish which is peculiar to Szechuan, where the strong and hot vegetables (chili, garlic, ginger, and onion) are used in quantity. The famous mixture of these four strong vegetables with black beans is called 'Yu Hsiang' (fish scent), probably because the ingredients are the same as those used for cooking fish.

This is well-known in China and is now becoming extremely popular in New York.

Hot Pepper Chicken

Serves 4–6, with other dishes

A 3–4 lb chicken

2½ teaspoons salt
2 dried chili peppers
3 fresh chili peppers
2½ tablespoons lard
2 tablespoons soy sauce
1½ tablespoons vinegar
1 cup superior stock
¼ teaspoon monosodium glutamate
2 teaspoons cornstarch

From the province of Kiangsi

Preparation Clean the chicken and chop it into about 20 pieces. Boil in water for 5 minutes and drain thoroughly. Rub the chicken pieces with salt and place them in a heat-proof bowl, skin-side down. Chop both the dried and fresh chili peppers, discarding the seeds.

Cooking Heat the lard in a small pan. Add the peppers and stir-fry over a medium heat for 2 minutes. Pour the lard and pepper mixture evenly over the chicken pieces. Blend the remaining ingredients in a bowl; then cook the sauce in a small pan over a low heat for 4–5 minutes until it thickens slightly. Pour the sauce evenly over the pieces of chicken. Place the bowl of chicken in a steamer and steam for 45 minutes. Turn out the contents of the bowl onto a dish, and serve. By this time, the chicken will have absorbed all the flavors of the combined ingredients, and should possess many of the local flavors of Kiangsi.

Crackling Aromatic Chicken Legs

Serves 4–6, with other dishes

2 lb chicken legs (drumsticks and upper legs)

2¼ teaspoons salt
2 medium-sized onions
4 slices ginger root
2 cloves garlic
¼ cup soy sauce
1½ tablespoons sugar
½ teaspoon five spice powder
2½ tablespoons dry sherry
2 tablespoons cornstarch
oil for deep-frying

This is a favorite dish in Peking.

Preparation Clean the chicken legs, rub them with salt, and leave them to season overnight. Chop the onions. Shred the ginger, crush the garlic, and chop them both. Put the chicken legs in a bowl with the onion, ginger, garlic, soy sauce, sugar, five spice powder, and sherry. Rub the mixture into the chicken legs thoroughly and leave them to marinate for 2 hours.

Cooking Place the marinated chicken legs in a heat-proof bowl. Steam vigorously for 25 minutes. When the chicken legs have cooled slightly, rub them with cornstarch and place them in a wire basket, four at a time. Deep-fry for 4–5 minutes. Drain well and continue deep-frying until all the legs have been fried.

Serving Place the crispy fried chicken legs on a chopping board and chop them in two. Arrange the pieces on a flat serving-dish and decorate by banking them with green vegetables (e.g. lettuce, quick-fried mustard greens, spinach, or broccoli). The brownness of the chicken legs and the greenness of the vegetables should make an attractive and happy combination.

Steamed Chicken in Ground Rice

Ground rice is often used in China in the same manner as breadcrumbs are used in the West; it is frequently used to coat pieces of meat for further cooking. When using ground rice (usually in coarse grains), it is often fried or roasted first until it is slightly brown and aromatic. When applied as a coating, ground rice definitely produces an aromatic effect on the final product.

Preparation Chop the chicken into 14–16 pieces, rub them with salt and sprinkle them with pepper. Beat the egg whites with a fork for 15 seconds. Dip the chicken pieces in egg white and roll them in roasted ground rice until evenly coated.

Cooking Place the pieces of chicken in a heat-proof bowl and steam for 2 hours. Pour off the chicken juice which has collected in the bowl. Heat the chicken fat in a small pan. Add the remaining ingredients including the liquid formed during steaming, and bring to the boil. Pour the mixture into two small sauce boats and use as a dip when the chicken is served.

Serves 4–6, with other dishes

A 3–4 lb chicken

2½ teaspoons salt
pepper to taste
2 egg whites
½ cup roasted ground rice (coarse grain)
2½ teaspoons chicken fat
2½ tablespoons light soy sauce
2½ tablespoons chicken stock
¼ teaspoon monosodium glutamate
¾ tablespoon vinegar
2 tablespoons dry sherry

Chinese Curried Chicken

Although curry powder is an imported ingredient, we Chinese have now adopted many curried dishes which are ideal for serving with rice.

Preparation Clean the chicken and chop it through the bone into 12–16 pieces. Peel the potatoes and cut them into chunks about the same size as the chicken pieces. Slice the onions thin.

Serves 4–6, with other dishes

A 3–4 lb chicken

½ lb potatoes
2 large onions

217

5 tablespoons vegetable oil
1 tablespoon salt
2½–4 tablespoons curry powder (or according to taste)
2½ tablespoons soy sauce
¾ cup secondary stock
¾ cup coconut milk
1¼ cups milk

Cooking Heat the oil in a large heavy saucepan. Add the onions, salt, and curry powder, and cook over a high heat for 2 minutes. Add the chicken pieces and continue to stir-fry for 5 minutes. Add the soy sauce, and stir-fry for a further 2 minutes. Pour in the secondary stock and coconut milk. Bring to the boil and simmer for 30 minutes. Add the potato pieces, and the milk. Bring to the boil and simmer for a further 30 minutes, turning the mixture over every 10 minutes.

Serving Serve in a bowl or tureen.

Hung Doo or 'Swinging Chicken'

Serves 4–6, with other dishes

A 3–4 lb fryer chicken

3 slices ginger root
3 dried chili peppers
¼ lb leeks
5 tablespoons lard
2 teaspoons salt
1 sheet dried tangerine peel
2½ tablespoons soy sauce
1½ tablespoons hoisin sauce
2½ tablespoons dry sherry
½ cup superior stock
2½ teaspoons sugar
¼ teaspoon monosodium glutamate
2 teaspoons sesame oil

'Hung Doo' is a Chinese literary expression which means 'the swinging capital'. The term was originally applied to the city of Nanchang, on the Yangtse, in the province of Kiangsi. Hung Doo chicken can therefore be called 'Swinging Chicken'.

Preparation Clean the chicken and chop it into 20 pieces. Shred the ginger and chili pepper. Cut the leeks into 1½ inch pieces.

Cooking Heat the lard in a large frying pan, add the chicken pieces, stir-fry for 5 minutes, then drain, letting the fat drip back into the pan. Place the chicken pieces on a heat-proof dish. Stir-fry the ginger, leeks, chili peppers, salt, and tangerine peel for 1½ minutes. Return the pieces of chicken to the pan. Add the soy sauce, hoisin sauce, sherry, stock, sugar, and monosodium glutamate. Turn the chicken in this mixture for 5–6 minutes over a high heat, until the liquid in the pan has become a thick sauce.

Serving Sprinkle with sesame oil, and serve on a well-heated dish.

Cantonese Crystal Chicken

Serves 4–6, with other dishes

A 3 lb broiler chicken

2½ teaspoons salt
2½ tablespoons dry sherry
¼ teaspoon monosodium glutamate
1½ teaspoons sugar
1½ tablespoons gelatin

This is a dish which can be made a day before it is used.

Preparation Clean and dry the chicken thoroughly. Mix the salt, sherry, monosodium glutamate, sugar, and gelatin into the stock until well-blended.

Cooking Boil the chicken for 30 minutes; then leave it to cool. Chop it into 20–24 pieces. Cut the ham into thin slices. Alternate the pieces of chicken and ham in overlapping rows

in a deep oblong or oval dish. Heat the stock mixture, stirring all the time until all solids are well dissolved. Cool for 15 minutes; then pour over the chicken and ham. Place the dish in a refrigerator to cool for at least 3 hours, or overnight.
Serving Turn the jellied chicken and ham on to a large flat dish and serve. In presenting this dish in China the jellied chicken is often surrounded by a bank of fresh vegetables and flowers. There is a version in which the chicken is banked all around with chrysanthemums and other flowers, and it is called 'South of the River 100 Flower Chicken'.

2½ cups superior stock
6 oz ham

Chicken Chinese Sausages

Preparation Clean the chicken; then boil it for 10 minutes in a shallow heat-proof dish. Sprinkle all over with salt. Soak the mushrooms for 20 minutes. Cut the sausages into ½ inch slices and place them on top of the chicken. Remove the mushrooms from the water in which they have been soaking and keep aside 2 tablespoons of this water. Cut off the mushrooms stalks and chop the caps into two to four pieces. Arrange these pieces among the pieces of sausage. Blend the retained mushroom water with the remaining ingredients and pour the mixture over the chicken, sausages, and mushrooms.
Cooking Place the dish in a steamer and steam for 40 minutes. Serve from the dish in which the meat has been cooked.

Serves 4–6, with other dishes

A 3–4 lb broiler chicken
3 Chinese sausages

2 teaspoons salt
4 large Chinese dried mushrooms
1½ tablespoons light soy sauce
1½ tablespoons dry sherry
¼ teaspoon monosodium glutamate
1½ teaspoons sesame oil

Turn-Out Chicken

This recipe is a simple peasant version from the province of Hopei, in which Peking is situated.

Preparation Clean the chicken and chop it through the bone into about 20 pieces. Boil for 10 minutes and drain thoroughly. Place the chicken pieces in a heat-proof bowl, skin side down, and sprinkle with salt. Cut the onions and Tsa T'sai into thin slices, and shred the ginger. Peel the potatoes, cut them into slices 1 inch thick, and cut the slices into rectangles 2 × 1 inch. Shred the ginger and sprinkle it over the chicken pieces; then place the onion and Tsa T'sai on top. Put the potato slices on top of the onion and sprinkle with soy sauce.
Cooking Steam the pudding in the heat-proof bowl for 70 minutes.
Serving Turn the contents of the bowl out like a pudding onto a large dish, and serve.

Serves 4–6, with other dishes

A 3–4 lb stewing chicken
1½ teaspoons salt

2 medium-sized onions
¼ cup Szechuan Tsa T'sai (pickled greens)
2 slices ginger root
1 lb sweet potatoes
2½ tablespoons soy sauce

Cantonese Braised Chicken

Serves 4–6, with other dishes

A 3 lb broiler chicken

2½ teaspoons salt
4 golden needles (tiger-lily buds)
1¼ tablespoons dried wood ears
8 large Chinese dried mushrooms
¼ lb leeks
3 scallions
2 cloves garlic
5 tablespoons vegetable oil
2 slices ginger root
¾ cup superior stock
¼ cup soy sauce
2½ teaspoons cornstarch
2½ tablespoons dry sherry
¼ teaspoon monosodium glutamate

Preparation Clean the chicken and rub it with salt, inside and out. Soak the golden needles and wood ears in warm water for 20 minutes. Soak the mushrooms in another bowl for 20 minutes and retain 6 tablespoons of the mushroom water. Chop the golden needles and leeks into 2 inch pieces. Cut the scallions into 1 inch pieces. Rinse the wood ears in fresh water. Crush and chop the garlic. Remove the mushroom stalks.

Cooking Heat the oil in a saucepan, add the chicken, and turn it in the oil for 6–7 minutes over a medium heat until evenly browned. Remove the chicken from the pan and add the ginger, golden needles, and garlic to the pan. Stir-fry for 1½ minutes. Add the wood ears, mushrooms, and leeks, and stir-fry for a further 2 minutes. Return the chicken to the pan. Blend together the stock, soy sauce, and retained mushroom water, and pour over the chicken. Bring the liquid in the pan to the boil, the insert an asbestos pad under the pan and simmer very gently for 30 minutes, turning the chicken over every 10 minutes.

Serving Remove the chicken from the pan and chop it into 20 pieces, through the bone. Arrange the pieces of chicken in a deep dish. Blend the cornstarch with 2 tablespoons water and add to the saucepan with the sherry, monosodium glutamate, and scallions. Stir constantly until the mixture comes to the boil; then pour it evenly over the chicken pieces, and serve on a well-heated dish.

Braised Chicken with Chestnuts

Serves 4–6, with other dishes

A 3–4 lb chicken

20 chestnuts
giblets from 2 chickens
6 medium-sized Chinese dried
  mushrooms
1 large onion
¼ cup vegetable oil
2 slices ginger root
¾ cup soy sauce
1½ tablespoons sugar
¾ cup chicken stock
¼ cup dry sherry
1½ teaspoons salt

Preparation Clean the chicken and chop it into 16–20 pieces. Boil the giblets in water for 5 minutes; then slice each of them into four. Soak the mushrooms in warm water for 30 minutes and retain the water at the end of this time. Cut off the mushroom stalks. Slice the onion thin. Boil the chestnuts for 25 minutes; then remove the shells and skins.

Cooking Heat the oil in a large saucepan. Add the ginger and onion, and stir-fry for 2 minutes. Add the chicken pieces and giblets and continue to stir-fry for a further 5–6 minutes. Pour in the soy sauce, mushroom water, sugar, stock, sherry, and salt. Bring to the boil and simmer for 10 minutes. Add the chestnuts and mix them with the other ingredients. Simmer, covered, for 30 minutes, stirring every 10 minutes; then serve.

Sliced Chicken

Diced chicken cubes, as we have seen, are usually used in pure chicken dishes, with only flavoring and seasoning ingredients added. Chicken cooked whole or chopped into large chunky pieces is usually served in dishes in which the supplementary ingredients seldom constitute more than 15% to 30% of the total ingredients. But in the case of sliced chicken dishes, the chicken meat may consist of up to 50% of the total ingredients. Because of the high regard we Chinese have for chicken (since it is always free-range and tasty, never mass-produced), dishes in which sliced chicken is combined with cheap and readily available vegetables are regarded as chicken dishes. Since chicken is one of the most versatile of meats and can be used in conjunction with many other ingredients, the number of dishes which can be created with chicken meat is practically inexhaustible. The following recipes are some of the best-known, most popular, or easiest to produce sliced chicken dishes.

Sliced Chicken with Mushrooms

Although this is quite a common and easy to produce dish, for those who like the distinctive flavor of mushrooms—especially the flavor of Chinese dried mushrooms—it is a dish one seldom gets tired of.

Preparation Cut the chicken meat thin into $1\frac{1}{2} \times 1$ inch slices. Rub them with salt and dredge with cornstarch. Soak the mushrooms in $\frac{3}{4}$ cup of warm water for 30 minutes. Retain 2–3 tablespoons of the mushroom water at the end of this time. Chop the onion fine.

Cooking Melt the lard in a frying pan, add the ginger and onion, and stir-fry for 2 minutes over a medium heat. Add the chicken slices, spreading them over the surface of the pan. Cook for $1\frac{1}{2}$ minutes, turning twice. Remove the chicken slices and keep them hot. Add the mushrooms to the pan and stir-fry for 1 minute. Add the mushroom water and all the remaining ingredients, and turn the mushrooms in this mixture. Return the chicken to the pan and increase the heat to high. Stir-fry the chicken and mushrooms together for $1\frac{1}{2}$ minutes; then serve.

If Chinese dried mushrooms are unavailable, substitute a larger quantity of well-rinsed fresh mushrooms and two tablespoons of ordinary dried mushrooms. Add an extra tablespoon of lard to the pan before stir-frying the mixed fresh and dried mushrooms, and cook them for 3 minutes before adding the other ingredients. When cooked in this way the dish can be almost as good as if Chinese dried mushrooms had been used. But it is important to give the fresh mushrooms a good rinsing before use so that all their blackness is washed away; otherwise black will become the dominant color of the dish.

Serves 4–6, with other dishes

6 oz chicken breast meat

$1\frac{1}{2}$ teaspoons salt
$1\frac{1}{2}$ tablespoons cornstarch
10 large Chinese dried mushrooms
1 small onion
$2\frac{1}{2}$ tablespoons lard
1 slice ginger root
2–3 tablespoons mushroom water
2 tablespoons soy sauce
2 tablespoons dry sherry
$2\frac{1}{2}$ tablespoons superior stock *or* chicken stock
$\frac{1}{4}$ teaspoon monosodium glutamate
$1\frac{1}{2}$ teaspoons sugar

Sliced Chicken with Pineapple

Serves 4–6, with other dishes

½ lb chicken breast meat
4 slices canned pineapple

2 teaspoons salt
pepper to taste
2 tablespoons cornstarch
1 slice ginger root
1 clove garlic
2½ tablespoons chicken stock
½ cup pineapple juice
1 tablespoon sugar
1½ tablespoons soy sauce
¾ tablespoon vinegar
1½ tablespoons vegetable oil
2½ tablespoons lard

This is in fact, a sweet and sour dish, more popular in the south, where more cooking with fruits and fruit juices is done, compared with the traditional cooking of the north.

Preparation Cut chicken thin into 1½ × 1 inch slices. Rub them with salt, sprinkle with pepper to taste, and dredge with 1 tablespoon of the cornstarch. Cut each slice of pineapple into six wedges. Shred the ginger, crush and chop the garlic. Mix the remaining cornstarch with the chicken stock, pineapple juice, sugar, soy sauce, vinegar, and vegetable oil until well-blended.

Cooking Heat the lard in a frying pan, add the garlic and ginger, and stir-fry for 30 seconds. Add the chicken slices and stir-fry for 2 minutes. Remove the chicken from the pan. Turn the pieces of pineapple in the pan two or three times, then pour in the sauce. Turn the pineapple in the sauce and cook gently until it thickens. Return the chicken slices to the pan and cook for 1 minute. Serve immediately. This is a sweet and sour dish which is popular with most Westerners.

Sliced Chicken with Cucumber

Serves 4–6, with other dishes

Preparation This is a variation of the recipe for Sliced Chicken with Bamboo Shoots (see page 223). Here the cucumber is cut into slices similar in size to the chicken slices; it should not be cut just across the vegetable, but along the skin, so that some slices will be wholly green. As cucumber requires very little cooking it does not require any separate frying; in other words, after the chicken slices have been stir-fried for the first time in the lard and impregnated with ginger and garlic, they do not need to be removed from the pan as the cucumber can then be added and stir-fried with the other ingredients. It is important not to use just any quantity of colored flavoring ingredients. All the best sliced chicken dishes leave the chicken extremely white to contrast sharply with the colors of the supplementary ingredients.

Tangerine Peel Chicken

From the province of Szechuan

The use of tangerine peel to flavor meat is typical of the south and west of China. It is used in much the same way as orange is used with duck in France—generally with a fairly strong tasting meat, such as beef, mutton, or duck. However, in this case it is used with chicken.

Preparation Cut the chicken thin into 1½ × 1 inch slices. Rub them with salt and dredge with 1 tablespoon of the cornstarch. Crush the garlic. Shred the ginger and chili peppers. Slice the onion thin. Soak the tangerine peel in water for 20 minutes; then drain.

Cooking Heat the oil in a frying pan, add the ginger, chili pepper, tangerine peel, and garlic, and stir-fry for 1 minute. Spread the chicken slices over the pan. Stir and turn them in the impregnated oil for 2 minutes. Add the stock and stir for 1 minute. Mix the remaining cornstarch and all the other ingredients together until well-blended. Pour the mixture over the chicken and stir until the sauce thickens. Remove the tangerine peel, and serve. This dish from the west of China is not only sweet and sour but also very hot.

Serves 4–6, with other dishes

10 oz chicken breast meat
2 pieces dried tangerine peel

2 teaspoons salt
2½ tablespoons cornstarch
2 cloves garlic
2 slices ginger root
2 dried chili peppers
1 medium-sized onion
3½ tablespoons vegetable oil
¼ cup chicken stock
1½ tablespoons sugar
1½ tablespoons vinegar
1½ tablespoons soy sauce
¼ cup water
1½ tablespoons dry sherry

Sliced Chicken with Bamboo Shoots

For this dish to have a really good flavor, it is necessary to use a percentage of dried bamboo shoots as well as the fresh or canned bamboo shoots.

Preparation Cut the chicken meat thin into 1½ × 1 inch slices. Rub them with salt and dredge with cornstarch. Soak the dried bamboo shoots for 30 minutes in 6 tablespoons of boiling water; then slice them thin. Cut the fresh or canned bamboo shoots into similar slices. Crush and chop the garlic.

Cooking Heat the lard in a frying pan; then add the ginger and garlic. Stir-fry over a medium heat for 1 minute, then add the chicken slices. Stir-fry for 1½ minutes. Remove the chicken slices and keep them hot. Stir-fry the dried bamboo shoots in the remaining oil for 2 minutes. Add the fresh bamboo shoots and stir-fry for 2 minutes. Pour in the soy sauce, sherry, chicken stock, monosodium glutamate, and hoisin sauce. Turn the bamboo shoots in this mixture for 1 minute. Return the chicken slices to the pan and increase the heat to high. Stir-fry all the ingredients together for 1½ minutes.

Serving Serve on a well-heated platter.

Bamboo shoots have, in fact, only a faint and subtle flavor which does not amount to very much to the majority of people. Many people just eat them for their crunchy texture. Even in China, bamboo shoots are interesting only when very well prepared and cooked. In this dish, the flavor of bamboo shoots is enhanced by using dried bamboo shoots, and made

Serves 4–6, with other dishes

6 oz chicken breast meat
¼ cup dried bamboo shoots
1 cup fresh or canned bamboo shoots

¾ teaspoon salt
1½ tablespoons cornstarch
1 clove garlic
2½ tablespoons lard
1 slice ginger root
2½ tablespoons light soy sauce
¼ teaspoon monosodium glutamate
1½ tablespoons hoisin sauce

more interesting by the addition of hoisin sauce, sherry, and chicken stock. Like bean curds, bamboo shoots can only be made tasty by the flavoring ingredients which are cooked with them, yet their own subtle flavor must be allowed just to suggest itself in the total orchestration.

Sliced Chicken with Green Pepper

Serves 4–6, with other dishes

Preparation Repeat the instructions given in the previous recipe, substituting 1 cup sliced sweet green or red pepper for the bamboo shoots. Stir-fry the pepper for 2 minutes before adding the soy sauce, sherry, chicken stock, monosodium glutamate, and hoisin sauce. Sweet pepper has quite a pronounced flavor and therefore requires the addition of all the flavoring ingredients to counter it and keep the flavor orchestration in balance.

Note It is essential that the ingredients added should not color the whiteness of the chicken slices, so that the alternating white chicken and the green pepper will provide a contrast. This is necessary if the dish is to look attractive.

Pan-Fried Chicken Sandwiches

Serves 4–6, with other dishes

6 oz chicken breast meat
1 cup bamboo shoots
6 oz pork fat

2 scallions
1 slice ginger root
1½ teaspoons salt
1½ tablespoons soy sauce
2 oz ham
1 egg
2¾ tablespoons cornstarch
1 cup vegetable oil
1 cup heart of mustard greens
2½ tablespoons water
2½ teaspoons sugar
2½ teaspoons vinegar
1½ tablespoons orange juice
2½ teaspoons soy sauce
dash of pepper

This is a rather unusual dish by Chinese culinary standards, again from the western province of Szechuan. It consists of thin slices of chicken meat, bamboo shoots, and pork fat, stuck together and fried; then sprinkled with chopped ham. It is a kind of small thin sandwich in which the bamboo shoots provide the crunchy 'heart', the pork fat the crackling base, the chicken the savory top, and the ham its saltiness. The frying in this case is mainly static (Tsien) as opposed to the normal stir-frying.

Preparation Cut the chicken meat thin into 12–15 slices 1½ × 1 inch. Chop the scallions and ginger as fine as possible, and mix them with the salt and 1 tablespoon soy sauce. Marinate the chicken slices in this mixture. Dip the bamboo shoots in boiling water for 3 minutes and cut them into pieces about the same size as the chicken slices. Boil the pork fat in water for 20 minutes and cut it into slices in the same way as the bamboo shoots. Chop the ham fine. Beat the egg and blend it with 1 tablespoon of the cornstarch to make a thin batter. Place the pork fat on a large plate and wipe each piece with a hot, damp cloth. Make sandwiches using the pork fat as the base, the bamboo shoots as the filling, and the chicken as the top. 'Cement' each layer together with the egg/cornstarch batter. Damp the top of each sandwich with the remaining batter and sprinkle with chopped ham.

Cooking Put the oil in a large, heavy frying pan over a moderate heat. Place the sandwiches in the pan and cook them for 3–4 minutes, splashing the top of each with a little hot oil. When the three layers have become well stuck together, turn the sandwiches over and cook them upside down for 1 minute. Turn them over once more until the pork fat turns brown and crackling; then drain them, and place in the center of a large well-heated dish. Meanwhile, prepare the greens to accompany the sandwiches. Cut each piece into four, dip in boiling water for 2 minutes; then stir-fry them in a small quantity of oil and salt for 1 minute. Blend 2 teaspoons of cornstarch with the remaining ingredients into a smooth sauce and pour it over the greens. Cook until the sauce thickens.

Serving Arrange the greens around the sandwiches on an attractive platter.

This makes an excellent and unusual party dish which can be prepared beforehand.

Braised Sliced Chicken with Pork Tripe

From Canton

Serves 4–6, with other dishes

Preparation Cut the chicken thin into 1½ × 1 inch slices. Rub with half of the salt and dredge with cornstarch. Take a sharp knife and score the tripe at ½ inch intervals crosswise, cutting half-way through the thickness. Turn the tripe over and repeat. Crush and chop the garlic, and slice the leeks thin. Combine the remaining salt, soy sauce, wine, garlic, and leeks and marinate the tripe in this mixture for 1 hour. Shred the ginger and chop the scallions fine, then sprinkle them over the chicken slices.

Cooking Put half of the vegetable oil in a frying pan over a medium heat. Add the chicken slices (with the ginger and scallions) and stir-fry for 1½ minutes. Remove the chicken from the pan. Add the remainder of the oil, increase the heat to high, and put the tripe in the pan. Stir-fry quickly for 5 minutes. Return the chicken to the pan and stir-fry with the tripe; then add the stock, sherry, and monosodium glutamate. Heat for 10 minutes, sprinkle with sesame oil, and serve.

6 oz chicken breast meat
½ lb pork tripe

2½ teaspoons salt
2 teaspoons cornstarch
2 cloves garlic
½ cup young leeks
1 tablespoon soy sauce
2½ tablespoons white wine
1 slice ginger root
2 scallions
5 tablespoons vegetable oil
1 cup superior stock
2½ tablespoons dry sherry
¼ teaspoon monosodium glutamate
1½ teaspoons sesame oil

225

Sliced Chicken with Smoked and Salted Fish

Serves 4–6, with other dishes

½ lb chicken breast meat
¼ lb smoked fish (salmon *or* white-fish)
3 tablespoons anchovy fillets

2½ slices ginger root
2½ tablespoons dry sherry
¾ tablespoon chicken fat
¾ cup chicken stock
1½ teaspoons salt
2 scallions
¼ teaspoon monosodium glutamate

From the south-east coast of China

Preparation Cut the chicken into about 12 thin slices, and arrange them on the base of a heat-proof dish, skin side down. Slice the smoked fish in the same way and alternate these pieces with the chicken slices in overlapping rows. Chop the ginger and sprinkle it over the chicken and fish with the sherry, chicken fat, 4–5 tablespoons of the stock, and half of the salt. Cut the anchovy fillets into six pieces and arrange them on top of the chicken and salmon. Chop the scallions.

Cooking Place the dish in a steamer and steam for 20 minutes. Heat the remainder of the stock in a small saucepan; then add the scallions, monosodium glutamate, and remaining salt. When the mixture comes to the boil, pour it over the chicken and salmon. Turn on to a serving dish, and serve immediately.

This is an unusual dish which possesses the unique flavor of chicken impregnated with flavor of smoky and salted fish.

Sliced Chicken with Pork Liver and Scallions

Serves 4–6, with other dishes

6 oz chicken breast meat
6 oz pork's liver
3 scallions

1 teaspoon salt
1½ tablespoons cornstarch
1 slice ginger root
1 clove garlic
1½ tablespoons chopped onion
1½ tablespoons soy sauce
¼ cup vegetable oil
5½ tablespoons chicken stock
2½ teaspoons sugar
2½ tablespoons white wine

This is another of those Chinese recipes where meats of different textures are quick-fried together. They are usually stir-fried over great heat. The blending by heat of two different types of meat flavor gives a new kind of dimension to savoriness as it strikes the palate during consumption.

Preparation Cut chicken thin into 1½ × 1 inch slices, rub them with salt, and dredge with cornstarch. Shred the ginger and rub it into the chicken slices; then leave to season for 15 minutes. Slice the liver in the same way as the chicken. Crush and chop the garlic, and mix with the chopped onion and soy sauce. Marinate the liver in this mixture for 15 minutes. Cut the scallions into 1 inch pieces.

Cooking Heat 2 tablespoons of the oil in a frying pan. Add the chicken slices and turn them in the oil for 1½ minutes; then remove them from the pan. Add the remaining oil and pour the liver and marinade into the pan. Increase the heat to high and stir-fry for 3 minutes. Return the chicken to the pan, and add the stock, sugar, and wine; stir-fry for 3 minutes. Mix in the scallions; turn and scramble them a few times with the liver and chicken; then serve.

Home-Cooked Hot Braised Sliced Chicken with Celery

From the province of Szechuan

Preparation Cut chicken thin into 1½ × 1 inch slices. Rub them with salt and dredge with 2 teaspoons cornstarch. Shred the ginger and chili peppers. Soak the black beans in water for 20 minutes; then drain. Cut the celery slantwise into ¾ inch slices. Mix the soy sauce, tomato puree, sugar, stock, monosodium glutamate, and remaining cornstarch until well-blended.

Cooking Heat the oil in a frying pan, add the ginger, chili, and black beans, and stir-fry for 1 minute over a high heat. Add the chicken slices, turn them for 2 minutes, then remove them from the pan. Put the lard in the pan and add the celery slices. Stir-fry and scramble for 3 minutes over a high heat. Return the chicken to the pan, pour in the sauce mixture and turn the chicken and celery in the liquid for 1½ minutes before serving.

Serves 4–6, with other dishes

½ lb chicken breast meat
1 bunch of celery

¾ teaspoon salt
1 tablespoon cornstarch
2 slices ginger root
2 dried chili peppers
1 tablespoon fermented black beans
2 tablespoons soy sauce
2½ teaspoons tomato puree
2½ teaspoons sugar
1 cup superior stock
¼ teaspoon monosodium glutamate
2½ teaspoons cornstarch
2½ tablespoons vegetable oil
1½ tablespoons lard

Cantonese Sliced Chicken in Fruit Sauce

It is more often the practice and tradition of the south to use fruits and fruit juices for cooking savory dishes. This dish is an example.

Preparation Cut chicken thin into 1½ × 1 inch slices. Rub them with salt and dredge with 1 tablespoon cornstarch. Mix all the remaining ingredients except the vegetable oil, and blend them to a smooth sauce.

Cooking Heat the oil in a frying pan and spread the chicken slices evenly over the pan; then turn them over. Stir-fry and scramble for 2 minutes. Pour the sauce into the pan and turn the chicken gently until the sauce thickens. Serve immediately.

This is a very fruity dish, combining the tender savoriness of chicken with the refreshing quality of the fruit juice. It should be a sensation to those who have never tried it before.

Serves 4–6, with other dishes

10 oz chicken breast meat

1½ teaspoons salt
1½ tablespoons cornstarch
2½ tablespoons orange juice
2½ tablespoons lychee juice
2½ teaspoons sugar
1½ tablespoons tomato puree
2½ teaspoons light soy sauce
1 tablespoon cornstarch
¼ cup water
2½ tablespoons vegetable oil

Sliced Chicken with Snow Peas

Serves 4–6, with other dishes

½ lb chicken breast meat
6 oz (2 cups) snow peas

1½ teaspoons salt
1½ tablespoons cornstarch
6 tablespoons chicken stock
1½ tablespoons light soy sauce
2½ tablespoons white wine
¼ teaspoon monosodium glutamate
2½ teaspoons cornstarch
2½ tablespoons vegetable oil
1 slice ginger root
1½ tablespoons lard

Preparation Cut chicken thin into 1½ × 1 inch slices. Rub them with salt and dredge with 1 tablespoon cornstarch. Blend together the chicken stock, soy sauce, wine, monosodium glutamate, and 2 teaspoons cornstarch.

Cooking Heat the oil in a frying pan and add the ginger. Stir-fry for 30 seconds, then discard the ginger. Put the chicken slices in the pan and stir-fry for 2 minutes over a high heat. Remove the chicken from the pan and keep it warm. Add the lard to the pan, then the snow peas. Stir-fry for 2 minutes. Return the chicken to the pan and mix with the snow peas. Pour in the sauce mixture and cook, turning and scrambling for 1½ minutes. Serve immediately.

Gold Coin Chicken

Serves 4–6, with other dishes

A 3 lb broiler chicken
2½ quarts master stock (*or* soy-herbal stock)

Preparation Clean the chicken thoroughly inside and out. Dip it in boiling water for 1 minute; then drain.

Cooking Bring the master stock to the boil in a large saucepan. Immerse the chicken completely and simmer in the stock for 20 minutes; then turn off the heat and let the chicken stand in the stock and hot marinade for 40 minutes. It will have turned a rich brown at the end of this time.

Serving Remove the chicken from the stock and place it on a chopping board. Cut the chicken thin into 2 inch rounds or 'coins' with a Chinese cleaver or a very sharp knife. Use the breast meat and the drumsticks; if using the latter, remove the leg bone first, and slice through the cross section. Place these 'coins' on an oval serving dish, arranged in three rows. The middle row should be the longest.

Shredded Chicken

As a rule in Chinese cooking, the foods are cut and reduced to harmonize with the natural size and shape of the bulk material of the dish. If the bulk food in the dish is noodles or spaghetti, the chicken has to be shredded into strips or threads. In the case of chicken itself, since much of its meat exists in strip form, we find it only natural to shape and trim it into more perfect strips or shreds, about the size of matchsticks or slightly larger. These strips can be used to fry and cook with such materials as bean sprouts, shredded bamboo shoots, asparagus, celery, ham, string beans, noodles, transparent bean-thread noodles, and numerous other things which exist naturally in strip or shred form, or which can be easily rendered into strips or shreds.

Chinese shredded chicken is not simply chicken meat torn from the bone into shreds. Breast meat, neatly cut into shreds, is often used. Smaller shreds are called 'chicken threads', and the larger strips are called 'willow leaf strips'. Chicken threads are about the length and thickness of matchsticks, perhaps a little thinner. Willow leaf strips can perhaps be termed chicken slivers. They are about 2–3½ inches long. The following section contains dishes were chicken meat is used in these shapes and sizes.

Breast meat is preferably for cutting into strips and threads, as it is easier to cut; but, of course, all other cuts of chicken can be used. With the inherent Chinese sense of economy in cooking, the whole carcase is, in fact, stripped for shreds, and these are used along with the neater, straight-cut strips for consumption at home. When producing dishes for banquets or party dinners, only the straight-cut shreds from the chicken breast are used, not only because the breast meat can be neatly cut more easily, but also because it is whiter. In the presentation of some dishes where color purity or contrast is paramount, the selection of white meat is an important consideration.

Slivered Chicken with String Beans

Preparation Cut the chicken into willow leaf strips. Rub them with salt, dampen with egg white, and dredge with cornstarch. Trim the string beans and slice them diagonally into strips the same length as the chicken slivers. Simmer in boiling water for 2 minutes; then drain.

Cooking Heat 2 tablespoons of the oil in a frying pan. Add the ginger and chicken, spreading the chicken strips evenly over the pan. Stir-fry over a medium heat for 2 minutes, then remove the chicken from the pan. Add the remaining oil and pour in the string beans. Stir-fry for 1 minute over a high heat. Pour in the chicken stock, sherry, sugar, soy sauce, and monosodium glutamate. Cook, stirring, for 2 minutes. Return the chicken to the pan, stir-fry for 1 minute; then serve.

Although quite simple, this is a satisfying dish which can be served either at a party dinner or for a home meal. The whiteness of the chicken and the greenness of the beans make an attractive contrast.

Serves 4–6, with other dishes

½ lb chicken breast meat
6 oz string beans

¾ teaspoon salt
1 egg white
1½ tablespoons cornstarch
¼ cup vegetable oil
2 slices ginger root
2½ tablespoons chicken stock
1½ tablespoons dry sherry
1½ teaspoons sugar
2 tablespoons light soy sauce
¼ teaspoon monosodium glutamate

Slivered Chicken with Hearts of Greens

Preparation Repeat the instructions given in the previous recipe, substituting mustard green hearts for the string beans. Cut the greens vertically into 2–3-inch strips, dip them in boiling water for a couple of minutes; then drain. Fry them with the ingredients used in the previous recipe, before adding the pre-fried chicken slivers.

Serves 4–6, with other dishes

229

Slivered Chicken with Broccoli

Serves 4–6, with other dishes

Preparation This recipe is a variation of Slivered Chicken with String Beans. Substitute broccoli sliced into strips for the string beans. Parboil the broccoli strips for 2–3 minutes before frying.

Slivered Chicken with Cucumber

Serves 4–6, with other dishes

Preparation Repeat the instructions given in the recipe for Slivered Chicken with String Beans, substituting cucumber for the string beans. Slice the cucumber lengthwise into strips about the same length and thickness as the chicken slivers. There is no need to simmer the cucumber before stir-frying it, as it requires very little cooking. Cucumber used in this way should not be peeled. Indeed, it should only be lightly scraped so that all its green coolness can be retained.

Slivered Chicken with Asparagus

Serves 4–6, with other dishes

Preparation This recipe is a variation of Slivered Chicken with String Beans. Use asparagus instead of string beans. Remove the hard coarse parts of the asparagus, split each spear into four, and cut into slivers the same size as the pieces of chicken. Parboil the asparagus strips for 5 minutes, and drain, before proceeding with the cooking instructions.

Slivered Chicken with Leeks

Serves 4–6, with other dishes

Preparation Follow the instructions given in the recipe for Slivered Chicken with String Beans, substituting leeks for string beans. Because leeks have a fairly pronounced flavor, 1½ tablespoons hoisin sauce should be added when stir-frying the chicken. This prevents the leeks from overpowering the chicken and other ingredients, and adds a touch of hotness to the dish.

In the previous six recipes, the lightly and quickly cooked vegetables retain a good deal of their own juices, distinctive flavors, and crunchy texture, which contrast well with the white, soft, savory tenderness of chicken. The vegetable strips are of a size where texture (as it feels to the mouth, tongue, and teeth), is easily apparent. The flavor, too, of each vegetable is very pronounced, since the vegetable juices have been freshly released through the sudden impact of heat, both from the oil and from the metal pan. This heat is maintained through the short but intense period of stir-frying. In each case, the contrast between the glistening greenness of the vegetables and the immaculate whiteness of the chicken increases the visual attractiveness of the dish.

In the following recipes, where the chicken meat and vegetables are reduced to very fine threads, the aim is to produce attractive 'woven' culinary tapestries: tapestries of color, texture, and taste, rather than the simpler contrasts achieved before.

Chicken Threads with Bean Sprouts

Preparation Use a razor-sharp knife to cut the chicken into threads or matchstick strips about 1½ inches long. Sprinkle them with salt, pepper, and cornstarch, discarding any excess cornstarch. Crush and chop the garlic.

Cooking Heat the oil in a large frying pan and add the ginger. Stir-fry for 30 seconds, then discard the ginger. Add the chicken threads and turn them in the oil for 1½ minutes over a medium heat. Remove them from the pan and keep them hot. Put the chicken fat and garlic in the pan and stir-fry for 30 minutes over a high heat, until they are all evenly coated. Add the soy sauce, chili sauce, and vinegar, and stir-fry for 1 minute. Return the chicken threads to the pan and sprinkle them with chicken stock, sherry, monosodium glutamate, and chives. Stir-fry for 1 minute, mixing all the ingredients together; then serve.

Serves 4–6, with other dishes

6 oz chicken breast meat
¾ lb bean sprouts

¾ teaspoon salt
pepper to taste
1½ tablespoons cornstarch
2 cloves garlic
2½ tablespoons vegetable oil
2 slices ginger root
2½ tablespoons chicken fat
2½ tablespoons light soy sauce
¾ teaspoon chili sauce
2½ teaspoons vinegar
2½ tablespoons chicken stock
1½ tablespoons dry sherry
¼ teaspoon monosodium glutamate
2½ tablespoons chopped chives

Chicken Threads with Sliced Peppers

Preparation Using a razor-sharp knife, slice the chicken into very thin threads 1½ inches in length. Sprinkle with salt and rub them with cornstarch, discarding any excess cornstarch. Slice the sweet peppers in the same way as the chicken, and shred the chili peppers.

Cooking Heat the oil in a large frying pan, and add the ginger. Stir-fry for 1 minute, then remove it from the pan. Add the chicken threads and stir-fry for 2 minutes; then remove from the pan and keep warm. Put the chicken fat and chili peppers into the frying pan, stir-fry for 1 minute; then add the green pepper threads and turn them in the fat for 2 minutes. Pour in the soy sauce, sugar, vinegar, and stock, and cook, stirring, for 1 minute. Return the chicken threads to the pan, and pour in the sherry. Mix and assembly-fry all the ingredients together for 1 minute; then serve.

Serves 4–6, with other dishes

6 oz chicken breast meat
2 large green sweet peppers
2 dried red chili peppers

¾ teaspoon salt
1½ tablespoons cornstarch
2½ tablespoons vegetable oil
2 slices ginger root
2½ tablespoons chicken fat
2½ tablespoons soy sauce
2½ teaspoons sugar
4 teaspoons vinegar
2½ tablespoons chicken stock
1½ tablespoons dry sherry

Chicken Threads with Bamboo Shoots

Serves 4–6, with other dishes

6 oz chicken breast meat
1 cup fresh or canned bamboo
shoots
1 cup dried bamboo shoots

¾ teaspoon salt
1½ tablespoons cornstarch
4 large Chinese dried mushrooms
2½ tablespoons vegetable oil
2½ tablespoons chicken fat
2 tablespoons soy sauce
3 tablespoons chicken stock
¾ teaspoon hoisin sauce
1½ teaspoons sugar
2½ teaspoons sesame oil

To make the dish extra tasty, both dried and fresh or canned bamboo shoots are used. Since chicken is white in color and bamboo shoots are ivory, black dried mushrooms are added to provide a color contrast, as well as to enhance the flavor.

Preparation Using a razor-sharp knife, slice the chicken meat into very thin matchstick shreds. Sprinkle them with salt and dredge with cornstarch. Cut the fresh or canned bamboo shoots into matchstick shreds. Soak the dried bamboo shoots in hot water for 30 minutes, then slice them into matchstick strips. Soak the mushrooms in 5 tablespoons warm water for 30 minutes. Remove the stalks and shred the caps fine. Retain 2 tablespoons of the mushroom water.

Cooking Heat the oil in a frying pan. Add the chicken threads and stir-fry for 2 minutes over a medium heat. Remove them from the pan and keep hot. Put the chicken fat in the pan; then add both types of bamboo shoots, and the mushroom threads. Stir-fry for 2 minutes over a high heat. Add the soy sauce, stock, hoisin sauce, mushroom water, and sugar. Return the chicken threads to the pan and cook, stirring, for 2 minutes. Sprinkle with sesame oil, and serve.

Chicken Threads with Chinese Cabbage or Celery

Serves 4–6, with other dishes

6 oz chicken breast meat
2 cups Chinese cabbage *or* Savoy
cabbage *or* celery

¾ teaspoon salt
1½ tablespoons cornstarch
2½ dried chili peppers
4 large Chinese dried mushrooms
2½ tablespoons vegetable oil
3 tablespoons chicken fat
1½–2½ teaspoons ground dried
shrimp
2 tablespoons soy sauce
3 tablespoons chicken stock
¾ tablespoon hoisin sauce
1½ teaspoons sugar
2½ teaspoons sesame oil

Preparation Using a razor-sharp knife, slice the chicken into thin matchstick threads. Sprinkle with salt and dredge with cornstarch. Shred the cabbage or celery (it need not be as finely shredded as the chicken), and the chili peppers. Soak the mushrooms in 5 tablespoons warm water for 30 minutes, remove the stalks, and slice the caps thin. Retain 2 tablespoons of the mushroom water.

Cooking Heat the oil in a frying pan. Add the chicken threads and stir-fry for 2 minutes over a medium heat. Remove them from the pan and keep hot. Put the chicken fat in the pan, and add the shredded peppers, mushrooms, and dried shrimp. Stir-fry for 30 seconds, then add the cabbage or celery. Stir-fry for a further 2 minutes. Pour in the soy sauce, stock, hoisin sauce, mushroom water, and sugar; then return the chicken threads to the pan and cook, stirring, for 2 minutes. Sprinkle with sesame oil, and serve.

Chinese Chicken-Celery Salad

Preparation Using a razor-sharp knife, cut the chicken into matchstick threads. Shred the ginger fine and scatter it over the chicken. Sprinkle with salt and pepper, and mix with the seasonings. Slice the celery into pieces about twice the size of matchsticks, sprinkle with soy sauce, sugar, vinegar, and chili oil, and toss the celery and seasonings together. Mix the chicken and celery in a salad bowl and sprinkle with the oil, monosodium glutamate, sherry, and sesame oil. Toss these ingredients together; then serve. This salad makes an interesting opening to a Western meal.

Serves 4–6, with other dishes

½ lb roast chicken meat
½ lb celery

1 slice ginger root
2 teaspoons salt
pepper to taste
2 tablespoons soy sauce
1 teaspoon sugar
2½ teaspoons vinegar
¾ teaspoon chili oil
1½ tablespoons vegetable oil
¼ teaspoon monosodium glutamate
1½ tablespoons dry sherry
2½ teaspoons sesame oil

Chopped Chicken Dishes

In Chinese cookery, the term 'Fu-Yung' indicates dishes prepared with beaten egg or egg white. The Chinese often blend finely chopped chicken with beaten egg or egg white, resulting in quite a large range of well known Fu-Yung dishes which can be cooked very quickly. This section contains a selection.

Tri-Color Scrambled Chicken Fu-Yung

The three colors making this an interesting dish. It originated in the former East Market in Peking. Serve with plain boiled rice.

Preparation Chop the chicken very fine. Separate the egg whites and yolks and put them into different bowls. Mix 1 cup of the chicken with the egg whites and ¼ cup of the stock. Add two thirds of the salt, 1 tablespoon wine, two thirds of the cornstarch, the monosodium glutamate, and pepper to taste. Blend these ingredients together well. Mix the egg yolks with the remaining chicken. Add the remaining stock, salt, wine, cornstarch, and pepper to taste.

Serves 4–6, with other dishes

½ lb chicken breast meat (use only white meat)
6 eggs

1 cup superior stock
1½ teaspoons salt
2 tablespoons white wine
2½ tablespoons cornstarch
¼ teaspoon monosodium glutamate
pepper to taste
6½ tablespoons lard
2 tablespoons tomato puree

233

Cooking Heat ¾ cup of the lard in a frying pan. When it is almost smoking-hot, remove from the heat for 4–5 seconds. Pour in the chicken and egg white mixture and scramble it quickly. Return the pan to a medium heat and continue to scramble and stir-fry for 30 seconds. Remove the pan from the heat and put half of the mixture along one side of a well-heated dish. Add the tomato puree to the remaining mixture and return the pan to the heat. Stir rapidly with a scrambling motion. After 10–12 seconds, spoon the resulting pink mixture on to the middle of the serving dish. Melt the remaining lard in a clean frying pan. Add the chicken and egg yolk mixture. Stir and scramble for 30–35 seconds, then spoon on to the serving dish.

This white, red, and yellow striped dish is very attractive.

Fu-Yung Chicken Slices

Serves 4–6, with other dishes

¼ lb chicken breast meat
2 oz white fish
3 egg whites

2½ teaspoons chopped onion
1½ teaspoons chopped ginger root
1½ tablespoons water chestnuts, chopped
¾ teaspoon salt
1 tablespoon cornstarch
1½ teaspoons flour
1 cup chicken stock
¼ teaspoon monosodium glutamate
2½ tablespoons white wine
½ teaspoon salt
½ lb lard

This is a pure white dish, consisting of chopped chicken blended with egg white (often with the addition of chopped white fish). It is cooked and presented in slices, and smothered in a white sauce.

Preparation Chop the chicken and fish very fine. Beat the egg whites with a fork for 10 seconds. Combine the cornstarch and flour. Mix together the chicken, fish, onion, ginger, water chestnut, egg white, and salt; then add 1½ teaspoons of the cornstarch and flour mixture and beat until the ingredients are well-blended and form a runny paste. Mix all the remaining ingredients, except the lard, to form a smooth sauce. Add ½ teaspoon salt.

Cooking Heat the lard in a large frying pan. Take a tablespoon of the chicken Fu-Yung mixture and slide it on to the surface of the boiling fat. (If it turns brown or curls up at the edges, the fat is too hot.) After 4–5 seconds frying, turn the piece of Fu-Yung with a wide spatula and fry the other side for the same length of time. Remove from the pan and place on a well-heated serving dish. Continue until all the Fu-Yung mixture has been used. Heat the sauce until it boils and thickens, then pour over the Fu-Yung Chicken Slices. This dish is best eaten immediately.

This is a typical dish from Peking, popular throughout the north but regarded with not quite the same enthusiasm in the south.

234

Corn and Velveteen Chicken

Some Chinese dishes are for accompanying wine, others lend weight to a meal, and others, like this one, function mainly as an aid to downing rice, which is very important in Chinese food consumption. Hence some dishes which may seem quite uninteresting to foreigners have a curious appeal to the Chinese. This is an example. It is essentially a domestic dish, of southern origin.

Preparation Chop the chicken fine. Beat the egg whites with a fork for 10 seconds, then mix well with the chopped chicken. Blend the cornstarch in a small bowl with 6 tablespoons of water.

Cooking Bring the chicken stock to the boil in a saucepan. Add the salt, sugar, monosodium glutamate, and cornstarch mixed with water. Stir until the liquid is somewhat thickened. Pour the chicken and egg-white mixture into the pan in a very thin stream, stirring constantly until the mixture is well blended. Add the corn and chicken fat and heat for 3–4 minutes. Give the mixture a final stir; then pour it into a large serving bowl and garnish with the chopped ham.

Serves 4–6, with other dishes

$\frac{1}{4}$ lb chicken breast meat
4 oz corn kernels

2 egg whites
2 tablespoons cornstarch
1$\frac{1}{4}$ cups chicken stock
1$\frac{1}{2}$ teaspoons salt
2$\frac{1}{2}$ teaspoons sugar
1$\frac{1}{2}$ tablespoons chicken fat
chopped ham
$\frac{1}{4}$ teaspoon monosodium glutamate

Chicken Fu-Yung Cauliflower

This is another example of how we Chinese expand the size and quantity of a dish with the use of vegetables and with only a limited use of the more expensive ingredient, chicken. This is a typical home-cooked dish, which is brought out to augment the normal domestic spread of dishes on the table when an unexpected guest arrives.

Preparation Chop the chicken fine. Add the egg whites, 1 teaspoon of the salt, monosodium glutamate, stock, and cornstarch, mixed with 2 tablespoons water. Beat with a rotary whisk until slightly puffed. Cut away the root of the cauliflower and break into branches. Simmer the vegetables in boiling water for 5–6 minutes; then drain.

Cooking Heat the chicken fat in a small saucepan. Add the cauliflower and sprinkle with the remaining salt, pepper, and white wine. Turn the cauliflower in the fat and wine for 2 minutes over a high heat. Meanwhile, heat the lard in a large frying pan. Add the chicken and egg white mixture and stir over a medium heat for 2 minutes. Pour the cauliflower back into the frying pan, and turn and mix it with the Fu-Yung mixture for 1$\frac{1}{2}$ minutes. Pour into a serving bowl and sprinkle with chopped ham.

Serves 4–6, with other dishes

$\frac{1}{4}$ lb chicken breast meat
1 medium-sized cauliflower

3 egg whites
2 teaspoons salt
$\frac{1}{4}$ teaspoon monosodium glutamate
$\frac{1}{4}$ cup chicken stock
2 teaspoons cornstarch
2$\frac{1}{2}$ tablespoons chicken fat
pepper to taste
2$\frac{1}{2}$ tablespoons white wine
2$\frac{1}{2}$ tablespoons lard
chopped ham

Chicken Fu-Yung
with Hearts of Greens

Preparation Follow the instructions given in the previous recipe, using ½ lb of the tender heart of mustard greens or 1 lb broccoli instead of the cauliflower. These vegetables will require 6–7 minutes of parboiling before being incorporated with the Fu-Yung. In contrast with the previous recipe, which results in an all white dish, this is a green and white dish.

Chicken Specialties

There are a number of miscellaneous chicken dishes which are difficult to classify under any precise category; however, they are distinctive and intriguing, and too interesting to miss or overlook. Indeed, many of them make frequent appearances on the Chinese dinner tables, both at home and during banquets.

Red, White, and Black
with Chicken Velveteen

Serves 4–6, with other dishes

8 large Chinese dried mushrooms
¾ lb chicken breast meat
¼ lb best ham

3 egg whites
1½ teaspoons salt
2 tablespoons cornstarch
1 cup chicken stock
¼ teaspoon monosodium glutamate
5 tablespoons white wine
oil for deep-frying

This is one of those Chinese semi-soup dishes which are served now and then during the long procession of courses at a Chinese party dinner. They help to break the monotony of quick-fried savory dishes, and they are particularly useful for eating with rice.

Preparation Soak the mushrooms in warm water for 30 minutes, then remove the stalks. Cut the chicken meat into about 20 thin slices. Trim the edges carefully so that each slice is a standard size of about 1 × 2 inches. Chop the trimmings fine. Add the egg whites, ½ teaspoon of the salt, and 2 teaspoons of the cornstarch, blended with 3 tablespoons of stock. Beat into a batter. Add the remaining salt and cornstarch, the monosodium glutamate, and wine to the rest of the stock. Mix until well-blended. Cut the ham into slices about the same size as the chicken slices.

Cooking Dip the chicken slices in the chopped chicken and egg white batter. Heat the oil in a deep-fryer and lower the pieces of battered chicken into the pan to fry at a low heat for 10–12 seconds, turning once. Remove, drain, and place in the bottom of a deep casserole or heat-proof dish. Insert the pieces of ham between the chicken slices. Arrange the mushrooms artistically in the dish. Add the remaining batter to the stock mixture and mix until well-blended. Heat the stock until it begins to boil, then pour it over the chicken, ham, and mushrooms. Place the casserole in an oven preheated to 350°F for 20 minutes, with the lid on. If you are using a dish, cover it with aluminum foil while it is in the oven. Serve from the casserole dish. This is a rather 'way-out' recipe, derived from east China.

Bean-Flower Velveteen of Chicken

This is another semi-soup dish which is called 'Soup Dish' (Tang Ts'ai) in China. This is not exactly a soup, but a main course with plenty of soup in it. It is usually served with rice.

Preparation Boil the chicken and pork for 15 minutes, and the fish for 10 minutes. Chop them separately and place them together in a bowl. Add the egg whites and ¾ teaspoon of the salt. Mix thoroughly until smooth and well-blended. Boil the onions and ginger in the stock for 7–8 minutes; then discard them, and allow the stock to cool in a bowl. When it is cool, pour in the meat and egg mixture. Blend well.

Cooking Add the remaining salt to the bean or pea soup and bring to the boil. Pour half into the meat, egg, and stock mixture and reserve the other half. Stir well. Put the bowl in a steamer and steam for 20 minutes; then pour the mixture into a serving bowl or soup tureen. Heat the remaining bean soup and add the monosodium glutamate and wine. As soon as it boils, pour it on top of the contents of the serving bowl or tureen. Sprinkle with pepper and sesame oil, and serve with rice.

In America, it is more convenient to use ready-made pea or bean soup. Bean soup, of varying thickness, can be prepared by prolonged simmering and straining, and the gradual adding of superior stock to the beans, but the preparation takes several hours.

Serves 4–6, with other dishes

¼ lb chicken breast meat
2 cups bean soup *or* pea soup

2 oz pork
¼ lb filleted white fish (sole, cod, halibut)

2 egg whites
2 teaspoons salt
2 medium-sized onions
2 slices ginger root
¾ cup superior stock
¼ teaspoon monosodium glutamate
2 tablespoons white wine
dash of pepper
2 teaspoons sesame oil

Paper-Wrapped Chicken

This was originally a southern Cantonese dish, but it is now popular throughout the country. Usually the chicken is wrapped in transparent cellophane paper, although recently there has been a drift to using rice paper, which is edible. Rice paper does not insulate the contents of the 'envelope'

Serves 4–6, with other dishes

from the deep-frying oil; furthermore, as it is non-transparent, it encloses the wrapped chicken in a parcel exactly the same as an egg roll, and indeed, it tastes like an egg roll! In this recipe, we adhere to the use of cellophane paper.

half 2–3 lb chicken

1 slice ginger root
3 tablespoons soy sauce
1½ tablespoons dry sherry
2½ teaspoons sugar
¼ teaspoon monosodium glutamate
4 large Chinese dried mushrooms
3 scallions

large sheet of cellophane or parchment paper

Preparation Cut and scrape the chicken meat from the bones. Shred the ginger coarse. Marinate the meat for 1 hour in a mixture of soy sauce, sherry, sugar, shredded ginger, and monosodium glutamate. Soak the mushrooms in a bowl of water for 30 minutes; then remove the stalks and slice the caps into thin strips. Cut the scallions into 1½ inch segments.

Wrapping The orthodox way of wrapping is envelope fashion. Cut the sheet of cellophane into pieces about 6 × 5 inches. Wrap about ¼–½ oz of the marinated chicken meat in each piece of cellophane, with two or three segments of scallion, and two or three mushroom strips. The cellophane should be made into an envelope, with a long tongue which can be well tucked in.

Cooking When all the chicken has been wrapped, deep-fry the packages, six at a time, for 3 minutes. Drain well. (Frying should never exceed 3½ minutes at once as that would blacken the cellophane paper.) When all the envelopes have been fried, give them a final deep-fry together for 1 minute, then drain thoroughly.

Serving When ready, arrange the packages on a round serving dish, radiating from the center, or pile them up in overlapping rows. They can be surrounded by a bank of green vegetables—lettuce, hearts of mustard greens, or watercress, if desired.

A novel way of wrapping, discovered recently by a British connoisseur who has lived a lifetime in China, and who employs a Chinese butler and chef at his home, is to make a long pack about 6 inches long, simply by screwing and twisting the paper to close at the ends when the stuffings have been inserted. When it is ready, each pack can be cut in half with a pair of scissors, and the chicken inside eaten without being unwrapped, thus preventing a lot of greasy fingers. In fact, each piece of wrapped chicken can be picked up by the fingers at the twisted end and the contents can be pushed into the mouth and conveniently eaten like an ice-cream cone! This way of wrapping can be highly recommended, although it is most unorthodox.

DUCK, PIGEON, TURKEY, AND FROGS

鴨 鴿 火 鷄 田 鷄

After chicken, duck is by far the most widely eaten fowl in China. Apart from the innumerable streams, canals, rivers, lakes, and waterways of China, every village has its pond, which helps in the rearing of this land-based waterfowl. On the dining table, its meat is considered one degree more special than chicken; and as it is a strong-tasting meat, many people regard it as more interesting than chicken, which is eaten almost every day by the well-to-do.

The most famous duck dish of China is, of course, Peking Duck. The duck used is, in fact, a mass-produced and manually fed white feathered-duck, especially raised for the purpose of providing the material for this famous dish. It has a long, broad back, short wings and short legs, and has the appearance of being strong and well-built. Despite the traces of fat in its muscle fibers, when the duck is cooked there is no sense of greasiness in its crimson/white flesh, compared with the dark tough meat of many other ducks. In the latter stages of their rearing, the birds are given little chance for exercise in water (as prolonged exercise might harden the muscles) and their feeding is partly left to nature and is partly artificial and forced. Because of the care taken, particularly in the last stage of fattening, the meat is especially appealing and tender.

This famous table-duck was first exported to England and America in 1875, to Japan in 1888, and to the U.S.S.R. in 1956, where it came to be known as the 'Moscow white-feathered duck'.

Pigeons are widespread throughout China; they are common both in the north and south. In Peking small pipes are often fitted to their feet, so that they make a piping noise or music as they swirl through the air. Since almost everything in China eventually lands on the dining table, including pigeons, there is quite a range of pigeon dishes. Unlike duck, pigeon is not considered a great dish, but when daintily prepared, many connoisseurs consider it a delicacy.

Turkey does not occupy the same place in the Chinese culinary world as in America. It appears to be mainly an imported bird, although it is obtainable in many parts of China. Its meat is considered too course and rough, and its flavor unsubtle.

Nevertheless, there are a number of Chinese turkey dishes which are attacked with massed chopsticks and great enthusiasm as something different from ordinary chicken. Basically it is inconvenient for Chinese cooking. It is too large a bird for a single dish, and when cut up or sliced there is less delicacy in the flavor of its meat than that of smaller birds. However, the Chinese way of dealing with turkey may contain useful hints for treating these birds in America. The Chinese term for turkey is 'fire bird' (or 'fire chicken') and the Chinese term for frogs is 'field chickens.' Since both are regarded as a kind of chicken by the Chinese, I have included a few recipes for turkey and frog in this chapter. Although frogs are not normally available in stores and supermarkets in the West, they may be of interest, especially in France, where this delectable item, imported in the main from India, appears to be consumed in some quantity as a delicacy.

Duck

There are many famous duck dishes in China. The following are some of the most popular or best-known. Since all fowl and meat can be red-cooked (which is simply cooked with soy sauce), we will start with Red-Cooked Duck.

Red-Cooked Duck

Serves 6–10, with other dishes, or is sufficient for 2–3 meals

4–5 lb duck

2 medium-sized onions
3 scallions
2 slices ginger root
1 piece dried tangerine peel
1 teaspoon salt
6 tablespoons soy sauce
2 teaspoons sugar
¼ cup dry sherry

This dish is very similar to Red-Cooked Chicken, but as duck is a stronger-tasting meat, more onion and scallions are used, and we usually cook the duck for slightly longer.

Preparation Clean the duck thoroughly inside and out. Slice the onions thin and cut the scallions into 2 inch segments. Place the onion, ginger, and dried tangerine peel inside the cavity of the duck.

Cooking Heat 5 cups of water in a heavy pan or casserole. When it boils, place the duck in it and boil for 4–5 minutes, turning the bird over a few times. Pour away three quarters of the water, and skim off impurities. Sprinkle the salt and half of the soy sauce over the contents of the pan; then insert an asbestos pad under the pan. Cover, and simmer gently over a low heat for 45 minutes, turning the bird over every 15 minutes. Add the remaining soy sauce, sugar, and half of the sherry, and continue simmering for 20 minutes; then add the remainder of the sherry. Scatter the scallions over the duck, and simmer for a further 20 minutes.

Serving Serve in the cooking pot or casserole, or in a deep dish or tureen. The duck should have become quite tender, and can be taken to pieces with a pair of chopsticks.

Dry-Fried Red-Cooked Duck

Serves 6–10, with other dishes

Preparation and Cooking Repeat the recipe for Red-Cooked Duck, but chop the duck into 2–2½ inch square pieces. After the initial pan boiling, which should be prolonged to 6–7 minutes, pour away three-quarters of the water. Add all the supplementary ingredients; then cover, and simmer gently for 45 minutes. Remove the lid and increase the heat; then turn the pieces of duck over and over until the liquid is almost gone. Add 2 tablespoons lard, 2 additional tablespoons of sherry, and all the scallion segments, and stir-fry over a medium heat for 4–5 minutes. Serve in a large flat serving dish or a deep dish.

Eight-Precious Duck

This is a party dish; it is called 'eight-precious' because eight different types of ingredients (or more) are usually used as stuffing for the duck. It is cooked by long-simmering.

Preparation Soak the mushrooms for 20 minutes, and remove the stalks. Boil the glutinous rice and barley for 5–6 minutes, then drain and rinse under running water. Blanch the chestnuts, lotus seeds, and gingko nuts; dice the bamboo shoots and chestnut meat, and shell the lotus seeds. Combine the mushrooms, rice, barley, chestnut meat, lotus seeds, nuts, pork, ham, and bamboo shoots in a bowl. Add 3 tablespoons of the soy sauce, $\frac{1}{2}$ teaspoon of the salt, and 3 tablespoons of the sherry; mix well. Wipe the duck clean with a damp cloth, and stuff it with the mixture. Sew and skewer it firmly closed. Cut the scallions into 2 inch segments.

Cooking Place the duck in a heavy pot or casserole, with the scallion segments and ginger. Add the stock, the remainder of the soy sauce, the salt, and the sherry. Bring to the boil, insert an asbestos pad under the pot; then cover, and simmer very gently for 1 hour, turning the bird over several times. Add the sugar, and some water if necessary in case the duck becomes too dry, and simmer gently for a further hour. Alternatively, the container can be placed in a steamer and steamed for 2 hours—no extra liquid should be added.

Serving Scoop out the stuffing and spread it on a well-heated serving dish as a bed. Quarter the duck and arrange the pieces neatly on top, or else carve it in American fashion. By this stage, the duck should be tender enough to be taken apart with chopsticks.

Serves 10–12

5–6 lb duck

6 Chinese dried mushrooms
5–6 tablespoons glutinous rice
3 tablespoons barley
$\frac{1}{4}$ cup chestnut meat
3–4 tablespoons lotus seeds
3–4 tablespoons gingko nuts
3–4 tablespoons bamboo shoots
$\frac{1}{4}$ cup roast pork
3–4 tablespoons smoked ham
6 tablespoons soy sauce
1 teaspoon salt
6 tablespoons dry sherry
3 scallions
3 slices ginger root
1 quart superior stock
2 teaspoons sugar

Cantonese Mustard Green and Onion-Simmered Family Duck

The main feature of this dish is the simmering of the onion inside the duck (as stuffing) and the greens outside the duck. Together, they counterbalance the richness of the bird.

Serves 6–10, with other dishes

4–5 lb duck

3 scallions
4 medium-sized onions
3 cups mustard green hearts
  (chopped)
6 Chinese dried mushrooms
½ cup Cantonese roast pork
2 teaspoons salt
2 tablespoons vegetable oil
2 tablespoons soy sauce
oil for deep-frying
1 quart superior stock
2 tablespoons oyster sauce

Preparation Soak the mushrooms for 20 minutes; then drain. Remove the stalks, then slice the caps into thin strips. Slice the onions thin, and cut the scallions into 1½ inch segments. Slice the pork crosswise into thin strips. Sprinkle these ingredients with ¾ teaspoon of the salt, and stir-fry for 2–3 minutes in the 2 tablespoons of vegetable oil. Rub the duck with soy sauce both inside and out, and stuff with this mixture. Close securely with skewers and string. Cut each mustard green heart into four pieces.

Cooking Heat the oil in a deep-fryer, and deep-fry the duck in the boiling oil for 3 minutes. Remove, and drain. Place the duck in a heavy pot or casserole, pour in the stock, add the oyster sauce and the remaining salt, and simmer gently for 1¼ hours. Lift the duck out. Line the sides of a large, heat-proof earthenware dish or casserole with the greens. Place the duck in the center of the dish or casserole and garnish it with scallion segments. Cover, and simmer in an oven preheated to 400°F for 30 minutes.

Serving Bring the dish or casserole to the table, and open the lid to let the steam rise just before serving.

Cantonese Roast Duck

Serves 6–10, with other dishes

4–5 lb duck

1 tablespoon salt
2 scallions
2 cloves garlic
2 tablespoons vegetable oil
3 tablespoons chopped onion
1½ tablespoons chopped parsley
2 teaspoons star anise
1 teaspoon peppercorns
2 tablespoons dry sherry
2 tablespoons soy sauce
2 teaspoons sugar
3 tablespoons honey
1 tablespoon vinegar
2 teaspoons cornstarch
¼ teaspoon monosodium glutamate

This dish is unique—the duck is filled with liquid or sauce, and then roasted.

Preparation Wipe the duck clean with a warm damp cloth. Tie the neck tightly with string, so that no liquid will drip out. Hang it up to dry for 2 hours; then rub it generously with salt, inside and out. Cut the scallions into 1 inch segments. Crush the garlic. Heat the oil in a small saucepan; then add the chopped onion, scallion segments, parsley, garlic, star anise, and peppercorns; stir-fry over a medium heat for 2 minutes. Pour in 1¼ cups water, bring to the boil and boil gently for 5–6 minutes. Add the sherry, soy sauce, and sugar; blend well. Pour this mixture into the cavity in the duck, sew up carefully, and make more secure with skewers, so that no liquid will run out. Mix the honey, vinegar, and ¾ cup boiling water.

Cooking Preheat the oven to 400°F. Roast the duck on a rack (or hang the duck tail-side up in the oven) for 10 minutes. Baste thoroughly with the honey/vinegar/water mixture. Reduce the oven temperature to 350°F and roast for 1 hour, basting at 30-minute intervals. Reduce the heat again, to 325°F and roast for a further 20 minutes. Allow the duck to cool slightly, then carefully remove the strings and skewers and pour the sauce into a bowl. Blend the cornstarch with 1 tablespoon water, and add to the sauce, with the monosodium glutamate. Heat the mixture in a small pan and serve as gravy.

Serving The duck may be carved or chopped as desired, and served in a well-heated, deep dish.

Red-Aromated Soy Duck

Herbal Soy Stock (or Master Stock) is a necessary prerequisite for this dish. When the stock is available, the cooking is comparatively simple.

Preparation Clean the duck thoroughly, inside and out. Simmer in boiling water for 5 minutes; then discard the water and rinse the bird under running water for 30 seconds. Slice the onions thin.

Cooking Place the duck in a heavy pan or casserole. Add the Herbal Soy Stock, and $2\frac{1}{2}$ cups water; then add the next six ingredients. Bring to the boil and simmer gently over a low heat for $1\frac{1}{4}$ hours, turning the bird over three times. Allow the duck to cool slightly. Cut off its wings and legs, and chop the body into oblong pieces, approximately 2 inches in size; arrange them on a plate in the shape of a duck. Strain one third of the duck stock into a small pan (keep the remainder for other uses). Blend the cornstarch with 1 tablespoon water and add it to the pan with the sugars and monosodium glutamate. Heat until the liquid thickens, stirring all the time. Pour this sauce over the pieces of duck; then serve.

Although only a small quantity of red coloring is used, it has a very marked reddening effect on the sauce and the duck. The tangerine peel and star anise in the stock produce a decidedly herbal and aromatic effect.

Serves 8–10, with other dishes

3–4 lb duck

2 medium-sized onions
1 quart Herbal-Soy Stock *or* Master Stock
$\frac{1}{4}$ cup soy sauce
2 pieces (about 3 tablespoons) Chinese dried tangerine peel
$\frac{1}{2}$ tablespoon star anise
3 slices ginger root
1 teaspoon salt
1 pinch red food coloring
1 tablespoon cornstarch
$\frac{1}{4}$ cup rock sugar
1 teaspoon sugar
$\frac{1}{4}$ teaspoon monosodium glutamate

Quick-Fried Ribbon of Duck with Shredded Ginger

Serves 4–8, with other dishes

¾ lb roast duck meat
4–5 slices ginger root

1 tablespoon fermented black
  beans
¾ cup celery
¾ cup young leeks
1 medium red sweet pepper
2 cloves garlic
2 red chili peppers
¼ cup lard
1½ tablespoons soy sauce
2 teaspoons sugar
1 tablespoon vinegar

Preparation Soak the black beans for 20 minutes; then drain. Slice the duck meat into matchstick strips. Cut the celery, leeks, sweet pepper, and ginger into similar strips. Crush the garlic and cut the chili peppers into four pieces.

Cooking Heat the lard in a large frying pan. Add the ginger and chili pepper and stir-fry for 1½ minutes over a medium heat. Add the black beans and garlic and stir-fry for a further 1½ minutes before adding all the other vegetables. Turn the heat up to maximum for 2 minutes; then add the duck meat, soy sauce, and sugar, and continue to stir-fry for 2 minutes. Finally, add the vinegar and stir-fry for 1 minute more.

Serving Dish out onto a well-heated plate; serve and eat immediately.

The dish is a great favorite in the western province of Szechuan, where most dishes are extremely hot. The hotness of this dish is derived from the chili-pepper-impregnated oil, and the addition of the vinegar. The heavy use of black salted beans is another typical Szechuan technique.

Quick-Fried Sliced Duck with Selected Vegetables

Serves 4–8, with other dishes

½ lb roast breast or leg of duck

6 medium-sized Chinese dried
  mushrooms
½ cup bamboo shoots
½ cup celery
¾ cup chicken stock
1 tablespoon cornstarch
2 tablespoons soy sauce
2 tablespoons dry sherry
1½ teaspoons sugar
¼ teaspoon monosodium glutamate
3 tablespoons vegetable oil
½ teaspoon salt
1 tablespoon duck fat

Preparation Soak the mushrooms for 30 minutes, then remove the stalks. Slice the duck meat into 1½ × 1 inch thin slices, and slice the bamboo shoots and celery similarly. Blend the stock, cornstarch, soy sauce, sherry, sugar, and monosodium glutamate.

Cooking Heat the oil in a large frying pan. Add the vegetables, sprinkle with salt, and stir-fry over a high heat for 5 minutes. Pour the sauce mixture evenly over the vegetables, and stir-fry together for 1½ minutes over a medium heat. Finally add the duck meat and duck fat. Stir and toss together for 1 minute. Dish out onto a well-heated serving plate and eat immediately.

Wine-Simmered Duck

Serves 8–10

4–5 lb duck

Preparation Clean the duck thoroughly, inside and out; then rub it both inside and out firstly with salt, and then with bean paste. Slice the onions and shred the ginger into strips. Stuff the duck with the onions and ginger and close the cavity securely with skewers and string. Leave to season for 2 days.

Cooking Bring the wine to the boil in a heavy pan or casserole and lower the duck into it. When it comes to the boil again, turn the heat down to minimum and insert an asbestos pad under the pan. Simmer gently for 3 hours, turning the bird over every 45 minutes. Serve in the pan or casserole. The meat should be so tender that it is possible to take the bird to pieces with a pair of chopsticks.

2 quarts white wine (Rhine, Grave, Moselle)

2 teaspoons salt
2 tablespoons brown bean paste
3 medium-sized onions
3 slices ginger root

Drunken Duck

Preparation Crush and chop the garlic, and shred the ginger and chili pepper. Clean the duck thoroughly. Cut the scallions into $\frac{1}{2}$ inch segments.

Cooking Heat 5 cups of water in a large pan. Add garlic, ginger, chili pepper, scallions, salt, and pepper. Bring to the boil, and lower the duck into the pan. When the liquid comes to the boil again, reduce the heat to low. Simmer for 30 minutes, turning the bird every 10 minutes; then allow it to cool in the liquid for several hours. Remove and drain the duck (reserve the stock for other uses) and place in the refrigerator overnight.

Marinating in Wine Cut off the legs and wings, and chop the body into four pieces. Place all the pieces of duck in a large container with a lid. Pour in the sherry or wine and cover the container tightly; refrigerate for 1–4 days.

Serving When ready to serve, remove all pieces of duck from the container. Drain and chop them into oblong pieces, about $1\frac{1}{2} \times 1$ inch, and serve cold.

This makes an excellent hors d'œuvre, and can also be used as a canapé at a cocktail party.

Serves 10–15 persons for a party meal, with many other dishes

3–4 lb duck

4 cloves garlic
4 slices ginger root
1 chili pepper
6 scallions
1 tablespoon salt
$\frac{1}{4}$ teaspoon freshly ground pepper
$2\frac{1}{2}$ cups sherry *or* Chinese rice wine

White-Simmered Duck with Ham and Leek

Preparation Repeat the recipe for White-Simmered Duck with Ham and Chinese Cabbage, using 4 cups leeks, instead of 6 cups cabbage.

One curious thing about the Chinese treatment of duck is that it is as often steamed first and then fried, as it is fried first and then steamed. Both processes seem to bring about equally beneficial results! The following are two examples:

Serves 6–10, with other dishes

245

Crispy and Aromatic Duck I

Serves 8–10, with other dishes

4–5 lb duck

2 teaspoons salt
½ teaspoon freshly ground black
   pepper
¼ teaspoon five spice powder
3 slices ginger root
3 scallions
2 tablespoons soy sauce
1 tablespoon vinegar
1 tablespoon honey
oil for deep-frying

The process here is to steam first, and deep-fry afterwards. This is a party dish.

Preparation Clean the duck thoroughly, inside and out. Make a mixture of the salt, pepper, and five spice powder, and rub the duck inside and out with this mixture. Shred the ginger, and cut the scallions into 1 inch segments. Stuff half of them inside the duck, and place the other half on top of it. Leave to marinate in a covered container overnight. Mix the soy sauce, vinegar, and honey.

Cooking Place the duck in a heat-proof dish, covered with a lid or aluminum foil (or wrap the bird in aluminum foil). Place it in a steamer to steam for 1½ hours; then remove. When cool, truss it, and brush liberally with the soy/vinegar/honey mixture. Allow to dry. Place the duck in a wire basket and double deep-fry it for 3–4 minutes (that is, deep-fry it twice: deep-fry for 3–4 minutes, drain; then repeat the deep-frying, again for 3–4 minutes, after which it should be golden-brown and crispy). The meat should be tender enough to be taken to pieces with a pair of chopsticks.

Serving Like Peking Duck, it should be eaten wrapped in pancakes, with strips of crunchy vegetables (scallion and cucumber) and brushed with soy paste and plum sauce.

Crispy and Aromatic Duck II

Serves 8–10, with other dishes

4–5 lb duck

3–4 quarts Herbal Soy stock *or*
   Master Stock
oil for deep-frying

The process here is to simmer first in Herbal Stock, and then to deep-fry. As Herbal Stock is a highly spiced liquid, it heightens the duck's aromatic qualities.

Preparation Clean the duck thoroughly.

Cooking Place the duck in a pan of boiling water and simmer for 10 minutes. Drain; then discard the water. Heat the stock, and when it begins to boil, lower the duck into it and simmer for 55 minutes. Lift the duck out to drain and cool for 15 minutes. Remove the joints of the bird with a cleaver, and quarter the body. Double deep-fry the pieces until golden and crispy: about 3–4 minutes for *each* frying.

Serving Serve on a well-heated, flat serving dish, banked with green vegetables. It is best eaten with pancakes.

White-Simmered Duck
with Ham and Chinese Cabbage

Preparation Soak the mushrooms in warm water for 20 minutes; then drain, and remove the stalks. Slice the ham and bamboo shoots into thin slices, 2 × 1 inch. Cut the cabbage or celery into 2 × 3 inch pieces. Clean the duck inside and out. Place it in a large pan and cover with water. Bring to the boil and simmer for 15 minutes; then skim off the fat and any impurities, and discard about one third of the liquid.

Cooking Add the ginger, bamboo shoots, ham, and mushrooms to the pan. Bring to the boil, reduce the heat to minimum; then insert an asbestos pad under the pan and simmer gently for 45 minutes. Allow the pan to cool; then refrigerate for 2 hours. Skim away the fat which has coagulated. Insert the pieces of cabbage under the duck, bring the contents of the pan to the boil, add salt and monosodium glutamate, and simmer gently for 35 minutes.

Serving The duck can be served in the cooking pot or casserole, or in a large soup tureen. When well-cooked, the dish is extremely rich, and at the same time sweet and refreshing—as a result of the large quantity of cabbage. The smoked ham and mushrooms provide that traditional earthy, smoky flavor which is always so recognizable in authentic Chinese dishes.

Serves 6–10, with other dishes

3–4 lb duck
½ lb smoked ham
1 lb Chinese celery cabbage *or*
   Savoy cabbage *or* celery

8 Chinese dried mushrooms
1 cup bamboo shoots
3 slices ginger root
2½ teaspoons salt
¼ teaspoon monosodium glutamate

West Lake Deep-Fried
and Steamed Duck

In this recipe, the duck is fried first and then steamed, and finally served doused in gravy.

Preparation Clean the duck thoroughly, and wipe dry with paper towels. Hang in an airy place for 3 hours. Rub the duck with half of the soy sauce, and truss. Blend the remaining soy sauce with the sherry, honey, and salt. Soak the mushrooms in warm water for 20 minutes; then remove the stalks and shred the caps. Slice the bamboo shoots, celery, and parsley fine. Shred the smoked ham.

Serves 8–10, with other dishes

4–5 lb duck

¼ cup soy sauce
3 tablespoons dry sherry
½ tablespoon honey
1 teaspoon salt
6 medium-sized Chinese dried
   mushrooms
½ cup bamboo shoots
½ cup celery
1½ tablespoons parsley
2 oz smoked ham

247

oil for deep-frying
3 slices ginger root
½ tablespoon star anise
¾ tablespoon cornstarch
¼ teaspoon monosodium glutamate

Cooking Heat the oil and deep-fry the duck for 9–10 minutes or until golden-brown. Drain, and rinse quickly under running water. Untruss the duck. Place the bird in a large heat-proof dish or casserole. Rub with the soy/honey/sherry mixture, and pour the remainder over the bird. Add the ginger and star anise. Pour 2½ cups of boiling water into the container, and cover tightly with the lid, or with aluminum foil. Place the dish in a steamer and steam for 1½ hours. Remove the duck from the dish, retaining the liquid. Take out its bones, and chop the meat into approximately 2 × 1½ inch pieces, leaving the skin attached to the meat. Skim the fat from the duck stock and strain one third back into the heat-proof dish. Arrange the pieces of duck, skin side up, in the dish, and place in a steamer to steam for 15 minutes. Meanwhile, place the bamboo shoots, celery, mushrooms, and parsley in a small saucepan. Add the remaining duck stock, and heat for 10 minutes. Arrange the vegetables on top of the duck and sprinkle with the smoked ham. Blend the cornstarch with 2 tablespoons water and add it, with the monosodium glutamate, to the liquid in the small saucepan. Stir over a medium heat until it thickens; then pour over the duck, and serve.

Deep-Fried and Steamed Eight-Precious Duck

Serves 10–12 people as a party dish

5–6 lb duck

2 cloves garlic
2 slices ginger root
6 tablespoons glutinous rice
4 dried oysters
4 dried scallops
6 Chinese dried mushrooms
1 Chinese sausage
3 tablespoons water chestnuts
3 tablespoons green peas
2 teaspoons sugar
1½ teaspoons salt
3 tablespoons soy sauce
oil for deep-frying
1¼ cups superior stock
2 heads of lettuce

Preparation Crush the garlic and shred the ginger. Soak the rice, oysters, and scallops separately for 1 hour, and soak the mushrooms for 30 minutes. Discard the mushroom stalks; then dice the caps, sausage, and water chestnuts into small cubes and mix them with the garlic, ginger, rice, oysters, scallops, peas, sugar, and salt. Blend well. Clean the duck thoroughly inside and out. Hang up to dry for 3 hours. Rub thoroughly with soy sauce, and then lower into boiling oil to deep-fry for 9–10 minutes, or until golden-brown. Rinse the duck quickly under running water; then drain.

Cooking Stuff the duck with the rice mixture, and then sew up and skewer firmly. Transfer the bird to a heat-proof bowl or casserole. Pour the stock over the duck; cover with lid or aluminum foil; and steam for 1¾ hours. Take the stuffing out of the duck, and spread in the center of a large, well-heated serving dish. Disjoint the duck with a sharp cleaver, and flatten the body with the side of the cleaver before placing it on the stuffing. Arrange the legs and wings around the body; place dish in a steamer, and steam for a further 10 minutes.

Serving Arrange lettuce leaves around the duck and stuffing, and bring the dish steaming to the table.

Sweet and Sour Duck

This dish comes from Canton.

Preparation Clean the duck inside and out. Hang it up to dry for 2 hours. Rub the duck with half of the salt and 1 tablespoon of soy sauce. Cut the cucumber into thin slices, and place in a bowl to marinate in 2 tablespoons of sugar, 1 tablespoon of the vinegar, and 1 tablespoon of the soy sauce. Remove the roots from the radishes, and cut down crosswise from the pointed end half-way to the base. Rub each radish piece with salt.

Cooking Preheat oven to 400°F, and roast duck for 45 minutes. Put aside to cool. Disjoint the end with a sharp cleaver, and cut the body into four pieces. Chop the legs and wings and the body quarters into 16–20 pieces, leaving some skin attached to each. Place four or five pieces in a wire basket, and deep-fry for 3 minutes. Drain, and arrange as the center of a large serving dish. Drain the cucumber, retaining the marinade, and arrange the slices around the duck, alternating with the pieces of radish. Blend the cornstarch with 3 tablespoons water, and add to the marinade, with the tomato puree, orange juice, and the remainder of the vinegar, sugar, and soy sauce. Mix well, and heat, stirring until the mixture thickens. Spoon this sweet and sour sauce over each piece of duck.

Serves 8–10, with other dishes

3–4 lb duck

2 teaspoons salt
2 tablespoons soy sauce
6 inch section of cucumber
3 tablespoons sugar
2½ tablespoons vinegar
1 cup large radishes
oil for deep-frying
1 tablespoon cornstarch
1½ tablespoons tomato puree
1½ tablespoons orange juice

Cold-Tossed Shredded Duck with Lychees

Southern Chinese cuisine is more inclined to use fruits with meat and savory dishes. Here is a Cantonese recipe, showing the Chinese advance from the French use of orange to the use of lychees with duck.

Preparation Slice the duck meat into very thin strips or shreds. Slice the ginger in a similar fashion. Cut the scallions into 2 inch segments. Toss them all together with soy sauce, sherry, and sesame oil for 1 minute. Add the lychee syrup, and toss again. Cut each lychee in half.

Serving Arrange the salad by spreading the duck meat out on a serving dish, and arrange the lychee halves on top, with the round side of each lychee facing up. This makes an intriguing and attractive dish.

Serves 6–8, with other dishes

Half a medium-sized roast duck
12 large lychees

3 slices ginger root
2 scallions
2½ tablespoons soy sauce
1½ tablespoons dry sherry
1 tablespoon sesame oil
3 tablespoons lychee syrup

Nanking Salt Duck

Serves 6–10, with other dishes

4–5 lb duck

6 tablespoons coarse salt
2 teaspoons freshly ground black
  pepper

Preparation Heat the salt in a dry frying pan over a low heat for 1½ minutes, spreading it thinly over the pan. Stir and toss several times; then add pepper to the salt, and continue to stir, heating for 1½ minutes. When this salt and pepper mixture is cool, put aside 1 tablespoon for use as a table dip. Use the remainder to rub thoroughly into the duck, both inside and out. Do this twice. Wrap the duck securely in aluminum foil, and refrigerate for 5–6 days.

Cooking Cook the duck by dipping it in boiling water for 5–6 seconds; then drain, and steam vigorously for 35 minutes. Or simmer it very gently (with an asbestos pad under the pan) for 40 minutes in 9 cups of water. Reserve this stock for other uses.

Serving Chop the duck through the bone into double-Mah-jong-size pieces (or serving pieces), and arrange on a serving dish.

The unique flavor of the duck comes from its cooking, most of which is achieved through seasoning and marinating in the salt and pepper mixture. The flavor of this mixture is increased by the heating. This method is unlike the usual hanging of birds, fowls, or meats which is found in Western cuisine. Although the actual cooking time is comparatively short, the meat is usually very tender.

Chinese Peppered Duck

Serves 6–10, with other dishes

Chinese Peppered Duck is prepared by rubbing the duck *once,* inside and out, with the same heated salt and pepper mixture as in the recipe for Nanking Salt Duck. Wrap in aluminum foil, and leave to season overnight in the refrigerator. Just before cooking, rub the duck over with 1½ tablespoons soy sauce.

Preheat the oven to 400°F and roast the duck for 1 hour. Chop through the bones into double-Mah-jong-size pieces, and arrange on a serving dish.

Peking Duck

Peking Duck is now a world famous dish. It owes its fascination and fame, I think, not only to the way it is cooked, but also to the way it is eaten, wrapped in a pancake or doiley with scallions and strips of sliced cucumber, and heavily dabbed with the appropriate sauces. It is this heavenly combination of fresh and crunchy raw vegetables with the crackling of the duck's skin, the tender meatiness of the duck's meat, and the sweet piquancy of the sauces, all wrapped in one roll, that gives the dish its distinction and inimitable quality.

Preparation Cut the scallions into 2 inch segments, and cut the cucumber into slightly thicker strips of the same length. Clean the duck inside and out, and lower it momentarily into a pan of boiling water for a quick scald: 2–3 seconds. Drain; wipe dry with paper towels, then hang it up to dry overnight in a cool, airy place. Prepare a bowl of sugar water by mixing the sugar with 1¼ cups water and 1 teaspoon salt, if desired; rub the duck with this sugar-salt solution several hours before roasting. Hang up to dry. When dry, the duck is ready for roasting.

Cooking Preheat the oven to 400°F. Place the duck on top rack and roast for exactly one hour, with a pan underneath to catch the drippings. After 60 minutes of roasting, the duck should be well-cooked and the skin very crispy.

Serving and Eating Peking Duck is the one thing which is carved beside the dining table in China; or to be more precise, it is peeled, for the motion of slicing the duck is one of peeling—a one-handed action, where the thumb and blade of the knife held in the same hand act in unison in a peeling action. In the initial carving, the peeling or slicing is restricted only to the crackling skin. The skin is first peeled off, then placed in a well-heated dish and passed around. Each diner will then open a pancake or doiley on the small dish provided in front of him. The pancake is brushed with sauce, and the diner places 2 pieces of crackling skin on the pancake, along with several segments of scallions, and some strips of cucumber. He wraps the pancake up like a jelly roll, turning in the sides so that nothing will fall or drip out; then uses his fingers to hold the roll, which is eaten like a hot dog. After the duck skin has been eaten, the carver peels off the meat: it is eaten in the same way as the skin—wrapped in a pancake with scallions and cucumber, and heavily brushed with sauce. Plum sauce and hoisin sauce for use with the duck should be served in separate sauce dishes. Soy bean pastes or jams should be blended with sesame oil and sugar, and stirred over a low heat for 2–3 minutes before being placed in a sauce dish for use.

Normally, a medium-sized duck will peel to make 1 dish of crackling skin, and 2 dishes of sliced duck meat. When these are complemented by other dishes (there are usually at least 6–10 dishes at a party or banquet), a 4–5 lb duck will be sufficient for 6–10 people.

Serves 6–10, with other dishes

4–5 lb duck

10 scallions
10 inch section of cucumber
1 tablespoon sugar
1 teaspoon salt
pancakes (see following recipe)
variety of sauces, including 3 tablespoons plum sauce and 2 tablespoons hoisin sauce
3 tablespoons soy bean jam *or* paste
1½ tablespoons sesame oil
1 tablespoon sugar

251

Pancakes for Peking Duck

Serves 6–10

2¾ cups flour
1¼ cups boiling water
3 tablespoons sesame oil

Preparation Sift the flour into a large bowl. Pour in the boiling water very slowly, and gradually work into a warm dough. Knead gently for 10–12 minutes, then leave to stand for 10–12 minutes. Form the dough into a roll 2 inches in diameter, then cut it into ½ inch thick slices. Brush one slice with sesame oil and lay another slice on top of it. Using a rolling pin, roll the double piece until it spreads out to a diameter of about 5–6 inches, rolling from the center out. Use up all the dough in this way. Heat a large heavy frying pan over low heat. When it is very hot, place the rolled pieces of dough evenly over the pan. Move the pan over the heat so that the heating is even and well spread. When any piece of dough starts to bubble, turn it over to heat the other side. When ready (i.e. both sides have patches of brown), pull each piece of dough apart into the two original slices. Fold each slice into a half circle on the side which has been greased. Pile the pancakes up on a plate, and steam them for 10 minutes, before they are used to wrap the duck.

In China, these pancakes are called 'thin pancake cakes' (bao pin) and they are indispensable for eating with Peking Duck. They can be kept in a refrigerator for several days, and re-steamed when required.

Lotus Leaf Rolls

Serves 6–10

3 cups flour
1 tablespoon sugar
1 tablespoon baking powder
¾ cup water *or* milk
¼ cup vegetable oil

Peking Duck is eaten with pancakes, but most of the other duck dishes, or red-cooked dishes which are often served with ample gravy, are usually accompanied by Lotus Leaf Rolls, which are more absorbent.

Preparation Sift the flour and mix with sugar and baking powder. Add water or milk very slowly; stir with fork into a soft dough. Knead for 5–6 minutes. Cover dough with a dry cloth, and allow to stand for 20 minutes. After the dough has risen, knead again for 2–3 minutes. Form the dough into a roll 1½ inches in diameter. Slice into 1 inch thick slices. Brush the top with a little oil, and fold over on the greased side into half moon shapes. Use a fork to press down the edges, making indentations all around.

Cooking Place the pieces of dough on a large heat-proof plate and steam for 12 minutes. Because of their absorbent quality they are extremely useful for soaking up gravy.

These Lotus Rolls can be kept for a day or two, and re-steamed for 7–8 minutes when required.

Pigeons

Red-Cooked Lemon Pigeon

Lemon, ginger, sherry and soy sauce combine to give this dish a really interesting flavor.

Preparation Clean the birds thoroughly and wipe dry with paper towels. Rub them inside and out with salt and 2 table-spoons of the soy sauce. Marinate for 30 minutes. Cut the lemon in half; squeeze out the juice from one half, and cut the other into thin slices for use on the serving dish.

Cooking and Serving Heat the lard in a heavy saucepan. When it has melted, add the pigeons. Fry for 6–7 minutes, turning the birds until they are evenly browned all over. Pour away excess fat, and add the lemon juice, stock ginger, 2 table-spoons of the sherry, the remainder of the soy sauce, the sugar, and the hoisin sauce. When the contents of the pan come to the boil, turn the birds over several times, cover the pan with the lid, and reduce the heat to low. Simmer the birds for the next 5–6 minutes, then turn them over and continue to simmer for another 5–6 minutes. Lift the pigeons onto a chopping board, chop each one into four pieces, and arrange them on a warm serving dish. Plac the sliced lemon on one side of the dish. Add the remaining sherry, mono-sodium glutamate, and sesame oil to the liquid in the pan. Increase the heat for a moment, and stir. Pour the gravy over each piece of pigeon on the serving dish.

In Canton, where pigeon is a popular dish, the birds are killed by drowning, not by having their necks wrung. Fortu-nately, there is no need to attend to these earlier and grimmer details when cooking pigeons in America.

Serves 4

4 pigeons (each about 1½ lb)
1 large lemon

1½ teaspoons salt
¼ cup soy sauce
5 tablespoons lard
¾ cup superior stock
2 slices ginger root
¼ cup dry sherry
2 teaspoons sugar
1½ tablespoons hoisin sauce
¼ teaspoon monosodium glutamate
2 teaspoons sesame oil

Deep-Fried Pigeon

Preparation Chop each bird into four pieces with a sharp cleaver. Rub each piece with a mixture of salt, soy sauce, and sherry, and sprinkle with pepper. Dust each piece with cornstarch.

Cooking Heat oil in the deep-fryer. When it is very hot, place eight pieces of pigeon in a wire basket, and double deep-fry them for a total of 6–8 minutes; that is, deep-fry them for 2–3 minutes first, and keep hot for 3–4 minutes while the next eight are being fried, and finally deep-fry them all together for another 3 minutes.

Serves 4

4 fat pigeons, total weight 4–5 lb

1 teaspoon salt
3 tablespoons soy sauce
1 tablespoon dry sherry
pepper
2 tablespoons cornstarch
oil for deep-frying

253

Serving The pieces of pigeon can be placed on a bed of 3 inch segments of scallions, and lemon slices. The usual dips for this dish are Salt and Pepper Mix, and Lemon Juice Soy-Ginger Mix (see Index).

Braised Pigeon in Fruit Juice

Serves 4

This is a highly savory Cantonese 'semi-soup' dish which is served among the earlier courses of a southern dinner to facilitate drinking.

Repeat the recipe for Red-Cooked Lemon Pigeon, but after the initial frying and draining away of excess fat, add 2½ tablespoons of apple sauce, 2 tablespoons of orange juice, 3 tablespoons of peeled and chopped tomato, 1 tablespoon of sweet chutney, and 1 tablespoon of chopped chives or scallions to the lemon juice.

When braised pigeons are arranged in quarters on the serving dish, they can be eurrounded not only by the slices of lemon, but also by slices of tomato, apple, orange; that is, all the constituents which make up the sauce.

Deep-Fried Aromatic Pigeons

Serves 4

4 fat pigeons, total weight 4–5 lb

1 teaspoon salt
pepper to taste
⅛ teaspoon five spice powder
3 tablespoons soy sauce
4 scallions
oil for deep-frying
2 slices ginger root
2 cloves garlic
2 cloves star anise
3 tablespoons dry sherry
1 tablespoon sesame oil
lettuce leaves

Preparation Mix the salt, pepper, and five spice powder together and rub on the pigeons, both inside and out; then rub with 1½ tablespoons of soy sauce. Marinate for 1 hour. Chop each pigeon into four pieces, and cut the scallions into 2 inch segments.

Cooking Heat the oil in a deep-fryer. When it is very hot, double deep-fry the pieces of pigeon until golden brown. Drain, and keep warm. Heat 2 tablespoons of oil in a frying pan. Add the ginger, garlic, and star anise, and stir-fry together for 1 minute; then add the scallions and the pieces of pigeon, and continue stir-frying for 1½ minutes. Add the remainder of the soy sauce, the sherry, and the sesame oil. Stir-fry for a further 1½ minutes.

Serving Arrange the pieces of pigeon on a serving dish lined with lettuce leaves.

Steamed Pigeons

Preparation Clean the pigeons and cut each into four pieces. Rub with salt and 1 tablespoon of the soy sauce; sprinkle with pepper to taste, and leave to season for 30 minutes. Soak the golden needles in warm water for 30 minutes, and cut into 3–4 inch segments. Soak the mushrooms and dates in warm water for 30 minutes, and slice into thin strips. Cut the scallions into 2 inch segments, and shred the ham.

Cooking Place the birds in a heat-proof dish, and add half of the mushrooms, the dates, half of the scallions, and the ginger; drape the golden needles over the pieces of pigeon. Place in a steamer, and steam, uncovered, for 40 minutes. Pour the liquid which has accumulated in the heat-proof dish into a small saucepan. Add the remaining soy sauce, mushroom strips, scallion segments, and the sugar, sherry, and monosodium glutamate. Bring to the boil, and boil for 15 seconds; then pour the sauce over the pigeon.

Serving Garnish the pigeon with the shredded ham, and serve from the heat-proof dish.

Serves 3

3 fat pigeons, each about 1½–2 lb

1 teaspoon salt
3 tablespoons soy sauce
pepper to taste
3 golden needles (tiger-lily buds)
6 dried Chinese mushrooms
4 Chinese dates
4 scallions
¼ lb smoked ham
2 slices ginger root
1½ teaspoons sugar
2 tablespoons dry sherry
¼ teaspoon monosodium glutamate

Casserole of Pigeon with Mushrooms

Preparation Slit each pigeon along the backbone with a sharp cleaver, and flatten with the side of the cleaver. Rub with salt and 2 tablespoons of the soy sauce. Slice the pork into four thin slices, and rub with the remaining soy sauce. Soak the dried mushrooms for 20 minutes, and remove the stems. Soak the golden needles in warm water for 30 minutes; then drain, and discard the water. Clean and rinse the fresh mushrooms under running water and remove the stems. Slice the sweet pepper thin, and blend the cornstarch with 2 tablespoons water.

Cooking Preheat oven to 375°F. Heat the oil in a large frying pan. Turn the pigeons in the hot oil for 3–4 minutes until slightly brown. Line a large heat-proof dish or casserole with slices of pork. Arrange the pigeons and ginger on top of the bacon, and place the dried mushrooms, the golden needles, the sliced sweet pepper, and the ham on the pigeons. Pour in 1 pint of boiling water, and place the dish or casserole in the oven for 1 hour. Open the casserole and scatter the fresh mushrooms over the contents. Sprinkle with half of the sherry, and the light soy sauce; then return to the oven for a further 30 minutes. Remove the casserole from the oven and pour the liquid into a small saucepan. Add the cornstarch

Serves 4

4 fat pigeons, total weight 4–5 lb
6 large Chinese dried mushrooms

12 medium-sized fresh mushrooms
1 teaspoon salt
3 tablespoons soy sauce
¼ lb slab bacon
4 golden needles (tiger-lily buds)
1 large sweet pepper
2 teaspoons cornstarch
5 tablespoons vegetable oil
2 slices ginger root
¼ lb ham
3 tablespoons dry sherry
2 teaspoons light soy sauce
¼ teaspoon monosodium glutamate

mixture, the remaining sherry, and the monosodium glutamate, and heat, stirring, until the sauce thickens.

Serving Arrange the pieces of pigeon and other ingredients decoratively on a large serving dish. Pour the sauce over, and serve.

Turkey

Turkey is neither a common nor a popular bird in China, although by Christmas time each year, we seem to encounter them; and every now and then there is a turkey dish on the table. As turkey is not a traditional food ingredient, the recipes for cooking it do not go back hundreds of years, but are improvisations of accepted well-tried methods, which, being traditional, usually have points to recommend them.

Steamed Roast Turkey

Serves 12–16 for a large party, or for several meals

10–14 lb turkey

¼ cup fermented black beans
12 scallions
6 slices ginger root
6 tablespoons dry sherry
½ cup soy sauce
1½ tablespoons sugar
3 teaspoons chili oil
3 tablespoons sesame oil

Preparation Wipe the turkey inside and out with a warm, damp cloth, and leave in an airy place to dry for 3 hours. Soak the black beans for 30 minutes; then drain and mash them, and put them in a bowl. Chop the scallions and shred the ginger; then add them to the bowl, with the sherry, soy sauce, sugar, and chili oil. Mix them well, then rub the turkey over twice, inside and out, with the mixture. Pile all the loose scallions on top of the bird, wrap securely in a large piece of aluminum foil, and place in the refrigerator overnight.

Cooking Place the turkey, still wrapped in aluminum foil, on a heat-proof dish, and steam in a steamer for 1½ hours. Preheat the oven to 400°F. Unwrap the turkey, and place it in a roasting pan. Rub it all over with sesame oil, and roast for 1¼ hours.

Serving Chop the bird through the bone with a sharp Chinese cleaver into double-Mah-jong-size pieces. Serve in two large serving dishes, banked with fresh or quick-fried green vegetables (lettuce, or hearts of greens).

There are enough turkey pieces here for at least two banquet tables. Hoisin sauce and plum sauce are good dips to provide.

Cold White-Cut Salted Turkey

Preparation Cut the wings and legs off the turkey, and chop the body into four pieces. Mix the salt and pepper, and heat the mixture in a dry frying pan for 2 minutes, stirring constantly. Rub the pieces of turkey with this mixture as soon as it is cool. Mix the sesame oil and chili oil, and rub the turkey with this. Wrap the bird securely in a long sheet of aluminum foil, and leave to season in a cool place for 2–3 days.

Cooking and Serving Bring a large pan of water to the boil. Unwrap the turkey, and place the pieces in the water. Bring back to a slow boil, reduce the heat to a rapid simmer, and cook for 20 minutes; then drain. Slice the meat into thin 2 × 3 inch pieces, and serve.

Turkey cooked this way is very savory and juicy, and does not fall to pieces like ordinary left-over turkey. Serve it cold as a Chinese hors d'œuvre, or as a main cold dish for a Western buffet.

Good dips for white-cut turkey are hoisin sauce, Plum Sauce, Chili-Soy Dip, and Salt and Pepper Mix (see Index).

Serves 12–16, or for more than one meal

10–12 lb turkey

3 tablespoons salt
2½ teaspoons pepper
3 tablespoons sesame oil
2 teaspoons chili oil

'Field Chickens' or Frogs

It is not without reason that frogs are called 'field chickens' in China. The meat is really very similar to chicken, but it is more tender and delicate. They are often served during banquets in south and east China where frogs thrive in the paddy fields. Definitely regarded as a delicacy.

Quick-Fried Frogs' Legs with Sweet Pepper

Preparation Rub the frogs' legs with salt. Blend the soy sauce, half of the hoisin sauce and tomato puree, and the sherry, and marinate the frog legs in this mixture for 30 minutes. Mix the cornstarch with the egg white and 1 tablespoon water. Batter the frog legs with this paste. Cut the sweet pepper into strips approximately the same size as the frog legs. Remove the seeds, and discard. Shred the ginger.

Serves 4 or 5, with other dishes

8–10 pair frogs' legs
2 medium-sized sweet pepper

½ teaspoon salt
3 tablespoons soy sauce
1½ tablespoons hoisin sauce

257

3 tablespoons tomato puree
1½ teaspoons chili oil
3 tablespoons dry sherry
½ tablespoon cornstarch
1 egg white
2 slices ginger root
3 tablespoons vegetable oil

Cooking Heat 2 tablespoons of the oil in a large frying pan. Add the sweet pepper and ginger, and stir-fry over a medium heat for 2 minutes. Put aside. Add the remainder of the oil to the pan, with the rest of the hoisin sauce, tomato puree, and chili oil. Stir and blend together. Turn the heat to high, and pour in the frogs' legs. Stir-fry quickly for 3 minutes, then add the sweet pepper; stir-fry together for a further minute, and serve.

Szechuan Home-Cooked Frogs' Legs

Serves 4–5, with other dishes

10–12 pairs frogs' legs

1 cup bamboo shoots
1 cup young leeks
1½ tablespoons black beans
2 cloves garlic
2 slices ginger root
½ tablespoon cornstarch
¼ teaspoon monosodium glutamate
¾ cup vegetable oil
2 tablespoons lard
2 tablespoons dry sherry
2 tablespoons soy sauce
¾ cup superior stock
2 teaspoons sesame oil

Preparation Clean and dry the frogs' legs. Slice the bamboo shoots into thin slices, and cut the leeks into 1 inch segments. Soak the black beans in water for 30 minutes; then drain. Crush the garlic and shred the ginger. Blend the cornstarch with 2 tablespoons water and the monosodium glutamate.

Cooking Heat the oil in frying pan, and when hot, add the frogs' legs. Stir-fry over high heat for 2 minutes, then set aside to keep warm. Add the leeks and bamboo shoots, and stir-fry in the remaining oil for 2 minutes. Drain away any excess oil. Add the lard and black beans to the pan. Stir-fry over a medium heat for 1½ minutes, then remove and discard the black beans. Add the crushed garlic, ginger, sherry, and soy sauce. After 10 seconds stirring and quick-frying together, pour in the frogs' legs, bamboo shoots, leeks, and stock. Cover and simmer for 5–6 minutes. Add the cornstarch mixture and stir-fry for a further ½ minute. Sprinkle with sesame oil, and serve.

Fried Steamed Frogs' Legs

Serves 4–5, with other dishes

10 pairs frogs' legs

1½ teaspoons salt
1½ tablespoons cornstarch
1 cup thin-stem bamboo shoots
2 scallions
4-inch section of cucumber
3 oz smoked ham
2 slices ginger root
3 tablespoons light soy sauce
2 tablespoons dry sherry

Preparation Rub the frogs' legs with salt, and dredge with cornstarch. Cut the bamboo shoots and scallions into 1 inch segments, and slice the cucumber thin. Cut the ham into six slices, shred the ginger, and parboil the bamboo shoots for 5 minutes. Drain. Mix the soy sauce with the sherry, chicken stock, monosodium glutamate, sugar, and sesame oil until well-blended.

Cooking Heat the oil in a frying pan. When hot, pour in the frogs' legs and stir-fry over a high heat for 2 minutes. Drain away the oil. Arrange the bamboo shoots and cucumber as a bed at the bottom of a heat-proof dish or casserole. Lay the frogs' legs on top, and sprinkle evenly with the scallions and the ginger, soy/sherry/chicken broth mixture, and the ham. Place the heat-proof dish in a steamer and steam vigorously for 30 minutes.

Serving Serve on the table in the heat-proof dish or casserole.

3 tablespoons chicken stock
¼ teaspoon monosodium glutamate
2 teaspoons sugar
2 teaspoons sesame oil
1 cup vegetable oil

FISH

In China, in the past, fish had to be eaten fresh or not at all as there was no refrigeration; except, of course, when it was salted and dried—a very different kettle of fish altogether.

When dried salted fish is fried it gives off a strong inimitable smell, which can only be adequately described in English with words which are unmistakably rude. In China we always fry this fish to such a degree of crispiness that even the bones become crispy and edible. Salted fish fried in such a way is very similar to concentrated cheese, except that it is crispy. But there is a unique 'melting' quality about its crispiness. It is one of the best-loved side-dishes for eating with soft or semi-soft (porridgy) rice, and is considered a delicacy by the Japanese.

The only way to keep fish fresh in China was to keep them alive in jars, vats, or ponds. Fish kept in this way are naturally immeasurably fresher and sweeter than frozen fish. It is strangely ironical that in a country where there was no refrigeration we ate fresh fish all the time, but in the West, where you have every modern aid and convenience, the only times most people ever see live fish are in aquariums, or else when they go fishing—and then even if they do catch any fish at all, they throw most of them back into the water! It seems that with the advance of civilization, and having got into the habit of only buying dead fish laid out on ice or marble slabs, we forget the quality of live or fresh fish.

Although China has a coastline of over three thousand miles with an abundance of salt-water fish, fresh-water fish play a much bigger part in the Chinese diet than fish from the sea. This is not only due to the fact that there are several mighty rivers and tens of thousands of miles of streams, tributaries, canals, and other waterways in China, as well as many fresh-water lakes, but also because we Chinese make a practice of fish-farming. There is a pond in most villages in which fish are reared, and grass and other natural fish foods are thrown in to keep the fish alive. Each year the ponds are drained, and the fish sifted; the smaller ones are returned to the re-flooded ponds for another season's growing, while the larger ones are taken out for food or sold to markets. These 'fish-farms' are undoubtedly a large source of fresh fish in China. To some extent, in supplying the necessary proteins, they must have partly compensated for the lack of dairies in China.

We Chinese eat all edible fish: the varieties are numerous, and some fish may not have any exact Western equivalent. Some of the favorites are bass, sea bass, sea bream, carp, flounder, halibut, mackerel, perch, pike, cod, salmon, sole, shad, trout, plaice, sardines, and herring.

The principal ways of cooking fish are to steam, clear-simmer, deep-fry, pan-fry, stir-fry, or braise them; or else they may be finely chopped or ground for making into fish balls and fish cakes.

Unlike meat, which often has to be aged to be tasty, fish are best cooked and eaten completely fresh. To retain that sweet, fresh juiciness in fish, they are best when cooked only for a short time. All the additional, supplementary seasonings and flavors are impregnated into the fish by a period of marinating, and then they are given a short, sharp blast of steam for about 10–20 minutes, or a sizzle in oil. Alternatively, after being cut into smaller pieces or slices, they are turned over a few times in hot oil, often preimpregnated with ginger, garlic, and onion; and then the various supplementary ingredients are added for a final stir-fry to give the flavor of the dish a balanced orchestration. Such cooking usually lasts no more than 2–3 minutes. Although fish cooked in this manner is very popular, it is suitable only for very fresh fish with firm flesh which does not break up too easily during the stir-frying.

Otherwise, we Chinese prefer to have fish cooked whole, especially a large freshwater specimen. We seem to have the same conception of a fish as Americans have of a roast: it is best served whole on a large serving dish, and brought in steaming, succulent, and garnished. Whole fish are steamed, clear-simmered, or deep-fried; draped with a few supplementary materials, and served covered with a rich sauce. In contrast to Western cooking, the Chinese sauce for fish is very seldom, if ever, a fish sauce. It is usually a meat sauce, or a hot sauce, incorporating pickles and dried mushrooms. The only times when any additional fish or seafood is introduced into a fish dish is when it is dried or pickled such as dried shrimp, dried scallop-mussels, or oyster sauce, when all the fishiness has gone out of them or has changed. One of the things we always try to avoid is adding more fishiness to a fish dish.

Because of our principle and practice of cross-cooking, we are much more inclined than Westerners to use non-fishy foods and ingredients, such as meat and strong-tasting vegetables, to cook with fish. Perhaps for this reason, the majority of Chinese fish dishes are noticeably less fishy and much more meaty in flavor than their Western counterparts.

One of the great secrets or strengths of Chinese fish cookery is to make a combined use of ginger, garlic, soy sauce (or fermented soy beans), and wine in most fish dishes. The combined use of these ingredients has a most salutary effect—and indeed they have the same effect on meat. It is almost justifiable to say that this quadruple combination of flavoring ingredients is the 'gunpowder' of Chinese cooking.

Coarse sea fish, which come in large chunks or pieces, are very often braised, which means that after an initial frying in oil with some salt, ginger, or garlic, they are cooked for a little while in a sauce consisting of a little soy sauce, sugar, a few scallions, and perhaps a few strips of dried mushroom. Only in the more elaborate recipes would wine, dried shrimp, ham, wood ears, and golden needles be added in the cooking or as a garnish. However, no matter how simple or elaborate the dish is, the quality and character of fish seems to approximate very closely that of meat after such treatment, and takes on the appetizing texture and flavor of meat especially when it is eaten with a bulk food such as boiled rice. Perhaps for this reason fish is as welcome a dish on a Chinese dinner table as meat. Could it be because both meat and fish share the 'gunpowder' as a common denominator that they have a common and unified quality and appeal?

Yet in the case of steamed or clear-simmered fish dishes, where the cooking is comparatively short and only a very limited amount of supplementary ingredients are added, the purpose is to bring out the sweet freshness of fish itself: in other words, to prepare fish as fish, rather than as an approximation to meat. The popularity and appeal of these dishes seems to stem from the purity of the fish flavor; from the soft, white delicacy of the texture of the flesh, and from that special savory-tastiness which is distinctive to fish, all of which are in contrast to the qualities of meat.

To sum up, it can perhaps be said that we in China appreciate fish both for its similarities to, as well as for its differences from, meat! The following recipes will illustrate some of the principal ways fish are cooked, and how these effects are brought about.

Red-Cooked Whole Fish

Serves 4–8, with other dishes

A 3 lb fish

4 large Chinese dried mushrooms
2½ teaspoons salt
2½ tablespoons flour
3 oz slab bacon
4 scallions
oil for deep-frying
4 slices ginger root
5 tablespoons soy sauce
¼ cup dry sherry
3¾ teaspoons sugar
½ cup chicken stock
pepper to taste

Carp, bream, bass, mullet, sea bass, red snapper, pike, perch, flounder, or salmon may be used for this recipe.

Preparation Soak the mushrooms in a small bowl of warm water for 30 minutes, remove the stalks, and retain ¼ cup of the mushroom water. Make five or six slashes on each side of the fish to enable the oil and heat to penetrate more easily during cooking. Rub the fish with salt, inside and out, and dredge it in flour. Slice the pork into thin strips and cut the scallions into 1½ inch segments.

Cooking Heat the oil in a deep-fryer, then lower the fish into it to fry for 5 minutes. If a deep-fryer is not available, semi-deep-fry the fish in the Chinese way by heating 1 inch of oil in a large frying pan. Fry the fish over a high heat for 1 minute on each side, then reduce the heat to medium and continue frying for 2½ minutes on each side. Drain, and keep it warm. Pour most of the oil away. Put the bacon, ginger, and half of the scallions into the remaining oil. Stir-fry for 1½ minutes, then add the mushroom water, soy sauce, sherry, sugar, chicken stock, pepper, and mushrooms. Bring to the boil and stir for 1 minute. Lower the fish into the boiling sauce and baste with the sauce for 2 minutes. Reduce the heat to low and carefully turn the fish over. Sprinkle it with the remaining scallions, cover the pan, and leave to cook gently for 4–5 minutes.

Serving Place the fish on a large oval dish and garnish with the bacon, scallions, and mushrooms, piling them on top.

Red-Cooked Fish with Vegetables

This is really a slightly more elaborate version of the previous recipe, using ham instead of pork, and with the addition of many more vegetables.

Preparation Soak the golden needles, mushrooms, and wood ears separately for 30 minutes. Cut the needles into 2 inch segments. Remove the mushroom stalks and cut the caps into strips. Retain ¼ cup of the mushroom water. Slice the bamboo shoots and sweet pepper into strips. Cut the onion and water chestnuts into thin slices. Cut the scallions into 2 inch segments. Cut the ham into strips. Make five or six slashes on each side of the fish, then rub it with salt, inside and out, and dredge with flour

Cooking Fry the fish in oil in a deep-fryer for 5 minutes, or semi-deep-fry it in a large frying pan in 1 inch of oil. If you use the latter method, cook the fish over a high heat for 1 minute on each side, then reduce the heat to medium and fry for 2½ minutes on each side. Drain the fish and keep it warm. Pour away most of the oil. Stir-fry the bamboo shoots, water chestnuts, green pepper, onion, mushrooms, wood ears, golden needles, and half of the scallions in the remaining oil for 2 minutes. Add the mushroom water, soy sauce, sherry, sugar, chicken stock, and pepper. Cook this sauce, stirring, for 2 minutes; then lower the fish into the enriched sauce to baste and cook gently for 5–6 minutes.

Serving Place the fish on a large oval dish and pile all the solid ingredients from the pan on top. Garnish with the strips of ham and the remaining scallions.

Serves 4–6, with other dishes

A 3 lb fish

3 golden needles (tiger-lily buds)
3 large Chinese dried mushrooms
1½ tablespoons dried wood ears
½ cup bamboo shoots
1 green sweet pepper
1 large onion
2–3 water chestnuts
3 scallions
3 oz ham
2½ teaspoons salt
2½ tablespoons flour
oil for deep-frying
5 tablespoons soy sauce
¼ cup dry sherry
1 tablespoon sugar
¾ cup chicken stock
pepper to taste

Red-Cooked Fish in Chunks

Large fish such as halibut, cod, or haddock, which are normally available in big pieces or chunks, can be red-cooked in a similar fashion to the method described in the two previous recipes. The fish should be cut into cubes about 1 inch square. As this is a home-cooked dish for domestic consumption, no mushrooms or bamboo shoots are used.

Preparation Cut the fish into cubes approximately 1–1½ inches in size. Rub them with salt and dredge with flour. Shred the ginger and cut the scallions into 1 inch segments.

Serves 4–6, with other dishes

2 lb fish

1¼ teaspoons salt
2¼ tablespoons flour
2 slices ginger root
3 scallions
5 tablespoons oil
3¾ tablespoons soy sauce
5 tablespoons meat *or* chicken stock
pepper to taste
2½ teaspoons sugar

263

Cooking Heat the oil in a frying pan. Fry the fish cubes for 2 minutes on each side. Remove them from the pan and keep warm. Add the ginger and half of the scallions to the pan. Stir-fry for 1 minute. Add the soy sauce, stock, pepper, and sugar, and stir-fry for 1 minute. Return the pieces of fish to the pan and baste them with the sauce for 1 minute. Cover the pan and cook the fish and sauce over a medium heat for 4 minutes.

Serving Place the pieces of fish on a serving dish and pour the sauce from the pan over them. Sprinkle with soy sauce and the remaining scallions; then serve.

This is a useful dish as it can be prepared and cooked in a very short time

Red-Cooked Small Fish

Serves 4–6, with other dishes

2 lb small fish

1¼ teaspoons salt
2½ tablespoons flour
2 slices ginger root
3 scallions
1 onion
5 tablespoons oil
3¾ tablespoons soy sauce
5 tablespoon meat stock *or* chicken
    stock
pepper to taste
2½ teaspoons sugar

Perch, whitings, smelts, or sardines may be used for this recipe. In cooking small fish which are difficult to bone, it is usual to fry them whole until both the heads and tails are crispy and can be eaten.

Preparation Rub the fish with salt and dredge with flour. Shred the ginger and cut the scallions into 1 inch segments. Slice the onion.

Cooking Deep-fry the fish in the oil for about 7–8 minutes, or until very crispy. Alternatively, you could shallow-fry them in oil over a medium heat for 8–10 minutes, turning them over three or four times. When the fish are very crispy, remove them from the pan and keep hot. Pour away most of the oil in the pan, then stir-fry the ginger and onion in the remainder. Add the soy sauce, stock, sugar, pepper, and the scallions. Return the fish to the pan and cook them in the sauce over a low heat for 10–12 minutes, turning them over every 3 or 4 minutes. When the pan is nearly dry, the fish will not only be crispy but also extremely tasty.

Small fish cooked in this way are a great attraction to the Chinese, who are all experts in extricating bones from their mouths. If the fish have been fried and cooked long enough, and the bones are all crispy, there is no need to extricate them, for the crispy bones can be chewed and eaten, thus giving added joy to consumption!

Red-Simmered Fish in Vinegar Sauce

Preparation Clean and scale the fish and wash them thoroughly in salt water. Shred the ginger, crush and chop the garlic, and cut the scallions into 2 inch segments.

Cooking Choose a thick-bottomed, heavy saucepan or heat-proof casserole. Place a heat-proof plate in the saucepan or casserole, to prevent the ingredients scorching. Cover the plate with the bacon strips and arrange the scallions and fish in alternate layers on top. Scatter the ginger and garlic evenly over these ingredients and pour in the vinegar, soy sauce, and red wine. Finally, pour in sufficient water to cover the top layer of food by $\frac{1}{2}$ inch. Bring the liquid to the boil and reduce the heat to a minimum, inserting an asbestos pad under the pan. Simmer gently for 2 hours; then place the pan or casserole in an oven preheated to 300°F for a further 2 hours, checking first to see that there is sufficient liquid. By the end of this time, the heads, tails, and bones should all be tender, delicious, and edible!

How true it is that Chinese cooking is either 'instantaneous' or 'interminable'; all quickly stir-fried dishes are instantaneous, and this recipe, like most long-simmered dishes, is interminable!

Serves 4–6, with other dishes

6 whitings *or* small carp (total weight 2½ lb)
¾ cup vinegar

3 slices ginger root
3 cloves garlic
12 scallions
4 bacon strips
¾ cup soy sauce
¾ cup red wine
1¼ tablespoons sugar

Sweet and Sour Red-Cooked Fish

In the majority of sweet and sour fish dishes, the fish is made crispy by frying before the sauce is added at the last minute, or towards the end of the cooking time. All red-cooked fish dishes can be converted into sweet and sour dishes by reducing the quantity of sauce in the original recipe and adding the sweet and sour sauce towards the end. The original sauce can be reduced simply by not including stock in the liquid ingredients and by reducing the quantities of sherry and mushroom water added. Through such elimination and reduction, the dish would become quite dry after a period of braising. The sweet and sour sauce is then poured over this comparatively dry dish. The ingredients for making the sauce are given in the following recipe.

Sweet and Sour Yellow River Carp

The term 'Yellow River' is used here mainly to provide a certain geographical nostalgia—to give the feeling that the dish and ingredients are something special, when, in fact, Yellow River carp is no different from or better than many other Chinese varieties of carp, except that it lives in muddier water and should be kept in clear water for a few days before consumption.

Serves 4–6, with other dishes

A 3 lb carp

2½ teaspoons salt
2½ tablespoons flour
1½ tablespoons wood ears
¼ cup bamboo shoots
3 cloves garlic
3 slices ginger root
4 scallions
1½ tablespoons water chestnuts
1 small sweet pepper
1½ tablespoons cornstarch
2½ tablespoons sugar
2½ tablespoons vinegar
1¼ tablespoons tomato puree
¼ cup orange juice
2½ tablespoons dry sherry
¼ cup stock *or* water
oil for deep-frying
2½ tablespoons lard

Preparation Wash the fish thoroughly, then slash it on both sides at 2 inch intervals, to a depth of about ¼ inch. Rub with salt and dredge lightly with flour. Soak and rinse the wood ears. Cut the bamboo shoots into strips. Crush the garlic and shred the ginger. Cut the scallions into 1 inch segments. Slice the water chestnuts thin. Cut the sweet pepper into thin slices. Mix the remaining ingredients, except the oil and lard, and blend well into a smooth sauce.

Cooking Heat the oil in a deep-fryer and deep-fry the fish for 8–10 minutes until quite crispy. Remove it and place it in the oven to keep warm, on a well-heated dish. Heat the lard in a frying pan. Add the ginger, garlic, and half of the scallions. Stir-fry for 2 minutes, then pour most of the impregnated lard over the fish. Put the bamboo shoots, water chestnuts, wood ears, sweet pepper, and remaining lard in the frying pan. Stir-fry together for 2 minutes. Pour in the sauce mixture. As soon as it thickens and becomes translucent, pour it and all the solid ingredients over the length of the fish, and serve.

This is a banquet dish, popular at most party dinners.

Deep-Fried Fresh Small Fish

Serves 4–6, with other dishes

2½ lb small fish (whiting, sardines, small trout)

2 slices ginger root
1 heaping tablespoon salt
1¼ tablespoons flour
oil for deep-frying

The usual Chinese treatment of small fish is to make them crispy and crackling, qualities which go well with boiled rice. In this case, the fish are salted as well.

Preparation Clean the fish thoroughly. Shred the ginger and chop it fine. Mix well with the salt and rub the fish thoroughly with the mixture. Allow about 1 hour to season; then sprinkle and dredge lightly with the flour.

Cooking Heat the oil in a deep-fryer. Place half of the fish in a wire basket and fry in the oil for 5 minutes. Remove and drain the fish, then fry the remainder for the same length of time. When all the fish have been fried and drained, put them in the wire basket and lower them into the oil for a second frying of 2–3 minutes. This should make the heads and tails really crispy and crackling.

Although not considered the most refined of dishes, this dish is very good with rice, especially when there are not a great many savory meat dishes available and the diners have to make do with mostly vegetable dishes.

Deep-Fried Fresh Salted Fish Steaks

Preparation Cut the fish into 2 × 1½ inch pieces. Shred the ginger and chop fine. Mix 2 teaspoons salt with the ginger. Rub each piece of fish with this mixture and leave to season for 2 hours. Mix the remaining salt with the flours. Beat the egg lightly. Wet the pieces of fish with the beaten egg and dredge with the seasoned flour.

Cooking Heat the oil in a deep-fryer. Lower three or four pieces of fish into the oil in a wire basket and fry for 3–4 minutes, or until lightly browned. Repeat until all the pieces of fish have been fried, then arrange them on a well-heated white serving dish in overlapping rows, and serve. A few leaves of lettuce or young cabbage can be used to garnish the fish, if desired.

The sharp saltiness on the surface of the fish contrasting with the freshness within makes this a very appealing dish for rice-eating fish-lovers, in spite of its apparent simplicity.

Serves 4–6, with other dishes

2 lb fish (cod, haddock, halibut)

2 slices ginger root
4 teaspoons salt
1¾ tablespoons flour
2 teaspoons self-rising flour
1 egg
oil for deep-frying

Roof-Tile Fish

This is just a simple dish of salted, fried fish in large pieces. It is popular in north China.

Preparation Shred the ginger and chop it fine. Mix with the salt. Cut the fish into 2 × 1½ inch strips. Rub them thoroughly with the salt and ginger mixture and leave to season for 30 minutes. Mix the plain flour with the self-rising flour. Beat the egg lightly. Wet the fish with the beaten egg and dust with flour.

Cooking Heat the oil in a deep-fryer. Place four or five pieces of fish in a wire basket and fry in the oil for 4–5 minutes; then drain. Repeat until all the pieces of fish have been fried. Finally, place all the pieces of fried fish in the wire basket and fry them together over a high heat for 1½ minutes. This should give the pieces of fish added crispiness just before serving.

Serving Arrange the pieces of fish like tiles or shingles on a roof on a well-heated serving dish.

Serves 4–6, with other dishes

A 3–4 lb piece of fish (cod, salmon, carp)

2 slices ginger root
3¾ teaspoons salt
2 tablespoons plain flour
2 teaspoons self-rising flour
1 egg
oil for deep-frying

Squirrel Fish

In contrast to Yellow River carp, this is a Yangtze River dish, well-known in the city of Nanking, which is situated on the great river.

Serves 4–6, with other dishes

A 3 lb carp *or* bream

1 heaping tablespoon salt
2½ tablespoons flour
6 Chinese dried mushrooms
2 slices ginger root
3 scallions
¼ cup bamboo shoots
1¼ tablespoons cornstarch
¼ cup water
2 tablespoons soy sauce
2 tablespoons sugar
3 tablespoons vinegar
6 tablespoons chicken stock
2½ tablespoons dry sherry
oil for deep-frying
2 tablespoons lard *or* butter

Preparation Chop off the head of the fish. Clean the rest of the fish and slice it open lengthwise. Remove the vertebrae and bones. Clean again thoroughly. Rub with salt and dust lightly with flour. Make ten slashes on each side of the fish. Leave it to season for 2 hours. Soak the mushrooms for 30 minutes, remove the stalks and shred the caps. Shred the ginger and cut the scallions into 1 inch segments. Slice the bamboo shoots into strips. Blend the remaining ingredients, except the oil and lard, into a smooth sauce.

Cooking Place the fish in a wire basket and lower it into the boiling oil for 5–6 minutes. When the sizzling stops, which means most of the water has evaporated, turn off the heat or remove the pan from the heat. The fish will now curl up like a squirrel. Allow it to continue cooking in the oil for 2 minutes without returning the pan to the heat; then turn the heat up to maximum and fry the fish for 2 minutes, which should turn it golden-brown and cause the tail to turn up even more like that of a squirrel. Meanwhile, prepare the sauce by frying the bamboo shoots and mushrooms in the lard over a medium heat for 1½ minutes. Pour in the sauce mixture. When it thickens and boils, drain the fish quickly and put it on a well-heated serving dish; then bring the fish and sauce to the table. Pour the sauce over the fish in front of the diners and the fish should emit a noise like a squeaking squirrel (does a squirrel squeak?). Anyway, the thought and description seem to tickle the Chinese fancy.

Deep-Fried Braised Fish Stuffed with Pork and Scallions

Serves 4–6, with other dishes

A 3 lb fish (carp, bream, bass)

¼ lb slab bacon
6 scallions
2½ tablespoons dried shrimp
2 cloves garlic
1¼ tablespoons sugar
1¼ teaspoons salt
2½ tablespoons flour
½ cup young leeks
2 slices ginger root
oil for deep-frying
2½ tablespoons lard
¼ cup soy sauce
1¼ tablespoons hoisin sauce

Preparation Clean the fish thoroughly and drain well. Soak the dried shrimp in water for 30 minutes; then drain. Cut the scallions into 2 inch segments, and crush and chop the garlic. Chop the bacon coarsely. Mix 1 teaspoon of the sugar with the salt, dried shrimp, scallions, garlic, and bacon to form a stuffing for the fish. Stuff the fish with the mixture and secure by sewing. Dredge the fish lightly with flour. Cut the leeks into 1½ inch segments and shred the ginger.

Cooking Heat the oil in a deep-fryer. Put the fish in a wire basket and lower it into the oil to deep-fry for 6 minutes; then drain well. Meanwhile, heat the lard in a heat-proof casserole. Add the ginger and leeks and stir-fry for 2 minutes. Add the soy sauce, hoisin sauce, remaining sugar, and vinegar, and continue to stir-fry for 30 seconds. Pour in the water and bring the liquid to the boil. Place the fish in the casserole, submerged in the sauce, and cook over a medium heat for 6–7 minutes. Turn the fish over and continue to simmer over a low heat for 7–8 minutes.

Serving Lift the fish carefully on to a serving dish. Pour the gravy in the casserole over the fish and garnish with the leeks from the casserole

2 tablespoons vinegar
¾ cup water

Carp Braised in Chicken Fat Sauce

Preparation Clean the carp thoroughly and rub with salt, inside and out. Leave to season for 1 hour. Dust and dredge the fish with the flour. Shred the ginger, crush and chop the garlic, and cut the scallions into 1 inch segments.

Cooking Heat the chicken fat in a large, oval, heat-proof casserole. Add the ginger, garlic, and half of the scallions. Stir-fry for 1 minute. Add the soy sauce, hoisin sauce, chili sauce, sugar, and sherry. Stir and mix well. When the mixture boils, lay the carp on the hot oil-sauce mixture to cook for 2 minutes. Turn the fish over and cook for another 2 minutes. Meanwhile, cut each bean curd cake into six pieces and place them against the sides of the casserole. Pour in the stock, sprinkle in the remaining scallions and cover the casserole firmly. Simmer gently for 10 minutes and serve from the casserole.

Serves 4–6, with other dishes

2½–3 lb carp
5–6 tablespoons chicken fat

2½ teaspoons salt
2 tablespoons flour
2 slices ginger root
2 cloves garlic
4 scallions
¼ cup soy sauce
1¼ tablespoons hoisin sauce
1¼ teaspoons chili sauce
2½ teaspoons sugar
2½ tablespoons dry sherry
2 cakes fresh bean curd
¾ cup chicken stock

Braised Fish Steaks in Red Wine Sauce

Preparation Cut each fish steak into three or four pieces about 2 inches square. Beat the egg. Rub the pieces of fish with the beaten egg, and dredge with the plain and self-rising flour. Cut the scallions into 2 inch segments.

Cooking Heat the oil in a frying pan. Add the ginger and half of the scallions, and stir-fry for 1 minute over a medium heat. Add the pieces of fish, spacing them evenly over the pan. Fry for 2½ minutes, then turn the pieces of fish over and fry for the same length of time on the other side. Mix 2 tablespoons of the red wine with the soy sauce, hoisin sauce, tomato

Serves 4–6, with other dishes

2 lb fish steaks
6 tablespoons red wine

1 egg
2½ teaspoons salt
2 tablespoons flour
2 tablespoons self-rising flour
3 scallions
¼ cup vegetable oil
2 slices ginger root

2½ tablespoons soy sauce
1¼ tablespoons hoisin sauce
1¼ tablespoons tomato puree
1½ teaspoons red bean curd cheese
2½ teaspoons sugar
1¼ tablespoons lard
2½ tablespoons chopped parsley

puree, bean curd cheese, and sugar. Pour this mixture evenly over each piece of fish. Turn the pieces of fish over and heat for 1 minute; then remove them from the pan with a spatula and place on a well-heated serving dish. Add the lard, parsley, remaining red wine, and the scallions to the pan. Turn the heat to high momentarily. Stir-fry the contents of the pan for 15 seconds.

Serving Pour the sauce over the pieces of fish and garnish with the solids from the pan.

This is another fish recipe with which one can be easily successful.

Pan-Fried Sliced Fish in White Sauce

Serves 4–6, with other dishes

1½ lb fillet of sole *or* flounder

1¼ tablespoons wood ears
2 teaspoons salt
1 egg white
1½ tablespoons cornstarch
1¼ tablespoons self-rising flour
1 cup chicken stock
¼ cup white wine
¼ teaspoon monosodium glutamate
2 teaspoons cornstarch
1¼ tablespoons chicken fat
1¼ tablespoons lard
2 slices ginger root

Preparation Soak the wood ears for 30 minutes, rinse and drain. Cut fish with a sharp knife into 2 × 1 inch strips. Rub them with salt. Beat the egg white with a fork for 10 seconds. Wet the fish slices with the egg white, then dust and dredge them with 2 tablespoons cornstarch, blended with the self-rising flour. Blend together ¼ cup of the chicken stock, the wine, monosodium glutamate, 1½ teaspoons cornstarch, and 1 tablespoon chicken fat, until a smooth sauce is formed.

Cooking Heat the lard, ginger, and remaining chicken stock in a frying pan and stir over a medium heat. Put the slices of fish into the liquid to heat for just over 1 minute on each side. Remove the fish carefully with a spatula, place on a well-heated dish, and keep hot in the oven. Pour away the remaining liquid from the pan. Add the chicken fat and wood ears to the pan and stir-fry quickly over a medium heat for 30 seconds. Pour in the sauce mixture and stir gently until the liquid thickens and becomes translucent. Pour the sauce and wood ears over the fish in the serving dish.

This is a delicate dish which requires precise timing to succeed. It is a very well-known and well-liked dish from Peking. The term 'pan-fried' is used here to distinguish the cooking method from quick-frying or stir-frying, where stirring, turning, mixing, and scrambling are involved. Pan-frying is static and the ingredients are handled carefully and slowly so that they do not break up. Usually the ingredients employed are few and all are cooked individually. They are not meant to be mixed up in a scramble. The sauce is the constituent part of the dish that combines all the ingredients together.

Pan-Fried Sliced Fish
in Sweet and Sour Sauce

Preparation Cut the fish with a sharp knife into 2 × 1 inch strips. Rub them with salt. Beat the egg white with a fork for 10 seconds. Wet the fish slices with the egg white, then dust 0and dredge them with 2 tablespoons of the cornstarch, blended with the self-rising flour. Blend together 3 tablespoons of the chicken stock with the soy sauce, sherry, tomato puree, orange juice, vinegar, sugar, and remaining cornstarch blended with ¼ cup water. Mix these ingredients together well, until a smooth sauce is formed.

Cooking Heat the lard and remaining chicken stock in a frying pan and stir over a medium heat. Put the slices of fish into the liquid to heat for 1½ minutes on each side. Strain off the excess liquid and pour the sauce mixture into the pan. Cook for 1½ minutes, basting the fish slices with the sauce and turning them over once.

Serving Put the slices of fish on to a well-heated serving dish, then pour the sauce from the pan over the fish. Garnish with chopped parsley if desired.

Various items, such as pickles, sliced peppers, carrots, and wood ears can be added during the frying and cooking with the sauce, if desired.

Serves 4–6, with other dishes

1½ lb fillet of sole *or* flounder

2 teaspoons salt
1 egg white
3 tablespoons cornstarch
2 tablespoons self-rising flour
½ cup chicken stock
2 tablespoons soy sauce
2½ tablespoons dry sherry
1¼ tablespoons tomato puree
¼ cup orange juice
2½ tablespoons vinegar
2 tablespoons sugar
2 tablespoons lard

Pan-Fried Sliced Fish
with Chicken and Sweet Pepper

This is a slightly spicy dish, and a natural extension of the Chinese tradition of cross-cooking.

Preparation Cut the fish with a sharp knife into 2 × 1 inch strips. Cut the chicken into slightly thinner pieces of a similar size. Beat the egg white with a fork for 15 seconds. Rub the fish and chicken slices with salt, wet them with egg white, and dredge in 1½ tablespoons of the cornstarch mixed with the self-rising flour. Crush the garlic and shred the ginger. Chop the chili pepper fine and slice the sweet pepper into strips. Mix the remaining cornstarch with the monosodium glutamate, ¼ cup of the chicken stock, and the wine, and blend into a smooth sauce.

Serves 4–6, with other dishes

1 lb fillet of sole
½ lb chicken breast meat
1 medium red sweet pepper

1 egg white
2½ teaspoons salt
2½ tablespoons cornstarch
1¼ tablespoons self-rising flour
2 cloves garlic
2 slices ginger root
1 dried chili pepper
¼ teaspoon monosodium glutamate
1 cup chicken stock
5½ tablespoons white wine
2½ tablespoons vegetable oil
1¼ tablespoons lard

271

Cooking Heat the oil in a large frying pan over a medium heat. Add the garlic and ginger and stir-fry for 1 minute. Add the chicken slices and spread them out over one half of the pan. Stir-fry for a few moments; then pour in the remaining chicken stock and mix it with the oil in the pan. Spread the fish slices over the other half of the pan. Fry for 1 minute; then turn the chicken and fish slices over and fry for a further minute. Remove the fish and chicken slices carefully from the pan. Put the lard into the pan, then add the chili pepper and sweet pepper. Stir-fry them together for 1 minute, then pour in the sauce mixture. Stir until the mixture thickens and becomes translucent. Return the fish and chicken slices to the pan and turn them in the sauce for 1 minute. Serve on a large well-heated dish.

Deep-Fried Fish Sandwich

Serves 4–6, with other dishes

2 fillets of fish (sole, carp, haddock, salmon)
1 lb slab bacon

2½ tablespoons soy sauce
2 scallions
2 teaspoons salt
3 eggs
2½ tablespoons flour
1¼ tablespoons self-rising flour
1½ tablespoons water
oil for deep-frying
parsley

This is a curious dish originating from the former Imperial kitchen. Apart from mixing and blending in cooking, it is also the Chinese tradition to laminate ingredients of different textures and qualities, in this case pork and fish. The pork should be cut into razor-thin slices.

Preparation Cut the fish into thin slices and pour the soy sauce over them to marinate for 30 minutes. Chop the scallions coarse. Cut the bacon into razor-thin slices, or ask the butcher to do it with a food slicer. Rub the slices of bacon with salt. Beat one of the eggs lightly. Mix the plain and self-rising flours with the remaining eggs and the water to form a light, runny batter. Wet the fish slices with the beaten egg and sprinkle with the chopped scallions. Dip two slices of bacon into the batter and make a 'sandwich' by placing a piece of fish in between them. Press together firmly. Continue to make these sandwiches until all the materials are used up.

Cooking Heat the oil in a deep-fryer over medium heat. Place two sandwiches in a wire basket at a time and lower them into the oil to deep-fry for 4 minutes; then turn the heat up to the maximum for a further 1–1½ minutes and continue to fry until they are distinctly brown. Repeat until all the sandwiches have been fried.

Serving Cut each sandwich into four pieces and arrange them neatly on a plain-colored serving dish. Garnish with sprigs of parsley.

This is a good dish to serve either as an hors d'œuvre or with drinks.

Smoked Fish

Chinese smoked fish is usually made with fish or pieces of fish which have already been thoroughly marinated and seasoned, then fried in oil until they are quite dry, so that they appear as if they have already been smoked. When smoke is actually used, it is applied only to provide a slight touch of flavor. This recipe describes the best way to go through the whole process in a modern kitchen. It sounds fairly complicated, but the result is well worth it.

Preparation Chop the scallions fine. Mix them with the soy sauce, soy paste, sherry, sugar, and monosodium glutamate. Rub the fish with the salt and leave the pieces to marinate in the mixed sauce for approximately 1 hour, turning a couple of times.

Cooking Heat the oil in a large, heavy frying pan. Spread the pieces of fish evenly over the pan and fry for 2 minutes on each side, over a medium heat. Reduce the heat to very low, pour the remainder of the marinade over the fish, and continue to fry very slowly and gently until nearly all the sauce has dried up, or is encrusted on the fish. The fish should now be dark brown in color.

Smoking Place the pieces of fish in a small roasting pan. Spread the brown sugar in the center of a large sheet of aluminum foil and place the dish containing the fish on top. Wrap the foil loosely over the dish of fish and seal over the top by twisting or screwing the edges together (thus forming a foil 'tent'). Repeat with another sheet of aluminum foil, but this time without sealing the top, and puncture a small hole in the top of the inner layer. Place the foil-wrapped dish of fish in a heavy saucepan or large roasting pan. Place the pan over a medium heat for 3–4 minutes, or until smoke starts to come out of the hole in the inner sheet of the foil. The smoke is caused by the burning sugar. Now seal the outer layer of foil, heat for a few more seconds; then turn the heat off and leave the fish to stand in the smoke-filled tent for 10 minutes.

Serving Unwrap the layers of aluminum foil, arrange the pieces of fish on a dish, brush with sesame oil, and serve.

This is a more elaborate type of Chinese smoked fish dish. The less elaborate method, as mentioned at the beginning of this recipe, does not require any smoking at all. All it requires is low-heat frying until all the marinade and fish have become dried enough for the fish to appear to have been smoked. The fish turns brown because of the soy sauce and other ingredients becoming encrusted on it during the slow process of gentle, low-heat frying.

Serves 4–6, with other dishes

4 fish steaks

2 scallions
2 tablespoons soy sauce
1 tablespoon soy paste
1¼ tablespoons dry sherry
2½ teaspoons sugar
¼ teaspoon monosodium glutamate
2 teaspoons salt
5 tablespoons vegetable oil
¼ cup brown sugar
1 tablespoon sesame oil

Double-Fried Eel

Serves 4–6, with other dishes

A 3–4 lb eel

3¾ teaspoons salt
2 slices ginger root
2 cloves garlic
4 scallions
oil for deep-frying
2½ tablespoons lard
2½ tablespoons soy sauce
2½ tablespoons dry sherry
5½ tablespoons chicken stock
¼ teaspoon monosodium glutamate
1½ teaspoons sugar
¼ teaspoon five spice powder
pepper to taste
2½ tablespoons chopped parsley

This is a rich, highly-spiced dish from Shanghai, and is an excellent accompaniment to rice.

Preparation Dip the eel in boiling water for 1 minute; then drain and dry it, and rub it with salt. Leave to season for 1 hour. Shred the ginger; crush and chop the garlic. Cut the scallions into 1 inch segments.

Cooking Heat the oil in a deep-fryer. Place the eel in a wire basket and deep-fry it for 4–5 minutes. Drain; then cut the meat neatly into 2 × 1 inch strips. Discard the head and tail. Place the pieces of eel meat in the wire basket, deep-fry for a second time over a high heat for 2–3 minutes until golden-brown; then drain thoroughly. Meanwhile, heat the lard in a frying pan. Add the ginger, garlic, scallions, soy sauce, sherry, chicken stock, monosodium glutamate, sugar, five spice powder, and pepper. Stir-fry together for 1 minute. Add the pieces of eel, spreading them over the pan. Turn and baste them with the sauce for 2½ minutes.

Serving Place the pieces of eel on a well-heated dish, pour the sauce over, and sprinkle with chopped parsley.

This dish is best served immediately.

Fried Fish Strips Tossed in Celery

Serves 4–6, with other dishes

1½ lb fish steaks (cod, salmon, haddock, pike, bass)
1 lb celery

1 egg
2½ teaspoons salt
1¾ tablespoons flour
1¾ tablespoons self-rising flour
2 tablespoons soy sauce
1¼ teaspoons chili sauce
¼ teaspoon monosodium glutamate
2½ teaspoons sesame oil
2 oz smoked ham
oil for deep-frying
juice of half a lemon

Preparation Slice the fish into thin sheets, and then cut the sheets along the grain into matchstick strips about 2 inches long. Beat the egg. Dip the fish strips into the beaten egg. Mix the salt with the plain flour and self-rising flour, and use it to dredge the fish. Cut the celery into strips about the same size as the fish strips, plunge into boiling water for 30 seconds; then drain. Add the soy sauce, chili sauce, monosodium glutamate, and sesame oil. Toss and mix well together. Slice the ham into matchstick strips.

Cooking Heat the oil in a deep-fryer. Pour in the fish strips and spread them out quickly with the help of a pair of chopsticks (or use a wire basket). After 2½ minutes of frying, the fish strips should float up to the surface of the oil. Remove quickly and drain.

Serving Lay the celery on a large oval dish or salad bowl as a bed. Pour the fried fish strips on top; toss and mix gently. Sprinkle with lemon juice, garnish with strips of ham; then serve.

Fish Balls in Soup

Fish balls, like meatballs, are often used in soups in Chinese cooking, or are cooked with various other items—both meats and vegetables—in mixed and 'made-up' dishes, which can be semi-soups or braised dishes.

Preparation Chop the onion and shred the ginger. Boil them in 6 tablespoons water for 1½ minutes. Strain away the onion and ginger and keep the water for later use. Beat the egg white. Chop and grind the fish into a paste. Add the ginger/onion water gradually to the fish paste, together with the beaten egg, cornstarch, salt, and pepper. Form the mixture into regular-sized balls, about the size of a small chestnut, by taking a fistful of seasoned fish paste and squeezing it through the hole made by crooking the index finger towards the base of the thumb. If necessary, make the balls rounder with the aid of wet hands and fingers. Chop the scallions.

Cooking Lower the fish balls into a pan of simmering chicken stock. When they have simmered for 4–5 minutes, add the monosodium glutamate and vinegar to the stock. (Further seasonings can be added if required.)

Serving Divide the stock and fish balls among eight bowls. Sprinkle each bowl with chopped scallions, and serve.

Serves 8

2 lb fish fillets
6¼ cups chicken stock

1 medium-sized onion
2 slices ginger root
1 egg white
1 tablespoon cornstarch
2½ teaspoons salt
pepper to taste
2 scallions
¼ teaspoon monosodium glutamate
1 tablespoon vinegar

Braised Fish Balls

Make the fish balls according to the instructions in the previous recipe, but reduce the quantity by one third. Cook them by immersing them in boiling water and simmering for 3–4 minutes. Drain them well.

Preparation Soak the mushrooms and golden needles separately for 30 minutes. Shred the mushrooms and cut the golden needles into 2 inch segments. Shred the pork into matchstick strips and rub these with salt. Cut the scallions into 1 inch segments. Chop the broccoli into 1 inch pieces.

Cooking Heat the lard in a frying pan or saucepan. Add the pork, dried shrimp, and scallions, and stir-fry over a high heat for 1 minute. Add the mushrooms, golden needles, wood ears, and broccoli. Continue to stir-fry over a high heat for 3 minutes. Add the soy sauce, then the stock. Bring to the boil and add the fish balls. Bring to the boil once more; then reduce heat to low and simmer for 6–7 minutes. Blend the cornstarch with 3 tablespoons water, sherry, and monosodium glutamate. Stir this mixture into the pan. Turn the mixture over two or three times, sprinkle with sesame oil, and serve.

Serves 6–8, with other dishes

fish balls (see previous recipe)

4 large Chinese dried mushrooms
2–3 stalks golden needles (tiger-lily buds)
2 tablespoons dried shrimp
½ lb lean pork
¾ teaspoon salt
3 scallions
1 cup broccoli
2½ tablespoons lard
1¼ tablespoons dried wood ears
2½ tablespoons soy sauce
¾ cup superior stock
2½ teaspoons cornstarch
2 tablespoons dry sherry
¼ teaspoon monosodium glutamate
2½ teaspoons sesame oil

Drunken Fish

Serves 4–6, with other dishes

2 lb very fresh cod *or* salmon

1 medium-sized onion
3 slices ginger root
1½ teaspoons salt
2½ tablespoons soy sauce
2½ tablespoons dry sherry
1 tablespoon brandy *or* Mowtai liqueur *or* Kaoliang liqueur
¼ teaspoon freshly ground black pepper
¾ teaspoon chili oil
2½ tablespoons chopped chives
1 heaping tablespoon sesame oil

It is in the Japanese tradition to eat raw fish. We Chinese also have some raw fish dishes. These are generally very well seasoned.

Preparation Chop the onion. Boil the ginger and onion in 6 tablespoons of water for 2 minutes. Retain the water. Cut the fish into very thin slices about 2½ × 1½ inches in size. Rub them with salt, then add the soy sauce, ginger/onion water, sherry, brandy or liqueur, pepper, chili oil, and half of the chives. Mix thoroughly. Leave to season for 3 hours in a refrigerator.

Serving Spread the pieces of fish on a flat serving dish. Brush them with sesame oil, sprinkle with the remaining chopped chives; then serve.

Stir-Frying, Steaming, and Simmering Fish

Fish is never stir-fried in the vigorous way in which pieces of meat, vegetables, or pasta are stir-fried in Chinese cooking. This is for the simple reason that pieces of fish would break up into uneven pieces if treated with such violence. Hence, slices of fish are usually cooked by static frying (Chien) or by wet frying (Liu) in a thickened sauce. To cook sliced fish either way, the actual cooking time is generally not more than 4–5 minutes, and all the flavorings and supplementary ingredients are generally added after the cooking has started. Apart from having to cut or slice the fish neatly and carefully to the required size, cooking by these methods is very quick—they are equivalent to quick stir-frying (Chow) in meat cookery, which produces an inexhaustible number of dishes; and although there are far fewer fish dishes in these categories than meat dishes, some of the best-known and best-liked fish dishes are wet-fried (Liu) dishes.

On the other hand, when fish is available fresh and whole, perhaps 'clear-steaming' or 'clear-simmering' are two of the simplest ways of handling it. Perhaps by not doing too much to fish, more of its native qualities, such as its sweet-freshness, can be retained. Here, the Chinese habit of adding fresh ginger root, with perhaps a few drops of wine and a sprinkle of sugar, can work miracles to reduce the fishiness in fish. Once again, the use of soy sauce or fermented salted beans, in conjunction with leeks, onions, and just a trace of garlic, seems to enhance the savory quality of fish in a way which few other flavors are able to surpass.

In contrast with wet-frying, when fish is steamed or simmered it is often well-marinated before cooking starts. In the cooking itself, the fish is simply subjected to a vigorous blast of steaming for 15–25 minutes, depending on the size or quantity of the fish to be cooked. It is cooked by 'open steaming', that is, without a lid. All the dressing and garnishing is usually arranged prior to the steaming, so once the cooking has been completed, the dish of fish can usually be brought direct from the steamer to the table, all spick and span and well-presented.

Clear-Steamed Fish

Various types of fish can be cooked by clear-steaming, including carp, fluke, mullet, bass, sea bass and sole. It is preferable to choose the thicker, chunkier varieties rather than the thin, flat type, such as flounder, which is more suitable for frying. The Chinese conception of a good fish dish is not unlike the Western conception of a good roast: something big, which can be carved on the table.

Preparation Soak the dried shrimp in a bowl of water for 1 hour. Soak the mushrooms, remove the stalks, and slice the caps into strips. Chop the ginger fine and mix with the salt and monosodium glutamate. Rub the fish with this mixture, inside and out, and leave to season for 30 minutes. Chop half of the scallions into fine pieces and the other half into 2 inch segments. Crush and chop the garlic and mix it with the scallions, soy sauce, sherry, sugar, stock, and cornstarch blended with 2 tablespoons water. Mix together well. Pour the mixture over the fish and turn it in the marinade a couple of times. Sprinkle the shrimp evenly over the fish, drape it with bacon and mushroom strips; then sprinkle lightly with pepper.

Cooking Place the fish in a deep heat-proof dish and steam vigorously for 20–22 minutes.

Serving Bring the dish from the steamer and serve in a cloud of steam. This is particularly effective on a winter's day. Although the cooking of this dish is simple, the unbiased opinion of many people is that this is one of the great fish dishes of the world.

Serves 4–6, with other dishes

A 3 lb whole fish

2 tablespoons dried shrimp
2 large Chinese dried mushrooms
3 slices ginger root
2½ teaspoons salt
¼ teaspoon monosodium glutamate
6 scallions
2 cloves garlic
¼ cup soy sauce
2½ tablespoons dry sherry
1 tablespoon sugar
¼ cup chicken stock
2½ teaspoons cornstarch
2 bacon strips
dash of pepper

Clear-Steamed Fish with Sub Gum Variety Toppings

Sub Gum means ten varieties, but as in many things Chinese, you do not have to be absolutely accurate in these fanciful specifications. You can do very well with seven or eight items.

Preparation Chop the ginger fine and mix with the salt and monosodium glutamate. Rub the fish with this mixture, inside and out, and leave to season for 30 minutes.

Cooking Place the fish in a deep heat-proof dish and steam vigorously for 20–22 minutes.

Serves 4–6, with other dishes

A 3 lb whole fish

3 slices ginger root
2½ teaspoons salt
¼ teaspoon monosodium glutamate
2½ tablespoons dried bamboo shoots
4 golden needles (tiger-lily buds)
4 large Chinese dried mushrooms
2½ tablespoons wood ears
3 oz slab bacon
2 young leeks

277

6 scallions
¼ cup water chestnuts
2 tablespoons lard
2 tablespoons soy sauce
1 tablespoon dry sherry
1 tablespoon vinegar
2 teaspoons cornstarch
2 tablespoons chicken stock

Preparation While the fish is steaming, prepare the toppings. Soak the bamboo shoots for 30 minutes, then cut them into strips. Soak the golden needles, dried mushrooms, and wood ears for 30 minutes. Cut the golden needles into 2 inch segments. Remove the mushroom stalks and shred the caps. Rinse the wood ears. Shred the bacon, cut the leeks and scallions into 2 inch segments, and cut the water chestnuts into thin strips.

Cooking Heat the lard in a small frying pan. Add the bacon and stir-fry over a high heat for 1½ minutes. Add all the other solid ingredients and continue to stir-fry for 3 minutes. Finally, pour in the soy sauce, sherry, vinegar, and cornstarch blended with 2 tablespoons chicken stock. Stir until the sauce thickens.

Serving Remove the fish from the steamer and pour the sauce from the frying pan along its length. Garnish with all the solid toppings from the frying pan. This is quite an easy fish dish to succeed with, and the end product can be extremely appealing.

Steamed Fish Steaks

Serves 4–6, with other dishes

1 large fish steak (about 2 lb)

2½ teaspoons salt
2½ teaspoons sugar
2½ tablespoons soy sauce
2½ tablespoons dry sherry
4 teaspoons vegetable oil
3 scallions
2 slices ginger root
half a lemon
2 oz smoked ham

Since fish does not always come whole, but often in fillets or steaks, the following is one way of steaming them. This is also the method used to steam flat fish, such as sole.

Preparation Cut the fish into pieces approximately 2 inches square, and rub them with salt. Mix together the sugar, soy sauce, sherry, and oil. Place the pieces of fish in a single layer in a heat-proof dish. Pour the sauce over, covering each piece of fish, and marinate for 30 minutes. Cut the scallions into 2 inch segments, shred the ginger, and cut the ham into strips. After the fish has been marinated, sprinkle some ginger and scallion over each piece of fish. Squeeze the juice from the half lemon over the fish, and garnish with the strips of ham.

Cooking Place the heat-proof dish in a steamer and steam vigorously for 20–22 minutes. Serve from the same dish.

Clear-Simmered Fish with Sub Gum Variety Toppings

The effect of clear-simmering is very similar to that of steaming, so far as fish is concerned. With fish, the simmering is seldom prolonged; the time required for simmering is often not more than half the time required for steaming

Preparation Clean and scale the fish and score it on both sides by slashing it at 1 inch intervals.

Cooking Heat the water in a fish poacher or in an oval or oblong heat-proof casserole (or even in a roasting pan). Add the ginger and salt. Bring the water to a vigorous boil, then lower the fish gently into the pan. See that the whole length of the fish is covered by water. As soon as the water comes to the boil again, reduce the heat. Place the lid on the fish poacher and allow the fish to simmer gently over a medium heat for 4 minutes. Insert an asbestos pad under the pan and reduce the heat to low. Simmer the fish slowly for a further 8 minutes. Drain away the water, and lift the fish out of the poacher. Place it on an oval well-heated serving dish.

Preparation While the fish is cooking, prepare the Sub Gum toppings. Soak the bamboo shoots for 30 minutes; then cut them into strips. Soak the golden needles, dried mushrooms, and wood ears for 30 minutes. Cut the golden needles into 2 inch segments. Remove the mushroom stalks and shred the caps. Rinse the wood ears. Shred the bacon, cut the leeks and scallions into 2 inch segments, and cut the water chestnuts into thin strips.

Cooking Stir-fry all the ingredients of the Sub Gum topping in the lard for 3½–4 minutes. Pour in the soy sauce, sherry, vinegar, and cornstarch blended with the chicken stock. Stir until the sauce thickens.

Serving Pour the sauce over the length of the fish and arrange the various solid items cooked in the sauce on top of the fish, as a garnish.

Serves 4–6, with other dishes

A 2½–3 lb fish

2 quarts water
4 slices ginger root
1½ tablespoons salt
¼ cup dried bamboo shoots
4 golden needles (tiger-lily buds)
4 large Chinese dried mushrooms
2½ tablespoons wood ears
3 oz slab bacon
2 young leeks
6 scallions
½ cup water chestnuts
5 tablespoons lard
5 tablespoons soy sauce
2½ tablespoons dry sherry
1½ tablespoons vinegar
1 tablespoon cornstarch
3 tablespoons chicken stock

SEAFOOD AND SHELLFISH

Not all shellfish can be classified as seafood in China. Most of the crabs and shrimp eaten are, in fact, fresh-water products from the lakes, rivers, canals, and ponds. Fresh-water shrimp and crabs are considered sweeter and more delicate than the coarser products of the sea, which are enjoyed by the coastal people.

Some of the shellfish or seafood are used mainly dried, as flavorers, rather than as a dish or food in themselves. There are few abalone dishes because it is most frequently used in small quantities just to give flavor. As a food, abalone is of no importance; as a flavorer it is one of the essential supplementary materials in Chinese cooking.

Although great quantities of shrimp and squid are eaten and cooked fresh, equal quantities of them are used dried as flavorers. The same applies to oysters and the root-muscles of scallops, which are considered to possess a very delicate taste. As cross-cooking and inter-blending of flavors are an integral part of Chinese cooking, these ingredients have a double function in Chinese food and cooking. They are always available as dried foods in Chinese markets, and should be found in any well-stocked Chinese pantry. They must always be soaked before being used for flavoring.

On the other hand, when shellfish and seafood are used fresh, they have to be very fresh (because, as mentioned before, it is only recently that refrigeration came to China). Some are even cooked alive—one of the best ways of eating oysters is to cook them in their own shells. It was the tradition of the coastal people of south-east China to stick bamboo-sticks in oyster beds, and over a period of time the sticks became encrusted with oysters. To harvest the oysters they had only to pull up the sticks. I remember many enjoyable and exciting winter evenings spent in grilling sticks of oysters (usually there were six to twelve oysters on a stick) over blazing braziers, and listening to the popping noise of the oyster-shells opening when they were cooked. This tradition and practice seems unknown elsewhere.

Cooking fresh, live crabs, lobsters, clams, shrimp, and scallops seems to be the practice wherever freshness is valued. As a rule they are only subjected to very brief cooking, usually by stir-frying, deep-frying, or steaming. In many parts of the world today, however, these shellfish and seafood are available only canned or frozen. The frozen varieties have to be completely thawed and drained before being used in Chinese cooking. There are some excellent canned varieties of crabmeat, but for shrimp to have any resemblance to the original fresh variety, it is best to buy them frozen.

As variety is the keynote to Chinese food, and since shellfish and seafood provide such a distinctive difference in taste and flavor from other types of materials, one almost invariably finds a dish or two made from shellfish during a multi-course Chinese dinner. In their use as flavorers—usually in small quantities in made-up dishes—they are to be found in almost every Chinese meal, if it is one which is above subsistence level. For these reasons seafood and shellfish are perhaps better known and more universally appreciated by the Chinese than by any other continental people.

Abalone

Abalone has a rubbery texture, is brownish-yellow in color, and has an extremely savory flavor. It is usually available canned—only occasionally in dried form. When the can is opened the liquid or abalone water should always be reserved for later use, especially for adding a savory flavor to soups and stewed or braised dishes.

In all normally available forms, abalone requires very little cooking—generally not more than a few minutes. Because of its rubbery texture, it becomes monotonous when chewed, and therefore is not a very interesting food to eat on its own. Although there are one or two pure abalone dishes, it is far more interesting when cooked with other ingredients.

Abalone Stir-Fried
with Mushrooms and Bamboo Shoots

Preparation Soak the dried mushrooms for 20 minutes, then drain, reserving ¼ cup of the mushroom water. Remove the stalks and cut each mushroom cap into four. Cut the abalone and bamboo shoots into ⅛ inch thick slices. Blend the cornstarch with 2 tablespoons of the abalone water. Chop the scallions into 1 inch segments.

Cooking Heat the oil in a frying pan, add the mushrooms and bamboo shoots, and stir-fry over a medium heat for 2 minutes. Add the soy sauce, hoisin sauce, sherry, and mushroom water; stir-fry gently for another minute. Pour in the abalone water and cornstarch mixture. As soon as the liquid thickens slightly, add the slices of abalone and scallions. Stir-fry for 2 minutes, then serve on a light-colored, well-heated dish, and eat immediately.

Serves 4–8, with other dishes

½–1 lb can abalone
6 Chinese dried mushrooms
1 cup bamboo shoots

2½ teaspoons cornstarch
2 scallions
3½ tablespoons vegetable oil
1½ tablespoons soy sauce
1¼ tablespoons hoisin sauce
1¼ tablespoons dry sherry

Abalone Braised with Transparent Noodles and Assorted Vegetables

Serves 6–8, with other dishes

½–1 lb can abalone
½ cup transparent bean-thread noodles

3 tablespoons wood ears
6 Chinese dried mushrooms
2 stalks celery
2 leeks
½ cup broccoli
½ cup bamboo shoots
1 heaping tablespoon cornstarch
2 scallions
5 tablespoons vegetable oil
1½ teaspoons salt
2 tablespoons soy sauce
1½ tablespoons dry sherry
2½ teaspoons hoisin sauce
1¼ cups chicken or superior stock

Preparation Soak the wood ears for 30 minutes, then rinse them in two changes of water. Soak the dried mushrooms for 20 minutes; then remove the stalks and cut each mushroom cap into quarters. Reserve 4–5 tablespoons of the mushroom water. Soak the noodles for 10 minutes in warm water, then drain. Cut the celery, leeks, and broccoli into 1–2 inch segments, and the abalone and bamboo shoots into ⅛ inch thick slices. Reserve all the abalone water, and blend in the cornstarch. Chop the scallions into 1 inch segments.

Cooking Heat the oil in a frying pan, then add the mushrooms, bamboo shoots, wood ears, celery, leeks, broccoli, and salt. Stir-fry for 2 minutes. Add the soy sauce, sherry, hoisin sauce, and mushroom water, and stir-fry gently for another minute. Add the abalone water/cornstarch mixture, the noodles, and stock. As soon as the liquid thickens slightly, add the slices of abalone and scallion. Simmer gently for 10 minutes.

Serving Pour into a large soup bowl or tureen. This is another semi-soup dish, with ample vegetable content.

Simmered Chicken with Abalone

Serves 8–10, with other dishes

3–4 lb chicken
¼–½ lb can abalone

1 lb broccoli
2 slices ginger root
2½ teaspoons salt
¼ teaspoon monosodium glutamate
5 tablespoons dry sherry

The flavor of chicken seems to combine well with most seafood, particularly with abalone. There are many dishes in which these two ingredients are used together with excellent effect. The following is one in which they are in 'wet combination'.

Preparation Cut the abalone into ⅛ inch thick slices, reserving the abalone water. Wash the broccoli and cut it into individual leaves and branches, discarding the outer, coarser parts.

Cooking Place the chicken in boiling water for 3 minutes, then discard the water. Remove the chicken to a large heat-proof casserole and pour in 5 cups of water. Add the ginger and salt, cover the casserole, and simmer the chicken gently, either over a low heat or in the oven for 1 hour. Put the broccoli and abalone into the liquid surrounding the chicken. Add the monosodium glutamate, and pour in the abalone water and sherry; then simmer, covered, for a further 30 minutes. Serve in the casserole or in a large soup bowl or tureen.

This makes a very attractive dish, with the greenness of the broccoli balancing the whiteness of the chicken. (Chinese celery cabbage can be used instead of broccoli.) The tastiness of the chicken, accentuated by the presence of abalone, causes the dish to rise to a degree of flavor which can only be described as 'the ultimate in savoriness'. This is a large dish, often made for dinner parties, and it is usually served in a tureen or 'ocean bowl'—the largest dish used on a Chinese dining table.

White-Cut Chicken with Abalone and Ham

This is an elegant party dish combining three contrasting flavors.

Serves 4–8, with other dishes

6 oz chicken breast meat
¼ lb abalone
¼ lb smoked ham

2 slices ginger root
2½ teaspoons salt
1½ tablespoons dry sherry
2 teaspoons soy sauce
2½ teaspoons sesame oil

Preparation and Cooking Add the ginger and salt to 2½ cups water and bring to the boil. Add the chicken meat and simmer for 6 minutes; then drain, reserving the water. Slice the chicken into ⅛ inch thick pieces. Reserve 1 tablespoon of the abalone water. Place the abalone in the chicken water, and simmer for 2 minutes. Drain, and cut into slices the same size as the chicken slices. Slice the ham in the same way. Arrange the slices of chicken, abalone, and ham on a white serving dish, alternating them in overlapping rows.

Serving Just before serving, mix the sherry with the abalone water, soy sauce, and sesame oil. Pour the mixture over the food on the dish.

Red-Cooked Abalone with Chicken, Mushrooms, and Bamboo Shoots

Preparation Soak the mushrooms for 20 minutes; then remove the stalks and cut the caps into quarters. Reserve ¼ cup of the mushroom water. Slice the chicken, bamboo shoots, and abalone into ⅛ inch pieces.

Serves 6–8, with other dishes

4 large Chinese dried mushrooms
1 chicken breast
½ cup bamboo shoots
¼ lb abalone

2½ tablespoons lard
1 slice ginger root
2 tablespoons soy sauce
2 teaspoons oyster sauce
2 teaspoons hoisin sauce
1¼ tablespoons dry sherry
1¼ teaspoons cornstarch
¾ teaspoon sesame oil

Cooking Heat the lard in a frying pan. Add the chicken, ginger, and bamboo shoots; stir-fry over a medium heat for 2 minutes. Add the abalone, mushrooms, soy sauce, oyster sauce, hoisin sauce, and sherry. Continue to stir-fry for 2 minutes. Blend the cornstarch with the mushroom water; then pour this mixture into the pan, add the sesame oil, and stir-fry gently for 5 minutes.

Serving Serve on a well-heated plate. This dish is considered a delicacy and is usually served only at party meals.

283

Bêche de Mer

Bêche de mer, also called sea cucumber, is considered a delicacy in China, and is served only during banquets and party dinners. It is quite tasteless in itself, but it is a great conveyor and orchestrator of other tastes and flavors. It has an interesting texture: jelly-like but firm. It is usually available dried, and requires long soaking before cooking.

Red Cooked Bêche de Mer with Pork, Mushrooms, and Bamboo Shoots

Serves 6, with other dishes

6 pieces bêche de mer (about 1 lb)
6 large Chinese dried mushrooms
½ cup bamboo shoots
¼ lb lean pork

1 scallion
2½ tablespoons lard
1 slice ginger root
¼ cup soy sauce
¾ cup dry sherry
1¼ tablespoons cornstarch
¾ cup chicken stock
¼ teaspoon monosodium glutamate
1¼ teaspoons sesame oil

Preparation Soak the bêche de mer overnight. Next day, dip it in boiling water for 15 minutes; then drain. Repeat the dipping. Soak the mushrooms for 30 minutes; then remove the stalks and cut the caps in half. Reserve ¾ cup of the mushroom water. Cut the bamboo shoots into ⅛ inch slices, shred the pork into matchstick strips, and cut the scallion into ½ inch segments.

Cooking Heat the lard in a covered frying pan. Add the bacon and ginger, and stir-fry over a medium heat for 3 minutes. Add the bamboo shoots and mushrooms, and continue to stir-fry for 2 minutes. Add the soy sauce, sherry, mushroom water, and bêche de mer. Leave to cook over a low heat for 40 minutes. Mix the cornstarch, chicken stock, and monosodium glutamate: pour the mixture into the pan, and simmer for a further 20 minutes.

Serving Pour the contents of the pan into a deep, heat-proof dish. Sprinkle with sesame oil and scallion, then place the dish in a steamer and steam for 30 minutes.

At the end of the steaming the bêche de mer has a rich, glistening gloss, and is tender but firm—highly palatable to connoisseurs.

Butterfly Bêche de Mer

Serves 6, with other dishes

10 pieces bêche de mer (about 1 lb)

Preparation Soak the bêche de mer overnight. Clean thoroughly, then cut the pieces into butterfly shapes. Dip them in boiling water and leave to soak. Hard-boil the eggs. Discard the yolks and cut the whites into thin slices. Slice the ham and chicken thin into 1½ × 1 inch pieces. Cut the scallions into 1 inch segments. Mix the bean sprouts with the cornstarch, monosodium glutamate, and 3 tablespoons water.

Cooking Boil the half chicken and the pigs' knuckle in water for 5 minutes. Discard the water. Place the chicken and pork in a heavy pan or heat-proof casserole with 1½ quarts water, half of the ginger, half of the salt, half of the sherry, and half of the scallions. Bring to the boil and simmer over a very low heat for 3 hours, with an asbestos pad under the pan. Strain the resulting 'soup', skim away the fat, and put the soup aside. Heat the lard in a deep-fryer and add the remaining ginger and scallions. Stir-fry for 2 minutes, then remove the ginger and scallions. Lower the bêche de mer into the impregnated oil to fry gently over a medium heat for 3 minutes, turning the pieces over a few times. Add the ham, sliced chicken, egg whites, pork/chicken soup, the remaining sherry, and the salt. Lower the heat and simmer gently for 35 minutes. Add the bean sprout mixture and cook for a further 2 minutes.

Serving Serve in a large soup dish or tureen.

2 eggs
1 oz smoked ham
2 oz cooked chicken breast meat
4 scallions
2½ tablespoons bean sprouts
4 teaspoons cornstarch
¼ teaspoon monosodium glutamate
half a small chicken
1 lb pigs' knuckle
2 slices ginger root
1 tablespoon salt
5 tablespoons dry sherry
2½ tablespoons lard

Clams

In contrast to bêche de mer, which needs long soaking and cooking with ingredients which have been cooked for a long time, clams are usually cooked very quickly, by steaming, simmering, poaching, or simply by pouring boiling water over them. The keynote for preparing clams in Chinese cookery is purity. The refinement comes with serving a wide range of dips and mixes on the dining table to accompany the dishes. The following are some of the most suitable dips and mixes to serve with clams: Soy-Mustard Dip, Soy-Sherry Dip, Ginger-Soy-Vinegar Dip, Soy-Chili Oil Dip, Dip for Clams, Plum Sauce, hoisin sauce, mustard, and tomato sauce (see chapter on Table Condiments).

Steamed Clams

Preparation Clean the clams thoroughly with a brush, under running water.

Cooking Place the clams on a flat, heat-proof dish. Put the dish in a steamer and steam for 7–8 minutes, until the shells open.

Serving Provide each diner with a bowl in which to mix his own dip from a selection of condiments arranged on the table. Let the diners cut the white meat from the shells and dip it into their dips and sauces.

Allow 4–6 steamer clams per person, depending on size

Clams Steeped in Chicken Stock

Serves 4

3–4 lb clams (yielding about ¾ lb clam-meat)

half a chicken (about 1½ lb)
¼ lb lean pork
2 slices ginger root
½ cup sherry
2 tablespoons light soy sauce
¼ teaspoon monosodium glutamate
pepper to taste

This is a dish from the province of Fukien, where the clams are large. Two clams per person would be sufficient for a multi-course meal

Preparation Shell the clams, remove the intestines and any impurities—only the meat should be used. Cut each piece of clam meat in half and soak in fresh water. Chop the half chicken into four pieces. Cut the pork into six pieces. Place the pieces of chicken and pork in a pan of boiling water. Boil for 3 minutes, then drain away the water and any impurities.

Cooking Place the chicken, pork, and ginger in a heavy pan or pot with 5 cups of water, and simmer gently for 2 hours. When the chicken/pork stock is almost ready, place the clam meat in a heavy soup bowl, pour in some boiling water, and steep for 1 minute. Drain away the water. Add the sherry to the clam meat and leave to marinate for 1 minute. Drain away the sherry. Remove the chicken and pork from the stock and skim away any fat and impurities. Heat the stock to boiling point. Pour 1¼ cups stock over the clams. Sprinkle with the light soy sauce, monosodium glutamate, and pepper; then serve.

This is a favorite dish in Fukien in the autumn, and is considered a great delicacy.

Pork-Stuffed Steamed Clams

Serves 4

16 steamer clams
½ lb slab bacon

1 slice ginger root
2 scallions
¾ teaspoon salt
4 teaspoons soy sauce
1¼ teaspoons sugar
1¼ teaspoons dry sherry

Preparation Steam the clams for 15 minutes. Chop the bacon. Remove the clam meat from the shells, reserving the shells for later use. Chop the clam meat coarse and mix with the minced pork. Chop the ginger root and scallions and add them to the clam/bacon mixture. Mix in the remaining ingredients, blend well, and stuff the mixture into the half-shells.

Cooking Arrange the shells on a heat-proof dish, place in a steamer and steam vigorously for 25 minutes. Alternatively, bake the stuffed clams in the oven for 20 minutes at 400°F.

Serving Serve the clams with a variety of dips and mixes.

Pork-Stuffed Deep-Fried Clams

Serves 4

Preparation Repeat the instructions given in the recipe for Pork-Stuffed Steamed Clams, adding 1 egg and 1½ tablespoons cornstarch to the pork/clam mixture.

Cooking Put the stuffed half-shells into a wire basket, six at a time. Lower into boiling oil and deep-fry for 4 minutes. Repeat until all the stuffed clams are cooked. Drain well; then serve, decorating each stuffed clam with a sprig of parsley, if desired.

An additional condiment which can be used with deep-fried clams is Salt-Cinnamon Mix (see Index).

Crabs

In Chinese cooking, crabs play a very different role from abalone, bêche de mer, and clams. They are eaten in much greater quantity, and although crab meat is sometimes used as a flavorer or cooked with other foods, it is most frequently eaten on its own. Indeed, there are a number of restaurants in Peking which serve nothing but crabs when they are in season. These are fresh-water river crabs which are served plain-steamed. On the rough table tops in the restaurant, each diner is issued with a wooden hammer with which to crack open the shells of the crabs. They are then eaten after dipping them in the dips and mixes which are amply provided in sauce dishes on the table. The meat is half-chewed, half-sucked out of the crabs while the diner holds on to the claws or feet. (We Chinese are past-masters at the art of extricating the shells and bones which get stuck between the teeth and in the mouth.) The claws are usually cracked last and eaten in the same manner. The favorite dip for crabs is Vinegar-Ginger Dip.

Stir-Fried Crabs in Egg Sauce

Preparation Remove the top shell from each crab and chop the body into four pieces. Leave a leg attached to each piece as a 'handle'. Reserve the shell for other uses. Shred the ginger and crush the garlic. Chop the scallions into ½ inch segments.

Cooking Heat the lard in a covered frying pan. Add the salt, ginger, garlic, and scallions, and stir-fry for 30 seconds over a medium heat. Put the crab pieces (including the shell) into the pan, turn the heat up to maximum, and stir-fry for 3 minutes. Pour in the Egg Sauce slowly. This causes almost an explosion of steam: the scallion/ginger/garlic impregnated steam shoots its way through the pieces of crab. Cover the pan and cook in this explosive situation for 1 minute. Serve immediately.

After the final explosive cooking with the crab, the Egg Sauce becomes extraordinarily tasty and makes a good accompaniment to rice. The dish should be eaten while very hot. It is a favorite dish with the southern Cantonese.

Serves 4–6, with other dishes

3–4 medium-sized crabs
¾ cup Egg Sauce (see Index)

3 slices ginger root
3 cloves garlic
3 scallions
3¾ tablespoons lard
2 teaspoons salt

Plain Deep-Fried Crabs

Serves 4–6, with other dishes

4 medium-sized crabs

3 slices ginger root
3 scallions
2 eggs
¼ cup flour
2½ teaspoons salt
oil for deep-frying

Preparation Steam the crabs for 10 minutes. Clean them, remove the top shell, and chop the body of each crab into six pieces, leaving each piece with a leg or claw attached as a 'handle'. Slightly crack the claws with the side or back of a chopper. Chop the ginger and the scallions fine. Beat the eggs lightly, blend with the flour, 2 tablespoons of water, ginger, scallions, and salt, and mix to a smooth batter. Dip the meat-end of each section of crab into the batter to coat.

Cooking Heat the oil in a deep-fryer. Place six sections of crab in a wire basket and deep-fry for 3–3½ minutes over a high heat, then keep warm on a heated plate. Repeat until all the crab sections are cooked.

Serving Serve hot with a variety of dips and mixes.

Crab Rice

Serves 6–8, with other dishes

2 large crabs
1 lb glutinous rice

2 scallions
2 slices ginger root
5 tablespoons dry sherry
5 tablespoons soy sauce
1¼ tablespoons vegetable oil
¾ teaspoon salt
¾ teaspoon sugar

Crab rice is a typical coastal dish, much loved by children but of doubtful value to Western infants, owing to the danger of broken shells becoming stuck in their throats, which somehow seldom happens to the Chinese!

Preparation Mince the scallions and ginger; then combine them with the sherry and 4 tablespoons soy sauce as a marinade. Chop one of the crabs into four to six pieces through the shell, and crack the other crab. Place them in a large basin with the marinade. Wash the rice in cold water until the water runs clear.

Cooking Place the rice in a saucepan and pour in 2 quarts water. Bring to the boil and boil for 5 minutes. Drain away the water. Pack the chopped crab at the bottom of a large heat-proof dish, which must be at least 4 inches deep. Pour the rice on top of the chopped crab, packing it down. Press the other crab on top of the rice. Mix the remaining marinade with 1 tablespoon soy sauce and the oil, salt, and sugar. Mix well, then sprinkle over the crab and rice. Place the dish in a steamer and steam for 35–40 minutes.

Serving Serve from the heat-proof dish. After eating the top crab, which now appears half-buried in the expanded rice, both children and adults enjoy digging for the pieces of crab buried in the rice. For crab connoisseurs, there is an attractive aroma about rice cooked in this manner, in addition to the general intrigue of the dish.

Quick Stir-Fried Crabmeat with Pork and Leeks

Preparation Shred the pork and ginger, crush and chop the garlic, and cut the leeks into ½ inch sections. Beat the egg lightly.

Cooking Heat the lard in a frying pan. Place the ginger, garlic, salt, and leeks in the pan, and stir-fry over a high heat for 2 minutes. Add the pork and continue to stir-fry for a further 2 minutes; then add the crabmeat and stir-fry for 2 minutes more, still over a high heat. Stir in the beaten egg, streaming it evenly over the pan. Mix the soy sauce with the sherry, 2 tablespoons of water, sugar, and cornstarch, and pour the mixture into the pan as soon as the egg has set. Stir gently over a low heat for 1½ minutes; serve on a well-heated dish.

Serves 6, with other dishes

½ lb lean pork
3 leeks
¾ lb lump crabmeat

2 slices ginger root
2 cloves garlic
1 egg
¼ cup lard
1½ teaspoons salt
2 tablespoons soy sauce
2½ tablespoons dry sherry
1¼ teaspoons sugar
1 tablespoon cornstarch

Stir-Fried Crabmeat with Eggs and Scallions

Preparation and Cooking Repeat the instructions given in the recipe for Quick Stir-Fried Crabmeat with Pork and Leeks, using half the amount of pork and crabmeat, substituting 4 scallions cut into 1 inch segments for the leeks, and using 6 eggs instead of one. No sauce mixture is required at the end, but sprinkle 1 tablespoon soy sauce and 1 tablespoon sherry over the mixture. After 1 minute of stir-frying, the mixture can be served. This is a quick, simple, but entirely effective dish.

Serves 6, with other dishes

Crabmeat in Steamed Eggs

Preparation Beat the eggs lightly and mix them with the stock and salt in a heat-proof serving bowl. Cut the scallions into 1 inch segments. Divide the crabmeat into two piles. Add half of the crabmeat to the egg mixture, together with the crab liquid. Stir to mix. Reserve the other half of the crabmeat for later use.

Cooking Place the heat-proof bowl in a steamer and steam gently for 25 minutes. Meanwhile, heat the oil in a frying pan. Add the ham, scallions, and remaining crabmeat. Stir-fry together for 1½ minutes.

Serving Remove the heat-proof bowl from the steamer. Garnish the top of the steamed egg and crab mixture with the stir-fried crab mixture. Serve from the heat-proof bowl.

Serves 4–6, with other dishes

3 eggs
4–5 oz lump crabmeat

2½ cups chicken stock *or* superior
stock (cold)
1¼ teaspoons salt
2 scallions
4 teaspoons vegetable oil
1 oz ham

Crabmeat with Braised Celery and Asparagus

Serves 6–8, with other dishes

½ lb celery
½ lb asparagus tips
½ lb lump crabmeat

3 tablespoons light soy sauce
2½ tablespoons crab liquid
5 tablespoons white wine
1 cup chicken stock
2 slices ginger root
1¼ tablespoons vegetable oil
¾ teaspoon salt
1¼ tablespoons cornstarch
¼ teaspoon monosodium glutamate

This makes an interesting party dish.

Cooking Parboil the celery and asparagus tips separately by simmering them in water for 5 minutes. Drain, then place them together in a saucepan. Add the soy sauce, crab water, 2 tablespoons of the wine, and half of the chicken stock. Bring to the boil, cover, and simmer gently until the liquid is reduced to about half its original quantity. This should take about 20 minutes. Turn the vegetables over a couple of times during this period. Shred the ginger. Heat the oil in a frying pan; add the ginger, salt, and crabmeat, and stir-fry gently for 2 minutes. Meanwhile, blend the cornstarch with the remaining chicken stock and the monosodium glutamate. Add the mixture to the crabmeat, with the remaining 2 tablespoons of wine. Allow to cook and thicken for 2 minutes. Spoon half of the crabmeat and liquid into the pan with the vegetables and cook for 1 minute.

Serving Pour the vegetable mixture into a deep serving dish. Pour the remaining crabmeat and gravy from the frying pan onto the vegetable mixture as a garnish. Serve immediately.

Lobster

Although popular in Western cuisine, lobsters do not occupy nearly so important a place in Chinese food and cooking as crabs do. This is mainly due to their much higher cost and lack of availability. Lobsters are called Lung Hsia or Dragon Crabs in Chinese, and almost all crab dishes can be prepared using lobsters, except for those in which flaked crabmeat is scramble-fried with eggs, as lobstermeat does not flake in quite the same manner as crabmeat.

Plain Deep-Fried Lobster

Serves 4–6, with other dishes

A 1½–2 lb lobster

1 slice ginger root
2 scallions
1 clove garlic

A rather extravagant dish with an excellent flavor.

Preparation Chop the ginger and the scallions, and crush the garlic. Beat the egg lightly and blend it with the flour, salt, 2 tablespoons water, ginger, garlic, and scallions. Slice the lobster in half through the shell lengthwise, using a sharp cleaver; then chop it into 1½ inch sections, including the claws. Dip each piece of lobster into the batter.

Cooking Heat the oil in a deep-fryer. Place half of the batter-coated pieces of lobster in a wire basket and deep-fry in the boiling oil for 3 minutes. Repeat this process with the remaining lobster pieces.

Serving When all the lobster pieces have been fried, serve them quickly on a well-heated dish. Eat with the usual array of table dips and mixes.

1 egg
5 tablespoons flour
1¼ teaspoons salt
oil for deep-frying

Lobster Stir-Fried with Pork

Sections of unshelled lobster, fried with chopped pork, are called 'Cantonese Lobster'.

Serves 4–6, with other dishes

A 2–2½ lb lobster
¼ lb pork

Preparation Slice the lobster in half lengthwise through the shell, using a sharp cleaver; then chop it into 1½ inch sections, including the claws. Chop the pork, ginger, and garlic fine; chop the scallions into ¼ inch sections.

Cooking Heat the oil in a covered frying pan. Add the pork, garlic, ginger, and salt, and stir-fry over a high heat for 2 minutes. Add the lobster pieces and the scallions, and continue to stir-fry for 2½ minutes. Pour in the chicken stock and soy sauce, and cook, covered, for 3 minutes. Meanwhile, beat the eggs lightly with 1 tablespoon water and the sherry; mix the cornstarch in another bowl with 5 tablespoons water. Add the cornstarch mixture to the frying pan and stir until the liquid in the pan thickens. Stir in the egg/water/sherry mixture, streaming it evenly over the contents of the frying pan. Stir, and dish out onto a well-heated serving plate.

2 slices ginger root
2 cloves garlic
2 scallions
5 tablespoons vegetable oil
1¼ teaspoons salt
¾ cup chicken stock
1¼ tablespoons soy sauce
2 eggs
2½ tablespoons dry sherry
1 tablespoon cornstarch

This is an excellent dish to eat when drinking wine or to accompany rice.

Steamed Marinated Lobster

Preparation Slice the lobster in half lengthwise through the shell, using a sharp cleaver; then chop it into 1½ inch sections, including the claws. Arrange the pieces of lobster, meat side up, on a large heat-proof dish. Chop the ginger, garlic, and scallions fine, and mix with the soy sauce, sherry, oil, and sugar. Beat them together lightly, then pour the mixture over the lobster sections. Leave to stand for 1 hour.

Serves 4–6, with other dishes

A 1½–2 lb lobster

2 slices ginger root
1 clove garlic
2 scallions
2 tablespoons soy sauce
2½ tablespoons dry sherry
4 teaspoons vegetable oil
1¼ teaspoons sugar
4 teaspoons chopped chives

Cooking Place the dish in a steamer and steam vigorously for 20 minutes, until the lobster turns bright red.

Serving Sprinkle the meat side of the lobster pieces with chopped chives; then serve.

Stir-Fried Lobster in Sweet and Sour Sauce

Serves 4–6, with other dishes

A 1½–2 lb lobster

2 slices ginger root
2 cloves garlic
2 scallions
2½ tablespoons lard
½ teaspoon salt
¼ cup chicken stock
1 tablespoon cornstarch
3 teaspoons soy sauce
3 teaspoons dry sherry
2 tablespoons vinegar
3 teaspoons tomato puree
1½ tablespoons sugar
2½ tablespoons water
2½ tablespoons orange juice

Preparation Slice the lobster in half lengthwise through the shell, using a sharp cleaver. Then chop it into 1½ inch sections, including the claws. Shred the ginger, crush and chop the garlic, and cut the scallions into ½ inch segments.

Cooking Heat the lard in a frying pan. Add the ginger, garlic, scallions, and salt; stir-fry for 1 minute over a medium heat. Place the pieces of lobster in the pan and stir-fry over a high heat for 3 minutes. Pour in the chicken stock and continue to stir for 30 seconds. Blend the remaining ingredients smoothly and stir the mixture into the pan. Continue to mix, stirring gently, for 1 minute. Serve immediately.

Lobster Meat Stir-Fried with Chicken and Vegetables

Serves 6–8, with other dishes

¾ lb lobster meat
½ lb chicken breast meat

¼ cup bamboo shoots
¼ cup cucumber
2 slices ginger root
2 scallions
2½ tablespoons vegetable oil
¾ teaspoon salt
¼ cup button mushrooms
2 tablespoons light soy sauce
¾ teaspoon chili oil
½ cup chicken stock
3 teaspoons cornstarch
¼ teaspoon monosodium glutamate
2½ tablespoons dry sherry
1 oz smoked ham, chopped

Preparation Cut the lobster meat and the chicken into ⅓ inch cubes. Cut the bamboo shoots and cucumber into similar pieces, after scraping (but not peeling) the cucumber. Shred the ginger and cut the scallions into 1 inch segments.

Cooking Heat the vegetable oil in a frying pan. Add the ginger, then the bamboo shoots, cucumber, salt, and chicken; stir-fry over a high heat for 1½ minutes. Add the lobster meat, mushrooms, and scallions, and stir-fry for a further minute; then add the soy sauce and chili oil; stir for 30 seconds. Pour in the chicken stock and leave to cook for 2 minutes. Mix the cornstarch with the monosodium glutamate, sherry, and 2 tablespoons water, blending well. Pour this mixture into the pan and stir to thicken.

Serving Pour the contents of the frying pan onto a serving dish. Garnish with chopped ham; then serve.

Stir-Fried Lobster with Red Wine-Sediment Paste

Serves 4–6, with other dishes

This is a dish from Fukien. In this south-east coastal province, red wine-sediment paste is a favorite cooking ingredient.

Preparation Slice the lobster in half lengthwise through the shell, using a sharp cleaver; then chop it into 1½ inch sections, including the claws. Shred the ginger, crush and chop the garlic, and cut the scallions into ½ inch segments.

Cooking Heat 2 tablespoons of the lard in a frying pan. Add the ginger, garlic, scallions, and salt, and stir-fry over a medium heat for 30 seconds. Add the pieces of lobster and stir-fry over a high heat for 2 minutes. Remove the lobster pieces from the pan, put them aside, and keep them warm. Put the remaining lard in the pan together with the hoisin sauce and wine-sediment paste (or substitute, below). Stir-fry over a medium heat for 30 seconds until the oil and sauces are well blended. Return the pieces of lobster to the pan. Raise the heat to maximum and stir-fry the lobster pieces in the oil and sauce for 30 seconds. Serve immediately.

A 1½–2 lb lobster
2½ tablespoons red-wine sediment paste

2 slices ginger root
2 cloves garlic
2 scallions
3¾ tablespoons lard
¼ teaspoon salt
1¼ tablespoons hoisin sauce

Wine-Sediment Paste Substitute

If you are unable to obtain red wine-sediment paste, use the following recipe to prepare a substitute.

Preparation Chop the onion, garlic, and ginger fine.

Cooking Stir-fry the onion, garlic, and ginger in oil for 2 minutes. Add all the remaining ingredients. Stir and mix for 1 minute. Allow the mixture (or paste) to stand and cool before use.

1 medium-sized onion
2 cloves garlic
2 slices ginger root
2½ tablespoons vegetable oil
1½ tablespoons soy bean paste
1¼ teaspoons sugar
2 tablespoons tomato puree
1¼ teaspoons red soy bean cheese
1½ tablespoons dry sherry
2½ teaspoons brandy

Oyster Dishes

Fresh oysters are a little-known food item to the Chinese population, except to people who live along or near the east coast of China. After all, China is an enormous continental country and fresh oysters could not travel very far and remain fresh before the days of refrigeration. To the majority of Chinese people oysters come only in dried form, and in that state they are used primarily for flavoring other types of food. As such, oysters are merely one among a number of similar types of dried sea food flavorers, the most important being abalone and squid.

It is not surprising, therefore, that there are not many fresh oyster dishes. Two of the most delicious ways of eating oysters are oyster omelets (or oyster cakes) and barbecued oysters. The following are several of the more widely-practiced dishes.

Deep-Fried Oysters in Batter

Preparation Shell the oysters. Chop the scallions fine, and season the oysters with salt, pepper, chili pepper, and half of

Serves 4–8, with other dishes

24 oysters

3 scallions
salt to taste
pepper to taste
chili pepper to taste
2 eggs
1 cup flour
vegetable oil for deep-frying

the chopped scallion. Mix the eggs, flour, and 6 tablespoons of water into a smooth batter. Dip the oysters into the batter.

Cooking Heat the oil in a deep-fryer (or Chinese semi-deep-frying pan), using ½–1 inch oil. Place a few oysters at a time in the boiling oil to fry for 2½–3 minutes until golden-brown. Remove them with a slotted spoon, and drain.

Serving Place the oysters on a well-heated dish, garnish with the remaining scallions, and serve.

Deep-Fried Oysters with Bacon

Serves 4–8, with other dishes

Preparation and Cooking Repeat the recipe for Deep-Fried Oysters in Batter, using an extra egg and ¼ cup extra flour in the batter. You will also need 6 strips of bacon. Cut each strip crosswise into four pieces; dip oysters and bacon pieces into the batter. Heat the oil in a deep-fryer. Wrap each oyster in 1 piece of bacon, and with the help of a pair of bamboo chopsticks (not plastic, as they would melt in the hot oil), immerse the bacon-wrapped oyster in the boiling oil. Repeat until six wrapped oysters are frying at the same time. Fry for 3 minutes; then remove with a slotted spoon and drain. Serve garnished with chopped scallions. The crispy bacon adds a new interest to the oyster.

Oysters with Pork, Vegetables, and Transparent Noodles

Serves 6–10, with other dishes

12 dried oysters
12 fresh oysters
½ cup lean pork
½ cup bamboo shoots
½ cup celery
½ cup broccoli
1 lettuce
6 golden needles (tiger-lily buds)
4 large Chinese dried mushrooms
½ cup transparent bean-thread
  noodles

¼ cup vegetable oil
¾ teaspoon salt
2½ cups chicken stock
2½ tablespoons soy sauce
2½ tablespoons dry sherry
¾ tablespoon cornstarch
¼ teaspoon monosodium glutamate

This is another Fukien dish which follows the Chinese tradition of flavoring fresh food with dried and pickled foods.

Preparation Soak the dried oysters for 1 hour, the golden needles and mushrooms separately in warm water for 30 minutes, and the transparent noodles for 20 minutes. Remove the mushroom stalks, shred the mushroom caps, and shell the fresh oysters. Shred the pork and bamboo shoots. Cut the celery, broccoli, and lettuce into 1 inch segments.

Cooking Heat the oil in a large saucepan. Stir-fry the pork, bamboo shoots, and salt for 3 minutes. Add the broccoli and celery; continue to stir-fry for 2 minutes. Then pour in the stock, add the golden needles, mushrooms, soy sauce, sherry, noodles, and dried oysters; bring to the boil and simmer gently for 20 minutes. Add the fresh oysters and lettuce, stir, and continue to simmer for 3 minutes. Mix the cornstarch, monosodium glutamate, and ¼ cup water until smoothly blended; stir into the pan, and after 1 minute of further cooking, serve in a large tureen or soup bowl.

This is a great dish to eat with rice.

Oysters with Pork, Vegetables, and Bean Curd

Repeat the recipe for Fresh and Dried Oysters with Pork, Vegetables, and Transparent Noodles, substituting 2–3 cakes of fresh bean curd, cut into slices, for the transparent noodles.

Serves 6–10, with other dishes

Red-Cooked Pork with Dried Oysters

Repeat the recipe for Red-Cooked Pork (see Index). Add 10 dried oysters (soaked for 1 hour and cleaned), placing them in between the pieces of pork, and simmering them together for 1¾ hours. Although oysters in pork is a cultivated taste, it is quite easily acceptable to the uninitiated. To the connoisseurs, the oysters add an inimitable richness of flavor to the already rich pork.

Serves 6–10, with other dishes

Scallops

Although scallops are frequently used dried, the flesh has a texture similar to that of clams, and can easily be stir-fried or steamed to excellent effect. The dried scallop used for flavoring is usually not a whole scallop, but the root muscles. Hence the regular shape of dried scallop is an amber-colored disc, with a diameter of ½–1 inch and a thickness of about ½ inch. It is considered to have a more delicate flavor than any other type of dried seafood, and is usually added to slow-cooking foods and dishes, such as soups, soft rice, and stewed dishes. Dried scallop must be soaked overnight, and when simmered and shredded, it can be used in various stir-fried combinations.

Steamed Scallops with Ham, Ginger, and Scallions

Serves 4–8, with other dishes

¾–1 lb scallops
2 oz smoked ham
1 slice ginger root
2 scallions

Preparation Cut each scallop into four pieces. Marinate them in sherry, sugar, and soy sauce for 30 minutes; then drain, reserving the marinade. Shred the ginger, and chop the ham and the scallions coarse.

Cooking Place the pieces of scallop neatly on a heat-proof dish. Sprinkle with ginger, scallions, ham, and the remaining marinade. Steam vigorously for 15 minutes, and serve.

5 tablespoons dry sherry
1¼ teaspoons sugar
2½ tablespoons soy sauce

Stir-Fried Scallops with Chinese Cabbage or Celery and Mushrooms

Serves 6–8, with other dishes

½ lb scallops
½ lb Chinese cabbage *or* celery
4 large Chinese dried mushrooms

2½ tablespoons vegetable oil
2 slices ginger root
¾ teaspoon salt
1¼ tablespoons light soy sauce
2½ tablespoons dry sherry
¼ teaspoon monosodium glutamate
5 tablespoons chicken stock

Preparation Soak the mushrooms in warm water for 30 minutes, remove the stalks, and cut the caps into quarters. Slice the scallops into quarters, and the cabbage or celery into 1½ inch segments. Blanch the cabbage or celery by immersing it in boiling water for 1½ minutes; drain.

Cooking Heat the oil in a frying pan. Add the ginger and salt, fry for 30 seconds, then add the pieces of scallop and stir-fry over a medium heat for 2 minutes; remove and put aside to keep warm. Discard the ginger. Add the cabbage or celery to the pan and stir-fry for 3 minutes; then add the mushrooms, soy sauce, and 1 tablespoon of the sherry. Continue to turn and stir-fry for 2 minutes more; then sprinkle with monosodium glutamate and pour in the chicken stock. Cover, and cook for 5 minutes; then return the scallops to the pan and stir-fry for 1 minute more, adding the remaining sherry. Serve and eat immediately.

Stir-Fried Scallops in Red Wine-Sediment Paste

Serves 4–8, with other dishes

¾ lb scallops
2½ tablespoons wine-sediment paste

1¼ teaspoons fermented black beans
2 slices ginger root
1 oz smoked ham
2 scallions
3¾ tablespoons vegetable oil
1¼ tablespoons hoisin sauce
1¼ tablespoons dry sherry
¾ teaspoon salt

Preparation Soak the black beans for 20 minutes, and mash. Shred the ginger, and chop the ham and the scallions coarse.

Cooking Heat the oil in a frying pan. Stir-fry ginger, scallions, and black beans for 1 minute over a medium heat; add the wine-sediment paste, hoisin sauce, and sherry, and stir-fry for 1 minute more, mixing the oil with the sauce. Add the pieces of scallop. Sprinkle with salt and ham, and stir gently, mixing the scallop with the sauce thoroughly for 2½ minutes over a high heat. Serve in a well-heated dish, and eat immediately.

Stir-Fried Scallops with Diced Chicken, Mushrooms, and Cucumber

Serves 4–8, with other dishes

¾ lb scallop meat
4 large Chinese dried mushrooms
6 oz chicken breast meat

Preparation Soak the mushrooms in warm water for 30 minutes. Drain, discard the stems, and cut the caps into quarters. Dice the scallops, chicken, and cucumber (unpeeled) into ⅓ inch cubes.

Cooking Heat the oil in a large frying pan. Add the cucumber, chicken, and scallops, and stir-fry over a high heat for 2 minutes. Pour in the mushrooms and soy sauce, lower the heat to medium, and stir-fry for another minute. Add the chicken stock and sherry, and stir-fry for a further minute. Mix the cornstarch, monosodium glutamate, and pepper with 3 tablespoons water, and stream evenly into the frying pan. When the contents of the pan thicken, pour onto a well-heated dish, and serve immediately.

quarter of a medium cucumber

4 tablespoons vegetable oil
2½ tablespoons light soy sauce
5 tablespoons chicken stock
1¼ tablespoons dry sherry
2 teaspoons cornstarch
¼ teaspoon monosodium glutamate
pepper to taste

Steamed, Dried Scallops with Cabbage, Ham, and Chicken Stock

Preparation Soak the scallops overnight in ½ cup water. Drain, reserving the water. Soak them in sherry for a further 6 hours, turning them over every 2 hours. Retain the sherry. Slice the ham thin into 1½ × ½ inch pieces. Blanch cabbage, cut it in half lengthwise, and trim away coarse leaves.

Cooking and Serving Place the cabbage in a saucepan, add the chicken stock, salt, scallop water, scallop sherry, soy sauce, and pepper, and bring to the boil. Simmer for 2 minutes, turning the cabbage over once. Transfer the cabbage to an oval or oblong heat-proof dish. Pour in the chicken stock mixture, and arrange the pieces of scallop and slices of ham alternately on top. Place the dish in a steamer and steam vigorously, uncovered, for 45 minutes. Serve in the original dish.

Serves 4–8, with other dishes

12 dried scallops
1 lb Chinese cabbage *or* celery
¼ lb smoked ham
1¼ cups chicken stock

½ cup dry sherry
¾ teaspoon salt
2½ tablespoons light soy sauce
dash of pepper

Squid

Although the squid is not considered the most refined seafood in China, it has many points to recommend it. Firstly, it is plentiful and cheap—it is eaten in quantity by poorer people. Secondly it is quick to cook. Thirdly, although it has less flavor than many other types of seafood, it can be made tasty very easily by seasoning or cross-cooking with other types of food; and fourthly, although its texture is like neither meat nor fish, it has a certain firmness which enables it to be chewed with great satisfaction, especially when eaten with rice.

Fresh Squid Stir-Fried with Vegetables

Preparation Cut the squid into 1½ × ½ inch strips. Chop the scallions into 1 inch segments, and shred the celery, bamboo shoots, and lettuce.

Serves 4–8, with other dishes

1 lb fresh squid
2 scallions

1 cup celery
2½ tablespoons bamboo shoots
¼ cup lettuce

¼ cup vegetable oil
2 slices ginger root
¾ teaspoon salt
1¼ tablespoons lard
1 tablespoon soy sauce
1¼ tablespoons hoisin sauce
2 teaspoons oyster sauce
1¼ tablespoons dry sherry
¾ teaspoon red bean curd cheese
1¼ tablespoons cornstarch
¼ teaspoon monosodium glutamate
½ cup chicken stock

Cooking Heat 2 tablespoons of the oil in a frying pan. Add the squid, scallions, ginger, and salt, and stir-fry for 3 minutes over a high heat. Remove the pieces of squid and put aside. Discard the ginger. Add the remaining oil, celery, bamboo shoots, and lettuce and stir-fry gently for 4 minutes over medium heat. Remove from the pan and put aside. Place the lard in the pan, add the sauces, sherry, and bean curd cheese, and stir until the fat and the sauces are well blended. Return the squid to the pan, stir-fry for 1 minute, then remove and keep hot. Return all the vegetables to the pan, toss and mix well with the gravy for 30 seconds; then blend the cornstarch and monosodium glutamate with the chicken stock and stir the mixture into the pan, mixing well with the contents. Heat for 2 minutes, and serve in a deep dish, using the vegetables as a base and piling the squid on top.

Fresh Squid Stir-Fried with Red-Cooked Pork and Mushrooms

Serves 5–6, with other dishes

1 lb squid
⅓ lb Red-Cooked Pork (see Index)
6 Chinese dried mushrooms

2 scallions
2½ tablespoons vegetable oil
5 tablespoons Red-Cooked Pork gravy
1¼ tablespoons dry sherry
2 teaspoons soy sauce
2 teaspoons cornstarch

Preparation Cut the squid into 1½ × ½ inch pieces. Soak the mushrooms for 30 minutes in warm water; drain and discard stalks, but reserve 4–5 tablespoons mushroom water. Cut each mushroom cap into four. Slice the pork thin and cut the scallions into 1 inch segments.

Cooking Heat the oil in a frying pan and fry the squid and scallions quickly over high heat for 1 minute. Add the pork, pork gravy, mushrooms, mushroom water, sherry, and soy sauce, and continue to stir-fry for 3 minutes. Blend the cornstarch with 3 tablespoons water and stir into the pan. Serve as soon as the liquid thickens.

This is a quickly cooked dish which can be prepared in a short time if the Red-Cooked Pork is available; this is why it often appears on a Chinese dinner table.

Red-Cooked Pork with Dried Squid

Serves 4–8, with other dishes

In the recipe for Fresh Squid Stir-Fried with Red-Cooked Pork and Mushrooms, the pork and pork gravy are used to flavor fresh squid. In this recipe, rich, golden-brown, dried squid, which is often hung in Chinese provision shops and restaurant windows, is used to add flavor to the pork. This is a kind of reversal process—a piece of Chinese culinary sophistication which is curiously effective.

Preparation Repeat the recipe for Red-Cooked Pork (see Index). Soak ⅓ lb dried squid overnight and cut into 1 inch squares. Place them alternately between the pieces of pork, and allow to simmer together for 1¾ hours from the commencement of cooking. The dried squid gives an additional savory flavor to the pork—a flavor beloved of the south-east coastal people of China. The flavor of dried squid is very similar to that of anchovy. It can be used not only to flavor meat, but even to flavor fresh squid itself.

Shark's Fin

Shark's fin, like bêche de mer, is a delicacy which belongs to the sphere of Chinese haute cuisine. It is only served at party dinners and banquets. The two materials have a curiously similar texture, jelly-like but firm. Shark's fin is somewhat stickier in the body and crunchier in the fin bones which makes it more interesting than bêche de mer. As both come in dried form, they need prolonged soaking and many changes of water before they are ready for cooking. In China, a shark's fin dish can almost be considered a culinary joke, for its takes 3 days to prepare, and only 3 minutes to eat. The reason why preparation of shark's fin takes such a long time is because in its original state, it is as tough as rhinoceros' horn. If it is to be softened into a jellified state without destroying or changing its essential texture, it requires very careful handling. Since this ingredient seems to intrigue Western fancy, we will go into it in some detail.

Braised Red-Cooked Shark's Fins

Preparation Soak the shark's fins overnight. Soak the dried shrimp for 30 minutes in warm water, then drain, discarding the water. Blanch the cabbage or celery, and drain. Soak the mushrooms for 30 minutes, remove the stalks, and shred the caps (discard the water). Shred the bamboo shoots and cut the scallion into 1 inch segments. Scrub, clean, and simmer the shark's fins gently in 5 cups of water for 1 hour; change the water and simmer for another 1½ hours; then drain.

Cooking Heat the chicken stock in a pan. Add the ginger and shrimp, simmer gently for 30 minutes; then drain and discard the shrimp and ginger. Add the cabbage to the stock, and simmer for 15 minutes. Heat the lard in another pan, and stir-fry the scallion, bamboo shoots, mushrooms, and salt for 1 minute; add the soy sauce, wine, shark's fins, and meat gravy. Simmer for 3 minutes; then pour in the chicken stock and cabbage, and simmer for a further 20 minutes. Blend the cornstarch and monosodium glutamate with 3 tablespoons water, add to the pan, and stir until the contents thicken. Sprinkle with sesame oil.

Serving Serve in a large soup bowl or tureen, arranging the fins on top of the cabbage.

Serves 6–10, with other dishes

1 lb dried shark's fins

1¼ tablespoons dried shrimp
¼ lb Chinese celery cabbage *or* celery
4 large Chinese dried mushrooms
¼ cup bamboo shoots
1 scallion
1¼ cups chicken stock
1 slice ginger root
2½ tablespoons lard
½ teaspoon salt
2½ tablespoons soy sauce
5 tablespoons white wine
1 cup Red-Cooked Meat gravy (see Index)
1 tablespoon cornstarch
¼ teaspoon monosodium glutamate
1¼ teaspoons sesame oil

Crab-Egg (Spawn) Shark's Fins

Serves 6–10, with other dishes

¾ cup crab eggs (*or* spawn)
3 lb dried raw shark's fins

4 slices ginger root
½ cup lard
½ cup white wine
10 cups secondary stock
2½ tablespoons dry sherry
5 cups superior stock
¼ lb crabmeat
2 tablespoons cornstarch
2½ tablespoons finely chopped ham

This is the recipe for the dish as prepared by the famous Lee Ho Foo Restaurant, Canton.

Preparation Trim and pare the shark's fins with a sharp knife. Soak them in water for 6 hours; drain and discard water. Transfer the fins to an earthen pot or casserole, add 5 cups water and simmer for one hour. Change the water and simmer gently for another hour. Remove the fins, clean and scrub away any impurities; then place them in fresh water and simmer gently for another 2 hours. Take out the fins for a final trimming, paring, and cleaning. Change the water again and simmer very gently for 8 hours. The fins are at last partially ready for cooking. Simmer the slices of ginger root in 8 tablespoons water for 6 minutes. Leave to stand for 1 hour, then discard the ginger. Heat 2 tablespoons of the lard in a heavy pot; add half of the white wine, 3 tablespoons of the ginger water, and 5 cups of the secondary stock. Place the fins in the pot and simmer for 30 minutes, then repeat, using equal amounts of the same ingredients, and simmering the shark's fins for another 30 minutes. Drain the fins, and keep warm.

Cooking Heat 1 tablespoon of the lard in a heat-proof pot over a medium heat. Add the sherry and superior stock, the fins, and the fresh crabmeat. Bring to a gentle boil, add the cornstarch, blended with 6 tablespoons water, stir for 30 seconds and remove from the heat. Add the crab eggs, and replace on the heat, and when the contents start to simmer again, add the remaining lard. (Lard is used in Chinese cooking to give smoothness.)

Serving Pour the contents of the pot into a large well-decorated soup bowl or tureen. Garnish with finely chopped ham and serve.

Shark's fins are appreciated for their texture and their savoriness.

Shark's Fin Omelet

Serves 4–8, with other dishes

¼ lb shark's fin
6 eggs

3 Chinese dried mushrooms

Preparation Prepare the shark's fin as in the recipe for Braised Red-Cooked Shark's Fins. Soak the mushrooms for 20 minutes, then shred them. Beat the eggs lightly, adding the salt. Shred the bamboo shoots, ginger, and ham. Cut the shark's fin into slivers.

Cooking Heat the lard in a small frying pan. Add the mushrooms, bamboo shoots, and ginger, and stir-fry for 30 seconds over a high heat. Add the shark's fin, soy sauce, and wine to the pan and stir-fry together over a medium heat for 2 minutes. Reduce the heat to low, and cook, covered, for a further 3 minutes. Meanwhile heat the oil in a larger frying pan over a high heat. Swirl the oil around a little so that it covers all the surface of the pan. Lower the heat and pour in the beaten egg; tilt the handle of the pan so that the egg is well spread, and heat for 1 minute. Pour in the shark's fin mixture from the small frying pan, sprinkle with the shredded ham, and spread down the middle of the eggs. Lift the edges of the eggs with a spatula. After lifting both edges and folding them over, turn the whole omelet with the aid of a spoon and spatula. Pour the sherry over the omelet, serve and eat immediately.

¾ teaspoon salt
2 tablespoons bamboo shoots
1 slice ginger root
1 oz ham
1¼ tablespoons lard
1¼ tablespoons soy sauce
¼ cup white wine
¼ cup vegetable oil
1¼ tablespoons dry sherry

Shrimp and Prawns

We make no distinction in China between shrimp and prawns. They are both called 'Hsia'. However, Hsia from the muddy coasts of Chile, usually known as Pacific Prawns in Britain, and very popular with restaurants both abroad and in Peking and Tientsin, are about ten times the size of the smaller fresh-water specimens from the lakes and rivers of the south.

Shrimp and prawns are very important items of the Chinese diet. This is partly because of their wide availability, and partly because of the quality of their flesh, which enables them to combine so well with numerous other items of food, both meat and vegetables. After pork and chicken, they are probably one of the most widely-used animal products for human consumption in China.

Although the demand for shrimp and prawns has shot up both in the West, and in the world as a whole in recent years (indeed there now appears to be a general shortage), they have been popular in China for centuries. Unlike other seafoods which are time-consuming to prepare, and still others which are in themselves tasteless and require a host of other materials to be cooked with them in order to make them palatable and appealing, shrimp and prawns are highly tasty, and can generally be prepared within a very short time. Because of their shape and size, they are particularly suitable for the Chinese practice of cross-cooking, requiring no further cutting, shaping, or reduction. Hence the number of recipes using these two items is inexhaustible. The following are a few of the more popular ones. Except for dishes in which very large shrimp are needed, prawns and shrimp are usually interchangeable.

Stir-Fried Shrimp with Green Peas

Preparation Shred the ginger, blend the cornstarch with the chicken stock, shell the shrimp, and cut the bamboo shoots into ¼ inch cubes.

Cooking Heat 1½ tablespoons of the oil in a frying pan over medium heat. Add the shrimp, ginger, and salt; stir-fry for 1

Serves 4–8, with other dishes

10 oz shrimp
1 cup green peas

1 slice ginger root

2 teaspoons cornstarch
5 tablespoons chicken stock
2 tablespoons bamboo shoots
3¼ tablespoons vegetable oil
½ teaspoon salt
1¼ tablespoons dry sherry
pepper to taste

minute, and set aside. Add the remaining oil to the pan together with the bamboo shoots and peas, and stir-fry gently over a high heat for 2 minutes. Return the shrimp to the pan and stir a few times. Add the cornstarch mixture, the sherry, and pepper, and stir-fry gently for 1 minute. Serve immediately, and eat while hot.

Stir-Fried Shrimp with Bean Sprouts and Shredded Ham

Serves 4–8, with other dishes

10 oz shrimp
1 cup bean sprouts
1 oz smoked ham

2 scallions
¼ cup vegetable oil
¾ teaspoon salt
1¼ tablespoons soy sauce
1¼ teaspoon sugar
1¼ tablespoons vinegar
1¼ tablespoons dry sherry

Preparation Shell the shrimp, blanch and drain the bean sprouts, shred the ham, and chop the scallions into 1 inch segments.

Cooking Heat 1½ tablespoons of the oil in a frying pan. Add the shrimp, scallions, and salt; stir-fry over a high heat for 1 minute, then remove from the pan and set aside. Pour the remaining oil into the pan. Add the bean sprouts, and stir-fry for 1 minute over a high heat. Add the soy sauce, sugar, and vinegar, and stir-fry for another 1½ minutes. Return the shrimp and scallions to the pan, and stir-fry together for a further 1½ minutes. Pour in the sherry, and stir once or twice. Garnish with the ham, and serve immediately on a well-heated platter.

As can be seen from the last two recipes, shrimp are usually stir-fried together with two or more vegetables. The following are some of the favorite combinations, and the shrimps are prepared and cooked in much the same way as when cooked with peas and bean sprouts; that is, they are first of all fried quickly with some ginger or scallions, or both, then put aside. The vegetables are stir-fried for a longer or shorter period (depending on their toughness) with the addition of some water or stock.

Finally, the shrimp and vegetables are returned to the pan and cross-fried together for a minute or two with sherry to make the dish aromatic. Cornstarch blended with water is added when the flavor of one or more of the ingredients is meant to be augmented and more widely spread in the ample gravy. It is not used if the dish is meant to be dry-fried. Shrimp used in dry-fried dishes are often fried without having been shelled. The Chinese believe that shellfish fried in their shells retain more of their own flavor than if they were shelled. But to enjoy such dishes as they should be enjoyed, you will have to be adept in shelling seafood within your mouth—a necessary technique for the complete enjoyment of Chinese food.

Stir-Fried Shrimp with Chinese Dried Mushrooms and Celery

Preparation Repeat the recipe for Stir-Fried Shrimp with Green Peas (see Index), using 6 Chinese dried mushrooms and ¾ cup celery instead of peas and bamboo shoots. Soak the mushrooms for 20 minutes in water, and dice them. Cut the celery into 1 inch segments. Stir-fry the vegetables for half a minute longer, before returning the shrimp to the pan for the final assembly.

Serves 4–8, with other dishes

Stir-Fried Shrimp with Green Pepper, Tomatoes, and Water Chestnuts

Preparation Repeat the recipe for Stir-Fried Shrimp and Green Peas (see Index), using 1 medium-sized green pepper, 2 water chestnuts, and 2 medium-sized tomatoes. Dice the green pepper into ⅓ inch cubes; cut the water chestnuts into ¼ inch cubes, peel the tomatoes and cut them into ½ inch cubes. Allow the pepper and water chestnuts to fry first for 1½ minutes before adding the tomatoes. You will need less chicken stock as the tomatoes will give off more liquid, which is strengthened by adding 1 tablespoon soy sauce.

Serves 4–8, with other dishes

The green pepper combined with the red tomatoes and pink shrimp makes a most attractive color combination.

Stir-Fried Shrimp with Bean Curd, Mushrooms, and Pork

Serves 4–8, with other dishes

Preparation Cut each cake of bean curd into eight pieces. Drain the button mushrooms and discard the water. Cut the scallions into 1 inch segments. Blend the cornstarch and monosodium glutamate with the chicken stock.

Cooking and Serving Heat 1½ tablespoons of the oil in a frying pan. Add the bacon, ginger, and salt, and stir-fry for 2 minutes over a high heat. Add the shrimp and continue to stir-fry for 1½ minutes. Remove the bacon and shrimp, and put them aside to keep warm. Pour the remainder of the oil into the pan. Add the onion and stir-fry for 15 seconds. Add the bean curd and stir-fry for 2 minutes, then add the soy sauce, sherry, oyster sauce, hoisin sauce, and mushrooms. Stir-fry for another minute. Pour in the stock mixture. Return the pork and shrimp to the pan. Cook, stirring gently, for 3 minutes; then sprinkle with sesame oil and serve in a deep dish.

8 oz (1½ cups) shelled shrimp
2 cakes bean curd
1 small can button mushrooms
2 oz slab bacon, finely chopped (¼ cup)
1 scallion
2 teaspoons cornstarch
¼ teaspoon monosodium glutamate
½ cup chicken stock
¼ cup vegetable oil
1 slice ginger root
½ teaspoon salt
4 teaspoons soy sauce
1 tablespoon dry sherry
2 teaspoons oyster sauce
2 teaspoons hoisin sauce
1¼ teaspoons sesame oil

Plain Stir-Fried Shrimp

Serves 4–8, with other dishes

1 lb (2 cups) shelled shrimp

1½ teaspoons salt
2 slices ginger root
5 tablespoons cornstarch
2 scallions
¼ cup vegetable oil
5 tablespoons white wine

For plain stir-frying, shrimp should be at least 2 inches long (before cooking), and weigh 1 lb after having been washed and shelled, if the dish is to have any bulk.

Preparation Chop the ginger fine. Sprinkle the shrimp with salt and ginger and leave to season for 30 minutes, turning the shrimp over a few times; then dredge with cornstarch (discarding any excess). Cut the scallions into ½ inch segments.

Cooking Heat the oil in a large frying pan. Add the scallions and stir-fry for 1 minute over a high heat. Add the shrimp and continue to stir-fry over a high heat for 2 minutes. Sprinkle with wine and stir-fry over a high heat for 30 seconds. Serve on a well-heated dish, and eat immediately.

Plain Stir-Fried Shrimp in Shells

Serves 4–8, with other dishes

1½ lb large shrimp

2½ teaspoons fermented black beans
2 cloves garlic
2 slices ginger root
2 scallions
¼ cup vegetable oil
¾ teaspoon salt
2 teaspoons soy sauce
2 tablespoons dry sherry
2½ tablespoons chicken stock
¾ teaspoon sugar
dash of pepper

Preparation Soak the black beans for ½ hour; then drain. Wash the shrimp thoroughly and leave the tails intact. Chop the garlic, ginger, and scallions fine.

Cooking Heat the oil in a frying pan. Add the salt, fermented beans, garlic, ginger, and scallions. Stir-fry vigorously over medium heat for 1 minute, mixing the ingredients together. Add the shrimp, raise the heat to maxmium, and stir-fry for another 2 minutes. Add the soy sauce, sherry, stock, sugar, and pepper, and continue to stir-fry for a further minute. Serve and eat immediately.

This is a famous Metropolitan Chinese dish, seen and served throughout China. Prawns or jumbo shrimp 3–5 inches long can be, and often are, cooked in precisely the same manner with the same ingredients, but with an increase in the cooking time of 1 minute.

Jumbo Shrimp in Shells, Stir-Fried with Wine-Sediment Paste

Serves 4–8, with other dishes

Repeat the recipe for Plain Stir-Fried Shrimp in Shells, substituting 2½ tablespoons of red wine-sediment paste and 1¼ tablespoons hoisin sauce for the fermented black beans and soy sauce. This is another dry-fried dish with a wonderful aromatic quality.

Deep-Fried Phœnix-Tail Shrimp

This way of cooking shrimp came to be so-called because the tail shell is left on and is not battered. When the shrimp are fried, the tails turn bright red, and can be conveniently used by the diners as 'handles'. This is a very popular way of presenting shrimp in Chinese restaurants abroad today; so prepared, the shrimp can be more easily managed by Westeners—yet it is an authentically Chinese custom.

Preparation Chop the ginger fine. Beat the eggs for 15 seconds, then fold in both types of flour, the salt, ginger, and ¾ cup of water. Beat for another minute into a light batter. Shell the shrimp, leaving the tail shells on. Clean them thoroughly, and remove the black vein.

Cooking Heat the oil in a pan. Hold each shrimp by its tail and dip it into the batter, then lower it into the boiling oil. Fry six shrimp simultaneously for 3 minutes, then remove them with a slotted spoon, draining off the excess oil. When the first batch has been fried, it can be kept hot and crispy in the oven while the remaining shrimp are being cooked. Repeat until all the shrimp have been cooked.

Serving Serve on a well-heated platter, garnished with parsley if desired.

The dips recommended for this dish are Salt and Pepper Mix and the dip recommended for shrimp (see pages 54 and 58).

Serves 4–8, with other dishes

1½ lb fresh jumbo shrimp

1 slice ginger root
2 eggs
½ cup flour
½ cup self-rising flour
2 teaspoons salt
vegetable oil for deep-frying

Deep-Fried Butterfly Shrimp

The term 'butterfly' simply means that after shelling, the shrimp's body is sliced open along two thirds of the inner curve, and spread-eagled into two butterfly wings. The tail shell is left intact. When shrimp are stuffed they are usually butterflied first. In Chinese cooking there are numerous items which could be stuffed into shrimp. Unstuffed butterfly shrimp are usually coated with batter.

Preparation Chop the ginger, garlic, and scallion fine. Beat the egg for 15 seconds. Add the chopped ingredients, cornstarch, and both types of flour to the eggs, and beat together for a further 30 seconds, making a light batter. Shell the shrimp, leaving the tail shells on, as in the previous recipe. Hold the shrimp by their tails and dip the bodies into the batter; then sprinkle with breadcrumbs to coat.

Serves 4–8, with other dishes

1½ lb fresh giant shrimp

1 slice ginger root
1 clove garlic
1 scallion
2 eggs
¼ cup cornstarch
2 teaspoons self-rising flour
1 cup breadcrumbs
oil for deep-frying
1 lemon
parsley sprigs

Cooking Heat the oil in a deep-fryer. Lower six shrimp at a time into the oil to fry for 3 minutes. Remove, and drain. When all the shrimp are ready, serve decorated with lemon wedges and parsley. The dips and mixes recommended for Deep-Fried Phœnix Tail Shrimp can be served.

Deep-Fried Shrimp with Stuffed Ham and Almonds

Serves 4–8, with other dishes

1½ lbs jumbo shrimp
1 oz smoked ham
2½ tablespoons chopped almonds

salt
parsley
3 eggs
¼ cup cornstarch
¼ cup self-rising flour
vegetable oil for deep-frying
1 lemon

Preparation Shell, clean, and butterfly the shrimp (see previous recipe), and sprinkle with ⅔ teaspoon salt. Chop the ham coarse. Blanch, toast, and chop the almonds. Chop the parsley, and beat one of the eggs. Mix half of the beaten egg with 1½ teaspoons of the cornstarch and the chopped almonds and ham. Stuff 1 teaspoon of the mixture into each of the butterflied shrimp. Close the shrimp by pressing the two wings together to seal. Beat the 2 remaining eggs and add to the unused half egg. Mix the remaining cornstarch with the self-rising flour. Dip each shrimp into the beaten egg to coat and dredge with the mixed flour.

Cooking and Serving Heat the oil in a pan and deep-fry the stuffed shrimp, six at a time. Decorate with parsley and serve with lemon wedges. Accompany with an assortment of dips, including Salt and Pepper Mix (see page 54).

Shrimp-Stuffed Shrimp

Serves 4–8, with other dishes

2 tablespoons dried shrimp
1½ lbs jumbo shrimp

1 strip bacon
2 water chestnuts
2 eggs
¼ cup cornstarch
¼ cup self-rising flour
¾ teaspoon salt

This is a useful dish to nibble when drinking wine, or to serve as one of the hors d'œuvre at a party dinner.

Preparation Soak the dried shrimp for 2 hours, then chop and mince them very fine. Chop the meat from 1 giant shrimp coarse. Chop the bacon and water chestnuts, and butterfly the remaining shrimp. Mix the minced dried shrimp with the chopped giant shrimp, the salt, bacon, and water chestnuts, together with half a beaten egg and ½ teaspoon of the cornstarch. Stuff this mixture into the bodies of the butterflied shrimp, and seal. From this point on, repeat the procedure for Deep-Fried Shrimp Stuffed with Ham and Almonds, and accompany with suggested dips.

Deep-Fried Shrimp Stuffed
with Crabmeat and Mushrooms

Repeat the recipe for Shrimp-Stuffed Shrimp, using ¼ cup crabmeat and 3–4 Chinese dried mushrooms for the stuffing. Soak the mushrooms for 40 minutes, remove the stalks, and chop the caps coarse. Mix with the chopped crabmeat, and stuff the mixture into the butterflied shrimp; then repeat as for previous recipe.

Serves 4–8, with other dishes

Shrimp Omelet

Although this is a simple dish, it is always appealing and goes extremely well with rice.

Preparation Cut each shrimp into three pieces. Sprinkle with ½ teaspoon of the salt. Beat the eggs lightly in a bowl, adding remaining salt, and sprinkle liberally with pepper. Chop the scallions into ½ inch segments.

Cooking Heat 2 tablespoons of the oil in a large frying pan. Add the shrimp and scallions and stir-fry for 1½ minutes over a high heat. Remove the shrimp and scallions, and keep warm. Add the remaining oil, which must be well spread over the surface of the pan. Pour in the beaten egg, and let it spread over the pan. Lower the heat. Tilt the pan a few times to loosen the egg; then leave to cook for 1¼ minutes. Return the shrimp and scallions to the pan, laying them down along the center of the eggs. Lift the edges of the eggs with a spatula, fold each side over the top, and finally, with the aid of a fork, spoon, or another spatula, turn the omelet over to fry for 45 seconds more. Pour the sherry over the omelet and lift out carefully on to a well-heated dish. Serve and eat immediately.

Serves 4–6, with other dishes

½ lb (1 cup) shelled shrimp
6 eggs

1½ teaspoon salt
dash of pepper
2 scallions
6 tablespoons vegetable oil
1½ tablespoons dry sherry

Cantonese Crystal Shrimp

Preparation Mix the salt in 2½ cups water. Soak the shrimp in this salted water, and place in the refrigerator for 2 hours. Drain, rinse quickly, and dry thoroughly. Mix the cornstarch or water chestnut flour with the chicken stock, white wine, and monosodium glutamate, blending until smooth. Chop the garlic and ginger fine, and cut the scallions into ¼ inch segments.

Serves 4–8, with other dishes

1 lb (1½ cups) shelled shrimp

2 tablespoons salt
2 teaspoons cornstarch *or* water chestnut flour
2½ tablespoons chicken stock
¼ cup white wine

¼ teaspoon monosodium glutamate
2 cloves garlic
2 slices ginger root
2 scallions
3 tablespoons vegetable oil
1½ tablespoons lard

Cooking Heat the oil in a pan over a high heat. Add the ginger, garlic, and scallions and stir-fry for 30 seconds. Pour the shrimp into the pan and stir-fry vigorously for a further 30–40 seconds. Drain, and put aside. Return the pan to the heat. Add the lard, and when it has all melted, pour the cornstarch mixture into the pan. Stir and mix gently until smooth and translucent. Return the shrimp to the pan, and stir and turn them for 30 seconds until they have taken on a glossy finish. Serve and eat immediately.

Basic Shrimp Balls

Makes 16 balls

Serves 4–8, with other dishes

1 lb (2 cups) shelled shrimp

¼ lb slab bacon
¼ cup water chestnuts
¼ cup cornstarch
2½ tablespoons soy sauce
2½ tablespoons dry sherry
¾ teaspoon salt
½ teaspoon sugar
1 egg
oil for deep-frying
parsley sprigs

The basic mixtures for Shrimp Balls and Shrimp Cakes are essentially the same; the difference lies in the way they are shaped.

Preparation Chop and mince the shrimp and pork; chop the water chestnuts very fine. Mix together with the cornstarch, soy sauce, sherry, salt, sugar, and egg. Form the mixture into balls the size of walnuts.

Cooking Place the shrimp balls in a wire basket. Heat the oil in a deep-fryer; then lower shrimp balls into the oil to fry for 2 minutes. Lift the wire basket from the oil to allow the balls a 2 minute break from the frying (as they might get burned), then fry them for 1½ minutes more. Drain. Serve, decorated with parsley.

A favorite dip to accompany this recipe is Salt and Pepper Mix (see Index).

Shrimp Balls with Spinach

Makes 16 balls

Serves 6–8, with other dishes

1 lb spinach
2 cloves garlic
2½ tablespoons vegetable oil
¾ teaspoon salt
dash of pepper
1¼ tablespoons soy sauce
1¼ tablespoons dry sherry

Preparation Repeat the recipe for Basic Shrimp Balls: prepare and fry them for the same length of time. Crush and chop the garlic. Wash the spinach and discard any coarse stems.

Cooking Heat the oil in a frying pan. Add the garlic and spinach, and stir-fry over a high heat for 2 minutes. Add the salt, pepper, soy sauce, and sherry; stir-fry for another minute.

Serving Arrange the spinach on a serving dish as a bed, and lay the fried shrimp balls on top. They can be served immediately, or the dish can be placed in a steamer for 5 minutes before being brought to the table.

Toasted Shrimp

This is a suitable dish for party dinners as well as for a family meal.

Serves 6–8, with other dishes

Preparation Using the ingredients given in the recipe for Shrimp Balls, make the shrimp paste by mixing the minced pork, water chestnuts, shrimp, etc. together. In addition, you will need 4–5 thin slices of bread. Cut each slice into four, and trim off the crusts. Three beaten eggs and 1 cup breadcrumbs or sesame seeds are also required. Spread shrimp paste mixture very thickly and firmly on one side of the bread, then wet with the beaten egg. Sprinkle and dredge with breadcrumbs. If you are using sesame seeds, sprinkle them on the spread, as they help greatly in providing a pleasant aroma.

Cooking Place four pieces of shrimp-spread bread at a time in a wire basket. Lower them to fry in hot oil for 2½–3 minutes; then drain. When all the pieces have been fried, arrange them on a well-heated dish, either decorated with parsley or built up in the form of a pyramid. Serve and eat immediately.

The crispness of the fried bread contrasting with the meatiness of the shrimp makes this a very appealing and interesting dish—yet one which is very easy to make.

Shrimp (Cantonese Style)

Preparation Rinse the shrimp thoroughly and dry them. Chop the scallions fine and crush and chop the garlic. Add to the shrimp, together with the salt, and leave to season for 2 hours. Shred the ginger and combine with the vinegar in a small sauce dish. Place the remaining ingredients in separate sauce dishes and arrange strategically on the table. Each diner should be provided with two small sauce bowls—one to combine ingredients in for his own particular dip, and one in which to put discarded shrimp shells.

Cooking and Serving After seasoning, place the shrimp in a large heat-proof bowl, and pour a kettleful of boiling water over them. Leave the shrimp to steep in the boiling water for 1 minute; then drain thoroughly, and bring to the table in a well-heated dish. The diner can either use his fingers or a pair of chopsticks to help himself to the shrimp. He should dip the shrimp into his own prepared dip and the shrimp should be half-chewed, half-sucked from the shell.

What is so appealing about a dish prepared in this way is its amazing freshness.

Serves 4–6, with other dishes

1½ lb shrimp

4 scallions
3 cloves garlic
1 tablespoon salt

3 slices ginger root
4–5 tablespoons wine vinegar
4–5 tablespoons soy sauce
3–4 tablespoons tomato sauce
2 tablespoons chili sauce
4–5 tablespoons rice wine *or* dry sherry

Drunken Shrimp

Serves 6–8, with other dishes

1¼ lb (3 cups) shelled shrimp

3 slices ginger root
3 scallions
¼ cup dry sherry
2 tablespoons brandy
2 teaspoons salt
¼ teaspoon black pepper
juice of half a lemon
2½ teaspoons sesame oil
4 teaspoons chopped parsley

Preparation Rinse and clean the shrimp thoroughly. Chop the ginger and scallion coarse. Prepare a marinade by adding the scallions and ginger to the sherry and brandy. Stir, and leave to mature for 1 hour. Place the shrimp in a flat-bottomed bowl. Sprinkle and rub with salt and pepper. Strain the impregnated sherry and brandy onto the shrimp, and mix well. Place the bowl in the refrigerator, and leave the shrimp to marinate for 3 hours; then drain and discard the marinade. Sprinkle the shrimp with lemon juice and sesame oil. Arrange them nicely on a plain white dish, sprinkle with chopped parsley, and serve.

This is an excellent dish to accompany wine. Favorite dips include Chili Sauce, mustard, hoisin sauce, Ginger-in-Vinegar, and Garlic-in-Vinegar (see the section on Table Condiments).

EGGS

Because there is an abundance of poultry in China, eggs are a universal dish. Egg dishes—usually the scrambled, stir-fried type—are those most likely to be brought to the table to add to the existing dishes if unexpected guests arrive. Since we live much more communally in China, unexpected guests are always arriving, and it is the custom to share your meal—if you can afford to eat at all. As stir-fried egg dishes are the quickest to cook, and as almost any other ingredient can be blended in, they are the most convenient to prepare at a moment's notice. Hence they are a favorite with housewives and restaurants with limited resources.

Another form in which eggs are frequently served is 'gravied eggs'—hard-boiled eggs which have been simmered in soy-meat stock. These are usually cut into slices with a thread (by sawing) and laid out neatly in wedges on a dish, their rich yellow yolk contrasting with the brownness of the skin. As hard-boiled eggs impregnated with soy sauce keep well, they are also the most common type of egg for taking on journeys, or buying from street-vendors, or from the sampans which crowd around ships and liners anchored in port. As we have seen in the chapter on Pork, a few hard-boiled eggs are usually added to the pan for simmering with the meat or gravy during the last stages of cooking. These eggs are often not all eaten at the table when the dish is first served, but kept for other meals, such as breakfast, or for other uses.

For breakfast, the type of eggs most frequently eaten is salted eggs, usually hard-boiled duck eggs which have been soaked in their shells in brine for varying lengths of time. As a rule, these are cut through the shells into four or six pieces and laid out on a dish without removing the shell. They have quite a distinctive taste, and their saltiness contrasts with the refreshing quality of the soft rice (congee) which we Chinese normally take at breakfast, to help freshen the mouth and stimulate the juices early in the morning.

As many Chinese dishes are created to go with rice, two types of egg dish are very popular in China: savory steamed egg-custards, and Yellow Running Oil-Scrambled Eggs (Liu Huang T'sai). This latter form of egg dish differs from ordinary stir-fried egg dishes (which are not very different from scrambled eggs), in that much more oil or lard is blended into the eggs during the final cooking stages, and they are usually very savory. The presence of oil acts as a lubricant for the downing of rice, which is an important function in the consumption of much Chinese food. For the same reason, when cooking Chinese fried and stir-friadiegg dishes, the eggs are seldom cooked until they are set and hardened. At least part of the egg mixture is left runny when the pan is removed from the heat: runny egg helps in the downing of rice. When a little rice wine or dry sherry is introduced into the eggs during the final cooking stage, it generates a wonderful aroma, reminiscent of the best home-cooking as served in courtyards, dining-rooms, or country restaurants in days gone by.

Steamed savory egg-custards are popular because they can be very light. Often, no more than a couple of eggs are used, combined with stock, for a large bowl of custard. In fact, egg-custards are part-egg and part-soup in composition (90% soup). Although they are solid dishes, they are very suitable for invalids and the aged. Furthermore, an egg-custard can be steamed on top of rice in a basket arrangement while the rice is being cooked.

In Chinese restaurants in the West, all Fu Yung dishes are egg dishes, either stir-fried or in the form of omelets or soufflés. But in China, Fu-Yung only refers to dishes prepared from egg whites beaten up with ground chicken or fish. They are usually very light and delicate dishes.

Finally, we have Tea Eggs and 1000 Years Old Eggs. Tea Eggs are very much an acquired taste. They are hard-boiled eggs which are again boiled in tea, with salt added. The shell is somewhat cracked, but not detached, during the second boiling.

1000 Years Old Eggs are not exactly antiques. They are duck eggs preserved in lime, pine, ash, and salt for about 50 days. They are normally obtainable from Chinese markets, coated with dried mud and husks, which gives them the appearance of dating from the Tang or Han dynasty. When the mud has been washed off and the shell removed, the egg is greenish-black in color, with a yellowish-green yolk. It has a pungent cheesy taste. Once you have acquired the taste, there can be no substitute!

Huang-Pu Scrambled Stir-Fried Eggs

Serves 6–8, with other dishes

10 eggs

1½ teaspoons salt
1½ tablespoons finely chopped chives
    or the green tops of scallions
¼ teaspoon monosodium glutamate
6 tablespoons vegetable oil

This is probably the best known plain, scrambled stir-fried egg dish. It originates from the boat-dwellers of Huang-Pu, which is a section of the Pearl River flowing past the city of Canton. Although originally what one might term a 'coolie dish'—a true product of the proletariat—it has come to be so well-liked that it is now on the menus of many famous restaurants in Kwangtung, for the delight of connoisseurs.

Preparation Beat the eggs in a bowl for about 10 seconds with a pair of chopsticks or a fork. Mix in the salt, chopped chives or scallions, and monosodium glutamate. Beat for a further 5 seconds.

Cooking Heat 3 tablespoons of the oil in a smooth, medium-sized frying pan over a low heat. Wait until the oil is very hot, then pour in one third of the egg mixture. Take the handle of the pan and maneuver it so that the egg flows and spreads evenly over the surface. Remove the pan from the heat as soon as most of the egg is solid. Stir once or twice; then lift the egg with a spatula onto a well-heated serving dish and keep it warm. Add 1 tablespoon of the oil to the pan and repeat the process. Repeat again until all the beaten egg has been used up, piling the scrambled omelets one on top of the other. In this way, you will have several layers of soft and runny egg sandwiched between firmer, well-fried eggs. Because of the conjunction of firm and soft layers, the highly savory flavor, the delicate egg quality, and the appealing scent of freshly fried chives, eggs cooked in this way are indeed a delicacy; yet they can be cooked quickly in any kitchen.

Scrambled Stir-Fried Eggs with Assorted Ingredients

Preparation Soak the mushrooms in water for 20 minutes, remove the stalks, and shred the caps. Cut the scallions into 1 inch segments. Beat the eggs and salt together in a bowl for 10 seconds.

Cooking Heat 2 tablespoons of the vegetable oil in a frying pan over a high heat. Add the shredded pork and stir for 1 minute. Add the scallion segments, mushrooms, and bean sprouts; stir-fry for 1 minute. Add the sugar and soy sauce, and stir-fry for 1 minute. Remove the mixture from the pan and keep warm on a heated plate. Add the remaining oil to the pan. Let it heat up for a few moments over a medium heat; then pour in the beaten eggs. Allow them to spread evenly over the pan. When most of the egg has become solid, return the shredded pork and rest of ingredients, except the sherry, to the pan, spreading the mixture fairly evenly over the egg. Scramble two or three times. Wait for 5–6 seconds; then sprinkle with sherry, scramble again, and serve on a well-heated dish.

This recipe can be used to make an omelet by turning the edges of the egg mixture on to the meat shreds, etc., during the second stage of frying. Turn the omelet over and cook for 7–8 seconds before sprinkling with sherry and serving. This is the way it is most usually done in Chinese restaurants in the West. A frequent and favorite variation is to sprinkle the omelet with about 6 tablespoons of Sweet and Sour Sauce (see Index) before serving. The sauce goes really well with eggs.

Serves 4–6, with other dishes

8 eggs

4 medium Chinese dried mushrooms
2–3 scallions
1½ teaspoons salt
5 tablespoons vegetable oil
½ cup shredded pork
½ cup bean sprouts
1½ teaspoons sugar
2 tablespoons soy sauce
1½ tablespoons dry sherry

Stir-Fried Eggs with Pork and Shrimp

Shrimp are another favorite for cooking with eggs. They can often be used in conjunction with pork.

Preparation Follow the instructions given in the previous recipe, using only ⅓ cup shredded pork and adding ¼ lb (⅔ cup) peeled shrimp. Substitute 2–3 tablespoons green peas for the mushrooms, which tend to have a blackening effect.

Serves 4–6, with other dishes

313

Scrambled Stir-Fried Eggs
with Shredded Ham

Serves 4–6, with other dishes

¼ lb cooked ham
8–9 eggs

¼ teaspoon monosodium glutamate
5 tablespoons vegetable oil
1½ tablespoons chopped chives *or*
    scallion tops
1½ tablespoons dry sherry

As Chinese cooking tends to go into cross-cooking, eggs are bound to be cooked with many other foods, resulting in a wide range of dishes. This is one of the favorites.

Preparation Slice the ham into strips about half the length of matchsticks. Beat the eggs in a bowl for 10 seconds with the monosodium glutamate.

Cooking Put the oil into a frying pan over a medium heat. When it is quite hot, pour in the beaten eggs and sprinkle with the chives or scallions, and ham. Lift the handle of the pan and maneuver the pan so that the eggs spread over the surface. When practically all of the egg is solid, sprinkle with sherry and remove the pan from the heat. Scramble the eggs a few times.

Serving Lift the 'omelet' on to a well-heated dish, and serve immediately.

Stir-Fried Eggs with Pork
and Crabmeat

Serves 4–6, with other dishes

6–7 eggs
½ cup shredded pork
½–¾ cup crabmeat

2 slices ginger root
3 scallions
2 medium-sized tomatoes
1½ teaspoons salt
5 tablespoons vegetable oil
½ cup bean sprouts
1 teaspoon sugar
¾ teaspoon salt *or* ¾ tablespoon
    light soy sauce
1½ tablespoons dry sherry

As crabmeat is even fishier than shrimp, the addition of 2 slices of ginger root is essential. To maintain contrast and brightness in color, the soy sauce should be eliminated and an additional ¾ teaspoon salt used instead. Light soy sauce could be used, if available. Tomato can be introduced here instead of mushrooms.

Preparation Shred the ginger root, cut the scallions into 1 inch segments, and peel and quarter the tomatoes. Beat the eggs and 1 teaspoon salt together for 10 seconds.

Cooking Heat 1½ tablespoons of the oil in a frying pan over a high heat. Add the pork and ginger, then stir-fry for 1 minute. Add the crabmeat, together with all the vegetables, and stir-fry for 1 minute. Add the sugar and ¾ teaspoon salt or the light soy sauce and stir-fry for a further minute. Remove the mixture from the pan and set aside to keep warm. Put the remaining oil in the pan and pour in the beaten eggs. Wait until most of the egg has become firm, then return the pork, crabmeat, and vegetable mixture to the pan, spreading it evenly over the eggs. After 10 seconds, stir two or three times. Pour in the sherry, stir once again; then serve immediately.

Vegetarian Scrambled Stir-Fried Eggs

Chinese vegetarian dishes are often more interesting than Western vegetarian dishes. Vegetables of different textures and colors are combined and cross-cooked with a selection of dried, pickled, or salted vegetables and sauces. Wine is added to enhance the flavor of vegetable dishes.

Preparation Soak the wood ears in warm water for 30 minutes, and clean them in two changes of water. Soak the mushrooms for 20 minutes, remove the stalks, and shred the caps. Retain 6 tablespoons of the mushroom water. Soak the noodles for 10 minutes; then drain. Clean the spinach and cut it into 1 inch pieces, discarding the coarse parts. Shred the ginger and cut the scallions into 1 inch segments. Cut the celery diagonally into ½ inch segments. Cut the cucumber into matchstick strips. Beat the eggs and salt together for 10 seconds.

Cooking Heat 3 tablespoons of the oil in a large frying pan. When quite hot, pour in the beaten eggs. Wait until most of the egg has become firm; then scramble lightly, and keep hot. Pour 1½ tablespoons of oil into the pan. Add the ginger and scallions, and stir-fry for 30 seconds. Add the mushrooms, celery, cucumber, bean sprouts, wood ears, and half of the soy sauce. Stir-fry together for 2 minutes over a high heat; then remove from the pan, and keep warm. Add the remaining oil to the pan, with the spinach and hoisin sauce. Stir-fry vigorously over a high heat for 2 minutes. Add the noodles, mushroom water, and remaining soy sauce; then return all the vegetables to the pan for a general fry-up. After 30 seconds, add the stir-fried eggs, sprinkle with sherry and monosodium glutamate; then stir-fry for a further 30 seconds. Serve immediately.

This is an extremely appetizing dish for vegetarians and non-vegetarians alike.

Serves 4–6, with other dishes

6 eggs

1 tablespoon wood ears
4 large Chinese dried mushrooms
1 cup transparent bean-thread
  noodles
½ cup spinach
1 slice ginger root
2 scallions
2 stalks celery
3 slices cucumber
1 teaspoon salt
6 tablespoons vegetable oil
½ cup bean sprouts
3 tablespoons light soy sauce
1 tablespoon hoisin sauce
1½ tablespoons dry sherry
¼ teaspoon monosodium glutamate

Chinese Omelets

As often as not, Chinese omelets come in miniature size (miniature by Western standards), and it takes eight to ten omelets to make a complete dish. Each omelet probably consists of no more than half an egg, with fillings. The fillings can consist of any of the wide variety of ingredients used in stir-fried eggs, together with such ingredients as lobster, oysters, and shrimp. These fillings have to be cooked or fried separately, and then added to the beaten eggs after the egg mixture has had a moment's frying. They should be added when the top of the omelet is still a little runny. This facilitates the sealing, when both sides, or just one side, of the omelet are turned over and the omelet is pressed lightly against the side of the pan. Some boiling oil is then poured over the omelet to seal it well and the whole omelet is turned over for 20–30 Xseconds of frying on the opposite side. Because of their size, these small omelets are intriguing to Westerners. They usually have some sauce (such as Sweet and Sour Sauce, a meat sauce, or Hot Sauce) poured over them when served.

Oyster Omelet

Serves 4–6, with other dishes

10 oysters
6 eggs

¼ lb lean pork
2 scallions
1 slice ginger root
½ cup bamboo shoots
1 teaspoon salt
6 tablespoons milk
dash of pepper
7 tablespoons vegetable oil
1 tablespoon soy sauce
2 teaspoons vinegar
2 teaspoons dry sherry
½ teaspoon sugar
2 teaspoons cornstarch

Oyster is used for cooking with other ingredients much more extensively China than is customary in America. In seaboard provinces such as Fukien, where I lived for over a decade, oysters were used for cooking with noodles, pancakes, and soups. Here is a recipe where they are cooked in an omelet. Albeit expensive, it is well worth a trial.

Preparation Shell the oysters, reserving 2 tablespoons oyster water. Finely chop the pork and the scallions; then shred the ginger and bamboo shoots. Beat the eggs and ½ teaspoon of the salt together for 10 seconds; then add the milk and pepper and beat for a further 5 seconds.

Cooking Heat 3 tablespoons of the oil in a frying pan, add about half of the pork, ½ teaspoon of the salt, and the ginger and scallion. Stir-fry for 3 minutes. Add the bamboo shoots and oysters, stir-fry for 2 minutes more, then remove the mixture from the pan and set aside. Wipe the pan and pour in the remainder of the oil. When it is quite hot, pour in a ladleful of beaten egg and spread it over the pan. When the bottom of the omelet has become firm, place a spoonful of the oyster/pork mixture in the center. Fold the omelet down the middle and push it with a spatula to one side of the pan. Push it lightly against the side of the pan and pour some hot oil over it to seal. Turn the omelet over and fry the other side for 20 seconds. Lift it from the pan with a slotted spoon, then drain and place it on a well-heated dish. Repeat this procedure until all the beaten eggs and filling are used up.

Serving While the omelets are keeping warm, drain away all the oil from the pan. Add the remaining half of the pork and fry it for 1 minute. Then add the soy sauce, vinegar, sherry, oyster water, sugar, and cornstarch blended with 1½ tablespoons water. As soon as the sauce thickens, pour it over the omelets and serve.

Crabmeat, Shrimp, and Lobster Omelets

True to the liberal tradition and high flexibility of Chinese cooking, any of the above seafoods can be substituted for oysters when making omelets.

Preparation Follow the instructions given in the previous recipe, but substitute either crabmeat, shrimp, or lobster for the oysters. It is a matter of choice whether or not to prepare a sauce to pour over the omelets before serving.

Serves 4–6, with other dishes

Yellow Flowing Eggs (Basic Recipe)

This is a favorite dish in Peking and the north, possibly created primarily to accompany rice. Its high savoriness and well-oiled lubricating qualities perform this function to perfection.

Preparation Beat the egg yolks, eggs, and monosodium glutamate together for 10 seconds. Add the cornstarch, blended with ¼ cup water, and the salt. Mix well together.

Cooking Heat the oil and 1½ tablespoons of the lard in a pan. When very hot, pour in the beaten eggs. Stir quickly in one direction, and reduce the heat to low. Add the remaining lard and continue to stir in the same direction until the mixture is glistening, smooth, and thick. Pour the mixture into a serving bowl or deep dish. Sprinkle with chopped ham; then serve.

Serves 4–6, with other dishes

4 egg yolks
3 eggs

¼ teaspoon monosodium glutamate
1½ tablespoons cornstarch
1 teaspoon salt
2 tablespoons vegetable oil
¼ cup lard
2 tablespoons chopped smoked ham

Yellow Flowing Eggs (Fancy Recipe)

As the majority of Chinese dishes and recipes are capable of a wide range of variations, the previous recipe can be made more elaborate in several ways:

1. Add the chopped ham to the beaten eggs before the initial stage of stir-frying.
2. Add 3 tablespoons cooked shrimp, 2 tablespoons diced, soaked, dried mushrooms, and 2 tablespoons wood ears which have been soaked and well-cleaned. These ingredients should be added during the final stage of fry-cooking. Add 1 tablespoon dry sherry just before serving.

These additional ingredients provide an interesting variety of textures and flavors, without detracting in any way from the primary function of the rice-downing dish.

Serves 4–6, with other dishes

317

Basic Steamed Eggs

Serves 4–6, with other dishes

3 eggs

1 teaspoon salt
2 teaspoons vegetable oil
¼ teaspoon monosodium glutamate
1¼ cups water
1½ teaspoons chopped chives *or* scallion tops
1 tablespoon soy sauce

Preparation Beat the eggs with the salt, oil, and monosodium glutamate for 10 seconds in a heat-proof bowl. Mix in the water and beat for 5 seconds.

Cooking Place the bowl in a steamer or in a large saucepan with about 1 inch of boiling water. Boil gently and steam for 20 minutes. Remove the bowl from the pan and sprinkle the surface of the eggs, which should now have hardened into a shimmering custard, with the chives or scallions and soy sauce. Serve from the bowl.

Fancy Steamed Eggs

Serves 4–6, with other dishes

3 eggs

1 teaspoon salt
¼ teaspoon monosodium glutamate
2 tablespoons chopped smoked ham
2 teaspoons vegetable oil
1½ cups chicken stock
¾ cup water
3 tablespoons crabmeat *or* shrimp
1 tablespoon chopped chives *or* scallion tops
1 tablespoon soy sauce

Preparation Beat the eggs with the salt, monosodium glutamate, ham, and oil for 10 seconds in a heat-proof bowl. Add the stock and water, and mix well.

Cooking Place the bowl in a steamer or in a large saucepan with 1 inch of boiling water. Steam for 18 minutes, by which time the surface of the egg mixture should have hardened. Arrange the crabmeat or shrimp on top of the eggs and sprinkle with chives or scallions, and soy sauce. Steam for a further 4–5 minutes and serve from the bowl.

To vary Mix flaked cooked or smoked fish, such as haddock or whitefish, with the eggs before steaming them. Garnish with chopped ham and chives.

Yellow Flower Pork

Serves 4–6, with other dishes

¾ lb slab bacon
5 eggs

2 tablespoons wood ears
1 slice ginger root
½ cup bamboo shoots
2 scallions
1 teaspoon salt
3 tablespoons vegetable oil
1 tablespoon light soy sauce
6 tablespoons superior stock
¼ teaspoon monosodium glutamate
1 tablespoon dry sherry
2 teaspoons sesame oil

Preparation Soak the wood ears for 30 minutes and rinse them in two changes of water. Slice the bacon into shreds. Shred the ginger and bamboo shoots. Cut the scallions into 1 inch segments. Beat the eggs with half of the salt for 10 seconds.

Cooking Heat 2 tablespoons of the vegetable oil in a pan. Pour in the beaten eggs. As soon as the mixture hardens and sets, scramble lightly, and set aside. Pour the remaining vegetable oil into the pan. Add the ginger, pork, and remaining salt. Fry for 2 minutes over a high heat. Add the bamboo shoots, soy sauce, wood ears, and scallions, and continue to stir-fry for another minute. Pour in the stock and add the monosodium glutamate. Cook, stirring gently, for 1 minute. Return the egg mixture to the pan and break it up into small pieces. Stir the ingredients together for 30 seconds. Sprinkle with sherry and sesame oil, and serve in a well-heated dish.

Yellow Flower Pork is a well-known favorite dish in the north, but it is not so popular in the south.

Oyster Cakes

I can never forget these 'oyster cakes' which were sold by street-vendors for a few coppers apiece in my boyhood days. They were just indescribably delicious when oysters were in season. In the coastal provinces, oysters are a common food, indulged in by everybody. Served in this way, they could be described as oyster pancakes but they were much thicker, more like flattened doughnuts, and *so* tasty!

Preparation Shell the oysters, reserving about 6 tablespoons of the liquid. Cut the scallions into ¼ inch segments. Beat the eggs in a bowl for 10 seconds. Stir in the oysters, salt, pepper, and scallions. Sift the flour, mix in the baking powder, and blend in the oyster water; then pour this mixture into the beaten eggs and blend well into a batter. Leave the batter to stand for 30 minutes.

Cooking Heat the oil in a deep frying pan until very hot. (The oil should be about 1 inch deep.) Fill a small ladle with batter, including at least one or two pieces of oyster. Slide the battered oysters sideways into the hot oil. Fry for 15 seconds, then when the oyster cake starts to float and sizzle, turn it over to fry on the other side for 30 seconds. Lift it out with a slotted spoon and place it in a wire basket suspended above the pan to drain and keep hot. Repeat this process until all the batter has been used up; then serve.

As these Oyster Cakes or waffles have never been seen in the West, they might be the answer to the dreams of many oyster connoisseurs. A good dip to serve with these cakes is a mixture of 1 teaspoon chili sauce with 3 tablespoons vinegar and 2 tablespoons soy sauce. In coastal China, Oyster Cakes are eaten as a snack, often at tea time, which is any time other than a fixed meal time!

Serves 4–6, with other dishes

15 oysters
4 eggs

4 scallions
1 teaspoon salt
dash of pepper
¾ cup flour
1½ teaspoons baking powder
vegetable oil for deep-frying *or* semi deep fry

Shrimp Cakes

Preparation Repeat the previous recipe using large shrimp instead of oysters. Shrimp water can be made simply by boiling the shells and tails in water. The dip recommended in the previous recipe can also be served with Shrimp Cakes. See also section on Table Condiments, Dips, and mixes.

Serves 4–6, with other dishes

Steamed Eggs

Steamed eggs, like the two previous recipes, are designed primarily for the accompaniment of rice. In contrast to Yellow Flowing Eggs, steamed eggs are very light dishes, made with only two or three eggs, and with a very small amount of oil, if any. The beaten eggs are usually mixed with stock or water before being steamed. Although stock is more savory, many people prefer the lightness of water. It is an ideal dish for invalids and the aged.

Steamed Three Variety Eggs

Serves 4–6, with other dishes

2 salt eggs
2 preserved '1000 Years Old Eggs'
3 fresh eggs

2 scallions
1 cup superior stock, heated
¾ teaspoon salt
dash of pepper
2 teaspoons vegetable oil
1 tablespoon chopped smoked ham

This is one of those domestic dishes which are sometimes served up as a change from the normal stir-fried egg dishes.

Preparation Dice the salt eggs and preserved eggs separately into small cubes or neat pieces. Cut the scallions into 1 inch segments. Beat the fresh eggs in a bowl.

Cooking Place the cubes of preserved egg at the bottom of a heat-proof dish. Mix the diced salt eggs with the beaten eggs. Stir in the heated stock, together with the salt, pepper, and oil. Pour the mixture into the heat-proof dish containing the preserved eggs. Place the dish in a steamer or a large sauce-pan with 1 inch of water, and steam for 20 minutes. Sprinkle with the chopped scallions and ham, and serve from the heat-proof dish.

Fancy Fried Eggs
with Sweet and Sour Sauce

Serves 4–6, with other dishes

6 eggs
¾ cup Sweet and Sour Sauce (see Index)

6 small crisp lettuce leaves
1 cup vegetable oil
2 tablespoons soy sauce
pepper

Fried eggs are a common enough dish, universal throughout the world. Yet when they are treated delicately, as they sometimes are in China, they can be a rather special dish.

Cooking and Serving Arrange selected lettuce leaves on a large serving dish. Heat a small pan of Sweet and Sour Sauce. Heat the oil in a frying pan until nearly smoking. Break an egg on to a greased plate, taking care to keep it intact, and slide it gently into the oil. Cook, covered, for just 1 minute. Pour a spoonful or two of boiling oil over the yolk to give it a thin skin. Pour two tablespoons of the hot Sweet and Sour Sauce into the center of each lettuce leaf. Lift the fried egg from the pan with a spatula and plonk it on top of the Sweet and Sour Sauce. Repeat this process until all the eggs are fried and there is an egg sitting on each piece of lettuce, swimming in the hot sauce. Sprinkle a teaspoon of soy sauce and some pepper on the yolk of each egg and serve.

This is a colorful dish, good enough to serve at a banquet.

Pork-Stuffed Eggs with Sweet and Sour Sauce

Cooking and Serving Simmer the eggs in boiling water for 10 minutes; then shell them. Finely chop the pork and mix in the cornstarch and salt. Chop the scallion and finely chop the ginger. Heat the oil in a frying pan and fry the scallion and ginger for 30 seconds. Add the pork, and stir-fry for 2 minutes. Add the soy sauce and sherry, and fry for a further 30 seconds. Cut each egg in half and slice a small, flat piece from the back of each half so that the half-eggs will be able to sit upright. Take a small scoop of yolk out of each half and fill the cavity with the fried pork mixture. Top this mixture with the scooped-out yolk. Shape and make firm with the fingers. Arrange the filled and topped half-eggs on a flat, heat-proof dish and place it in a steamer for a 5 minute blast of steam. Alternatively, put the dish in an oven preheated to 400°F for a few minutes. To serve, pour 1 tablespoon of Sweet and Sour Sauce over each half-egg, or top each one with a sprig of parsley and a cooked shrimp.

Serves 4–6, with other dishes

6 large eggs
¼ lb lean pork
¾ cup Sweet and Sour Sauce (see Index)

2 teaspoons cornstarch
½ teaspoon salt
1 scallion
1 slice ginger root
2 tablespoons vegetable oil
1 tablespoon soy sauce
1 tablespoon dry sherry

Iron Pot Grown Eggs

Originally, these eggs were cooked in iron pots, but nowadays it should be an advantage to cook them in a large ovenproof glass dish with a cover, so that the 'growing' of the eggs will be more visible.

Preparation Beat the eggs for 10 seconds with a fork in a large bowl. Stir in all the other ingredients and beat with a rotary beater for a further 15 seconds. Pour the mixture into a heat-proof dish and cover with a lid.

Cooking Place the dish on top of an asbestos pad over a medium heat. After 3 minutes, reduce the heat to very low and allow the cooking to proceed for 25 minutes. The egg mixture inside the dish will be seen to 'grow' until it has risen almost to the top of the dish. Serve immediately, removing the lid at the table to prevent the raised egg from collapsing.

Serves 4–6, with other dishes

6 eggs

¼ lb (⅓ cup) lean pork, finely chopped
¾ teaspoon salt
1 tablespoon soy sauce
dash of pepper
1¼ cups water
4 teaspoons melted lard *or* butter
1 tablespoon finely chopped chives

Tea Eggs or Marbled Eggs

Serves 6

6 eggs
2 tablespoons Indian tea leaves

Preparation and Cooking Hard-boil the eggs for 10 minutes, then slightly crack the shells but do not remove them. Boil tea leaves in 1 cup water for 5 minutes or until it becomes very strong and dark. Immerse the cracked-shell eggs in the tea for 45 minutes or until cool. When you remove the shells from the eggs you will notice that some of the tea has seeped through the cracks and formed a marbled pattern on the whites of the eggs. The tea also gives the eggs a very distinctive flavor.

Soy Eggs

Soy Eggs are made by simmering hard-boiled eggs in soy sauce for 15–20 minutes. Drain, cool, and slice them lengthwise into four to six wedges. Hard-boiled eggs can also be simmered in the gravy of red-cooked dishes, such as Red-Cooked Pork or Beef (see Index), during the last 30–40 minutes of cooking time.

Thousand Year Old Eggs

Use 3–4 eggs at a time, with other dishes

2 dozen duck eggs

6 tablespoons salt
2½ cups water
30 tablespoons pine ash
6 tablespoons lime

We cannot allow a chapter on eggs to end without dealing with and giving a picture of Thousand Years Old Eggs. These eggs are, in fact, seldom made at home in China. They are almost always bought from food markets. They are nowadays frequently obtainable from Chinese food stores in America. In China, for some reason, they are called 'Pine Flower Eggs' (Sung Hwa Dan). Is it because pine ash is used in the making of them?

Preparation First of all, dissolve the salt in the water in a large bowl. Gradually add the pine ash and then the lime. Stir into a thick, consistent, muddy mixture with a spoon or stick. Wash the eggs in hot water. Coat them completely in a ¼ inch layer of 'mud-pack' from the bowl (as they do with ladies' faces in facials). See that they are completely coated. Roll the mud-covered eggs in a tray of husks (rice or any other dry husk) so as to take on a coating, thus preventing the eggs from sticking to each other or anything else. Place the eggs in a pile at the bottom of a large earthenware jar and cover with a lid.

After 3 days, take the eggs out and rearrange them, placing those on the top at the bottom of the pile and vice versa. Repeat the procedure five times in 15 days. After 15 days of changing, seal the jar by placing the lid on firmly, and leave the eggs to stand for 1 month. At the end of the total 45 day period, the Thousand Years Old Eggs should be ready. The mixture of salt, lime, and ash provides a process of 'slow cooking' which acts as a time-machine to shorten the time from 1000 years to 50 days. The eggs, covered in husks and grey dried mud, appear remarkably like antique eggs.

Serving To eat the eggs, wash off the mud under running water and crack the shells gently. Remove the shells and slice the eggs lengthwise into quarters. The eggs should be greenish-yellow in color and they taste pungent and cheesy. There is nothing quite like them in the Western culinary world.

SWEETS AND SNACKS

Sweets or desserts do not really have the same function in China as in the West where the dessert ends the meal. At an ordinary Chinese dinner, the dessert does not occur at all: in fact there is no sweet after any Chinese meal.

Sweets are eaten in China on two occasions. Firstly, during a multi-course party dinner or banquet, where they have the same function as soups, that is to punctuate the long, endless procession of savory dishes. In many cases, Chinese sweets not only have the function of soups, they *are* soups—sweet soups! (Some are such thick soups that they are really creams or custards!) Sweets are also eaten between meals, as snacks. Then they are often simply dumplings or steamed buns stuffed with sweet fillings. Sometimes they are sprinkled or studded with sesame seeds to give them an aromatic flavor. They are either steamed or deep-fried; if deep-fried they are called 'crispies'.

Compared with the enormous range and sophistication of Western desserts, Chinese sweet dishes are almost primitive. They can only be of purely academic interest to the Western connoisseur. Nonetheless, some of the Chinese practices could contribute to Western concepts and experiments with desserts.

On the other hand, we Chinese have a vast tradition of savory snacks. The majority are steamed, poached, simmered, fried, dry-fried or dry-heated. There are not many Chinese pies and tarts for the simple reason that there are very few ovens in China in which to cook them.

Savory snacks are eaten in China not only between meals, but also at the numerous tea-houses which serve them all day long. The tea-houses are, in a way, Chinese cafés or coffee-houses, where people—the lazy bourgeoisie who can afford the time and money—can sit and nibble all day long!

Almond Tea

Serves 4–6

1 cup shelled almonds

½ cup rice
4–5 tablespoons sugar

Preparation Soak the almonds in boiling water, then remove the skins. Grind the rice and almonds together with 2½ cups water, which should be added gradually. Strain the resulting smooth, thin paste through a fine sieve or cheesecloth. Put the paste and the strained rice and almonds through the grinder a second time. Add the sugar and 1¼ cups water to the strained mixture. Stir until smoothly blended.

324

Cooking Put the mixture into a heavy saucepan. Bring to the boil slowly (it burns very easily), and insert an asbestos pad under the pan. Stir continually. As the liquid thickens, add 2 tablespoons water (or use milk or cream if you prefer) at a time to prevent it getting too thick. Continue to stir for 30 minutes.

Serving Pour the Almond Tea into individual bowls, one for each diner.

Walnut Soup

Preparation Blanch the walnuts and remove the skins. Grind them to a powder, then add 1 quart water.

Cooking Bring the mixture to the boil and simmer gently for 40 minutes. Strain through cheesecloth. Add the sugar, powdered rice, and 1¼ cups water to the strained walnut 'milk'. Put the mixture into a heavy saucepan and bring to the boil, stirring constantly. Insert an asbestos pad under the pan and continue to stir for 25 minutes. Serve in soup bowls.

Serves 4–6

2 cups shelled walnuts

5 tablespoons sugar
1 cup powdered rice *or* rice flour

Lotus Seed Soup

Preparation Blanch the dry lotus seeds, then remove the skins. Grind them into a powder, then add 1 quart water.

Cooking Bring the mixture to the boil very gently in a heavy pan. Insert an asbestos pad under the pan. Simmer very gently for 30 minutes, then strain. Place the candied lotus seeds in another heavy pan. Add 1¼ cups water. Bring to the boil and simmer for 20 minutes. Pour in the strained lotus seed 'milk' and insert an asbestos pad under the pan. Bring the mixture slowly to the boil, add the sugar, and reduce the heat to low. Stir continually for 15 minutes. Serve in soup bowls.

To vary this recipe, add canned chopped pineapple instead of, or as well as, the candied lotus seeds.

Serves 4–6

1 cup dry lotus seeds
1 cup crystallized candied lotus
  seeds

5 tablespoons sugar

Peanut Cream

Preparation Roast the peanuts and grind them to a powder as fine as powdered sugar.

Serves 6–8

2 cups shelled peanuts

1 cup powdered rice
¾ cup sugar

Cooking Mix the powdered rice and peanuts in a heavy pan. Pour in 6¼ cups water. Stir, and bring to the boil slowly; then insert an asbestos pad under the pan. Simmer gently, stirring continually, until the mixture thickens. Add the sugar, bring to a slow boil once more, and stir for a further 5 minutes.

Serving Serve in bowls, like custard. In the West, a small amount of cream could be poured over the custard to make it even more interesting and acceptable.

Almond Junket

Serves 4–6

1 cup almonds
½ cup rice
4½–5 tablespoons sugar
1 envelope unflavored gelatin powder
¾ cup evaporated milk

Preparation Repeat the recipe for Almond Tea.

Cooking In the final boiling, instead of adding water, stir in 1 envelope of plain gelatin powder, blended with ¼ cup water, and ¾ of a cup of evaporated milk. Stir slowly for 3 minutes, then pour the liquid into a square heat-proof dish. Let it cool for 30 minutes; then place in refrigerator for 3 hours.

Serving After 3 hours, the liquid will have set into a jelly. Cut it up into neat pieces. Dissolve 1½ tablespoons sugar in 6 tablespoons water, then pour over the junket and serve on an attractive platter.

Potato Cream

Serves 6–8

2½ lb potatoes

4 tablespoons butter
6 tablespoons sugar

Preparation Peel the potatoes.

Cooking Just cover the potatoes with water and boil gently for 1 hour, adding water when necessary. Drain; then add the butter and mash into a cream. Sprinkle with sugar and serve as a kind of potato-custard cream.

The flavor can be made somewhat more interesting by adding a little vanilla or banana extract and cream (a 20th century Chinese concession to Western modernity!).

Sugared Potato Chips

We Chinese do not appear to regard potatoes in quite the same light as Americans. In the West, they are served as a kind of bulk ballast. Not having to eat them quite so often, we seem to regard them more as a cross between a vegetable and an apple, and therefore more suitable for making into a sweet.

Preparation Peel the potatoes and cut them crosswise into very thin slices.

Cooking Deep-fry the potato chips in the oil for 8–10 minutes to cook through. Drain well. Heat the butter in a large frying pan. Turn the chips in the pan a few times to coat them with butter.

Serving Place the buttered chips on individual serving dishes and sprinkle with sugar.

Sugared Potato Chips can be made into Sugared Potato Fritters simply by dipping the fired chips in egg and flour batter before frying them in the butter; then sprinkle with sugar.

Serves 4–6

1½ lb potatoes
¼ cup sugar

vegetable oil for deep-frying
2½ tablespoons butter

Steamed Pears in Honey

This is an attractive sweet and can well be served as a Western dessert.

Preparation Peel the pears, leaving the stems as 'handles'.

Cooking Stand the pears in a pan and barely cover with water. Simmer for 30 minutes, sprinkle the pears with sugar, and simmer for a further 5 minutes. Reserve half of the water in the pan for later use and pour away the remainder. Refrigerate the pears for 2 hours; then add the honey and liqueur to the reserved water and stir until well-blended. Put the mixture in the refrigerator.

Serving Place each pear in a dessert bowl and pour over the chilled liqueur/honey mixture. Serve with whipped cream if desired.

This is a very refreshing dessert to have after the 'long hot summer' of a multi-course Chinese dinner.

Serves 6

6 pears
¼ cup honey

⅛ cup sugar
2½ tablespoons liqueur (Chinese Rose Dew, Kirsch, Cherry Brandy *or* Crème de Menthe)

Chilled Melon Bowl

This is simply serving a chilled fruit salad in a scooped-out melon, which is a very attractive way of serving a dessert. The full Chinese title for the dish is 'Ten Variety Chilled Melon Bowl', but it is not absolutely necessary to have ten different types of fruit in the salad.

Serves 4–10

1 large melon

½ cup Almond Junket (see Index)
variety of fresh and canned fruit

Preparation Slice an inch off the top of a large melon and scoop out the inside of the fruit carefully in large pieces with a spoon. Cut the scooped-out pieces into regular triangular shapes. Cut the Almond Junket into similar pieces. Mix the pieces of melon and Almond Junket with six or more types of canned and fresh fruit, such as strawberries, honeydew melon, cherries, peaches, pears, apples, pineapple, lychees, grapes, plums, etc. Pack the cavity of the melon with this mixture. Chill the melon in the refrigerator for at least 2 hours.

Serving If desired, the pile of fruits in the melon can be topped with a piece of ice.

This dish can be a magnificent dessert if well-presented and decorated, especially if you use a watermelon. A similar type of dessert could be concocted using a fresh pineapple instead of a melon.

Honeyed Apples

Serves 4–6

4 apples
5 tablespoons honey

¾ teaspoon salt
¼ cup flour
¼ cup self-rising flour
2 eggs
oil for deep-frying
5 tablespoons vegetable oil
2½ tablespoons sesame seeds

Preparation Peel the apples and cut each of them into eight wedges. Sprinkle with salt. Mix the plain flour, self-rising flour, eggs, and 2 tablespoons water into a batter.

Cooking Dip the apple wedges in the batter and deep-fry in hot oil for 3 minutes at about 375°F. Drain well. Heat the vegetable oil in a frying pan and add the honey. Mix until well-blended. Turn the apple wedges in the hot honey/oil until well-covered. Sprinkle with sesame seeds, and serve.

Orange Tea

Serves 4–8

6 large oranges

6 tablespoons sugar
2 tablespoons cornstarch
1 quart water

Although this is an extremely simple dish, it serves a useful purpose during a multi-course Chinese dinner, in that the slight sharpness in the taste of oranges has the refreshing effect of cleansing and clearing the mouth for the next series of savory dishes to be served.

Preparation Cut the oranges in half, loosen the peel with a sharp knife, and scoop out the flesh into a bowl. Cut it into small, regular-sized pieces.

Cooking Mix the sugar, cornstarch, and water in a saucepan and bring to the boil. Add the pieces of orange. Remove from the heat as soon as the mixture comes to the boil again.

Serving Orange Tea may be served hot or chilled in small bowls during a multi-course dinner.

Peking Dust

This is a dessert which was invented by the European residents of Peking during the 1920s and 1930s. It has now become part and parcel of 'Old China Hands' Peking nostalgia (there are a number of European restaurants in Peking).

Preparation Score each chestnut by cutting a criss-cross on the flat side.

Cooking Simmer the chestnuts in boiling water for 40 minutes. Drain, cool, and shell them. Grind them into a light, flaky powder. Blend this powder with the salt and ¼ cup sugar.

Serving Divide the 'dust' among five or six serving bowls or plates, forming each mound of dust into a pyramid. Whip the cream to the desired consistency and fold in the superfine sugar. (You can add a little vanilla extract at this point, if desired.) Top the pyramids of dust with the whipped cream; then serve.

Serves 5 or 6

2 lb chestnuts

¼ teaspoon salt
¼ cup sugar
¾ cup heavy cream
2½ tablespoons superfine sugar

Eight Precious Rice

This is the traditional Chinese steamed pudding, studded with a variety of candied fruits and nuts. It is often served during a banquet.

Preparation Cook the rice by boiling or steaming. Grease a large heat-proof bowl, about 8 inches in diameter, with half the lard. (The lard should be cold.) Stick the candied fruits and nuts on to the walls of the bowl as decoratively as possible, and arrange the remainder at the bottom of the bowl. Add the sugar and remaining lard to the cooked rice and mix well. Spoon half of the rice into the bowl, covering the fruits and nuts on the bottom but without dislodging those studded on the walls. Spoon in the sweetened red bean paste on top of the rice. Cover the paste completely with the remaining rice, leaving nearly 1 inch space at the top of the bowl for expansion.

Cooking Place a cloth or piece of aluminum foil over the bowl and put it in a steamer to steam vigorously for 60–70 minutes, or until cooked through.

Serving Invert the pudding onto a dish and serve. The fruits and nuts showing on the top and sides should make an interesting pattern. Eight Precious Rice is almost a kind of Chinese Christmas pudding!

Serves 10–12

1½ lb glutinous rice

5 tablespoons lard
1 cup candied fruit (raisins, cherries, ginger, dates, prunes, dragon eye meat, dried lychee meat *or* mixed glacéed fruit)
5 tablespoons nuts (almonds, chestnuts, walnuts, melon seeds, ginkgo nuts)
½ cup sugar
1 cup sweetened red bean paste *or* date purée

Drawn Thread Toffee Apples

Serves 4–6

4 crisp apples

1 egg
1 cup flour
oil for deep frying
½ cup sugar
¼ cup vegetable oil
¼ cup syrup

This is a popular Peking sweet. It came to be so called because when the pieces of apple immersed in hot, sticky syrup are pulled apart, they draw with them long threads of thick syrup, which rapidly begin to harden into brittle caramelized sugar. The process begins as soon as the pieces of apple are dipped into ice-cold water, giving each piece of apple a very sweet, but thin, encrustation.

Preparation Peel and core the apples, slice each into six wedges, then cut each wedge in half. Blend the egg, flour, and ¾ cup water to make a smooth batter. Dip each piece of apple in the batter

Cooking Deep-fry the pieces of apple in the oil for 2½–3 minutes, then drain. Heat the sugar, vegetable oil, and 2 tablespoons water in a heavy saucepan over a gentle heat for 5 minutes, stirring constantly. Add the syrup and stir for a further 2 minutes. Add the fried apple-fritters and stir slowly, covering each piece of apple completely with the syrup.

Serving Bring the pan to the dining table and quickly spoon the hot, syrup-covered apple slices into a large bowl of ice-water. Remove them quickly and distribute the apple slices among the dessert bowls of the diners. Alternatively, if the diners are adept with chopsticks, put the syrup-covered apple slices in a well-heated bowl in the center of the table, and let the guests use their chopsticks to pick up slices and dip them in the ice-water.

In pulling an apple slice away from the other pieces, the diner will find long, thin threads of syrup trailing from the piece of fruit. Before eating, he must remember to plunge the piece of apple into the ice-water, which transforms the syrup instantly into a brittle coating with dangling threads (a kind of sugar stalactite!). The coating and threads are extremely fragile. They crackle when bitten into, which, together with the sensation of instant sweetness, creates an interesting experience which most Westerners enjoy.

Drawn Thread Toffee Apples are frequently served as a dessert in Chinese restaurants abroad.

Snacks

Chinese snacks or 'small eats' (T'ien Hsin) consist principally of noodles (which have already been dealt with in a separate chapter), dumplings (which are very thin-skinned, small raviolis, usually cooked by boiling, poaching, or steaming), the larger steamed buns (which are a meal in themselves), and pancakes. The majority of these are stuffed with savory foods, but a few have sweet stuffings. In preparing 'small eats' of this type, there are usually four steps to be considered: making the dough, rolling or shaping the pastry, making the filling, and the final heating or cooking.

Chiao Tzu (Stuffed, Boiled or Steamed Dumplings)

These dumplings are normally made 50–100 at a time. Wrapping dumplings is a kind of pastime in China. At festival seasons, Chinese women are often to be seen wrapping them on trays without looking at them—just like Western women knitting! Children are asked to join in.

Preparation Mix 1¼ cups of water with 2¾ cups of sifted flour and knead until smooth. Cover with a wet cloth and let it stand for 30 minutes. Form the dough into a 14 inch roll about 1 inch in diameter. Cut the dough into ½ inch thick slices. Roll the slices on a board lightly dusted with flour, until each piece is about 3 inches in diameter. Place a heaped teaspoon of the filling in the center of each dough circle. Fold over and seal the edges by pressing them together.

Cooking Bring a gallon of water to the boil and tip in all the dumplings. When the water comes to the boil again, let it boil for 10 seconds, then pour in 2 cups of water. Repeat this process three times in the course of about 10 minutes, by which time the dumplings should be ready. Remove them with a slotted spoon, drain and arrange them on a well-heated serving dish.

Serving These dumplings are usually eaten dipped in soy sauce or vinegar, or both. In north China, savory dumplings are frequently served as a full meal, in which case each person will need at least 18–24 of them. The 'dough-soup', which is the water in which the dumplings are boiled, is served in small bowls to accompany the dumplings. Because of its total neutrality (there being no seasonings added), it has the refreshing 'washing' effect which we Chinese love, especially when the dumplings are eaten with pickles and other salted dishes. For the more 'degenerate', chicken broth could be served instead of the dough-soup.

These dumplings can also be steamed. To do this, a piece of cheesecloth is spread out on the bottom of a steamer and the dumplings are arranged on top of the cloth. In China we usually use a round basket-like steamer. The dumplings

Makes approximately 30 dumplings

1¼ cups water
1½ cups flour
1½ cups self-rising flour
filling for the dumplings (see following pages)
soy sauce *or* vinegar or both

331

should be steamed for 20–25 minutes (depending on the strength of the steam).

Some suggested fillings for Chiao Tzu are Pork and Chinese Celery Cabbage Filling, Shrimp, Crabmeat, or Beef and Water Chestnut Filling (recipes on following pages).

Kuo T'ieh (Steam-Fried Dumplings)

Makes approximately 30 dumplings

¾ cup water
1½ teaspoons sugar
1½ tablespoons soy sauce
1½ tablespoons vinegar
2½ tablespoons vegetable oil

When dumplings are steam-fried in the special way peculiar to north China they are called 'Kuo T'ieh'.

Preparation Make the dumplings according to the instructions in the previous recipe. Blend together the water, sugar, soy sauce, and vinegar.

Cooking Grease a flat frying pan, griddle, or roasting pan with the vegetable oil. Place pan over a medium heat and arrange the dumplings on it in one layer. Allow the dumplings to 'Tsien' (fry steadily) for 4–5 minutes until they are beginning to get brown at the bottom, moving the pan now and then to ensure even heat. Sprinkle the dumplings with the soy sauce mixture, cover the pan with a lid, and heat the dumplings for a further 2–3 minutes.

This method of multi-process heating produces the desired effect of softness at the top, juiciness inside, and crispiness at the bottom, which makes these 'Kuo T'ieh' certainly one of the most interesting and appealing raviolis in the world. They are usually eaten with soy-vinegar dips, which are arranged in small saucer-style sauce dishes on the dining table.

Shao Mai (Steamed Open Dumplings)

Makes approximately 36 dumplings

While 'Chiao Tzu' and 'Kuo T'ieh' are the favorites of the north, the dumpling which is very popular in the south, especially in Canton, is the 'Shao Mai'. Since this is an open dumpling, 'Shao Mai' must be steamed rather than boiled. As the Cantonese are fond of seafood, more often than not shrimp, and crabmeat are incorporated into the fillings.

Preparation Make the dough skins according to the instructions in the recipe for Chiao Tzu, adding 1 egg and 1 cup cornstarch for every 2 cups flour. After kneading, form the dough into a 12 inch roll, 1 inch in diameter. Cut off slices about ⅛ inch thick from this dough roll and roll them out to circles about 2½ inches in diameter. Form a ring by joining your index finger with the thumb on your left hand. Place dough circle on top of this ring, and make a hollow by gently pressing down the center of the ring with the fingers of your right hand. The tucked-down part of the dough-sheet can then be supported by the remaining fingers and the rest of the hand. A small dough-bag is thus formed, with the index finger and thumb acting as a support to the mouth of the bag. When the bag is stuffed with the filling, the mouth is somewhat tightened. Push the filling into the dough-bag with a pair of chopsticks or the handle of a wooden spoon.

Cooking When the dumplings have been prepared, arrange them in a steamer covered with cheesecloth and steam vigorously for 15–20 minutes.

Serving Often these Shao Mais are decorated with a single shrimp placed on top of the filling so as to protrude slightly from the top of the casing. This hints at the abundance of fillings inside.

Pork and Chinese Celery Cabbage Filling for Dumplings

Fillings for dumplings can be cooked or uncooked, but fresh ones are preferred. In the north, the favorite fillings are made of pork or lamb with Chinese celery cabbage. In the south, seafood such as shrimp and crabmeat are frequently used.

Preparation Chop the pork, cabbage, scallions, and ginger root. Place all the ingredients in a bowl, then stir and mix well. Allow the mixture to stand for 30 minutes before using as a filling for dumplings.

For 40–50 dumplings

½ lb pork
½ lb Chinese celery cabbage

2 scallions
1 slice ginger root
¾ teaspoon salt
¼ teaspoon monosodium glutamate
1½ tablespoons soy sauce
2½ teaspoons sesame oil

Shrimp or Crabmeat Filling

Preparation Soak the dried mushrooms for 30 minutes, remove the stalks and chop the caps. Chop the shrimp or crabmeat, pork, scallions, and ginger root. Place all the ingredients in a bowl, stir and mix well. Allow the mixture to stand for 30 minutes before using as a filling. This should be sufficient for 40–50 dumplings.

½ lb (1¼ cups) shelled shrimp *or* crabmeat
3 Chinese dried mushrooms
2 oz pork
2 scallions
2 slices ginger root
¾ teaspoon salt
2 tablespoons soy sauce
1¼ tablespoons dry sherry
2½ teaspoons sesame oil

333

Beef and Water Chestnut Filling

8 oz beef
½ cup water chestnuts
2 oz fat pork
2 scallions
1 slice ginger root
½ cup watercress
4 teaspoons soy sauce
4 teaspoons oyster sauce
1¼ teaspoons sugar
dash of pepper and salt
¼ teaspoon monosodium glutamate
2½ teaspoons sesame oil

Preparation Chop the beef, pork, water chestnuts, scallions, ginger root, and watercress. Place all the ingredients in a bowl; stir and mix well. Allow the mixture to stand for 30 minutes before being used as a filling. Sufficient for 40–50 dumplings.

Hun Tuns or Wontons

Makes about 30 dumplings per ½ lb flour

These miniature dumplings are called 'Wontons' in Cantonese. They are made more or less in the same manner as ordinary dumplings, except that the dough skin used is much larger in relation to the stuffing inserted. The large dough skin trails a 'skirt' which the Chinese think resembles a cloud. 'Hun Tun' means in Chinese 'swallow a cloud'! Hun Tuns are either used in soups, or deep-fried and eaten as snacks. When deep-fried, they are frequently served with Sweet and Sour Sauce (see Index).

Preparation Hun Tun skins are usually made with one portion of water to three portions of flour, with an egg added for every ½ lb flour. The dough is then kneaded until smooth and left for 30 minutes. Form the dough into a roll about 14 inches in length and about 1 inch in diameter. Cut ½ inch thick slices from the roll on a flour-dusted board. Roll them out into thin pancakes about 3½ inches in diameter. Try to roll out the dough until it is paper-thin. Cut these round dough-skins into quarters, and wrap some of the filling in each quarter. After the filling has been wrapped and sealed into the skin, the two extremities of the skin should be brought together and pressed against each other. Thus the skin is double-folded.

Hun Tun skins, or Wonton wrappings, are available frozen in Chinese markets and are an excellent substitute for homemade dumplings.

Chicken Filling for Hun Tuns

¼ lb chicken breast meat
4 large Chinese dried mushrooms
2 scallions

Hun Tun fillings can be of the same ingredients as the fillings for other types of dumpling. But, being smaller in size, often daintier things such as chicken or bêche de mer are used.

Preparation Soak the mushrooms for 30 minutes, remove the stalks and chop the caps. Chop the chicken, scallions, and ginger root. Place all the ingredients in a bowl. Stir and mix well. Allow the mixture to stand for 30 minutes before using as a filling. Sufficient for 30–40 Hun Tuns.

1 slice ginger root
4 teaspoons soy sauce
½ teaspoon salt
2½ teaspoons sesame oil

Shrimp and Bêche de Mer Filling

Preparation Soak the bêche de mer overnight. Chop the shrimp, bêche de mer, chicken meat, scallion, and ginger root. Place all the ingredients in a bowl. Stir and mix well. Allow the mixture to stand for 30 minutes before using as a filling. Sufficient for 30–40 Hun Tuns.

¼ lb (¾ cup) shelled shrimp
2 oz bêche de mer
2 oz chicken meat
1 scallion
2 slices ginger root
1½ tablespoons soy sauce
4 teaspoons vinegar
dash of pepper and salt
2 teaspoons sesame oil

Sweet Dumplings

There are vast varieties of sweet dumplings, which are usually made and served during festivals. The two recipes given here are the most popular and best-known.

T'ang Yuen (Sweet Soup Balls)

Preparation Soak the tapioca for 4 hours; then drain thoroughly. Mix the rice flour with the tapioca. Knead until the tapioca and rice flour are very well-blended. Mix the brown sugar with the bean paste and blend well. Take a piece of dough and form it into a ball the size of a large cherry; then flatten it slightly. Make a deep indentation in the middle of the ball and place some of the sweetened black bean paste inside. The paste should amount to about one third of the quantity of dough in the ball. Fold the edges of the dough-ball round the filling, completely enveloping the black bean paste. Seal the edges carefully and shape the dough into a ball once more, rolling it until it is quite round. Repeat this process untill all the dough and black bean paste have been used up.

Cooking Heat the sugar and ginger in 2 quarts of water. Bring to the boil and simmer for 2 minutes. Drop all the balls carefully into the simmering liquid. Continue to simmer gently for 20 minutes, by which time the balls should have floated up to the surface.

Serves 10–12

½ cup tapioca
1¼ cups glutinous rice flour

¼ cup brown sugar
1 cup sweetened black bean paste
2½ tablespoons sugar
3 slices ginger root

Serving Divide the balls among the serving dishes, which should be half-filled with the sugar/ginger soup.

Be very careful when biting into the balls or gulping them down, as the sugared bean filling is inclined to retain its heat for a great length of time.

Yuan-Hsiao

Makes approximately 30 dumplings

½ cup walnuts
½ cup almonds
1½ tablespoons melon seeds
1½ tablespoons sesame seeds
1 oz pork fat
½ cup sugar
1½ lb glutinous rice flour

This is also known as 'The New Year Festival Sweet Dumpling'. The interesting thing about Yuan-Hsiao is that it is not wrapped like other dumplings.

Preparation Grind the walnuts, almonds, and melon seeds. Roast and crush the sesame seeds and chop the pork fat. Put all the ingredients in a bowl, except the glutinous rice flour, and mix together until well-blended. Form the mixture into balls about ½ inch in diameter and dampen them by sprinkling water over them. Divide the glutinous rice flour between two trays, spreading it evenly out over both of them. Place the damp balls on one of the trays, then tilt it slightly one way, then the other, so that the wet balls pick up the dry flour as they roll around. After a period of rolling, the surface of the balls will have become so dry that they will no longer pick up the flour. Remove them from the tray and wet them again by sprinkling more water over them. Alternatively, you could put them in a wire basket and sink them into water. Place the balls on the fresh tray of flour and roll them again to pick up more flour. After two or three sessions of rolling, when all the rice flour has been used up, the Yuan-Hsiao balls are ready for cooking.

Cooking Heat 2 quarts of water in a saucepan. Bring to the boil, then carefully add all the Yuan-Hsiaos. Boil them for 5 minutes, then pour in 1¼ cups of water. Boil for a further 3 minutes, at the end of which time the dumplings will be cooked.

Serving Place four or five of the dumplings in a bowl and pour in enough of the dough-soup from the saucepan to cover the balls.

Once again, you are warned not to bite into the dumplings as soon as they are served, as the heat inside the filling can be very high. It is rumored that people have expired swallowing them!

Steamed Buns

Chinese steamed buns are principally of two types, those with fillings and those without. Those without fillings are eaten with meal, fish, vegetable, and savory dishes. Among unfilled buns, the best known are the Man Tou and the Hua Chuan. Man Tou buns are made from wheat flour and are second in importance only to rice as the bulk food of China. Indeed, in the wheat-producing regions of north China, the consumption of Man Tou undoubtedly exceeds that of rice per head of population. If you walked into any dining hall north of the Yellow River, you would see Man Tou piled up in small, steaming mountains for the diners to fetch and bring to their own tables. Hua Chuan is a more refined form of Man Tou. It is, in fact, a steamed roll made in layers of raised dough, used more often during dinner parties and in restaurants than at ordinary meals.

Man Tou (Plain Steamed Buns)

Preparation Heat 6 tablespoons of the water until warm, add the yeast, and stir until dissolved; then blend into the flour, and mix well. Add the remaining water gradually. Knead well for 7–8 minutes. Allow the dough to stand in the bowl in a warm place for 2 hours, until it has expanded to twice its original size. Knead for a couple of minutes and repeat. Shape the dough into a roll 24 inches long and 2 inches in diameter. Cut off slices about 2 inches thick and form them into flat-bottomed buns.

Cooking Place the buns on a damp cheesecloth in a steam basket or steamer. Steam vigorously for 15–20 minutes.

Serving Hot Man Tou buns are served for breakfast, lunch, and dinner.

Serves 10–12

1 cup water
2 tablespoons dried yeast
1 lb flour

Hua Chuan (Flower Rolls)

Preparation Make the dough according to the instructions for Man Tou (Plain Steamed Buns). Divide dough into two portions and roll out each portion to a sheet ⅛ inch thick Sprinkle each sheet with about ½ teaspoon salt, and brush the surface of each with 1 tablespoon of sesame or vegetable oil. Place one sheet on top of the other, oiled surface against the non-oiled surface. Roll the two sheets into a scroll about 1½–2 inches in diameter. Trim the ends and cut the scroll into 2½ inch segments. Press down the middle of each segment with a pair of chopsticks so that the opened ends will open out further.

Serves 10–12

Cooking Place these open-ended rolls in a steamer on top of a damp cheesecloth and steam vigorously for 15 minutes.

Serving Hua Chuan are essential and excellent for accompanying red-cooked meats and, indeed, all rich dishes.

Pao Tzu (Stuffed Steamed Buns)

Serves 6–10

There are two types of Pao Tzu or stuffed, steamed buns—those with savory fillings and those with sweet fillings. Stuffed steamed buns are never served during meals; they are always eaten as snacks.

The dough used for stuffed buns is the same as Man Tou dough, except that 1¼ tablespoons of sugar is added. The presence of the sugar seems to have a very salutary effect. Since stuffed buns are eaten on their own, and not used just for soaking up the savoriness from the other dishes on the table, they have to be in themselves more appealing than unstuffed buns. Westerners take to these stuffed buns much more readily than to the plain Man Tou.

As in the making of Man Tou buns, the dough is first of all formed into a roll 2 inches in diameter, then sliced into thick disks. These disks are then rolled out again into 3 inch diameter rounds. Between ½ and 2 teaspoons of the filling is placed at the center of each piece of dough, then the sides should be drawn up to a point and sealed. In this way, the filling is completely enveloped in the center of a flat-bottomed ball. These flat-bottomed balls of dough are placed in a steamer on top of a damp cheesecloth and steamed vigorously for 25 minutes.

The stuffings for these buns can be made from any combination of meat and vegetables, either fresh or cooked.

1 lb pork
2 scallions
1½ lb Chinese cabbage
2½ tablespoons soy sauce
1¼ teaspoons salt
2½ teaspoons sugar
1 tablespoon sesame oil

Savory Stuffing for Pao Tzu (1)

Preparation Chop the pork coarse. Chop the scallions and cabbage. Place all the ingredients in a bowl and mix well. Leave the mixture to stand for 30 minutes before using. Sufficient for 30–40 buns.

338

Savory Stuffing for Pao Tzu (2)

Preparation Chop the roast pork and chop the scallions. Place all the ingredients in a bowl and mix well. Allow the mixture to stand for 30 minutes before using. Sufficient for 30–40 buns.

1½ lb Cantonese roast pork
3 scallions
2½ tablespoons soy sauce
1¼ teaspoons salt
2½ teaspoons sugar
1 tablespoon sesame oil

Sweet Stuffing for Pao Tzu

Preparation Roast the sesame seeds in a dry frying pan for 1 minute, then crush them. Grind the walnuts and almonds. Chop the pork fat into tiny cubes. Mix all the ingredients together in a bowl and use the mixture as a filling. Sufficient for 30–40 buns.

2½ tablespoons sesame seeds
1 cup walnuts
¾ cup almonds
2 oz pork fat
1 cup sugar
4 teaspoons lard

Sugar and Black Bean Filling for Pao Tzu

For approximately 40 buns

Cooking Stir-fry the ingredients together in a frying pan for 5 minutes over a gentle heat. Allow to stand and cool, then use as a filling.

1 cup sugar
12 oz black *or* red bean purée
¼ lb lard

Ping or Pancakes

The Chinese word 'Ping' refers to pancakes as well as to cakes of a much greater thickness, which have been cooked by frying with a little oil or on a dry pan or griddle. Although there are numerous types of cakes and pancakes, the majority of them are extremely mundane, usually incorporating a small amount of onion, grated radishes, or sesame seeds to provide flavor, pungency, or aroma. They are really only a poor man's way of making wheat flour edible. Through tradition or habit, many Chinese people have come to regard them with respect or even nostalgia, but they really enjoy them only if they are accompanied by quantities of wholesome, rich, savory foods. To Westerners, only the following types of Chinese pancakes are likely to be of much interest. Suggested fillings are given on page 341.

Spring Rolls, Pancake Rolls, and Egg Rolls

The above three are in fact the same thing. Spring rolls *are* pancake rolls, but in China they are called spring rolls because they are served and eaten on and after the Old New Year Day, usually falling sometime in February, which is getting fairly near to spring in many parts of the country. Egg rolls are pancake rolls with a little extra egg in the dough. The pancake rolls or egg rolls made and served by Chinese restaurants abroad are usually about 5 or 6 inches in length and about ¾ inch in diameter, which is larger than those usually served in China. In America, the egg rolls are usually cut into three pieces or into 1½ inch sections when served. As probably more pancake rolls are eaten abroad than spring rolls are in China, the overseas version deserves a mention. I shall call the original Chinese version the spring roll and the overseas version the egg or pancake roll.

Egg or Spring Roll Skins

Makes 12–15 pancakes

½ lb flour
¾ teaspoon salt
2 eggs
oil

Egg or spring roll skins are made in a way very similar to the method for making ordinary pancakes. The intention is simply to make a batter and produce extremely thin pancakes, which are then filled.

Preparation Combine the flour and salt. Beat the eggs lightly and add to the flour. Beat steadily in one direction, gradually adding 1⅔ cups water. Continue beating until a thin, smooth batter is obtained.

Cooking Pour a small quantity of oil into a frying pan, swirl it around, and pour away the excess. Stir the batter, then place 2 tablespoons of it in the middle of the pan. Lift the handle of the pan and move it around until the batter has spread evenly over the whole surface of the pan. Pour away any excess batter. Place the pan over a low heat, and as soon as the dough skin starts to peel and shrink from the sides, lift it from the pan and put it aside, covered with a damp cloth. Repeat this process until all the batter has been used, re-oiling the pan lightly by rubbing it with an oil-soaked cloth after each pancake has been made.

Wrapping the Rolls

Place about 2 tablespoons of filling just below the center of the dough skin or pancake, spreading it lengthwise. Fold the edge nearest to you over the filling, then roll up fairly tightly. When the pancake is rolled up, turn in the edges of the two ends. Continue to roll away from the body. Finally, fold the farthest side or corner inwards and seal it down with beaten egg.

340

Deep-Frying the Rolls

Fry the filled egg or spring rolls four or five at a time by placing them in a wire basket and lowering them into boiling oil, at a temperature of about 375°F. After frying for 2 minutes, remove the pan from the heat for 1 minute, then replace it for a further 2 minutes. Alternatively, egg rolls and spring rolls can be pan-fried in shallow oil, just like sausages, by turning them in the oil and frying on all sides.

When the filling is composed of fresh, raw ingredients, it is sometimes advisable to steam the egg or spring rolls for 10 minutes before deep-frying. In such cases, the rolls are sometimes dipped in beaten egg or batter before deep-frying.

Meat Fillings for Egg or Spring Rolls

As a rule, egg roll and spring roll fillings have to be cooked first before they are packed into the rolls. This is because the rolls are too thick for the meat ingredients to be thoroughly cooked during the 4–5 minutes the rolls are deep-fried. The majority of Chinese stir-fried dishes can, in fact, be packed into the rolls as fillings. The following recipes are only a few of the more usual combinations.

Chicken and Vegetable Filling

Preparation Soak the dried mushrooms for 30 minutes, then shred them. Shred the bamboo shoots, blanch the bean sprouts, and chop the scallions. Shred the chicken meat.

Cooking Heat the oil in a frying pan. Add the chicken, bamboo shoots, and scallions. Stir-fry over a high heat for 1 minute; then add the bean sprouts and mushrooms. Stir-fry for a further minute. Add all the other ingredients and continue to stir-fry for 1 minute. Remove the mixture from the pan and put it in a colander to cool and drain. Use as a filling for egg or spring rolls when it is thoroughly cooled and drained.

For 12–15 rolls

½ lb chicken meat, cooked *or* uncooked
3 Chinese dried mushrooms
2½ tablespoons bamboo shoots
½ cup bean sprouts
2 scallions
2 tablespoons vegetable oil
¾ teaspoon salt
3¾ teaspoons soy sauce
1¼ teaspoons sugar
1¼ teaspoons cornstarch

Stir-Fried Pork and Vegetable Filling

Cooking Repeat the previous recipe, substituting 1¼ cups shredded pork for the chicken. Stir-fry the pork and salt together over a high heat for 1 minute before adding any other ingredients. Otherwise, the procedure is the same as in the previous recipe. The mixture must be thoroughly cooled and drained before use.

For 12–15 rolls

Roast Pork and Cooked Shrimp Filling

For 12-15 rolls

Cooking Use the same vegetables and seasonings as in the recipe for Chicken and Vegetable Filling (see above). Stir-fry the vegetables over a medium heat for 2 minutes, then add 3 oz shrimp and 1 cup shredded roast pork. Stir-fry for 1 minute, then add the seasonings for a final general stir-fry.

Glossary

Abalone A rubbery-textured, limpet-like shellfish, available in cans, which is used extensively for flavoring soups, mixed-fried foods, and red-cooked dishes. Occasionally cooked and presented as principal material of a banquet dish. It is ivory yellow in color.

Bamboo Shoots The young shoots of the bamboo plant which are harvested in the spring. They sometimes reach 2–3 inches in diameter, are crunchy in texture, and have a mild and subtle flavor. Available cleaned and trimmed in cans, they are used extensively in Chinese cooking.

Bean Curd Ground soy beans which have been lightly cooked with water and then left to set into a semi-solid 'custard'. This is cut into cakes approximately 2 inches square, and about 1 inch deep. With its high protein content, it is a mainstay of Chinese (and Japanese) vegetable and vegetarian cooking.

Bean Curd Cheese A type of fermented bean curd which has a very strong, savory, cheesy taste. It is used extensively for flavoring, and is often eaten in small quantities with congee (plain, boiled rice-porridge) for breakfast in China.

Bean Sprouts Young sprouts of the mung bean, sold fresh and in cans. The fresh ones have husks that must be removed before using.

Bird's Nest The regurgitated fish and seafoods that sea swallows in south-east Asia deposit in their nests for their young. An expensive delicacy, used in Bird's Nest Soup.

Black Beans (Fermented) Small, black, salted soy beans, which may be soaked for about 15 minutes in water before use.

Chili Sauce (and Chili Oil) Chili sauce is a hot sauce made from small chili peppers. It is very similar in flavor to Tabasco. Chili oil, which is even hotter, is made from small red peppers which are slowly fried in oil. The oil becomes colored by the peppers in the process of the heating, and the chili oil, when ready for use, is reddish in color.

Chinese Cabbage A firm and flavorsome lettuce-like plant with long, crisp leaves. It can be braised, stir-fried or made into a salad.

Chinese Dried Mushrooms These are dark brownish-black in color, and must be soaked in water for about 30 minutes before use. The stem should be removed as it is so

343

tough that even one hour's cooking will not tenderize it. Dried mushrooms have a much more pronounced flavor than fresh mushrooms; they also have a much meatier texture.

Chinese Parsley Fresh coriander leaves (also known as cilantro) that look like parsley but have a different, much stronger taste. They are often available in Italian and Latin American markets as well as Oriental markets.

Chinese Sausages Smoked pork sausages, 4–8 inches long, often steamed or lightly fried, or cross-cooked with vegetables or other ingredients.

Cloud Ears A form of fungus, usually available dried, that has to be soaked for at least 30 minutes before use. These fungi are cloud-shaped—hence their name. Cloud ears are used mainly for their textural effect—a sort of slippery crunchiness.

Congee Rice Congee is a word used in the Far East to describe rice-porridge, or watery rice, or rice which has been cooked for a long time in at least four to eight times its own weight of water. It is usually served for breakfast, or cooked by people who must augment their meager rice ration with a very large content of water.

Crackling Rice The scrapings of rice from the bottom of the rice pot, which have been further dried, then finally deep-fried until really hot and crackling. Often served with soup or sauce.

Double-Mah-jong-Size An average Mah-jong-size piece measures about $1 \times \frac{2}{3} \times \frac{1}{4}$ inch, so a double-Mah-jong-size piece is double that. It would probably have to be cut or bitten in half before being eaten.

Egg Noodles Spaghetti-type noodles made from eggs and wheat flour.

Five Spice Powder A mixed, ground, herbal powder used in Chinese cooking. It consists of five types of ground, dried spices: usually star anise, Szechuan or anise pepper, fennel, cloves, and cinnamon.

Ginger Root A gnarled fresh root available in Oriental, Greek and Latin American stores. Ginger root can be stored indefinitely in the freezer, or it can be peeled and sliced and stored in a sealed jar, covered with dry sherry. Ginger root is invariably used in the preparation of seafoods, fish, and all the stronger tasting meats such as lamb or chicken.

Glutinous Rice A variety of round, small-grained rice which becomes sticky when cooked. It is usually used in sweet dishes, but it is also used for Lotus Leaf Wrapped Rice.

Golden Needles See Tiger-Lily Buds.

Hoisin Sauce Literally translated it means 'Sea-Fresh Sauce'. It is made from soy sauce, soy paste, ground yellow beans, garlic, sugar, and vinegar. Sweet and spicy, it is frequently combined with other sauces for use as a dip. Used in the cooking of seafoods, meats, and vegetables.

Kumquats Like very small oranges or tangerines. Available in cans, or occasionally fresh.

Light Soy Sauce Soy sauce in China is like wine in the West, in that it comes in numerous grades, strengths, colors, and flavors. The light-colored variety is mostly used for preparing light-colored dishes.

Lotus Leaves Often used to wrap up food materials before cooking—much the same as aluminum foil is used in America these days, except that lotus leaves impart a special flavor and aroma to the food. Poultry is frequently wrapped in a lotus leaf, then steamed or roasted.

Lotus Roots When fresh, these are usually used to prepare a sweet dish. Dried lotus roots require soaking, then may be used along with other vegetables in a mixed-fried or mixed-assembled dish.

Lychees Fleshy, white fruit with reddish-brown skin and a large stone. Has a sweet and very subtle flavor. Sold fresh, in cans or dried.

Monosodium Glutamate A flavor-enhancing powder available in Oriental markets and also sold as MSG and Ac'cent. Although a very small amount of the powder undeniably helps to bring out the flavor of food, larger amounts may sometimes cause headaches and other minor symptoms. It can be eliminated from the recipes if desired.

Oyster Sauce A rich sauce made from oysters, oyster water, and soy sauce. Used to flavor seafood, meat, poultry, and vegetable dishes.

Plum Sauce (Duck Sauce) A spicy, fruity sauce made from plums, chili, vinegar, and sugar. Frequently used as a dip.

Red Bean Curd Cheese A variety of Bean Curd Cheese.

Red-in-Snow Pickled Greens A variety of salted, pickled greens which are most often used coarsely chopped, and sprinkled over meaty or cross-cooked dishes, giving them a more piquant flavor.

Rice Stick Noodles Long, thin noodles made from rice flour. Can be boiled, stir-fried, or used in soups.

Rice Wine The most common type of wine used in Chinese cooking. It is made from rice, and tastes like medium dry sherry, which can be used as a substitute.

Sesame Oil This is the oil produced from sesame seeds. It has a very strong nutty flavor, more often used in small quantities for flavoring than for cooking.

Shark's Fin The dried cartilage of a shark's fin Very delicate flavor. Available processed, boned, skinned and washed.

345

Silver Ears A type of fungus similar to Cloud Ears, except that they are usually white in color. Most often used in sweet dishes.

Snow Peas Tender young peas eaten pod and all. They are often quickly stir-fried into extremely attractive, glistening vegetable dishes.

Soy Jam (Soy Bean Paste) This can almost be described as a solid version of soy sauce, but is somewhat less salty, often tastier, and should be applied in small quantities when cooking. It can often be used in conjunction with soy sauce.

Star Anise A dark brown eight-pointed seed called the 'eight point' in China. Used as a flavoring ingredient as it has a very distinctive flavor.

Stocks: Superior; Secondary; Master; Herbal Superior Stock is a meat broth produced by simmering pork, chicken, bacon, and bones together. Secondary Stock is usually produced by simmering just bones. Master Stock is made from good quality meat simmered with soy sauce, wine, sugar, and a variety of spices. Herbal Stock is a Master Stock where a much greater proportion of herbs is used in the preparation for cooking.

Szechuan Pickled Greens A hot pickle, to which a quantity of ground red chili pepper has been added. Very hot. Often used in small quantities to flavor meats, vegetables, and soups.

Tangerine Peel The dried skin of tangerines. Used for flavoring duck and red-simmered dishes.

Tiger-Lily Buds (Dried Lily Buds or Golden Needles) These are long, yellow strips of stem-like vegetables. Small quantities are often used in vegetable and semi-vegetable dishes, as they have a very distinctive (moldy) flavor.

Transparent Noodles (Cellophane or Bean-Thread Noodles) These are white-colored noodles which, when soaked, become transparent. Usually cooked with meat or vegetables. Because they tend to absorb a lot of liquid, the noodles become very meaty and flavorsome—ideal for consuming with plain rice.

Vinegar The Chinese use rice vinegar, but if this is unobtainable, red wine vinegar closely resembles rice vinegar in flavor and color.

Water Chestnuts An aquatic plant with white meat grown in East Asia. Usually available canned. They have a crunchy texture, and are often used in stir-fried braised or steamed dishes. Often chopped coarse and mixed with chopped meat or shrimp into meatballs or shrimp balls.

Wood Ears The more usual type of fungus which grows on trees, of which Cloud Ears and Silver Ears are different varieties. Wood Ears are usually black in color and have to be soaked before use. They have very little taste or flavor, and are usually used in cooking for their color and textural effect.

Choice of Dishes

Selecting dishes for a Chinese meal requires some thought—even for the Chinese. Most Chinese choose the dishes simply out of habit; few do so with any system or deliberation. They are used to having certain foods, or enjoy certain basic dishes, and all they do for a special occasion is add a few extra dishes using foods that are in season, dishes appropriate to the occasion, or those likely to be appreciated by the principal guests.

On the whole, the range of dishes depends largely on the food materials available. At a small informal dinner in a restaurant you are likely to have a chicken dish, a pork dish, a fish dish, a beef or lamb dish, a seafood dish, a vegetable dish, a made-up dish, and perhaps a soup or two. At a larger dinner, some of the favorite food materials such as chicken or pork may be repeated, but in different forms. If chicken is cooked whole—long-simmered, for example—part of it can be served as a semi-soup dish, and the rest diced into small cubes and stir-fried in a hot thick sauce made from reduced soy sauce or soy paste. Although the chicken is basically the same in each case, because of the different methods of cooking and presentation, the character of the two dishes is entirely different. Pork, for instance, can be slowly red-cooked (in soy sauce), and served in a large 4 to 5 lb chunk, or shredded into threads and quickly stir-fried with vegetables or transparent noodles into a dish which bears no resemblance at all to the first pork dish. The emphasis is always on difference and contrast. When you have eaten several dishes with sauce you will long for some dry ones; after a succession of dry dishes you will appreciate a semi-soup dish. The contrast and difference are brought out not only by the variety of food materials used, but also by the way in which they are cooked. The situation gives great scope to keen and sophisticated cooks.

At a formal banquet, the Chinese meal is transformed from being a spread to a sequence of dishes or courses. The succession of dishes generally follows a set pattern: it usually starts with a selection of cold dishes (or a whole array of cold meats and other items arranged on a single large platter), followed by three, four, or five quick stir-fried dishes, which could either be in a rich sauce, or else dry and crispy. This course is followed by the main dishes, which might include a magnificent roast, a long-simmered semi-soup dish—Whole Duck Soup, for example; a casserole or a red-cooked dish, or even a fish cooked whole such as Sweet and Sour Yellow River Carp. To conclude such a banquet, several very plain dishes are often served with rice. These are meant to act as a ballast to the meal, to counteract the richness of the food which has gone before. Fruit is sometimes served towards the end of the whole proceeding.

One of the first things Americans should avoid doing when ordering Chinese food is to repeat similar types of dishes: they should aim at difference and variety. Variety can be achieved not only by alternating the food materials used in the dishes, but also by alternating the cooking methods used in producing the dishes. For example, after a quick-fried dish, it may be salutary to have a crispy deep-fried one; after a dry-fried dish it is recommendable to have a semi-soup dish, and after steamed duck, which can be jelly-like in tenderness, it may be time to have a crackling roast of pork, which is partly aromatic in its appeal. Dishes where the constituent materials are all shredded into threads and tossed together may be suitable to follow a dish where a large piece of meat or fish is simmered whole.

Apart from the ways in which the food materials are cooked, contrast and difference can also be achieved by the way Chinese foods are cut—for they can be chopped either fine or coarse, shredded into large or small pieces, or cut into paper-thin slices or willow strips. Larger slices can be cut through the skin into thin lean-and-fat slices, suitable for dipping into mixed garlic and vinegar dips, or quick-fried into double-cooked pork. The thicker and squarer pieces which are carved from similar cuts of meat, and which contain several layers of lean-and-fat, must always be cooked for a long time, and to such a degree of tenderness that they will melt in the mouth.

The main disadvantage of eating in Chinese restaurants abroad is that the majority of the dishes—probably over 90% of them—are usually of the quick stir-fried variety. As most of these dishes only require to be cooked for 3 to 4 minutes they are great time-savers, but severely limit the methods of cooking used, and in this way limit the choice available to the customer. However, despite the comparatively small scope for maneuvering, it is still possible, thanks to the enormous range of Chinese dishes, to achieve some degree of variety in a menu, and any slightly above average Chinese restaurant should be able to offer an imaginative selection of dishes.

Another factor which is highly relevant when choosing dishes in a Chinese restaurant in America is, of course, to check whether the restaurant specializes in Peking or Cantonese cooking, or whether it is an average run-of-the-mill Chinese restaurant. Bearing this in mind, I shall endeavor to choose dishes for two alternative menus for 4 to 6 people in each type of restaurant.

Menu 1

Barbecued Spare Ribs
Fish Balls and Watercress Soup
Deep-Fried Phœnix-Tail Shrimp
Shredded Beef Stir-Fried
with Sweet Peppers
Sweet and Sour Pork
Plain Stir-Fried Bean Sprouts
Fried Rice (with Ham, Egg, Onion,
Peas)

Menu 2

Sweet and Sour Spare Ribs
Chicken and Corn Soup
Crispy Shrimp Balls
Cantonese Cha Shao Roast Pork
Beef Chop Suey
Braised or Quick-Fried
Mustard Greens or Mixed
Vegetables
Fried Rice

Peking Restaurant
for 4–6 people

Menu 1

Hot and Sour Soup
Deep-Fried Diced Chicken with
Soy Jam
Sliced Fish in Wine Sauce
Quick-Fried Shredded Lamb
with Scallions
Peking Duck (half) served with
Pancakes
White-Cooked Cabbage
(flavored with Dried Shrimp)
Drawn-Thread Toffee Apples

Menu 2

Imperial Hors d'Oeuvre
(an assortment of cold meats,
abalone, shrimp,
pickled vegetables, etc.)
Quick-Fried Diced Pork in
Soy Paste Sauce
Dry-Fried Jumbo Shrimp in
Garlic-Flavored Oil
Sweet and Sour Fillet of Pork
(Peking Style)
Aromatic and Crispy Duck (half)
served with Steamed Buns
Boiled Duck Soup with
Fresh Chinese Celery Cabbage

Menu 1

Wonton Soup
Cantonese Barbecued Roast Pork
Fresh Shrimp Plain Steamed in
Shells,
served with Piquant Sauce
Sliced Willow-Cut Beef in Oyster
Sauce
(or Cantonese Steak)
Lemon Duck
Quick-Fried Broccoli in
Oyster Sauce

Menu 2

Sliced Pork and Cucumber Soup
or
Abalone and Fish Ball Soup
Quick-Fried Sliced Beef in
Oyster Sauce
Chopped Lacquered Duck
(Barbecued)
Steamed Bass in Soy and
Ginger Sauce
Quick-Fried Crabmeat with
Mushrooms
Plain Quick-Fried Snow Peas

The reader will note from the foregoing selection that there are few long-cooked and clear-simmered dishes to contrast with the quick-cooked variety, which is to be regretted. But, to recap, when choosing Chinese dishes, the main thing the American should bear in mind is to select dishes which include a wide variety of food materials—after shrimp, for example, choose chicken, beef, fish, pork, vegetables, etc., and whenever feasible the methods employed in cooking these dishes should also vary: if two dishes are quick-fried, the others should be steamed, long-simmered, deep-fried, red-cooked, barbecued, slow-stewed, or casseroled. Invariably, different methods of cooking produce different textures and flavors. The keynote is variety and contrast.

Index